MASTERING LABOR LAW

CAROLINA ACADEMIC PRESS MASTERING SERIES

RUSSELL WEAVER, SERIES EDITOR

For other titles, please go to caplaw.com.

Mastering Administrative Law, Second Edition
Linda D. Jellum

Mastering Adoption Law and Policy
Cynthia Hawkins DeBose

Mastering Alternative Dispute Resolution
Kelly M. Feeley, James A. Sheehan

Mastering Appellate Advocacy and Process, Second Edition
Donna C. Looper, George W. Kuney

Mastering Art Law, Second Edition
Herbert Lazerow

Mastering Bankruptcy
George W. Kuney

Mastering Civil Procedure, Fourth Edition
David Charles Hricik

Mastering Constitutional Law, Second Edition
John C. Knechtle, Christopher J. Roederer

Mastering Contract Law
Irma S. Russell, Barbara K. Bucholtz

Mastering Corporate Tax, Second Edition
Gail Levin Richmond, Reginald Mombrun, Felicia Branch

Mastering Corporations and Other Business Entities, Second Edition
Lee Harris

Mastering Criminal Law, Third Edition
Ellen S. Podgor, Cynthia E. Jones, Peter J. Henning, Neil P. Cohen, Sanjay K. Chhablani

Mastering Criminal Procedure, Volume 1: The Investigative Stage, Third Edition
Peter J. Henning, Cynthia E. Jones, Ellen S. Podgor,
Karen McDonald Henning, Sanjay K. Chhablani

Mastering Criminal Procedure, Volume 2: The Adjudicatory Stage, Third Edition
Peter J. Henning, Cynthia E. Jones, Ellen S. Podgor,
Karen McDonald Henning, Sanjay K. Chhablani

Mastering Elder Law, Third Edition
Ralph C. Brashier

Mastering Employment Discrimination Law, Third Edition
Jeffrey M. Hirsch, Joseph A. Seiner, Sandra F. Sperino

Mastering Environmental Law
Joel A. Mintz, Tracy D. Hester

Mastering Evidence
Ronald W. Eades

Mastering Family Law, Second Edition
April Carroll Meldrum

Mastering First Amendment Law
John C. Knechtle

Mastering Income Tax, Second Edition
Gail Levin Richmond, Christopher M. Pietruszkiewicz

Mastering Intellectual Property
George W. Kuney, Donna C. Looper

Mastering International Sales Law
Herbert Lazerow

Mastering Interviewing and Counseling
Kelly M. Feeley, Rebecca C. Morgan

Mastering Labor Law, Second Edition
Anne Marie Lofaso, Joseph E. Slater, Jeffrey M. Hirsch

Mastering Legal Analysis and Communication
David T. Ritchie

Mastering Legal Analysis and Drafting, Second Edition
George W. Kuney, Donna C. Looper

Mastering Legislation, Regulation, and Statutory Interpretation, Third Edition
Linda D. Jellum

Mastering Native American Law, Third Edition
Angelique Wambdi EagleWoman, Stacy L. Leeds

Mastering Negotiable Instruments (UCC Articles 3 and 4) and Other Payment Systems, Second Edition
Michael D. Floyd

Mastering Negotiation
Michael R. Fowler

Mastering Partnership Taxation
Stuart Lazar

Mastering Products Liability, Second Edition
Tim Kaye

Mastering Professional Responsibility, Second Edition
Grace M. Giesel

Mastering Property Law, Second Edition
Darryl C. Wilson

Mastering Sales
Colin P. Marks, Jeremy Kidd

Mastering Secured Transactions: UCC Article 9, Third Edition
Grace M. Giesel

Mastering Tort Law, Third Edition
Russell L. Weaver, Edward C. Martin, Andrew R. Klein, Paul J. Zwier, II, John H. Bauman

Mastering Trademark and Unfair Competition Law, Second Edition
Lars S. Smith, Llewellyn Joseph Gibbons

Mastering Trusts and Estates, Second Edition
Gail Levin Richmond

MASTERING LABOR LAW

SECOND EDITION

Anne Marie Lofaso

PROFESSOR OF LAW
UNIVERSITY OF CINCINNATI COLLEGE OF LAW

Joseph E. Slater

EUGENE N. BALK PROFESSOR OF LAW & VALUES
UNIVERSITY OF TOLEDO COLLEGE OF LAW

Jeffrey M. Hirsch

GENEVA YEARGAN RAND
DISTINGUISHED PROFESSOR OF LAW
UNIVERSITY OF NORTH CAROLINA SCHOOL OF LAW

CAROLINA ACADEMIC PRESS
Durham, North Carolina

Library of Congress Cataloging-in-Publication Data

Names: Lofaso, Anne Marie author | Slater, Joseph E. author | Hirsch, Jeffrey M. author
Title: Mastering labor law / Anne Marie Lofaso, Joseph E. Slater, Jeffrey M. Hirsch.
Description: Second edition. | Durham, North Carolina : Carolina Academic Press, 2026. | Series: Mastering series | Includes bibliographical references and index.
Identifiers: LCCN 2025051014 | ISBN 9781531034610 paperback | ISBN 9781531034627 ebook
Subjects: LCSH: Labor laws and legislation — United States
Classification: LCC KF3319 .S434 2026
LC record available at https://lccn.loc.gov/2025051014

Carolina Academic Press, LLC
700 Kent Street
Durham, NC 27701
Telephone (919) 489-7486
www.cap-press.com

Printed in the United States of America

Dedicated to —

Jim Heiko, Giorgi Heiko, Penny Lofaso, and Toni Lofaso — AML
Krista, Isaac, Paris, and Chadwick — JES
Lynn, Noah & Naomi — JMH

CONTENTS

TABLE OF CASES

B

C

D

N

O

P

Q

R

S

T

U

SERIES EDITOR'S FOREWORD

The Carolina Academic Press Mastering Series is designed to provide you with a tool that will enable you to easily and efficiently "master" the substance and content of law school courses. Throughout the series, the focus is on quality writing that makes legal concepts understandable. As a result, the series is designed to be easy to read and is not unduly cluttered with footnotes or cites to secondary sources.

In order to facilitate student mastery of topics, the Mastering Series includes a number of pedagogical features designed to improve learning and retention. At the beginning of each chapter, you will find a "Roadmap" that tells you about the chapter and provides you with a sense of the material that you will cover. A "Checkpoint" at the end of each chapter encourages you to stop and review the key concepts, reiterating what you have learned. Throughout the book, key terms are explained and emphasized. Finally, a "Master Checklist" at the end of each book reinforces what you have learned and helps you identify any areas that need review or further study.

We hope that you will enjoy studying with, and learning from, the Mastering Series.

Russell L. Weaver
PROFESSOR OF LAW &
DISTINGUISHED UNIVERSITY SCHOLAR
UNIVERSITY OF LOUISVILLE,
LOUIS D. BRANDEIS SCHOOL OF LAW

PREFACE

The field of U.S. labor law faces uncertain times in 2026, the year this second edition was published. In the private sector, ninety years after the passage of the National Labor Relations Act (NLRA), labor and management remain stuck in a legislative stalemate—the last major amendment to the NLRA was in 1959, and the most recent amendment was in 1974. As a result, students and labor law practitioners are left trying to make statutory language enacted well over sixty years ago work in the global and more service-oriented economy of the 21st century. This also means that the rules and decisions of the National Labor Relations Board (NLRB), the administrative body charged with interpreting and enforcing the often quite general language of the statute, are especially important. The increasingly dramatic shifts of the NLRB, depending on which party controls the Presidency, have become even more pronounced since the 2014 date of the first edition, and this adds to the unpredictability frequently encountered by parties to labor disputes. Beyond that, as of this writing, courts are considering constitutional challenges to the very structure of the NLRB itself.

In the public sector, apart from a federal statute governing most federal agencies and their employees, state and local laws continue to set labor law rules. These laws vary tremendously. To pick just the broadest splits, some states simply do not authorize collective bargaining for most or all public employees; some authorize collective bargaining, but do not permit any public employees to strike; and some authorize collective bargaining and permit most public employees to strike (although often only after going through various procedures not required in the private sector). Public-sector rules also diverge significantly regarding the scope of bargaining and in other key areas. Public-sector labor law also differs from private-sector law in that even in the 21st century, and even since the first edition of this book, statutes are frequently passed, amended, and repealed, sometimes restricting or eliminating the collective bargaining rights of public employees, and sometimes expanding such rights. Further, a crucial constitutional development came in 2018, when the U.S. Supreme Court held that, in the public sector, union security clauses in labor contracts that require members of union bargaining units to pay any dues to the union that represents them violate the First Amendment. *Janus v. AFSCME*, 575 U.S. 878 (2018).

With both private- and public-sector labor law, commentators continue to seek new ways to accommodate the interests of labor and management regarding the wages, hours, and working conditions of employees. In the private sector, labor law also attempts to determine how best to divide profits among workers, shareholders, and executives. In the public sector, it seeks to balance worker rights and voice with democratic accountability for government decisions that affect the public. This book does not delve into these policy debates. It seeks only to present law students, legal practitioners, and other interested parties with a basic understanding of private- and public-sector labor law as it exists, both to aid in actual labor relations and to provide a basis for informed opinions in debates over how labor law rules could best structure the future American workplace.

This book covers the major points that are normally discussed and analyzed in most labor law courses, plus it provides additional coverage of public-sector topics that are often covered in a separate, advanced course or seminar. It has been updated to include significant changes in both the private and public sectors that have occurred since the first edition. Although a book of this length cannot capture all facets of U.S. labor law, it does cover the primary procedural and substantive issues occurring under the NLRA, related federal statutes (such as the Norris-LaGuardia Act), and various representative state public-sector collective bargaining statutes. The authors hope this book will provide an instructive overview of labor law and offer a more straightforward method for mastering this often complex subject matter area.

There are many to thank, including Series Editor Russ Weaver; the University of Toledo College of Law and its Eugene N. Balk Professorship Fund; the University of North Carolina School of Law; and the University of Cincinnati College of Law.

Anne Marie Lofaso
Joseph E. Slater
Jeffrey M. Hirsch

MASTERING LABOR LAW

CHAPTER 1

Introduction to Private and Public Sector Labor Law

ROADMAP

- Describing what the subject of labor law is (and is not) about
- Understanding the basic differences between labor law in the private sector and labor law in the public sector
- Reviewing the objectives of this book

Labor laws are the legal rules governing unions in their relations with employers, employees in their relations with unions, and employees covered by a labor law statute who engage in what is called "concerted activity" in matters involving wages, hours, and working conditions. While much of labor law involves interactions between employers and employees either in unions or trying to organize unions, labor law does provide some important protections for employees who are neither in a union nor trying to form one. This chapter discusses what the subject of labor law constitutes and what it does not, underscores the most important differences between private-sector and public-sector labor law, and concludes by laying out the objectives of this book.

A. Labor Law Defined

Labor laws should be distinguished from what are often called "employment laws." Employment laws establish various rules and standards for employers and employees, usually without regard to whether the employer is unionized or whether employees are combining to take collective action. Employment laws include, e.g., Title VII of the Civil Rights of 1964 and other federal and state anti-discrimination laws, the Fair Labor Standards Act (governing minimum wages, child labor, and overtime), the Occupational Safety and Health Act, workers' compensation laws, and unemployment compensation laws. In many law schools, not only will there be a separate course for employment law or work law, but also for employment discrimination law, employee benefits law, and sometimes even workers' compensation law.

Labor laws remain very important. Although overall union density (the percentage of eligible employees who are represented by a union) has slipped in recent decades, unions in the United States still represent around 16 million employees. Further, as noted above, labor law rules can and do apply to employees who are not in unions or seeking to join one. In the private sector, challenges for unions and employers are clear, and both sides are using new, inventive, and sometimes aggressive tactics in both traditionally unionized industries and also in new sectors of the economy. In the public sector, unionized workplaces are common: union density in the public sector was 36 percent in 2024. Thus, those interested in laws governing the workplace should have at least a basic understanding of labor laws in both the public and private sectors.

B. Public-Sector vs. Private-Sector Labor Law

This book, unlike other hornbooks and guides to labor law, covers both private- and public-sector labor law rules. This is important because in the 21st century, public employees have made up nearly half of all union members in the U.S. Those who practice labor law should be prepared to handle clients in both sectors, as legal rules in the two sectors can differ significantly in some very important areas.

Most labor law in the private sector is governed by the National Labor Relations Act (NLRA), a federal statute. However, most private-sector employers and employees in the airline and railway industries are covered by the Railway Labor Act (RLA), a separate federal statute. The RLA contains rules that are often, but not always, similar or identical to those in the NLRA. This book, when discussing private-sector labor law, will primarily focus on NLRA rules, but will also occasionally discuss RLA rules, particularly when the NLRA rule originated with the RLA.

In contrast, public-sector labor law is set by many state and even local statutes (although a federal statute sets labor law rules for most eligible employees of the federal government). These public-sector laws vary considerably. A few states do not permit any public employees to bargain collectively; another minority of states only allows a few types of public employees to bargain (typically police and/or firefighters). By the middle of the first decade of this century, thirty states and the District of Columbia allowed collective bargaining for all major groups of public employees, twelve states allowed only one to four types of public workers to bargain, and eight did not allow any public workers to bargain. Major changes in coverage have continued since then. For example, in the past fifteen years, Wisconsin and Iowa almost completely eliminated bargaining rights for public employees who are not "public safety" employees, and Florida created onerous "recertification" rules for public-sector unions. On the other hand, in the past decade, public-sector collective bargaining rights were significantly expanded in, for example, Colorado and Virginia. Unlike practitioners in the private sector, those in the public sector must be aware of *statutory* changes in labor law rules, not just changes made by agency and court decisions.

Rules in public-sector labor laws are often based on private-sector rules, but in some important areas, public-sector rules differ dramatically. For example, most states do not allow any public employees to strike and instead use alternative processes to resolve bargaining impasses, including but not limited to "fact-finding" and "interest arbitration." Also, the "scope of bargaining"—what topics unions and employers may be obligated to bargain about—is often significantly more constrained in the public sector than in the private sector. This book cannot, of course, be a comprehensive guide to all the various public-sector labor laws in the U.S. But it will describe the most important areas in which public-sector law varies from private-sector law and cover the main different approaches states use.

In the private sector, although there have been no statutory amendments in many decades, labor law has undergone significant turbulence and change in the 21st century, largely due to decisions of the National Labor Relations

Board (NLRB), the agency that administers the NLRA in the first instance. The NLRB under President George W. Bush changed several significant labor law doctrines to be more employer-friendly. The NLRB under President Obama took a different approach, reversing some of the Bush NLRB cases and creating some new, union-friendly rules. The Trump NLRB swung back hard toward favoring employers, and then the Biden NLRB reversed course and issued a number of union-friendly rules and decisions. The second Trump administration certainly will reverse course again.

C. Objectives of Mastering Labor Law

Legal rights remain vital in labor relations, both in dramatic, well-publicized events and in routine daily relations. Labor law has a profound impact on the working lives of millions of people, on business strategy, and on large segments of the economy and government.

This book explains the most important aspects of both the NLRA and public-sector laws. These include union organizing (and the related rights of employees not currently represented by a union to engage in concerted action); collective bargaining; administration and enforcement of labor contracts ("collective bargaining agreements"); the economic weapons both sides may use (e.g., strikes, lockouts, and pickets); methods to resolve bargaining impasses; and the rights of individual union members *vis-à-vis* their unions.

This book also describes the procedural mechanisms to enforce labor law rights. Notably, labor laws are generally enforced at least in the first instance by agencies: the NLRB in the private sector, and analogous federal, state, and local government labor agencies in the public sector. In most labor law cases, litigation must begin with the agency. It is only after the agency acts that most labor cases may go to court. Finally, this book also discusses remedies for various types of labor law violations.

CHECKPOINTS

- Labor law governs relations between unions and employers, unions and employees represented by unions, and employees engaged in collective action regarding wages, hours, and working conditions.
- In the private sector, labor law is set by federal statute, but in the public sector, labor law is set by state or even local statues (as well as the federal government with regard to federal workers).
- Public-sector labor laws generally have many provisions and rules in common with each other and with private-sector labor law, but public-sector laws vary considerably from private-sector law and among themselves on a number of important topics, including but not limited to what types of employees are covered, how bargaining impasses are resolved, and what topics unions have a right to bargain about.
- The objective of this book is to explain the most important aspects of both the NLRA and public-sector laws.

CHAPTER 2

History and Background of Labor Law in the Private and Public Sectors

---

ROADMAP

- Overview of the early development of unions and labor relations before modern labor statutes
- Types of problems that the National Labor Relations Act and state public-sector labor laws were trying to solve
- History of some important, recurring issues in labor law
- Discussion of different assumptions about the economy, fairness, the role of government, and the rights of workers, unions, and employers that predated modern labor law and which sometimes inform modern interpretations of labor statutes
- Description of the basic structure of modern labor statutes
- Distinctions between development and histories of private-sector labor law and public-sector labor law

---

The history of labor relations before modern legislation is important in understanding modern labor law for three reasons. First, modern labor statutes use broad, general language, leaving courts and labor boards to both interpret the language and to fill in gaps. Often, doing so involves policy judgments that are based on values with deep historical roots. Second, much modern law was designed to address problems in labor relations that predate labor law statutes by decades, so understanding the goals of labor law is central to understanding labor law's application in a given situation. Third, much of the debate in public-sector labor law concerns the extent to which the problems and solutions developed in the private sector are appropriate in the public sector. Thus, seeing the origins of both together deepens our understanding of that issue.

A. Introduction

In some ways, the history of private-sector labor relations and labor law is quite separate from the history in the public sector. Private-sector unions won statutory protections and the right to bargain collectively in the 1930s, and union density in the private sector, which peaked in the 1950s, has been declining for decades. By contrast, public-sector unions only began winning statutory rights in some states in the 1960s, and public-sector union density, which was low before then, has been relatively high since the 1970s. But the histories also have important similarities. Unions in both sectors were active before they won formal collective bargaining rights; public-sector unions, like their private-sector counterparts, attempt to improve compensation and working conditions for those they represent; many legal rules in the two sectors are similar (although important differences remain); and many tactics and concerns on both sides are similar.

B. Private-Sector Unions and Labor Law Through the Creation of the NLRA

1. The Beginnings of Labor Law in America and Use of Criminal and Civil Conspiracy Law

Even before the American Revolution, some workers had organized into groups and taken collective action to try to better their working conditions. The first reported labor case in the U.S. was the "Philadelphia Cordewainers' Case," *Commonwealth v. Pullis*, 3 Commons & Gilmore 59 (Mayor's Court 1806). This case held that a strike for higher wages was an illegal criminal conspiracy. Union activity of all kinds was often held to be a criminal conspiracy through at least the mid-nineteenth century. Although in *Commonwealth v. Hunt*, 45 Mass. (4 Metc.) 111 (1842), the Massachusetts Supreme Court did hold that the mere act of forming a union and refusing to work for employers who hired workers who were not union members was not a criminal conspiracy. Still, courts continued to find that most activities by unions were illegal. Cases in the later 19th and early 20th centuries generally used civil conspiracy theories as opposed to criminal conspiracy. In both types of cases, courts looked at whether unions were using "legal means" to pursue a "legal end," and in both types of cases, the range of legal means and ends were quite narrow. For example, in *United Shoe Machinery Corp. v. Fitzgerald*, 237 Mass. 537 (1921), the court found illegal a strike for the "end" of making the employer agree to bargain with the union.

2. The Freedom of Contract and the Impact of the Industrial Revolution on Unionism

At the same time, however, the economy was changing, and unions began attracting more members. The industrial revolution brought more factory work, less skilled artisanal and agricultural work, and a new, specialized, managerial class keen on controlling the work process. The new industrial jobs often involved very long hours, low pay, and dangerous working conditions. In reaction, many workers sought to organize into unions. The American Federation of Labor (AFL) formed in 1886 as an umbrella group for various craft unions (unions organized by trade), and it grew dramatically in the late 19th and early 20th centuries. By the end of 1904, over two million workers in the U.S. were union members. Employers frequently reacted with great hostility to union organization, and labor relations in these decades were stained with a remarkable amount of violence (mostly, but not entirely, directed by employers at unions).

These conflicts also featured debates over what constituted "freedom" in work relations. Employers and their supporters emphasized the freedom of business owners to set employment terms as they saw fit through the "at-will" employment rule and "freedom of contract" principles. Under "at-will" rules, employers could fire employees for any reason at all (including union sympathies) or no reason, and employees could quit at any time for any or no reason. Freedom of contract arguments were also used to oppose legal limits on at-will rules, including laws giving rights to unions and their supporters, in cases such as *Coppage v. Kansas*, 236 U.S. 1 (1915) (holding unconstitutional a state law barring "yellow dog" contracts in which employees agreed not to join unions as a condition of employment); and *Lochner v. New York*, 198 U.S. 45 (1905) (striking down as unconstitutional a state law capping the number of hours that bakers could work).

Unions and their supporters, on the other hand, defined "freedom" to include the right to associate into worker organizations (much as doctors did with the American Medical Association and lawyers with the American Bar Association) without fear of being fired. They further stressed that without such organization, "freedom of contract" was illusory due to grossly unequal bargaining power between most employees and employers. Also, the argument continued, unions helped bring democracy into the workplace. Additionally, in the late 19th and early 20th centuries, unions tried to achieve some goals through legislation (often at the state level): minimum wages and maximum hours laws most famously, but also workplace safety laws and laws preventing employers from discriminating against union members. From 1885–1930, however, courts struck down as unconstitutional more than 150 such laws. *See* William Forbath, Law and the Shaping of the American Labor Movement (1989), 178–92.

3. Union Responses to Impact of Industrial Revolution on Workers

Courts' rejection of workplace legislation led unions to engage in more direct economic action (strikes and boycotts), but these were often held to be illegal as well. For example, in *Vegelahn v. Gunter*, 167 Mass. 92 (1896), the court majority upheld a broad injunction against a peaceful labor picket designed to discourage potential employees from working with an employer with whom the union had a dispute. Notably, even a peaceful picket often maintained by only two people was considered an improper means (the majority found it "intimidating"), and the majority also found the ends improper, characterizing it as interfering with the rights both of the employer and potential employees to form a contract. In a noteworthy dissent, Justice Holmes would have allowed somewhat more union activity. Further, he analogized union actions toward an employer to different employers competing against each other (which was legal, even if the competition caused harm to one or both of the employers).

Judges were especially hostile to the "end" of a union security clause: an agreement between the union and the employer that the employer would only hire those who were already union members (the "closed shop"); or require union membership as a condition of employment after the employee was hired (the "union shop"). For example, in *Plant v. Woods*, 176 Mass. 492 (1900), the Massachusetts Supreme Court found the goal of a closed shop illegal, and it issued a very broad injunction against any sort of union activity in pursuit of that goal.

Throughout this era, employers aggressively pursued injunctions against union activity (often seeking them *ex parte*), and courts routinely granted them. This was true not only in stopping strikes and boycotts, but also with regard to yellow-dog contracts and union organizing. After all, under at-will rules, employers did not need a contract violation in order to fire a pro-union employee. Instead, yellow-dog contracts were used as a basis to seek injunctions against union organizers looking to organize employees who had signed such contracts, on the grounds that such activity interfered with the contracts. *See, e.g.*, *Hitchman Coal & Coke Co. v. Mitchell*, 245 U.S. 229 (1917).

Despite these anti-union judicial attitudes, union membership continued to grow. To avoid unionization, employers increasingly began to use the tactic of creating what were called "company unions": employee organizations ostensibly created to deal with the employer over workplace issues that were actually entirely controlled by the employer.

The most controversial tactic of unions in this era remains a contentious subject today (complete with some rather complicated legal rules, *see* Chapter 16): secondary activity. Secondary activity is, broadly, any action a union takes to further its position in a dispute with the employer that employs the union's members (the "primary" employer) that is designed to appeal to or influence the behavior of anyone other than the members of that union at the primary employer and the primary employer itself. Other employers, employees of other employers, and the general public, are all "secondary" parties. This includes, of course, potential individual consumers and customers of the primary employer, other employers who are suppliers and/or customers of the primary employer, and workers at customer and supplier employers.

Unions liked secondary activities because they were often effective tools to pressure primary employers; employers disliked them for that reason and because they often entangled "innocent" employers, meaning employers who had no way to resolve the labor dispute with the primary employer themselves. Courts, prior to the NLRA, were quite hostile to such actions, frequently granting injunctions against them. This included injunctions against peaceful consumer boycotts, in which unions would urge the public not to patronize stores that carried a struck employer's products (*see, e.g.*, *Matthews v. Shankland*, 56 N.Y.S. 123 (Sup. Ct. 1898)) and even appeals to boycott the primary employer (*see, e.g.*, *Gompers v. Bucks Stove & Range Co.*, 221 U.S. 418 (1911)).

4. Employer Antitrust Arguments against Unions

Courts also often used antitrust laws to enjoin secondary activity. For example, in *Loewe v. Lawlor*, 208 U.S. 274 (1908) (the "Danbury Hatters" case), a union and its individual members were held liable (for treble damages) under the Sherman Antitrust Act of 1890 for urging consumers not to buy products from stores that sold hats made by the primary employer. Under modern law, some appeals to the public are still barred, or appear to be barred, by section 8(b)(4) of the NLRA (*see* Chapter 16), but this issue is made more complicated by modern First Amendment law.

Labor then successfully lobbied for amendments they hoped would protect unions in the Clayton Antitrust Act of 1914. Specifically, section 6 of that Act stated that "the labor of a human being is not a commodity or article of commerce," and that antitrust laws did not bar unions "from lawfully carrying out the legitimate objects thereof." Also, section 20 of the Clayton Act barred injunctions in cases involving disputes between employers and employees involving terms or conditions of employment. These hopes, however, were dashed. Notably, *Duplex Printing Press Co. v. Deering*, 254 U.S. 443 (1921), found an antitrust violation and allowed an injunction in a case involving a boycott aimed at secondary employees and at secondary employers who were customers of the primary employers. The majority in *Duplex Printing* held that the only permissible objects of union appeals were parties who were "proximately and substantially concerned as parties to an actual dispute." This effectively limited union appeals to the primary employer and to employees of the primary employer. The dissent noted that in this case, there were four companies in the area who made printing presses; all but Duplex were already unionized; and the unionized employers had stated that they could not preserve current wages at Duplex if they faced a nonunion competitor. Thus, the dissent concluded Duplex was not an unrelated employer. This case foreshadows another important issue under modern law: cases in which employees at a primary and a secondary employer share some economic interests. In some cases, these interests are sufficient to defeat a charge of illegal secondary activity; in some cases, they are not (*see* Chapter 18 for additional discussion on this topic).

The 1920s was a difficult decade for organized labor. There was a backlash against some radical strikes in 1919 (e.g., the Seattle general strike and the Boston police strike, discussed below). The Clayton Act offered no protection. Courts issued literally thousands of injunctions against labor activities, and employers were still free to fire employees for joining unions and to use yellow-dog contracts. Some courts did hold that peaceful primary strikes over wage and hour issues were legal. Unions had no statutory protections. But they were still organizing.

C. The Creation of Modern Labor Law

1. Modern Private-Sector Labor Law

a. The Railway-Labor Act of 1926 and Norris-LaGuardia Act of 1932

Modern private-sector labor law began with the Railway Labor Act of 1926 (RLA). This book will not focus on the RLA, which mostly covers private employers in the railroad and airline industries. The rules are often the same or similar to NLRA rules, although important differences exist, notably regarding strikes.

More important here was the Norris-LaGuardia Act of 1932. First, this Act barred courts from issuing injunctions in at least most peaceful labor disputes. *See* Sections 1, 4, 7, 9, and 10. Second, it made yellow-dog contracts unenforceable (although there was still no affirmative right to join a union). *See* Section 3. It also specifically reversed a main part of the holding in *Duplex Printing*, stating that its ban on injunctions applied "whether or not the disputants stand in the proximate relation of employer or employee." Section 13. The Act also contained some strong pro-union language, e.g.: "the individual unorganized worker is commonly helpless to exercise actual liberty of contract and to protect his freedom of labor...." Further, "it is necessary that he have full freedom of association, self-organization, and designation or representatives of his own choosing, to negotiate the terms and conditions of his employment ... for the purposes of collective bargaining or other mutual aid or protection." Section 2.

The Norris-LaGuardia Act later helped to resolve unions' antitrust problem. In *Apex Hosiery Co. v. Leader* 310 U.S. 469 (1940), and *United States v. Hutcheson*, 312 U.S. 219 (1941), the Supreme Court found an implicit "labor exemption" from antitrust laws. This exemption arose from the purposes of the Clayton and Norris-LaGuardia Acts, along with the language of section 13 of the Norris-LaGuardia Act. Thus, it appeared, at least for the moment, that secondary activities might be legal. As shown below, this moment would not last long. But unions remain essentially exempt from antitrust laws. *See* Chapter 21 for further discussion of this issue.

b. The National Labor Relations Act (Wagner Act) of 1935

The next step was the creation of the National Labor Relations Act (NLRA), specifically the Wagner Act of 1935. This Act was passed at the height of the Great Depression, and amidst significant labor unrest. In 1932, there were 840 strikes; in 1933, there were 1,700; and in 1937, there were 2,200. In 1934, approximately 1,500,000 workers went on strike at some point. Some of these strikes were led by radicals, and many more of them were met by significant violence from employers and their agents. Among other things, the law on the books and the reality on the ground were significantly out of synch.

Section 1 of the Wagner Act set out the following policies:

> [T]he denial by employers of the right of employees to organize and the refusal by employers to accept the procedure of collective bargaining lead to strikes and other forms of industrial strife or unrest, which have the intent of the necessary effect of burdening or obstructing commerce....
>
> The inequality of bargaining power between employees who do not possess full freedom of association or actual liberty of contract, and employers who are organized in the corporate or other forms of ownership association substantially burdens and affects the flow of commerce, and tends to aggravate recurrent business depressions, by depressing wage rates and the purchasing power of wages earners....
>
> It is hereby declared to be the policy of the United States to eliminate the causes of certain substantial obstructions to the free flow of

> commerce ... by encouraging the practice and procedure of collective bargaining....

The NLRA had four main goals: labor peace and stability; encouraging the practice and procedure of collective bargaining; providing a fair but neutral playing field on which unions and employers could settle their disputes without the government setting terms; and finally, to bring the law into conformity with the realities of unions as they actually existed.

Section 7 of the Wagner Act provided some of the most important rights of employees: "the right to self-organization, to form, join, or assist labor organizations, to bargain collectively through representatives of their own choosing, and to engage in other concerted activities for the purposes of collective bargaining or other mutual aid or protection." Section 8 of the Wagner Act, which is now Section 8(a) of the NLRA, made illegal certain acts by employers, known as "unfair labor practices" or "ULPs." For example, section 8(1), now section 8(a)(1), made it a ULP for employers to interfere with, restrain, or coerce employees in the exercise of their rights under Section 7. This meant, for example, that it was now illegal to fire an employee because that employee was a member of a union. Other employer ULPs included a ban on company unions and a duty to bargain with the union in good faith (these and other ULPS are discussed in more detail in later chapters of this book).

Section 9 of the Act discussed representation elections and created the "majority, exclusive representative" model central to U.S. labor law. Under this model, a union may only be recognized as a representative if a majority of the relevant employees supports the union; and if the union is a representative, it is the exclusive representative for the entire group of employees in matters concerning wages, hours, and working conditions.

The Wagner Act also created the National Labor Relations Board (NLRB). Its main functions are to oversee union representation issues and to adjudicate in the first instance claims of unfair labor practices (ULPs). It has five board members, appointed by the president; a general counsel; and currently over thirty regional offices. *See* Chapter 3.

The Supreme Court rejected constitutional challenges to the Wagner Act in *NLRB v. Jones & Laughlin Steel Corp.*, 301 U.S. 1 (1937), holding that it was a proper exercise of Congress's power under the Commerce Clause

This, the end of the Depression, and World War II mobilization, contributed to a significant increase in union membership. In 1933, fewer than 2,700,000 workers were in unions; in 1937, the total was over 7,000,000; and by 1945, it was more than 14,300,000. Also, beginning in 1938, a new labor organization had formed: the Congress of Industrial Organizations (CIO), which had split from the AFL. The CIO organized more unskilled workers (including more minorities and women). It also tended to organize on a "wall-to-wall" model, with all a plant's eligible employees in one bargaining unit, whereas the AFL had tended to organize employees by craft/occupation. In the 1950s, the AFL and CIO merged into the AFL-CIO, which is still the main national "umbrella" organization for unions in the U.S. today. By 1954, more than 17,000,000 workers were in unions, which was almost 35 percent of the non-agricultural workforce.

c. The Labor-Management Relations Act (Taft-Hartley Act) of 1947

Meanwhile, in 1947, the Labor-Management Relations Act (also known as the Taft-Hartley Act) added union ULPs and other rules designed to curb the power of the growing labor movement. Congressional Republicans enacted Taft-Hartley over the veto of President Harry Truman, and these amendments redefined the role of the government in labor relations away from explicitly favoring collective bargaining. The Act's supporters stressed "freedom of choice," referring to whether an employee wished to be represented by a union. Section 7, as amended, now states that, in addition to having the rights to organize, collectively bargain, and engage in concerted activities for mutual protection, employees also have the right to refrain from engaging in any of these activities.

More substantively, employer ULPs were now recodified in Section 8(a) of the NLRA, and new Section 8(b) added union ULPs. Some of the union ULPs were, at least mostly, the mirror of employer ULPs: e.g., Section 8(b)(1) barred union coercion of an employee's exercise of Section 7 rights, and Section 8(b)(3) imposed a duty on unions to bargain in good faith. But the Taft-Hartley Act added unique union ULPs as well. Notably, Section 8(b)(4) made almost all secondary activities illegal.

This Act also added Section 14(b) to the NLRA, which created the "right to work" option, allowing individual states to choose to outlaw union security clauses in collective bargaining agreements. *See* Chapter 19. Currently, about half the states in the U.S. have chosen that option.

Also, Taft-Hartley excluded supervisors from the NLRA's coverage. Further, Taft-Hartley's Section 301 created federal court jurisdiction over suits alleging a violation of a collective bargaining agreement. These and other rules from Taft-Hartley will be discussed in later chapters of this book.

d. The Labor-Management Reporting and Disclosure Act (Landrum-Griffin Act) of 1959, 1974 Healthcare Amendments, and Recent Attempts at Reform

The final major amendment to the NLRA came in 1959, with the Labor-Management Reporting and Disclosure Act (also known as the Landrum-Griffin Act). This Act mostly focused on the rights of individual union members *vis-à-vis* their unions; its purpose was to ensure more union democracy and combat union corruption. It also added further restrictions on secondary activities, notably by barring certain "hot cargo" clauses. As Chapter 18 discusses, these are clauses in collective bargaining agreements providing that union bargaining unit members are not required to work on or with products from "unfair" secondary employers. This amendment also limited the use of recognitional and organizational picketing under Section 8(b)(7) of the Act.

In 1974, the NLRA was amended to extend jurisdiction to hospitals. It also created a few special rules for employers and employees in the health care industry: most importantly, Section 8(g) requires a 10-day notice before such employees are legally allowed to strike.

In more recent decades, union density in the private sector has declined significantly. In 2024, union density as measured by actual union membership (as opposed to the percentage of employees covered by union contracts) was around 6%. This is in stark contrast to union density in the public sector, which (measured the same way) is more than five times larger. While an explanation for these opposing trends is beyond the scope of this book, readers might consider whether any of the legal rules they encounter here provide part of the explanation.

2. The History of Unions and Labor Law in the Public Sector

Public-sector labor law developed differently than private-sector law. First, laws authorizing collective bargaining in the public sector came significantly later (typically 30–50 years after the NLRA). Second, because public-sector labor law, unlike private-sector law, is mainly state and local law, public-sector law developed much more unevenly. Even today, states vary dramatically in what, if any, rights to bargain collectively they grant to public-sector unions.

Still, like private-sector unions, public-sector unions organized and were active before they won the formal right to bargaining collectively.

a. The Impact of the Boston Police Strike on Public Sector Unionism

Why did public-sector law labor develop on such a different track than private-sector law? One key event was the Boston police strike of 1919. While some public workers organized into unions as early as the 1830s, throughout the 19th century, most unionized public employees were members of private-sector unions, e.g., carpenters employed by naval yards. But in the late 19th and early 20th century, some public employees began to organize their own unions, and these unions began to affiliate with the AFL. In 1906, the AFL chartered the first national union of government employees, the National Federation of Post Office Clerks. From 1916–18, the AFL formed the American Federation of Teachers, the National Federation of Federal Employees, and the International Association of Fire Fighters; also, two major postal unions (the National Association of Letter Carriers and the Railway Mail Carriers) affiliated with the AFL. Union density in the public sector grew from under 2 percent in 1905, to 4.8 percent in 1915, to 7.2 percent in 1921.

The Boston police strike, however, helped end this burst of union organizing in the public sector. In 1919, the AFL for the first time began chartering locals of police unions; by the fall of that year, it had chartered thirty-seven such locals, including one in Boston. The Boston Police Department then barred its officers from affiliating with the AFL. Police Commissioner Steven O'Meara, backed by many local and national business groups, voiced concerns over "divided loyalty" if unionized police were called to deal with strikes. O'Meara suspended several union leaders for refusing to leave the AFL, and this prompted a strike by essentially all Boston police officers. This strike led to lawlessness in the city's streets for two days, with considerable property damage, hundreds injured, and at least nine killed (reportedly by state guards called in to quell the situation). All the strikers were fired.

This disastrous event left a lasting legacy in the history of public-sector labor relations. For many decades, the image of government employees was fused with the image of the Boston strike. In 1981, Ronald Reagan cited the strike as precedent for firing illegally striking members of a federal-sector union, the Professional Air Traffic Controllers Organization (PATCO). More generally, courts and legislatures often cited the Boston strike as a reason why public-sector workers of any kind should not have any type of collective bargaining rights.

A less obvious effect of the strike was that many public employers that allowed some form of employee organization still banned those organizations from affiliating with organized labor. Thus, some very important public-sector unions were not, and still are not, affiliated with the AFL-CIO (e.g., the National Education Association and the Fraternal Order of Police).

b. Public Sector Unionism Prior to Modern Laws

Other factors contributed to the different path taken by public-sector law. Judges remained very hostile to public-sector unions even after the New Deal. Notably, courts assumed that public-sector unions would behave exactly as private-sector unions did, including striking. This fear was routinely displayed in cases that barred public employees from *organizing* into unions, even though the union had expressly renounced any right to strike. Indeed, this was true even though public-sector unions, from the 1920s through at least the early 1960s, rarely struck.

It was also likely true that a *federal* law giving state and local public employees NLRA-style rights in the mid-20th century would have been held unconstitutional, beyond Congress's power under the Commerce Clause and/or a violation of the 10th Amendment (which reserves unenumerated powers to the States). State and local governments, in turn, were direct employers of workers themselves, which made it less likely they would want to authorize the existence of unions. A number of courts held that public-sector bargaining would also violate the more obscure constitutional "non-delegation" doctrine (forbidding the delegation of exclusively governmental power to private parties such as unions or arbitrators). *See, e.g.*, *Nutter v. City of Santa Monica*, 168 P.2d 741 (Cal. App. 1946).

Because both the Norris-LaGuardia Act and the NLRA excluded the public sector, government employers routinely used yellow-dog contracts into the 1960s, and courts routinely upheld them. *See, e.g.*, *AFSCME Local 201 v. City of Muskegon*, 120 N.W.2d 197 (Mich. 1963). Through the mid-1960s, courts rejected union arguments that such bars on joining unions violated the First Amendment rights of public employees, on the theory that while public employees had the right to discuss politics, they did not have an accompanying right to public employment, citing *McAuliffe v. New Bedford*, 155 Mass. 216, 219 (1892).

c. *The Rise of Public-Sector State Bargaining Statutes*

Finally, in 1959, Wisconsin passed the first state law in the nation that gave the right to organize and (limited) collective bargaining rights to public workers, the Municipal Employees Relations Act. While this law still barred strikes, as amended in 1962, it provided that if bargaining reached an impasse, a state agency could conduct mediation and fact-finding. The law was later amended to permit binding arbitration (often called "interest arbitration") to resolve contract negotiation impasses. These techniques are now common in modern public-sector law.

The Wisconsin law was the first of a wave of public-sector labor laws. Also in 1962, President Kennedy issued Executive Order 10988, providing limited union rights to most federal employees (in 1978, these rights were significantly expanded by the Federal Service Labor Management Relations Act). By 1966, sixteen states had enacted laws granting the right to organize and some collective bargaining rights to public employees. By the 1980s, over three-quarters of the states provided some or most public employees with the right to bargain collectively. By 2000, twenty-nine states and the District of Columbia allowed collective bargaining generally for public employees; thirteen states authorized collective bargaining for certain types of public employees only (typically teachers, firefighters, and/or police); and eight did not authorize any form of public-sector collective bargaining.

Beyond that, the laws themselves varied. The scope of bargaining (what unions have a right to negotiate over) is sometimes significantly more restricted in the public sector than it is in the private sector. Further, in 2000, only twelve states allowed any public employees to strike (and no state allowed police or fire employees to strike). Employees not allowed to strike were typically provided with some combination of some forms of mediation, fact-finding, and interest arbitration. The variations in state law will be addressed in the relevant chapters of this book. Coverage varies, not just in what types of public employers are and are not covered, but also in that some state public-sector labor laws cover supervisors. And many other variations exist (including, e.g., some states adopting the "mandatory card check recognition" rule that is not used in the private sector or even most public-sector jurisdictions).

Also, in the late 1960s, courts began holding (for the first time) that the First Amendment protected the right of at least most public-sector employees to join or support unions, meaning they could not be disciplined or discharged for so doing. This spelled the end for yellow-dog contracts and employer policies barring public employees from joining unions affiliated with the

AFL-CIO. *See, e.g., Atkins v. City of Charlotte*, 266 F. Supp. 1068, (W.D. N.C. 1969); *American Federation of State, County & Municipal Employees, AFL-CIO v. Woodward*, 406 F.2d 137 (8th Cir. 1969). Significantly, though, this First Amendment right is limited to the right to organize. It does not include the right to bargain collectively or the right to strike. Indeed, in *Smith v. Arkansas*, 441 U.S. 463 (1979) (*per curiam*), the Supreme Court found no First Amendment violation when an employer refused to take grievances from a union (insisting instead on taking grievances from individual employees only). But generally, public employees now had a constitutional right to form, join, or support a union.

d. Recent Developments in Public-Sector Bargaining Law

The 21st century has seen an ebb and flow of public-sector bargaining rights, with some states limiting or eliminating them, and others creating or expanding them. Perhaps most famously, Wisconsin passed a law (Act 10) in 2011 that practically eliminated collective bargaining for the public employees it covered, while "public safety" employees (primarily law enforcement and firefighter employees) were excluded from the changes. Among other things, the law limited the scope of bargaining to wages, and even as to wages, unions could only ask for an increase up to the rise in the cost of living; it imposed a "mandatory recertification" system under which unions had to be recertified in an election each year, and would only be recertified if the union received 51 percent or more of the votes of the entire union bargaining unit (see Chapter 10 to understand how unusual and radical this rule is); and made the state a "right to work" jurisdiction for the public sector (meaning clauses in collective bargaining agreements requiring the payments of any dues to the union were illegal, see Chapter 19). A number of other states in 2011 also passed laws limiting public-sector union rights, albeit to a lesser degree. Along the same lines, in 2017 Iowa passed a law similar to Wisconsin's Act 10, House File 291. Florida has recently enacted various measures making it significantly more difficult for unions to remain certified. Florida SB 256, enacted in 2023, requires that affected unions maintain at least 60% of union membership in their bargaining units or be decertified (this rule does not apply to police and firefighter unions).

On the other hand, in the past decade (and thus after the first edition of this book), several states have significantly expanded public-sector labor rights. For example, in 2017 and 2019, in SB 493 and SB 135, Nevada extended collective bargaining rights to school administrators and state employees. In 2020 and 2022, Colorado enacted HB20-1153 and SB22-230, which grant collective bargaining rights to state and (most) county workers. Virginia had long not only refused to grant a legal right for public-sector unions to bargain collectively but had also affirmatively held that such bargaining was illegal even if the employer and union voluntarily wished to engage in it. But in 2020, Virginia enacted HB 582, which permits local governments in the commonwealth to allow collective bargaining. Statutory changes to public-sector labor laws, often significant ones, will almost certainly continue.

In both the public and private sectors, the history of labor relations has played, and continues to play, a major role not only in the crafting and amendment of statutes, but also in court and agency interpretations of statutes. As you read the following chapters, you will likely note some areas in which the statutory interpretations in court and labor board decisions seem at least somewhat detached from actual statutory language. Such rulings often reflect historical practices, understandings, or ideologies.

CHECKPOINTS

- Before the enactment of NLRA, unions organized and engaged in a wide variety of actions, from primary strikes to secondary activities and boycotts, in attempts to win rights for unions and improve the wages, hours and working conditions of their members. Employers fought strongly against unions, from using "yellow dog" contracts to actual violence.
- Courts often sided with employers, e.g., finding many union activities illegal under the law of conspiracy and later antitrust, and striking down laws banning "yellow dog" contracts.
- Labor law in the private sector is governed by the National Labor Relations Act (NLRA), as amended. It provides covered employees with the right to form and join unions, bargain collectively, and engage in other concerted activities for mutual aid and protection.
- The NLRA also provides a list of employer unfair labor practices (ULPs) in Section 8(a) and union ULPs in Section 8(b). The NLRA also sets out mechanisms for union representation proceedings, and

it created the National Labor Relations Board (NLRB) to enforce the law in the first instance.

- Labor laws in the public sector developed later and more unevenly. They usually are a matter of state law, and state laws vary considerably regarding what rights, if any, they grant public sector unions (e.g., as to what employees they cover, what topics unions may negotiate about, and how bargaining impasses are resolved).
- The First Amendment of the Constitution grants most public employees the right to organize into unions, but does not grant further rights; e.g., it does not grant the right to bargain collectively.
- Public-sector labor statutes have been, and continue to be, amended much more frequently than private-sector laws in the past few decades.

CHAPTER 3

Overview of the National Labor Relations Board's Organization and Its Unfair Labor Practice and Election Procedures

---

ROADMAP

- What is the National Labor Relations Board?
- What constitutes an unfair labor practice charge?
- What is the process for bringing a case before the NLRB?
- What is the process for obtaining a Board-conducted, secret-ballot election?

This chapter gives a basic overview of the National Labor Relations Board (NLRB or Board) and the two fundamental processes that the NLRB administers—the unfair labor practice (ULP) hearing and the secret-ballot election for determining whether a union will represent a particular group of employees. In the public sector, state labor boards are typically structured much like the NLRB. Practices and procedures before state labor boards are generally similar except that, in most jurisdictions, parties litigate their own ULP charges before the labor board, rather than having board attorneys prosecute the case.

A. What Is the National Labor Relations Board?

The National Labor Relations Board is an independent federal agency that protects the rights of most private-sector employees to engage in concerted activity with or without the help of a union. Independent federal agencies, such as the NLRB, are created by an act of Congress, in this case, by Section 3 of the National Labor Relations Act (NLRA), 29 U.S.C. § 153. The NLRB is independent of the Department of Labor and does not come under the jurisdiction of the Secretary of Labor.

The NLRB consists of two sides: the General Counsel, or GC-side, and the Board or Board-side.

1. The GC-Side

The GC-side enforces the NLRA. This office investigates and prosecutes ULPs and conducts secret-ballot elections. The General Counsel, appointed by the President with the advice and consent of the Senate for a term of four years, runs the GC-side. The General Counsel leads four legal divisions on the GC-side: (1) the Division of Operations Management; (2) the Division of Advice, which advises the regional offices; (3) the Division of Enforcement Litigation; and (4) the Division of Legal Counsel.

The Division of Operations Management oversees the twenty-six regional offices and several other sub-regional and resident offices across the country. These offices have geographic jurisdiction. For example, Region 10 has jurisdiction over parts of eight states—Alabama, Georgia, Kentucky, North Carolina, South Carolina, Tennessee, Virginia, and West Virginia—with a regional office in Atlanta, Georgia; a sub-regional office in Winston-Salem, North Carolina; and two resident offices, one in Birmingham, Alabama, and the other in Nashville, Tennessee. By contrast, Region 9 has only one regional office in Cincinnati, Ohio, but it has jurisdiction over parts of four states—Indiana, Kentucky, Ohio, and West Virginia. Any person who believes that an employer or a union has violated the NLRA may file charges alleging specific ULPs with the appropriate office. Attorneys and field agents in these offices will investigate those charges, and the regional office under the General Counsel's authority will issue a complaint upon reasonable cause to believe that a ULP has occurred. The regional offices also conduct secret-ballot elections to determine whether employees in a particular bargaining unit wish to be represented by a union.

The Division of Advice houses two offices: the Regional Advice Branch and the Injunction Litigation Branch. Regional Advice advises the regional offices on challenging cases, helping those attorneys assess whether to recommend issuing a complaint. The ultimate decision rests with the General Counsel, but the Regional Advice Branch attorneys and regional attorneys work together to determine the theory of the case. The Injunction Litigation Branch represents the Board in Section 10(j) and 10(l) appeals for injunctive relief involving actions brought before a United States Court of Appeals.

The Division of Enforcement Litigation houses the Office of Appeals and the Appellate and Supreme Court Litigation Branch. The Office of Appeals oversees all administrative appeals from Regional Office decisions not to issue a complaint. The Appellate and Supreme Court Litigation Branch defends the Board's final decisions and orders before the federal courts of appeals and the United States Supreme Court.

In August 2013, the NLRB created the Division of Legal Counsel. This new Division consists of three branches: (1) the Ethics, Employment, and Administrative Law Branch; (2) the Contempt, Compliance and Special Litigation Branch; and (3) the Freedom of Information Act (FOIA) Branch. According to an NLRB news release dated August 22, 2013, available at https://www.nlrb.gov/news-outreach/news-story/national-labor-relations-board-creates-division-of-legal-counsel-at:

> The Ethics, Employment and Administrative Law Branch provides the NLRB with legal counsel and advice in the areas of ethics, labor relations, employment and personnel law, government contracting and Federal Tort Claims Act matters.
>
> The Contempt, Compliance and Special Litigation Branch provides compliance and contempt advice and conducts litigation when external statutes, programs or outside proceedings threaten the Agency's ability to carry out its mission. It also provides advice and engages in litigation to attain compliance with outstanding court judgments and initiates ancillary collection proceedings. It protects the Board's remedial orders in bankruptcy courts or against attachments, garnishments, and liens. It also assists with defending Agency employees when they have been sued in their individual capacity for actions taken in their official capac-

ity, and assists Regions regarding compliance work related to potential derivative liability.

The Freedom of Information Act (FOIA) Branch coordinates the processing of all FOIA requests in the Regional Offices and directly handles all FOIA requests in Headquarters, as well as all FOIA appeals. In the near future, it is anticipated that all FOIA work will be centralized at the NLRB Headquarters, and, at that time, the FOIA Branch will be responsible for processing all FOIA requests nationwide.

In addition, the Division of Legal Counsel's Lead Technology Counsel renders advice and assistance regarding e-litigation and e-discovery matters.

This Division reorganizes branches formerly in the Divisions of Enforcement and Advice to "eliminate[] duplication of functions, improve the delivery of services, streamline operations and integrate services." *See id.*

2. The Board-Side

The Board-side has three main divisions: The Division of Judges, the Office of Representational Appeals, and the Board. The Division of Judges houses the administrative law judges who, after hearing cases, make decisions and recommend orders to the Board. The Office of Representational Appeals "reviews... election-related decisions, including dismissals of petitions and pre-election decisions by Regional Directors." *See* NLRB, Conduct Elections, https://www.nlrb.gov/about-nlrb/what-we-do/conduct-elections.

The Board is a five-member administrative tribunal, with one member serving as the "Chairman." The Board "primarily acts as a quasi-judicial body in deciding cases on the basis of formal records in administrative proceedings. Board Members are appointed by the President to 5-year terms, with Senate consent, the term of one Member expiring each year." *See* NLRB, The Board, https://www.nlrb.gov/about-nlrb/who-we-are.

The history of presidential appointments to the Board explains how the NLRB has become one of the most politicized and polarized federal agencies. This history illustrates how ideology has come to play an influential role in policymaking. In a practice known as oscillation, national labor policy changes as the political composition of the Board changes, typically with a shift in party control of the presidency. *See generally* Joan Flynn, *A Quiet Revolution at the Board: The Transformation of the NLRB, 1935–2000*, 61 Ohio L. J. 1361 (2000).

Under the Wagner Act, presidential appointments to the Board came strictly from government or academia (neutrals). President Eisenhower became the first President to appoint Board members with a history of representing one side or the other—in this case, he appointed three Board members with management-side experience. Presidents Kennedy and Johnson returned to the practice of appointing neutrals. President Nixon appointed one representative with a management-side background. President Ford appointed one representative with a management-side background and one who had represented both management and labor. President Carter returned to the practice of appointing neutrals.

President Reagan's Board marked the start of the modern Board's reputation for political decision-making. By the time President Reagan entered office, a custom had developed whereby no more than three of the five Board members would belong to the same political party as the sitting president. Regardless of political affiliation, all of President Reagan's appointees were representatives from either management (mostly in-house corporate labor counsel) or government. These appointments resulted in the most political Board to date. The Dotson Board (1983–1987) (named for its Chairman, Donald L. Dotson) issued what academics have come to view as some of the most pro-management decisions in the Board's history—at least up to that point. President George Bush continued this practice but also appointed one Board member with a labor background.

President Clinton was the first president to appoint truly pro-labor Board members in a way that would make an impact. Clinton had the opportunity to make nine appointments to the Board. Three hailed from management, three came from unions, two were career attorneys with the NLRB (neutrals), and one, William B. Gould IV, who served as Chairman, was an academic with ties to labor unions. During the Clinton era, the Gould Board set out to reverse the Dotson Board's pro-management decisions and issue its own pro-labor decisions. Accordingly, although policy oscillation has always been a part of the Board's practice, it became its modus operandi with the Dotson and Gould Boards.

The George W. Bush (Bush II) and Obama Boards followed suit. President George W. Bush had the opportunity to appoint eight board members: five of the six Republicans had management-side backgrounds; one Republican, Alex Acosta, was a neutral government/academic who later became the United States Attorney for the Southern District of Florida in the Bush administration and then the Secretary of Labor in the Trump administration;

and the two Democrats had a labor background. President Obama appointed eleven board members: six of the seven Democrats had union backgrounds; one Democrat was a career government employee who had worked for both administrations; and the four Republicans all had management backgrounds.

The Bush II and Obama Boards ushered in a brand-new type of gamesmanship. During George W. Bush's presidency, as Board member terms expired, those spots remained vacant. As of January 1, 2008, the Board had only two members—Peter Schaumber, a Republican with a pro-management arbitration background, and Wilma Liebman, a Democrat with a union background. The ideology of these two Board members represented the relative extremes of the U.S. political landscape at that time, so it was hard to imagine that they would agree on much. Nevertheless, they kept the Board functioning and managed to decide almost 600 cases over the following twenty-seven months until March 27, 2010, when then-President Obama was able to appoint three more members (two pro-union Democrats and one pro-management Republican).

In *New Process Steel v. NLRB*, 560 U.S. 674 (2010), the United States Supreme Court reversed the Seventh Circuit's enforcement of one of those two-Board-member decisions because the Board lacked the three-person quorum required under Section 3(b) of the NLRA. The practical import of this decision was twofold. First, the Obama Board had to re-decide and re-issue those cases decided by the Schaumber-Liebman Board. Second, this decision legalized a do-nothing strategy for those interested in not enforcing the NLRA. Because the NLRA is mostly a pro-union statute, this do-nothing strategy works for those with a pro-business, anti-union agenda, historically, the Republican Party.

On January 4, 2012, President Obama, faced with the prospect of another two-member Board, used his constitutional recess appointment powers to make three intra-recess appointments—a common presidential practice since the Reagan administration. *See* U.S. Const. Art. II, sec. 2 ("The President shall have Power to fill up all Vacancies that may happen during the Recess of the Senate, by granting Commissions which shall expire at the End of their next Session."). These recess appointments, however, were controversial for two reasons. First, the appointments were made during a recess within a Congressional session (intra-session) rather than during a recess between congressional sessions (inter-session). Second, the Republican-controlled House of Representatives refused to give its consent to the Democratic-controlled Senate to go into recess to try to prevent any intra-session appointments. *See* U.S. Const. Art. I, sec. 5 ("[n]either House, during the Session of Congress, shall, without the Consent of the other, adjourn for more than three days...."). In response, the Senate held very brief, *pro forma* sessions in which no business was conducted.

The newly constituted Board—two Board members appointed with the consent of the Senate and three Board members appointed without Senate consent, while the Senate was in intra-session recess—began to decide cases. One of those cases made it to the Supreme Court, once again, not on the merits, but on the questions of what constitutes a recess and whether the Senate was "in recess" under the Recess Appointments Clause when the President made these appointments. *See NLRB v. Noel Canning*, 573 U.S. 513 (2014). A unanimous Court affirmed the D.C. Circuit's opinion, concluding that the President's appointment of those Board members was invalid under the Recess Appointments Clause. In so holding, however, the majority (Breyer, J.) did not limit the President's recess-appointment power as much as the D.C. Circuit would have. Instead, the Court held that recess appointments could be made during both intra-session and inter-session breaks, but that the breaks had to be of sufficient length. All nine justices agreed that the three-day break, during which time the President made the three recess appointments, was insufficient to count as a recess, and thus that these recess appointments were invalid.

With the appointments of three Board members invalid, the remaining two-member Board was without a quorum. Therefore, under *New Process Steel*, *supra*, all Board decisions made during that time (between January 4, 2012, and August 5, 2013) were invalid. On July 18, 2014, shortly after *Noel Canning* was decided, the Board notified the public that it "unanimously ratified all administrative, personnel, and procurement matters [it took] from January 4, 2012[,] to August 5, 2013," the date on which the Board regained its quorum. It explained that the Board acted "to remove any question concerning the validity of [its] actions undertaken during that period." *See* NLRB, News and Publications, *NLRB Officials Ratify Agency Actions Taken During Period When Supreme Court Held Board Members Were Not Validly Appointed*, Aug. 4, 2014, https://www.nlrb.gov/news-outreach/news-story/nlrb-officials-ratify-agency-actions-taken-during-period-when-supreme.

During President Donald Trump's first administration (2017–2021), the Board consistently maintained a quorum. Over that period, it adopted its most pronounced pro-business stance since the Reagan era, thereby raising the stakes of an oscillation policy.

On January 20, 2021, just minutes after taking the oath of office as the 46th President of the United States, Joe Biden dismissed Peter Robb, the Trump-appointed NLRB General Counsel, Robb still had ten months left on his four-year term. In a letter delivered that day, Robb was given until 5:00

p.m. to resign or be removed. Robb refused—and was promptly fired. President Biden then appointed longtime NLRB attorney Peter Ohr as Interim General Counsel. Ohr served in that role until the Senate confirmed Biden's nominee, Jennifer Abruzzo. G.C. Abruzzo, a veteran of the NLRB and former senior official at the Communications Workers of America, brought extensive labor relations experience to the position.

Robb's sudden dismissal raised important legal questions. Critics argued that the President may have overstepped his authority by removing a Senate-confirmed official before the end of their term. Supporters countered that the General Counsel serves at the pleasure of the President and can be removed, especially here, where there were no statutory removal protections. Although the issue never reached the Supreme Court, every federal court of appeals that reviewed the case agreed: President Biden's decision to remove Robb was constitutional and fell within his executive authority under Article II of the U.S. Constitution. *See, e.g.*, *Rieth-Riley Constr. Co. v. NLRB*, 114 F.4th 519, 529–31 (6th Cir. 2024).

President Donald Trump took a page from President Biden's book during Trump's second term. On January 27, 2025, President Donald Trump fired Gwynne Wilcox, the first Black woman to serve on the NLRB, triggering legal and political backlash. Wilcox, a longtime labor attorney and newly appointed chair, was dismissed via late-night email for allegedly misaligning with the administration's goals. Trump also removed General Counsel Jennifer Abruzzo and installed Marvin Kaplan, a former management-side lawyer, as chair—leaving the Board without a quorum, with only Kaplan and labor-side member David Prouty remaining.

Wilcox sued, citing the NLRA's removal protections, which require notice, hearing, and a showing of neglect or malfeasance. *See* 29 U.S.C. § 3(a); *see also Humphrey's Executor v. U.S.*, 295 U.S. 602 (1935). In March, Judge Beryl Howell ruled in her favor, calling the dismissal a "blatant violation of the law" and declaring, "An American president is not a king." *Wilcox v. Trump*, 775 F. Supp. 3d 215 (D.D.C. 2025). The court reinstated Wilcox and restored the Board's quorum, but the Trump administration appealed. The Supreme Court issued a temporary stay, allowing her removal to stand pending review. *See Trump v. Wilcox*, 145 S. Ct. 1415 (2025). The case has raised urgent questions about executive authority and the independence of federal agencies, making Wilcox's firing a defining moment in labor law and constitutional governance.

Finally, in recent years, a growing wave of constitutional challenges has targeted the structure and enforcement mechanisms of the NLRB. One claim—that the agency's denial of jury trials in backpay proceedings violates the Seventh Amendment—has not met with any success. However, a particularly consequential line of attack concerns the statutory removal protections afforded to NLRB ALJs and Board Members—protections not extended to the General Counsel—which critics argue impermissibly constrain the President's Article II removal power.

Just before this book went to press, the Fifth Circuit issued a sweeping decision in *Space Exploration Technologies Corp. v. NLRB*, Case No. 24-50627 (5th Cir. Aug. 19, 2025), affirming preliminary injunctions that halted ULP proceedings against SpaceX and two other employers. The court held that ALJs are "inferior officers" who, under *Jarkesy v. SEC*, 34 F.4th 446 (5th Cir. 2022), *aff'd and remanded*, 603 U.S. 109 (2024), must be subject to presidential removal. It further concluded—relying on the Supreme Court's temporary stay in *Trump v. Wilcox* and its longstanding precedent in *Humphrey's Executor v. United States*, 295 U.S. 602 (1935)—that the for-cause removal protections for Board Members under Section 3(a) of the NLRA similarly violate the separation of powers principle by unduly restricting executive oversight. In the court's view, subjecting parties to proceedings before such insulated officials constitutes irreparable harm, thereby justifying the injunctions.

Crucially, while the Fifth Circuit found these removal protections unconstitutional, it declined to sever Section 3(a), rendering the NLRA unenforceable within its jurisdiction. No other circuit has adopted this position, thereby creating a circuit split on an important federal issue and setting the stage for likely Supreme Court review. Should the Court affirm the Fifth Circuit's reasoning, it may choose to sever the offending portion of Section 3(a), thereby preserving the remainder of the Act, which does contain a severability clause under Section 503. This decision marks a pivotal moment in administrative law, raising profound questions about the future of independent agency adjudication and the constitutional limits of executive control.

B. What Constitutes an Unfair Labor Practice Charge?

A prerequisite to any NLRB action is a ULP charge. A charge is a formal filing with the Region where the charging party identifies the right under the NLRA that allegedly has been violated. The Board's Rules and Regulations provide that "[a]ny person" may file a ULP charge. Rules & Regulations, 29 C.F.R. § 102.9. Such "charge must be filed with the Regional Director for the

Region in which the alleged unfair labor practice has occurred or is occurring." *Id.* at § 102.10. Forms for filing a charge are available on the NLRB's website.

Charges must "be in writing and signed, and ... shall be sworn to ... under the penalty of perjury that its contents are true and correct." *Id.* at § 102.11. Charges must contain the following information:

(1) The full name and address of the person making the charge.

(2) If the charge is filed by a labor organization, the full name and address of any national or international labor organization of which it is an affiliate or constituent unit.

(3) The full name and address of the person against whom the charge is made (referred to as the Charged Party).

(4) A brief statement of the conduct constituting the alleged unfair labor practices affecting commerce.

Id. at § 102.12(a).

C. The NLRB Unfair Labor Practice Process

1. Timeliness of the Charge

In NLRA Section 10(b), Congress established a short statute of limitations; a ULP charge must be filed within six months of conduct that constitutes the basis for the charge. *See* 29 U.S.C. § 160(b).

2. Investigation of the Charge and Determination Whether to Issue a Complaint

Once a charge is filed with the NLRB, attorneys or field agents in the Regional Office investigate the charge to determine whether to issue a complaint. *See* NLRB RULES & REGULATIONS, 29 C.F.R. § 102.15. If the Regional Office declines to issue a complaint, then the charging party may appeal to the General Counsel. *See id.* at § 102.19; NLRB Form 4767 (available at https://www.nlrb.gov/guidance/fillable-forms). The Office of Appeals manages those appeals. Although those appeals are rarely granted, the General Counsel's ultimate decision not to issue a complaint is unreviewable. *See NLRB v. UFCW, Local 23*, 484 U.S. 112, 122–23 (1987).

If a complaint issues, it must contain the following information:

> (a) A clear and concise statement of the facts upon which the Board asserts jurisdiction, and
>
> (b) A clear and concise description of the acts which are claimed to constitute unfair labor practices, including ... the approximate dates and places of such acts and the names of Respondent's [Charged Party's] agents or other representatives who committed the acts.

NLRB Rules and Regulations, § 102.15. The Respondent has "14 days from the service of the complaint" to "file an answer" in which Respondent must "admit, deny, or explain" or state that it is "without knowledge" of "each of the facts alleged in the complaint." *Id.* at § 102.20.

In general, neither charging parties nor respondents have any discovery rights. By contrast, the General Counsel has limited discovery rights primarily through the Board's statutory power to issue subpoenas. 29 U.S.C. § 161. In particular, the General Counsel will issue (1) subpoenas *ad testificandum* or to order witnesses to testify or (2) subpoenas *duces tecum* to order parties to produce documents at hearing.

3. The Hearing

An administrative law judge (ALJ) conducts hearings to take evidence on a complaint. NLRB Rules & Regulations, 29 C.F.R. § 102.34. The ALJ's primary duty is to "regulate the course of the hearing," which includes, among other things, a duty to "inquire fully into the facts" to determine whether the respondent has engaged in a ULP. *Id.* at § 102.35(a)(6). The ALJ is required to conduct the hearing in accordance with the federal rules of civil procedure and evidence only "so far as practicable." 29 U.S.C. 160(b); NLRB Rules & Regulations, 29 C.F.R. § 101.10(a), 102.39. The ALJ has authority like a trial tribunal. The judge has power to, among other things, rule on applications for or petitions to revoke subpoenas; rule on offers of proof; hold settlement conferences; dispose of motions; and approve stipulations. *See id.* at § 102.35.

4. The Administrative Law Judge's Decision (ALJD)

The ALJ issues a decision "[a]t the conclusion of the hearing." That decision must state "findings of fact and conclusions, as well as the reasons for the determinations on all material issues, and making recommendations as to action which should be taken in the case. The [ALJ] may recommend dismissal or sustain the complaint, in whole or in part, and recommend that the respondent cease and desist from the unlawful acts found and take action to remedy their effects." NLRB Rules & Regulations, 29 C.F.R. § 101.11(a); *see also id.* at § 102.45(a). The ALJD is thereupon filed with the Board in Washington, D.C., and by Board order the case is transferred to the Board. *Id.* at §§ 101.11(b), 102.45(a).

5. Exceptions

Once the ALJD issues, the parties have two courses of action. The parties may either comply with or challenge the ALJD. NLRB Rules & Regulations, 29 C.F.R. §§ 101.11(b), 101.12, 101.13. To challenge an ALJD, the parties must file exceptions within 28 days of the service date for the order transferring the case to the Board. *Id.* at § 102.46. In response to exceptions, any party may file an answering brief or cross-exceptions. *Id.* at § 101.11(b).

Parties must be careful in filing exceptions because it is the exceptions, not the briefs in support of exceptions, that courts will ultimately review in determining whether a party properly preserved an issue for appeal. *See* 29 U.S.C. § 160(e); NLRB Rules & Regulations, 29 C.F.R. §§ 101.12(b), 102.46(a)(1)(ii); *Woelke & Romero Framing Inc. v. NLRB*, 456 U.S. 645, 665–66 (1982). The Board has set out the following four guidelines for filing exceptions:

> Each exception must (A) Specify the questions of procedure, fact, law, or policy to which exception is taken; (B) Identify that part of the Administrative Law Judge's decision to which exception is taken; (C) Provide precise citations of the portions of the record relied on; and (D) Concisely state the grounds for the exception....

NLRB Rules & Regulations, 29 C.F.R. § 102.46(a)(1)(i). Parties may put argument and legal citation in the exceptions or in a brief in support of exceptions. *Id.* at § 102.46(a)(2). If no exceptions are filed, then the ALJD becomes the Board's order. *See* 29 U.S.C. § 160(c); NLRB Rules & Regulations, 29 C.F.R. §§ 101.12(b); 102.48(a).

6. The Board's Decision and Order (D&O)

The Board issues a final order for purposes of appellate jurisdiction in a federal court of appeals. There are two ways in which a final order might be issued. As explained above, if no timely or proper exceptions are filed, the ALJD becomes the final Board order. *See* 29 U.S.C. § 160(c); NLRB Rules & Regulations, 29 C.F.R. §§ 101.12(b); 102.48(a). If timely and proper exceptions are filed, however, the Board will issue a final order only after it "reviews the entire record, including the administrative law judge's decision and recommendations, the exceptions thereto, the complete transcript of evidence, and the exhibits, briefs, and arguments." NLRB Rules & Regulations, 29 C.F.R. § 101.12(a).

7. The Appellate Process

Once the final Board D&O issues, regional attorneys work with the parties to secure compliance. At this point, the aggrieved party or parties have five main options. First, the aggrieved party could comply with the Board's order. Second and relatedly, the parties could try to settle the case with the Regional Office. Third, the aggrieved party could do nothing. Because Board orders are not self-executing, an aggrieved party who has been found to have violated the NLRA and who has been ordered to remedy a ULP is not in contempt unless the Board's order is court-enforced. For this reason, the parties will typically seek court enforcement of the Board's order, which brings us to options four and five. Fourth, the aggrieved party may file a petition for review "in any United States court of appeals in the circuit wherein the unfair labor practice ... was alleged to have been engaged in or wherein such person resides or transacts business, or in the United States Court of Appeals for the District of Columbia, by filing" a petition for review with that court. 29 U.S.C. § 160(f). Fifth, the aggrieved party could refuse to comply with the order and wait for the Board's Appellate Court counsel to apply for enforcement of the Board's order in any court of appeals of the United States "... wherein the unfair labor practice ... occurred or wherein such person resides or transacts business" by filing an application for enforcement with that court. 29 U.S.C.

§ 160(e). Most aggrieved parties will not do this because they lose the privilege to forum shop.

Once a Board order is court-enforced, aggrieved parties must comply, or they will be in contempt. The Board's Contempt Branch generally handles these cases, which includes suing non-complying parties in district court for civil or contempt proceedings. Filing a petition for *certiorari* with the Supreme Court does not automatically stay enforcement of the Board's order.

D. The NLRB Secret-Ballot Election Process

The NLRB has exclusive jurisdiction over union election procedures. In particular, the NLRB regulates the process by which an employee forms, joins, or decertifies a union. The election process has five stages: pre-petition, petition for election, pre-election/hearing (or election agreement), election, and certification/post-election. This section explains these procedures primarily within the context of union certification.

1. Pre-Petition

During the pre-petition stage, the union seeking to represent employees commences an organizing campaign. To obtain a Board-conducted secret-ballot election, a union must petition for election with the appropriate Regional Office. That petition must be accompanied by evidence, typically signed authorization cards, that at least 30 percent of employees in an appropriate unit are interested in having an election (showing of interest). Although only a 30 percent showing of interest is needed for the union to obtain an election, it will usually aim for at least 70 percent showing of interest, knowing that union support wanes in the weeks leading up to an election.

2. Petition

Once the union has completed the petition for a representative election, which can be obtained on the NLRB website, it will file the petition with the appropriate regional office. The union will then serve the petition, along with a blank Statement of Position form and a description of the election procedures (both available on the NLRB website), on the employer.

3. Pre-Election

During the pre-election stage, three events could occur: (1) the union can withdraw the petition with the Regional Director's approval; (2) the Regional Director could dismiss the petition (which is an appealable decision); or (3) the Region could investigate the claim. If the Region investigates the claim, it can make one of two main decisions. The Region may (1) obtain a consent or stipulated election agreement or (2) hold a formal hearing. A consent election agreement means that the parties waive a hearing and agree that the Regional Director's rulings on challenged ballots and election objections are final and binding. A stipulated election agreement means that the parties waive a hearing and agree that the Regional Director will resolve any post-election disputes subject to Board review. If a formal hearing is elected, it will be conducted by a Hearing Officer, and a record of the hearing goes to the Regional Director, who issues a Decision Directing Election, Decision Dismissing Case, or Decision Reopening Record.

During the pre-election investigation, agents in the NLRB's Regional Office determine (1) whether the Board has jurisdiction over the election; (2) whether there is a qualified union; and (3) whether there is an election bar. (These topics are discussed in Chapter 10.)

4. Election

Assuming the Board has jurisdiction, the union is qualified, and there is no election bar, the Board will conduct a secret-ballot election, typically (or at least aspirationally) within five weeks of the election petition filing. The Region's agents will hold the election per the Election Agreement or the Regional Director's Decision Directing Election.

5. Post-Election/Certification

A union can only win the election if it obtains a majority of those valid ballots cast during the election. If the results of the election are conclusive (there are no challenged ballots or the challenged ballots are not determinative), the

Board will certify the results of the election, meaning the Board will certify whether the union wins or loses the election. If the results of the election are inconclusive, then there may be a post-election hearing to resolve challenged ballots and other factual issues.

Suppose, for example, the union receives support from a majority of those who vote in the election. In that case, the union wins the election, and the Board will certify the union as the exclusive representative. At this point, the employer must bargain with the union upon the union's request. If the union fails to receive support from a majority of those who vote—including a tie—the union loses the election.

The employer (or the union if it loses) may challenge the election results directly by filing election objections within seven days of the election or indirectly by filing ULP charges challenging the Region's findings during the pre-election hearing or based on conduct that occurred during the campaign. If the union loses an election, it can file election objections and hope for a re-run election, but it cannot file ULP charges. These procedures are explained in greater detail in Chapter 10.

CHECKPOINTS

- The NLRB protects the rights of private-sector employees to engage in concerted activity with or without the help of a union.
- The NLRB consists of two sides: the General Counsel, or GC-side, and the Board, or Board-side.
- The GC-side enforces the NLRA by investigating and prosecuting ULPs and by conducting secret-ballot union-representation elections. A presidentially appointed General Counsel leads the GC-side.
- The Board is a five-member administrative tribunal that "decid[es] cases on the basis of formal records in administrative proceedings."
- Regional Offices investigate charges to determine whether there is reasonable cause to issue a complaint.
- If a complaint is not issued, the charging party may appeal the decision to the General Counsel through the Office of Appeals. If the General Counsel issues a complaint, the case is transferred to an ALJ for a hearing.

- After the hearing, the ALJ prepares a decision (ALJD), to which the parties may file exceptions. If no exceptions are filed then the ALJD automatically becomes the final Board decision and order (D&O). If exceptions are filed, then the Board reviews the entire record before issuing a final D&O.
- Any party aggrieved by the final D&O may, among other things, petition an appropriate court of appeals to review the Board's order. If the court of appeals enforces, in whole or in part, a Board D&O, then the parties must comply with that order. Failure to comply with a court-enforced Board order could result in civil or criminal contempt proceedings.
- Filing a petition for *certiorari* does not automatically toll enforcement of the Board's order.
- The Board's Regions conduct secret-ballot elections to determine whether employees want union representation. To obtain a secret-ballot election, a union must file a petition for election with the appropriate Regional Office, accompanied by a showing of interest of at least 30 percent, typically in the form of signed authorization cards.

CHAPTER 4

Jurisdiction of the NLRA

ROADMAP

- Employers covered by the NLRA
- Employers excluded from the NLRA, including public-sector, RLA-covered, unions, religious, and small employers
- Employees covered by the NLRA
- The distinction between covered employees and independent contractors
- The distinction between covered employees and students
- Other employee exemptions, including managers and confidential employees
- Distinction between private-sector and public-sector approaches to supervisors
- Extraterritoriality of the NLRA

An initial question in any labor law dispute is which, if any, laws apply. This question can be critical because if no labor law covers a dispute, the alleged victim has no legal recourse. In the private sector, this means that if the NLRA or the Railway Labor Act (RLA)—which applies to railroad and airline employees—lacks jurisdiction, the workers involved lack a right to unionize and lack protection if their employer decides to retaliate against them for their collective activity. In the public sector, most but not all states and the federal government provide collective bargaining rights to at least some groups of public employees.

An inquiry into whether the NLRA or other labor laws apply generally relies on three questions: (1) is the employer covered by the NLRA; (2) is the worker covered by the NLRA; and (3) does the NLRA apply in the geographic area where the challenged action occurred? This chapter will primarily focus on the NLRA's jurisdiction, although these three questions are also the central focus for other labor laws.

A. Who Is an "Employer"?

Generally, employees can successfully challenge only actions by their statutory employer (their union is the most significant exception). Therefore, if a given employer falls outside the NLRA's jurisdiction, victims of even the most egregious employment actions will be left without a legal remedy under the NLRA.

Section 2(2) of the NLRA broadly defines "employer" as including "any person acting as an agent of an employer, directly or indirectly, but shall not include the United States or any wholly owned Government corporation, or any Federal Reserve Bank, or any State or political subdivision thereof, or any person subject to the Railway Labor Act ... or any labor organization (other than when acting as an employer), or anyone acting in the capacity of officer or agent of such labor organization." 29 U.S.C. § 152(2). We explore these statutory exclusions below, as well as some additional exclusions created by the NLRB or courts.

1. Exclusion of Public-Sector Employers

Section 2(2)'s explicit exclusion of public-sector employers is quite significant, as government workers make up approximately 15 percent of all workers in the U.S.

At times, it can be difficult to determine whether to classify an employer as public or private, such as when a private entity is performing work for the government on a contract basis. The NLRB used to carefully review the contractual relationship between the public and private entity in deciding whether contract employees work for a public employer that is excluded from the NLRA. *See Res-Care, Inc.*, 280 N.L.R.B. 670 (1986). However, in *Management Transportation Corp.*, 317 N.L.R.B. 1355, 1358 (1995), the Board changed course and held that, in deciding whether or not to assert jurisdiction over an employer with ties to the government, it would "only consider whether the employer meets the definition of employer under Section 2(2) ... and whether such employer meets the applicable monetary jurisdictional standards." (Section A.5 discusses the monetary jurisdictional standards).

The NLRA's exclusion of the public sector does not leave all government workers without protection. Federal workers are covered by the Federal Service Labor-Management Relations Statute. Although this statute is mostly outside the scope of this book, it provides most basic collective bargaining rights, albeit with a limited scope of bargaining. For example, a covered federal agency may not interfere with federal employees' statutory labor rights. *See* 5 U.S.C. § 7116(a). Moreover, many public-sector workers are covered by state labor statutes, which are discussed throughout this book. However, in states without such laws, public-sector workers lack any labor rights.

2. Exclusion of Railway and Airline Workers

Section 2(2) also explicitly excludes "any person subject to the Railway Labor Act [("RLA")]." Recognizing the importance of railroads to the United States economy, Congress enacted various laws in the late 1800s to reduce the likelihood of work stoppages and other types of labor unrest that would interfere with the rail system's transport of freight and people. In 1926, the laws were reformed into the RLA and, in 1936, Congress added airlines to the RLA's jurisdiction. This jurisdiction is exclusive; therefore, any labor disputes that involve the railway or airline industries fall under the RLA, not the NLRA. *See* 45 U.S.C. § 151. However, it can be difficult at times to determine whether an employer falls under the RLA, such as an airplane manufacturer like Boeing. Typically, the NLRB concludes that it has jurisdiction over employers like Boeing because the employees are working in the manufacturing, not the airline, industry.

Despite their different jurisdictions, there are many similarities between the RLA and NLRA. In particular, the RLA's and NLRA's core protections for employees' collective action often parallel each other. But there are significant differences. For instance, reflecting its heightened concern with labor disruptions, the RLA regulates strikes and other work stoppages more heavily than the NLRA. Moreover, the two statutes have different rules for electing unions. This book, while focusing on the NLRA, will point out some of the more significant RLA differences.

3. Exclusion of Labor Unions

The final explicit exclusion under Section 2(2) is for "any labor organization (other than when acting as an employer), or anyone acting in the capacity of officer or agent of such labor organization." The need for this exclusion will become self-evident as you learn about the structure of the NLRA and its regulation of labor relations. In particular, Section 8 of the NLRA sets forth various unfair labor practices that employers and unions can commit. 29 U.S.C. § 158. But the NLRA clearly separates employer unfair labor practices in Section 8(a) and union unfair labor practices in Section 8(b). Although some of those unfair labor practices are similar, they are exclusive and do not contemplate unions being treated as employers. However, as Section 2(2) states, when there is a labor dispute that involves a union acting in its capacity as an employer, the exclusion will not apply. For example, administrative employees who work for the Teamsters union may vote for union representation by the Laborers union. In such a case, the Teamsters is an employer under the NLRA, but the Laborers is not.

4. Exclusion of Certain Religious Employers

In addition to the explicit statutory exclusions under Section 2(2), the NLRB and courts have carved out other exclusions based on various grounds. A prominent example is the non-statutory exclusion for certain religious employers. The primary driver of this religious-employer exception is the First Amendment's protection of religious freedom. In *NLRB v. Catholic Bishop of Chicago*, 440 U.S. 490 (1979), the Supreme Court recognized this exception under the NLRA.

At issue in *Catholic Bishop* was an NLRB rule that excluded teachers in religious schools only when the schools were "completely religious." The Court rejected that rule as not adequately protecting against the infringement of religious schools' First Amendment rights. Rather than make judgments about which schools would generally be entitled to First Amendment protection and which would not, the Court simply concluded that in enacting the NLRA, Congress did not intend for the statute to apply to any teachers in the religious school at issue in *Catholic Bishop*.

Faced with this lack of guidance, appellate courts have developed their own tests for excluding religious employers. One prominent example is the D.C. Circuit's decision in *University of Great Falls v. NLRB*, 278 F.3d 1335, 1347

(D.C. Cir. 2002), which held that the religious exemption will apply if a school: "(a) holds itself out to the public as a religious institution; (b) is non-profit; and (c) is religiously affiliated." For many years, although the NLRB declined to officially adopt the *Great Falls* test, it applied it in cases without determining whether an alternate test would be more appropriate. Then, in 2014, the Board adopted a test that was similar, but not identical to *Great Falls*, under which it would decline jurisdiction over a higher education employer for religious reasons only if the institution (1) "holds itself out as providing a religious educational environment," and (2) "holds out . . . faculty members as performing a religious function." *Pacific Lutheran University*, 361 N.L.R.B. 1404 (2014) (stressing that for faculty members to perform religious functions, they must have a specific role in creating or maintaining the school's religious education). In 2020, the Board shifted its analysis again by explicitly adopting the *Great Falls* test. *See Bethany College*, 369 N.L.R.B. No. 98 (2020).

In non-education cases, the religious exemption is generally limited to employers that are primarily religious in nature, rather than a for-profit enterprise that follows certain religious tenets.

If the religious employer exemption applies, its impact is significant. When the NLRB classifies an employer as religious, all employees—even employees who do not engage in any religious work—lose the NLRA's protection.

5. Exclusion of Certain Small Employers

Unlike many employment statues, the NLRA does not require covered employers to employ a minimum number of employees. (By contrast, for example, Title VII of the Civil Rights Act, the primary employment discrimination statute, applies only to employers with fifteen or more employees.) Despite the lack of a statutory small employer exception, the NLRB has created a policy that excludes certain small employers.

Because Congress chose to enact the NLRA pursuant to, and co-extensive with, its power to regulate interstate commerce, the NLRB has declined to assert jurisdiction in situations that suggest that an employer is not engaging in such commerce. Under this policy, the NLRB will exercise its jurisdiction over employers who operate retail businesses only if they have annual gross receipts of $500,000 or more. In addition to more obvious types of retail business, the NLRB will also include in this rule employers who run apartment and condominium buildings, cemeteries, casinos, home construction, hotels, restaurants, taxis, and amusement parks. Shopping centers and office buildings are considered retail business as well, but they are subject to a higher threshold of $100,000 or more in annual gross receipts.

When faced with a matter involving an employer that operates a non-retail business, the NLRB uses a different metric. Instead of gross receipts, the NLRB looks to the employers' interstate commercial activity. If either an employer's annual sales outside of its state or annual purchases from a different state do not amount to at least $50,000, the NLRB will decline to assert jurisdiction over the employer. When making this calculation, the NLRB will include sales or purchases that occur through a third party. Moreover, the NLRB has created several special thresholds for various industries, including health care ($250,000); childcare ($250,000); nursing homes ($100,000); legal services ($250,000); and cultural and educational institutions ($1,000,000).

6. Joint Employers

In contrast to the various employer exclusions, the joint employer doctrine is a way in which an employer can be added to a labor dispute. This doctrine may be implicated when workplace terms and conditions are impacted or determined by more than one employer. For instance, imagine an employee of a garment manufacturer who produces clothes almost exclusively for a national clothing store chain. The contract between the clothing chain and the garment manufacturer includes various workplace requirements that the manufacturer must implement and enforce, such as a rule prohibiting employees from discussing their pay. In this situation, where such a "pay gag" rule is unlawful under the NLRA, the NLRB could likely file an unfair labor practice charge against not only the garment manufacturer but also the clothing chain because both entities are acting as employers. Another example is a claim brought by the NLRB's General Counsel in 2022 alleging that the NCAA and PAC-12 are joint employers of some collegiate athletes at the University of Southern California.

Joint employer cases typically hinge on questions about how closely two facially separate employers act together to impact a group of employees' terms and conditions of work. Although the joint employer doctrine is not new, it has become more relevant as businesses have increasingly embraced workplace arrangements in which employees' work is an important part of more than one employer's business. Arrangements such as temporary staffing, subcontracting, franchising, and gig work have been on the rise and can often implicate questions about joint employment.

Mirroring the rise in potential joint employment situations has been a heightened, and often fraught, focus by the NLRB on its test for determining whether a business is a joint employer. As is often the case, the Board's approach has flip-flopped. In 2015, the NLRB issued its decision in *Browning-Ferris Industries of California, Inc.*, 362 N.L.R.B. 1599 (2015), *enf'd in relevant part* 911 F.3d 1195 (D.C. Cir. 2018), which used a common-law-based focus on a business's right to control working conditions. Under *Browning-Ferris*, joint employment would exist if two or more businesses "share or codetermine those matters governing the essential terms and conditions of employment." A joint employer only needs to "possess the authority to control employees' terms and conditions of employment"; a joint employer does not have to actually exercise that authority in a direct and immediate manner. In 2020, the NLRB abandoned the *Browning-Ferris* analysis through rulemaking, which required a joint employer to exercise actual control over working conditions—"substantial direct and immediate control" that is not "limited and routine." Then, in 2023, the NLRB reversed the 2020 rule through new rulemaking that returned the standard to the *Browning-Ferris* analysis. *See* NLRB, Standard for Determining Joint-Employer Status, 29 C.F.R. § 103 (2023). The 2023 rule also clarified that when collective bargaining is at issue, a joint employer will only have to bargain "with respect to any term or condition of employment that it possesses the authority to control or exercises the power to control (regardless of whether that term or condition is deemed to be an essential term or condition of employment under the rule)." At time of this book's publication, the 2023 rule was being litigated.

B. Who Is an "Employee"?

Even if the NLRA covers an employer, the same is not necessarily true for all of its workers. Like other jurisdictional issues, this one has a substantial impact. Any worker who is not classified as a covered employee under the NLRA (or RLA or public-sector labor law) lacks any right to engage in collective labor action. Thus, excluded workers cannot unionize or act in concert with other workers without the risk that their employer may lawfully retaliate against them for engaging in such activity.

The NLRA provides a basic definition of employee that has been used as the model for many other labor and employment statutes, which is somewhat curious given its lack of clarity. Under Section 2(3), "[t]he term 'employee' shall include any employee"—a definition that the Supreme Court has described as having "striking" breadth. *See Sure-Tan, Inc. v. NLRB*, 467 U.S. 883, 891 (1984). This basic definition is often used to distinguish a covered employee from someone who does work for a business but is not considered an employee, such as an independent contractor or student. In those cases, the NLRB and courts have turned to a traditional agency law test that tries to determine whether the relationship between the worker and business is more like an employee-employer relationship or something else that falls outside the concern of the NLRA.

Section 2(3) elaborates on this basic definition of employee to make clear that, among other things, employees who are on strike or were fired are still covered by the NLRA, that job applicants are considered employees, and that certain types of employees are excluded from the NLRA's coverage:

> The term "employee" shall include any employee, and shall not be limited to the employees of a particular employer, unless the Act explicitly states otherwise, and shall include any individual whose work has ceased as a consequence of, or in connection with, any current labor dispute or because of any unfair labor practice, and who has not obtained any other regular and substantially equivalent employment, but shall not include any individual employed as an agricultural laborer, or in the domestic service of any family or person at his home, or any individual employed by his parent or spouse, or any individual having the status of an independent contractor, or any individual employed as a supervisor, or any individual employed by an employer subject to the Railway Labor Act ... or by any other person who is not an employer as herein defined.

This statutory language raises several commonly litigated issues, such as the distinction between covered employees and independent contractors; classification of graduate student workers and college athletes; the classification of union salts; and the exclusion of managerial, supervisory, and confidential employees.

1. Employee or Independent Contractor?

The distinction between employees and independent contractors has been a significant issue for the past several decades. Employers have been aggressive in trying to classify workers as independent contractors because the consequences are so significant. In addition to independent contractor status excluding a worker from protection under most labor and employment laws, it also relieves the employer of paying employee tax contributions for that worker or providing employee benefits. Many employers have had success in pushing the independent contractor classification, as the multi-part test used to answer this question leaves much room for interpretation, and it usually requires substantial time and resources for workers or government agencies to challenge possible misclassifications. Moreover, a worker can be classified as an employee for one statute and an independent contractor for another.

In the first iteration of the NLRA, the Wagner Act of 1935, there was no mention of independent contractors. Congress added the exclusion of these workers to Section 2(3) in the Taft-Hartley Act of 1947, mainly in reaction to the 1944 Supreme Court case, *NLRB v. Hearst Publications*, 322 U.S. 111 (1944). In *Hearst*, the Court agreed with the NLRB's conclusion that "newsboys"—workers, usually adult, who sold newspapers on streets—were covered employees under the NLRA. The controversy over this holding centered on the newspaper publisher's lack of control over the manner and timing of the newsboys' work, which was a central focus of the common-law agency test used to determine when an individual is a "servant." In *Hearst*, both the NLRB and Court rejected the argument that the common-law test should apply to the NLRA. Instead, according to the Court, a worker's coverage under the NLRA should be based on the "history, terms and purposes of the legislation." Because the NLRA was intended to broadly reduce industrial strife, which could include disputes with independent contractors, the Court held that the NLRB could find that workers are covered by the NLRA even if the common-law definition of servant would exclude them.

By excluding independent contractors from Section 2(3)'s definition of employee, Congress intended to overturn *Hearst* and require the employee classification question to turn on the common-law agency test. This test relies on a set of factors that are to be viewed in totality, with the purported employer's right to control the work as the most critical factor in most cases:

(a) The extent of control which, by the agreement, the master may exercise over the details of the work.

(b) Whether or not the one employed is engaged in a distinct occupation or business.

(c) The kind of occupation, with reference to whether, in the locality, the work is usually done under the direction of the employer or by a specialist without supervision.

(d) The skill required in the particular occupation.
(e) Whether the employer or the workman supplies the instrumentalities, tools, and the place of work for the person doing the work.
(f) The length of time for which the person is employed.
(g) The method of payment, whether by the time or by the job.
(h) Whether or not the work is part of the regular business of the employer.
(i) Whether or not the parties believe they are creating the relation of master and servant.
(j) Whether the principal is or is not in the business.

Roadway Package System, Inc., 326 N.L.R.B. 842, 849 n.32 (1998) (quoting Restatement (Second) of Agency, § 220).

The NLRB briefly altered this traditional test by holding that "entrepreneurial opportunity ... has always been at the core of the common-law test" and, therefore, "is a principle by which to evaluate the overall effect of the common-law factors on a putative contractor's independence to pursue economic gain." *SuperShuttle DFW, Inc.*, 367 N.L.R.B. No. 75, at *1 n.4 (2019) (citing *FedEx Home Delivery v. NLRB*, 563 F.3d 492 (D.C. Cir. 2009)). In 2023, the NLRB reversed *SuperShuttle* and reiterated that the traditional factors will be used to determine whether a worker is an employee or an independent contractor. *See The Atlanta Opera, Inc.*, 372 N.L.R.B. No. 95 (2023).

In *The Atlanta Opera*, the NLRB described its approach to arguments that a worker's entrepreneurial opportunity supports a finding that they are an independent contractor. The Board rejected the claim that mere theoretical entrepreneurial opportunity supports an independent contractor classification. Instead, an independent contractor is someone who typically has "significant entrepreneurial opportunity" and "(a) has a realistic ability to work for other companies; (b) has proprietary or ownership interest in their work; and (c) has control over important business decisions, such as the scheduling of performance; the hiring, selection, and assignment of employees; the purchase and use of equipment; and the commitment of capital." *Id.* at *18. These considerations, which "synthesize[] the full constellation of considerations that the Board has addressed under the rubric of entrepreneurialism," will be weighed along all of the traditional common-law factors to determine if the worker is an employee or independent contractor. *Id.*

One classic situation giving rise to the independent contractor question involves insurance agents, such as the employees in *NLRB v. United Insurance*

Co., 390 U.S. 254 (1968), a post-Taft Hartley case. *United Insurance* involved a union's attempt to organize "debit agents" of an insurance company. The Supreme Court, agreeing with the NLRB, held that the agents were employees rather than independent contractors. Despite the agents' autonomy to fix their hours of work and their absence from the workplace, the Court held that they were more like employees because the totality of the circumstances showed that they lacked the independence, initiative, and decision-making authority of an independent contractor. For instance, the agents did not have their own businesses, were trained by the company, did business in the company's name, performed essential functions of the company, and were subject to terms and conditions of employment that were under the company's unilateral control.

Delivery drivers have also been the subject of significant litigation regarding their classification as employees, including drivers who work for gig companies. One of the leading NLRB cases on the employee-independent contractor question is *Roadway Package System, Inc.*, 326 N.L.R.B. 842 (1998), which involved the classification of package delivery drivers. In *Roadway*, the NLRB used the *United Insurance* common-law factors to classify the drivers as employees. Among the many facts that the NLRB considered to be important in this case were the drivers' role in performing essential functions of the business, lack of prior training or experience, submission to the company's control over their work, and lack of entrepreneurial opportunity.

2. Employee or Student?

Another classification that has been contentious in recent years involves graduate students who also do work for their universities, such as teaching assistants, research assistants, and medical residents. The issue with these workers is not whether they perform work as an independent contractor—there is usually no dispute that some of their role with the university involves the work of an employee. Rather, the issue centers on whether that work is economic in nature (that is, work performed in exchange for compensation). The NLRB could attempt to establish a rule that triggers NLRA coverage for any level of employment, but it has declined that option and instead asks whether a student-worker's overall relationship with the university is better characterized as that of an employee or that of a student.

One of the difficulties in tracking the NLRB's approach to this area is that the outcome of student-employee cases frequently turns on the political lineup of the Board members. For instance, in *Boston Medical Center Corp.*,

330 N.L.R.B. 152 (1999), a Democratic-majority NLRB overturned an earlier Board decision and found that medical residents were covered employees under the NLRA even though part of their purpose in working at the hospital was educational. The NLRB stressed that common-law agency principles pointed to employee status, particularly factors such as the residents' compensation for their work, including fringe benefits; that the residents spent a majority of their time on patient care; and that the residents did not pay tuition or otherwise engage in classroom activity.

In contrast to *Boston Medical*, a Republican-majority NLRB found graduate students to be excluded in *Brown University*, 342 N.L.R.B. 483 (2004), which was also a reversal of an earlier Board decision. Then, in 2016, a Democratic-majority Board reversed course again, concluding that graduate students could be employees under the NLRA. *See The Trustees of Columbia University in the City of New York*, 364 N.L.R.B. 1080 (2016). Since 2016, there has been a sharp rise in graduate student organizing, with numerous union wins—often by very large margins—in the early 2020s.

In *Columbia University*, the NLRB disagreed with the *Brown University* finding that graduate students were more like students than employees and should therefore be excluded from the NLRA. Instead, the *Columbia University* Board stressed that it had statutory authority to classify graduate students as employees "where they perform work, at the direction of the university, for which they are compensated," even if they also performed educational work. *Id.* at 1080. Given the NLRA's policy to encourage collective bargaining, "coupled with the very broad statutory definitions of both 'employee' and 'employer,' it is appropriate to extend statutory coverage to students working for universities covered by the Act unless there are strong reasons *not* to do so." *Id.* at 1081. The Board rejected the conclusions of *Brown University* that classifying graduate students as employees would improperly intrude on the educational process. Moreover, it stressed that even when the economic relationship "may seem comparatively slight, relative to other aspects of the relationship between worker and employer, the payment of compensation, in conjunction with the employer's control, suffices to establish an employment relationship for purposes of the Act." *Id.* at 1085. The NLRB then applied a common-law test that looked to whether the employer has the "right to control the employee's work, and that the work be performed in exchange for compensation," *id.* at 1094, finding that the research and teaching assistants at issue in the case were employees. That said, the Board was careful to point out that all graduate students are not automatically classified as employees. *Id.*

at 1083. Although most share relevant working conditions with the graduate students at issue in *Columbia University*, the Board will examine the facts of each case.

Finally, a couple of recent NLRB cases raise significant issues about whether certain collegiate athletes can be classified as employees under the NLRA. One case involves a Regional Director's decision that basketball players at Dartmouth College were employees and could, therefore, seek an election to unionize. *See Trustees of Dartmouth*, Case 01-RC-325622 (Feb. 5, 2024). The election was held in 2024, which the union won in a 13–2 vote, but Dartmouth challenged the employee classification issue. The *Dartmouth* decision relied heavily on *Columbia University* to find that the players were employees. In particular, the Regional Director found that there was a significant amount of control over the players' work, the work benefited the school, and the work was done in exchange for compensation (primarily an easier admission path, equipment and apparel, and special support programs). *Dartmouth* also relied on an earlier Regional Director decision to find Northwestern University scholarship football players to be employees—a conclusion that the NLRB later vacated in an exercise of its ability to decline jurisdiction when it would not promote law stability, which it found to be the case given the number of public schools over which it lacked jurisdiction. *See Northwestern Univ. & College Athletes Players Ass'n*, 362 N.L.R.B. No. 167 (2015). However, *Dartmouth* promised to be more far-reaching than *Northwestern* because the basketball players at Dartmouth, like other Ivy League schools, do not receive athletic scholarships. In the end, however, the union withdrew its petition after the 2024 presidential election to avoid an adverse ruling that would create a precedent. In a second matter, the NLRB General Counsel pursued a case seeking to get around the NLRB's concern in *Northwestern* about having jurisdiction over only private schools. The General Counsel filed unfair labor practice charges against the University of Southern California, alleging that it unlawfully misclassified athletes on the football and men's and women's basketball teams. But the General Counsel also added the NCAA and PAC-12 to the case as joint employers. *See University of Southern California*, Case No. 31-CA-290326 (2022). If successful, this joint employer theory could result in a union entering into a collective-bargaining agreement with the NCAA and conferences, which could apply to public universities through their agreement with those institutions. But, like the *Dartmouth* case, the union withdrew its petition after the 2024 election.

3. Union Salts

One controversial employee classification issue involves what are referred to as union "salts." This term refers to union employees who apply for jobs with the intent of organizing ("salting") the workplace. As discussed in more detail in Chapter 9, which examines discrimination charges filed against employers under Section 8(a)(3), the Supreme Court in *NLRB v. Town & Country Electric, Inc.*, 516 U.S. 85 (1995), ultimately resolved the issue by holding that salts can be employees under the NLRA.

Salting also presents employee classification issues before such salts are hired. This topic is discussed in detail in Chapter 9's description of discriminatory refusals to hire. The key classification issue in such cases is currently controlled by *Toering Electric Co.*, 351 N.L.R.B. 225 (2007), in which the NLRB established a new rule requiring the General Counsel to show that salts submitted bone fide applications for employment and were "genuinely interested in seeking to establish an employment relationship with the employer" before they can be considered employees.

4. Managerial Employee Exclusion

The NLRA's exclusion of managerial employees, although not explicit, has been assumed since the Wagner Act. The exclusion is viewed as necessary to ensure that the employer's most important officials do not have a conflict of loyalty between the employer and a union. However, while the existence of the exclusion has not been open to serious debate, its boundaries have been in flux.

The NLRB had long taken the position that managers should be excluded only if there was a "labor nexus"—that is, only if those workers had a role in the formulation and implementation of the employer's labor policies. In *NLRB v. Bell Aerospace Co.*, 416 U.S. 267 (1974), the Supreme Court rejected the labor nexus requirement, holding that the NLRA should not cover any worker who has a managerial role in their workplace. The Court's rationale was that employees who were high in the managerial structure have discretion to implement and to act independently of the employer's policies and, therefore, must remain aligned with the employer rather than a union.

Following *Bell Aerospace*, the NLRB abandoned its labor nexus rule and now determines when a worker is managerial on a case-by-case basis. Among the factors the NLRB looks for are the ability to "formulate and effectuate management policies by expressing and making operative the decisions of their employer" and "discretion in the performance of their jobs independent of their employer's established policy." *Bell Aerospace Corp.*, 219 N.L.R.B. 384, 385 (1975). The managerial classification is reserved for executive-level workers who are the true representatives of management, not rank-and-file employees.

One set of workers that can raise difficult managerial questions are university faculty members. Because faculty members are often involved in policy decisions, they are at risk of being excluded from the NLRA as managerial employees. The Supreme Court addressed this issue in *NLRB v. Yeshiva University*, 444 U.S. 672 (1980), where a union sought to represent faculty at several Yeshiva University-affiliated schools in New York City. The NLRB rejected the University's argument that the faculty were managerial employees, finding them to be professional employees who exercised collective judgment in the interest of the employer (an aspect of Section 2(12)'s definition of professional employees, which will be discussed in the next section) and stressing the board of trustees' final authority to make decisions. The Supreme Court ultimately reversed the NLRB, holding that, no matter their professional status, the faculty members met the definition of managers.

In *Yeshiva*, the Court elaborated on its description of the exclusion in *Bell Aerospace* by holding that managerial employees "exercise discretion within, or even independently of, established employer policy" and are aligned with management. Moreover, the managerial exclusion typically applies only when an employee "represents management interests by taking or recommending discretionary actions that effectively control or implement employer policy." In applying these factors in *Yeshiva*, the Court emphasized the faculty's absolute authority over academic policies. That the faculty exercises its authority through its independent professional judgment, which the NLRB thought to be key, was of no import to the Court, which stressed that the professional interests of the faculty and university administration were aligned. Thus, the "divided loyalty" problem that underlies the managerial exclusion was present. The Court nevertheless stressed that the Board should continue to review questions of a faculty's status on a case-by-case basis and that the Board could find employee status in instances where, for example, the faculty's managerial authority is merely routine or significantly limited by higher officials.

Later, in *Pacific Lutheran University*, 361 N.L.R.B. 1404 (2014), the NLRB elaborated on how it would make case-by-case determinations of faculty members' status as employees or managers. Under *Pacific Lutheran*, when deciding whether faculty possessed the "broad and substantial" decision-making authority that would make it managerial, the NLRB will consider five categories of university decision-making. Three of these categories are considered "primary," or essential to the university as a whole: academic programs, finances, and enrollment management. The two "secondary categories" are less critical to the university as a whole: academic policy, as well as personnel policy and decisions. Under the *Pacific Lutheran* analysis, the NLRB will consider faculty members' actual exercise of control or their ability to effectively recommend decisions within the five categories to help determine whether the faculty has enough broad and substantial decision-making authority to be considered managerial.

5. Confidential Employee Exclusion

One additional employee classification issue addresses the problem of confidential employees. The NLRB has long concluded that confidential employees cannot be members of bargaining units with other employees. However, as explained below, it remains an open question whether such employees are protected by the NLRA at all.

The NLRB, with the Supreme Court's approval in *NLRB v. Hendricks County Rural Electric Membership Corp.*, 454 U.S. 170, 190 (1981), defines confidential employees with regard to a "labor nexus." In other words, the NLRB will classify as confidential only those employees who have access to confidential information related to the employer's labor relations. For instance, an Apple employee who knows the secret new color for a future version of the iPhone will not be a confidential employee under the NLRA, but an employee who knows how the employer plans to negotiate with a union will.

The policy rationale for the labor nexus is that an employee with access to confidential labor relations information faces a conflict of interest if they are also in a union that would benefit from having that information. Because that conflict of interest is less apparent if confidential employees are merely organized in a different unit from other employees, the NLRB has concluded that confidential employees still enjoy protection under the NLRA. *Grove Valve & Regulator Co.*, 262 N.L.R.B. 285, 304 (1982) (citing *Ford Motor Co.*, 66 N.L.R.B. 1317 (1946)). However, some circuit courts have rejected the Board's position and held that confidential employees are wholly excluded from the NLRA. *See Peerless of Am. v. NLRB*, 484 F.2d 1108, 1112 (7th Cir. 1973); *NLRB v. Wheeling Electric Co.*, 444 F.2d 783 (4th Cir. 1971).

6. Supervisor Exclusion

a. Supervisors in the Private Sector

Although the NLRB and courts interpreted the Wagner Act as excluding managers, no such exemption existed for lower-level supervisors. That changed with the passage of the 1947 Taft-Hartley Amendments, which explicitly excluded supervisors from the NLRA's jurisdiction. This change was codified in Section 2(11):

> The term "supervisor" means any individual having authority, in the interest of the employer, to:
>
> - hire,
> - transfer,
> - suspend,
> - lay off,
> - recall,
> - promote,
> - discharge,
> - assign,
> - reward, or
> - discipline other employees, or
> - responsibly to direct them, or
> - to adjust their grievances, or
> - effectively to recommend such action,
>
> if in connection with the foregoing the exercise of such authority is not of a merely routine or clerical nature, but requires the use of independent judgment.

A supervisor need only have the authority to engage in one of the listed duties, as long as that authority requires independent judgment and is in the interest of the employer.

Many of the Section 2(11) duties are relatively straightforward and easy to apply, such as an employee with the independent authority to hire and fire other employees. The meaning of other duties, such as the ability to assign or responsibly direct, is less obvious and has led to a great deal of litigation. Adding to the confusion is the meaning of "independent judgment" and "interest of the employer," which have also been the source of contention among various Board members and between the NLRB and courts.

Despite the long history of litigation over the meaning of supervisor, the definition is currently more stable than it has been for many years—although there is still quite a bit of dissatisfaction with the prevailing interpretation. One reason for the sharp disagreements over the meaning of "supervisor" is that the changing American workplace has dramatically expanded the exclusion's breadth. In the 1940s, the line between employees and supervisors was relatively clear. However, in the modern economy, employers often give even lower-level workers far more discretion and input than they once did. The result is a much larger set of workers who arguably have the authority to perform one or more Section 2(11) duties. One example of such workers are nurses, who often help oversee the work of nursing assistants and less senior nurses, especially as health care facilities have cut back on the number of more expensive doctors. This expanded authority, coupled with nurses' traditionally high rate of unionization, has meant that nurses have often been at the center of Section 2(11) litigation.

To understand the current Section 2(11) definition, it is important to consider the history of litigation over the supervisory exclusion, particularly in the health care industry. Recognizing the growing problem of nurses and other health care workers losing NLRA protection, the NLRB issued decisions trying to interpret Section 2(11) in a manner that would prevent most rank-and-file nurses from being classified as supervisors. Yet, the Supreme Court has rejected the NLRB's interpretation each time. In one such case, *NLRB v. Health Care & Retirement Corporation of America*, 511 U.S. 571, 579 (1994), the NLRB concluded that many nurses who could "assign" or "direct" others' work were not supervisors under Section 2(11) because their authority was an "exercise of professional judgment incidental to patient care," rather than supervisory authority in the interest of the employer. In *Health Care & Retirement*, much like it did in rejecting the NLRB's definition of manager in *NLRB v. Yeshiva University*, 444 U.S. 672 (1980), the Court held that authority performed with nurses' professional judgment still qualified as work done in the interest of the employer.

After the Court in *Health Care & Retirement* rejected the NLRB's reliance on Section 2(11)'s interest-of-the-employer requirement, the Board turned to the independent-judgment prong. The NLRB argued that nurses and other professional and technical workers exercised their supervisory authority as a matter of routine professional or technical expertise, rather than with independent judgment. The Court disagreed with this argument in *NLRB v. Kentucky River Community Care*, 532 U.S. 706 (2001), where it held that the

NLRB's "categorical exclusion" of professional and technical judgment lacked support from the text of Section 2(11). Thus, despite Section 2(12)'s explicit recognition that some professional employees are covered by the NLRA (the NLRA has special bargaining unit rules that apply to professional employees), the NLRB could not broadly avoid supervisory status for professional and technical workers.

Despite the loss in *Kentucky River*, there were two aspects of the decision that provided some solace for the NLRB. First, the Court agreed with the NLRB that the party arguing that an employee should be excluded as a supervisor bears the burden of proof. Second, the Court suggested that the NLRB might be able to limit the reach of the "responsibly to direct" supervisory duty by distinguishing employees who "who direct the manner of others' performance of discrete *tasks* from employees who direct other *employees*." This somewhat cryptic invitation led the NLRB to issue what is its latest word on Section 2(11)'s more controversial provisions.

Following *Kentucky River*, the NLRB heard arguments in three supervisor cases known as the *Oakwood* trilogy, after the lead case of *Oakwood Health Care, Inc.*, 348 N.L.R.B. 686 (2006). In *Oakwood*, the NLRB addressed the interpretation of three aspects of Section 2(11): "assign," "responsibly to direct," and "independent judgment." The NLRB in *Oakwood* also looked to employees who engage in supervisory duties part-time, concluding that they should be considered supervisors only if they spend "a regular and substantial portion" of their work—generally, at least 10–15 percent of work time—on those duties. *Id.* at 694.

The NLRB in *Oakwood* defined "assign" as meaning "the act of designating an employee to a place (such as a location, department, or wing), appointing an employee to a time (such as a shift or overtime period), or giving significant overall duties, i.e., tasks, to an employee." *Id.* at 689. According to the NLRB, examples of assigning an overall task might include an order to restock shelves, but not an order to perform a discrete task such as restocking toasters before coffeemakers. A similar distinction the NLRB noted would be a charge nurse assigning a subordinate nurse the overall task of regularly giving medication to a group of patients, but not an order to immediately give medication to a specific patient. In contrast, the dissent interpreted "assign" to encompass only a supervisor's determination of employees' basic terms and conditions of work, such as their position, work site, and work hours. Thus, under the dissent's view, daily task assignments would not trigger a supervisory classification.

The *Oakwood* majority defined "responsibly to direct" as requiring the purported supervisor to "be accountable for the performance of the task by the other [employee], such that some adverse consequence may befall the one providing the oversight if the tasks performed by the employee are not performed properly." *Id.* at 692. This means that the supervisor must have the power to direct other employees' work, take corrective action as needed, and face adverse consequences if the work is not satisfactory. The dissent would interpret "responsibly to direct" as covering only workers, like foremen, who are in charge of department-level work units. In particular, the dissent would find that a purported supervisor has responsibility to direct others only when the supervisor has substantial authority to make sure that a work unit, which they are in charge of, meets the employer's objectives; is accountable for others' work; and has significant discretion and judgment in directing the work unit.

The NLRB in *Oakwood* also addressed the broader mandate that supervisors must have the authority to perform one of the Section 2(11) duties with independent judgment. According to the NLRB, independent judgment is the ability to act, or effectively recommend an act, "free of the control of others and form an opinion or evaluation by discerning and comparing data." *Id.* at 693. However, even when this freedom exists, it will only constitute independent judgment when it is not "merely routine or clerical in nature." The question whether judgment is independent hinges on the purported supervisor's degree of discretion. Thus, judgment will not be independent if it must follow detailed instructions or there is only one obvious choice. Yet, as the NLRB stressed, even when relevant instructions exist, a purported supervisor's judgment may be independent if they have enough discretion, such as the ability to recommend new hires based on their view of applicants' experience, character, and aptitude.

b. Supervisors in the Public Sector

Although many states protect the right of public-sector employees to engage in concerted activity, those states may still by statute or otherwise exclude some of their workers from coverage. For example, the managerial and confidential exemptions in the public sector usually follow NLRA rules. By contrast, a significant number of public-sector jurisdictions treat supervisors differently. Essentially, there are three models in the public sector for supervisors. First, some public-sector jurisdictions follow the NLRA rule: excluding supervisors from coverage and using essentially the same definition of "supervisor" as has evolved under the NLRA. Second, some public-sector statutes exclude supervisors but use a narrower definition of "supervisor" that excludes fewer employees. Third, some public-sector jurisdictions do not exclude supervisors at all.

Iowa and Rhode Island are examples of states that follow the NLRA approach for supervisors. *See State, Dept. of Personnel v. Iowa Public Employment Rel. Bd.*, 560 N.W.2d 560 (Iowa 1997) (approving use of NLRA precedents in interpreting who is an excluded "supervisory employee"); *Bd. of Tr., Robert H. Champlin Mem'l Library v. Rhode Island,* 694 A.2d 1185 (RI 1997) (same for Rhode Island public-sector statute covering municipal employees).

Illinois is an example of a state that excludes supervisors but uses a narrower definition. The Illinois Public Relations Act defines "supervisor" as follows:

> A "Supervisor" is an employee whose principal work is substantially different from that of his subordinates and who has authority, in the interest of the employer, to hire, transfer, suspend, lay off, recall, promote, discharge, direct, reward, or discipline employees, or to adjust their grievances, or to effectively recommend such action, if the exercise of such authority is not of a merely routine or clerical nature, but requires the consistent use of independent judgment. Except with respect to police employment, the term "supervisor" includes only those individuals who devote a preponderance of their employment time to exercising such authority ...

5 Ill. Comp. Stat. 315/3(r) (2001). Note that for most employees this statute covers, an employee is only a supervisor if that employee spends the majority of their time exercising supervisory authority.

Ohio's statute, Oh. Rev. Code Sections 4117.01(c)(10) and 4117.01(f), explicitly exclude supervisors using the definition in the NLRA. But then Section 4117(f)(1)–(3) specifies that certain types of employees who would otherwise meet that definition are *not* supervisors

> (1) Employees of school districts who are department chairpersons or consulting teachers shall not be deemed supervisors; (2) with respect to members of a police or fire department, no person shall be deemed a supervisor except the chief of the department or those individuals who, in the absence of the chief, are authorized to exercise the authority and perform the duties of the chief of the department; and (3) with respect to faculty members of a state institution of higher education, heads of departments or divisions are supervisors; however, no other faculty

member or group of faculty members is a supervisor solely because the faculty member or group of faculty members participate in decisions with respect to courses, curriculum, personnel, or other matters of academic policy.

Finally, some public-sector statutes do not exclude supervisors at all. One example is New Jersey's public sector law, Chapter 303. *See New Jersey Turnpike Authority v. American Federation of State, County, and Municipal Employees, Council 73*, 696 A.2d 585 (1997). In addition, Alaska, California, Florida, Michigan, Minnesota, and New Hampshire all have public-sector labor laws that do not exclude supervisors.

States that allow supervisors to bargain collectively generally do not allow them to be in the same bargaining unit as employees they supervise. This rule is designed to avoid conflicts of interest in, for instance, disciplinary matters. *See, e.g., Appeal of New Hampshire Retirement System*, 167 N.H. 685 (2015).

C. The Extraterritorial Reach of the NLRA

Although questions regarding the NLRA's jurisdiction are dominated by issues regarding a given employer's or employee's coverage, the NLRA's extraterritorial reach can also cause confusion. Under Section 10 of the NLRA, the NLRB's power extends to the commission of unfair labor practices that affect commerce. Included in Section 2(6)'s definition "commerce" is trade and other types of commerce "between any foreign country" and a part of the United States. For the NLRB, this definition is sufficient to provide extraterritorial jurisdiction when an American employee is on a temporary assignment in a different country, as long as the employee expects to return to the United States after the assignment.

This "work station" rule has gained acceptance among some circuit courts, but not all. For example, in *Asplundh Tree Expert Co. v. NLRB*, 365 F.3d 168 (3d Cir. 2004), the Third Circuit held that the general presumption against a statute's extraterritorial reach outweighed the NLRA's reference to foreign commerce. In particular, such "boilerplate" language—especially given that the NLRA contains no mechanism for extraterritorial enforcement—was similar to the Supreme Court's rejection of extraterritorial jurisdiction for Title VII of the Civil Rights Act. *See EEOC v. Arabian American Oil Co.*, ("*ARAMCO*"), 499 U.S. 244 (1991) (Congress later amended Title VII to make its extraterritorial jurisdiction more explicit). Despite *Asplundh*, this issue remains an open question in other circuits and the NLRB continues to apply its work station rule.

CHECKPOINTS

- The NLRA covers only private-sector employers.
- Employers in the railway and airline industries are covered by the Railway Labor Act, not the NLRA.
- Labor unions are not usually considered employers under the NLRA, except when there is a labor dispute that involves a union acting in its capacity as an employer.
- Certain religious employers are excluded from the NLRA's coverage.
- An employer covered by the NLRA must be engaged in an industry affecting interstate commerce, as measured by the NLRB's monetary threshold rules for small employers.
- Independent contractors are not covered employees under the NLRA, and the test for independent contractor status is based on the common-law factors.
- The NLRA covers most graduate students and could even cover certain collegiate athletes.
- Union salts are covered employees under the NLRA, as long as they have a genuine interest in being an employee for the employer being organized.
- The NLRA does not cover managers who formulate and effectuate the employer's management policies and can perform their jobs with independent discretion.
- Confidential employees, who are privy to confidential labor relations or personnel records, cannot be in the same bargaining unit as other employees, and might be excluded from the NLRA's coverage.
- The NLRA does not cover any worker who performs one of the twelve supervisory duties in the interest of the employer and with independent judgment.

- State public-sector labor laws vary in that some apply the NLRA definition of supervisor, some use a narrower definition of supervisor, and some do not exclude supervisors at all.
- The NLRB will claim jurisdiction over American employees temporarily working in foreign countries, although some circuit courts disagree.

CHAPTER 5

Section 7 Rights to Engage in Protected Conduct: Union Employees

ROADMAP

- The crucial distinction between protected and unprotected conduct under § 7
- The three elements that constitute protected conduct
- The multi-layered meaning of concerted activity under *City Disposal Systems*
- Legitimate employer-related ends under the *Eastex* test
- Union employee *Weingarten* rights to assistance in disciplinary investigations
- The lack of *Weingarten* rights for nonunion employees under *IBM*
- Determining disloyalty and illegitimate means under *Jefferson Standard*

A. Section 7 and Protected Conduct

Having set out labor law history and the procedure, organization, and jurisdiction of the National Labor Relations Board (NLRB or Board) in the previous chapters, the first substantive question to address is: What statutory rights do employees have under the National Labor Relations Act (NLRA or Act)? The heart of the NLRA, and the location where these statutory rights can be found, is Section 7 of the NLRA. As originally enacted in the Wagner Act of 1935, Section 7 gives "employees" four essential rights: (1) the right to "self-organization"; (2) the right to "form, join, or assist labor organizations"; (3) the right to "bargain collectively through representatives of their own choosing"; and (4) the right "to engage in other concerted activities for the purpose of collective bargaining or other mutual aid or protection." The Taft-Hartley Act of 1947 expanded Section 7 to clarify that employees have the right to refrain from engaging in any of these activities.

From an initial consideration of Section 7's language, two points can be made immediately. First, Section 7 uses the word "employees," not "unionized employees" or "employees looking to form a union." Consequently, Section 7 rights do not apply only to unionized employees or those employees seeking to unionize; they apply to *all* employees the NLRA covers (see Chapter 4 for the NLRA's definition of "employee" and exclusions, such as public-sector employees). Indeed, this use of Section 7 rights in the nonunionized environment has become such an important topic in the current economy that Chapter 6 is dedicated to consideration of the Section 7 rights of nonunion employees. For now, we will set aside this "universal" aspect of Section 7.

Second, protected activity under Section 7 must be distinguished from unprotected activity. Employees have the right to organize themselves into a union, to seek recognition from their employer to engage in collective bargaining over terms and conditions of employment, and even to apply various forms of economic pressure for these purposes (including strikes, pickets, and boycotts), but only if such activity is undertaken in a *protected* manner. As described below, three elements—concertedness, legitimate purpose, and legitimate means—must be met before employee conduct is considered protected under Section 7.

Section 8(a)(1) provides the primary enforcement action for employees' Section 7 rights by stating that "[i]t shall be an unfair labor practice for an employer to interfere with, restrain, or coerce employees in the exercise" of their Section 7 rights. (Section 8(b)(1) is analogous to Section 8(a)(1) except that it applies against unions and only prohibits restraint and coercion.) For a so-called "independent" Section 8(a)(1) ULP, the NLRB must find that employees' Section 7 rights are at issue. In most cases, like those discussed in this chapter, an employer has taken some form of adverse action against employees because of their Section 7 activity (e.g., firing employees for contacting a union). In other cases, an employer may violate Section 8(a)(1) for implementing policies that "interfere with" or "restrain" employees' ability to engage in Section 7 activity (e.g., a "pay gag" policy that prohibits employees from discussing pay with each other). As discussed in Chapter 7, the NLRB may use different tests for specific scenarios, but at the heart of all Section 8(a)(1) ULPs is a finding that an employer has somehow interfered with, restrained, or coerced Section 7 activity (usually requiring a finding that employees would reasonably view the employer's action as chilling their Section 7 rights). Thus, establishing that an employee or employees were engaged in "concerted and protected activities" under Section 7 is a crucial first step to proving a Section 8(a)(1) ULP.

Finally, in contrast to the "independent" Section 8(a)(1) ULP just discussed, there is also a so-called "dependent" or "derivative" Section 8(a)(1) ULP. Whenever the NLRB finds that an employer has violated any of the other Section 8(a) provisions (Sections 8(a)(2) through 8(a)(5)), it will automatically add a "dependent" Section 8(a)(1) ULP. This doesn't have much of a practical impact beyond adding to the ULPs listed in the notice posting and cease-and-desist order. Still, the dependent Section 8(a)(1) reflects the NLRB's position that an employer's violation of any of the Section 8(a) provisions will also reasonably lead employees to feel that the employer is chilling their Section 7 rights.

B. The Elements of Section 7 Protected Conduct

Although the statutory language of Section 7 provides the limits of protected activity, most of the factors discussed below have been largely developed through Board or judicial interpretation of that section. For example, the first element of protected conduct, "concertedness," derives directly from statutory language. By contrast, the third element of engaging in legitimate means in undertaking protected activity is not found directly in the statutory text. Of course, just because the term "concerted" is found in Section 7 does not mean that it is any less difficult to interpret as a legal matter than the notion of legitimate means.

In all, an activity is protected under Section 7 of the NLRA if employees engage in concerted activity for legitimate purposes using legitimate means. The following three sections are divided into these three essential elements of Section 7 protected conduct: (1) concertedness; (2) legitimate ends or purpose; and (3) legitimate means.

1. Concertedness

Section 7 expressly states: "Employees shall have the right ... to engage in other concerted activities for the purpose of collective bargaining or other mutual aid or protection...." Yet the definitional section of the NLRA, Section 2, does not clarify the meaning of "concerted." A narrow way of understanding this word is to say that employees engage in concerted activities when they act together to achieve a mutually desired result within the workplace. Under such a definition, two or more employees would literally have to be engaged in an activity together for concertedness to be present and for the activity to be potentially protected under Section 7.

There is no dispute that concertedness is met when two or more employees act together to achieve a common employment-related goal. However, it is also true that most courts recognize that an individual employee acts in a concerted manner when they speak as a spokesperson for a group of employees or are trying to persuade other employees to take group action. But what if the individual is merely referencing rights bargained for under a collective bargaining agreement? Can an individual employee acting on their own in this situation meet the "concertedness" prong of the Section 7 protected conduct? The answer is "yes."

In *NLRB v. City Disposal Systems, Inc.*, 465 U.S. 822 (1984), the Supreme Court held that an employee's honest and reasonable assertion of his right under a collective bargaining agreement to refuse to drive a truck he believed to be unsafe constituted "concerted activity" under the Act. In reaching this result, the Court deferred to the NLRB's *Interboro* doctrine, enunciated in *Interboro Contractors, Inc.*, 157 N.L.R.B. 1295 (1966), *enforced*, 388 F.2d 495 (2d Cir. 1967). Under the *Interboro* doctrine, if a single employee asserts a right found under the collective bargaining agreement, then the action qualifies as concerted protected activity. The doctrine's rationale is that by relying upon the collective bargaining agreement to vindicate their workplace rights, an employee is acting in tandem with those who collectively bargained the contract in the first place. Put another way, by individually invoking a collectively bargained right, the employee is continuing the group process that led to the right being part of the CBA. Importantly, the employee need not invoke any magic words or the exact provision to take advantage of the collective bargaining rights that they are calling upon for protection. It is enough that the employee makes clear that they are relying on the collective bargaining agreement in protesting hours, wages, or other working conditions.

Justice O'Connor dissented in *City Disposal* on the basis that even if the right the employee asserts can be grounded in the collective bargaining agreement, it is not enough to make the individual's self-interested action concerted. Justice O'Connor goes on to point out that labor laws were designed to encourage employees to act together. While she conceded that it was possible for one employee to act on behalf of other employees, and the activity could still be considered concerted under the *Interboro* doctrine, she did not feel that the particular facts of *City Disposal* suggested anything other than the truck driver was acting for his own personal benefit.

After the Court's decision in *City Disposal*, many "concertedness" cases involved an employer's argument that the employee was making only a personal gripe rather than engaging in concerted activity for the purpose of mutual aid or protection. The employee usually responds that their complaint concerned wages, working conditions, or hours, and that all these topics are protected as concerted activity regardless of whether it is part of a group complaint. Ultimately, the decision in *City Disposal* benefits employees by giving broader statutory meaning to what constitutes protected concerted activity and protects individual protests directed at one's own wages and working conditions.

However, as broad as the definition of concerted activity is, it is still true that an employee expressing purely personal concerns should not be considered to have engaged in concerted activity. If an employee is not engaged in concerted activity, they can be fired without the employer having to worry about committing a ULP. (Recall that ULPs only come into play when an employee is engaged in protected Section 7 conduct.) Also, if an individual employee is making complaints about working conditions during the organizational phase, and there is not yet a collective bargaining agreement in place, such an employee is not individually invoking rights that have been bargained for by the whole and thus would not be engaged in concerted activity under the theory espoused in *City Disposal*. However, as noted above, if an individual employee is attempting to initiate, induce, or prepare for group action—such as trying to start a union campaign—the individual's conduct would be considered concerted. *See Mushroom Transp. Co. v. NLRB*, 330 F.2d 683, 685 (3d Cir. 1964).

2. Legitimate Ends or Purposes

In addition to the threshold requirement of concertedness, activity qualifying for Section 7 protection must be directed toward a legitimate end or purpose. In this regard, Section 7 says the activity must be directed toward "collective bargaining" or "mutual aid or protection." Whether the activity is directed toward collective bargaining is usually readily discernible. Questions more often arise regarding whether activity is directed toward "mutual aid or protection."

If the purpose of the concerted activity is directed toward conditions of employment, such as hours, wages, or benefits, then this prong of the Section 7 protected activity test is met. But what if the purpose for the concerted activity is not directly related to an employee's own workplace? Is that activity carried out for a legitimate purpose?

In *Eastex, Inc. v. NLRB*, 437 U.S. 556 (1978), the Supreme Court considered a case where workers were handing out leaflets encouraging their fellow workers to support the union and criticizing both a proposal to incorporate the state right-to-work statute into the state constitution and a recent presidential veto of an increase in the federal minimum wage. In other words, the workers' activity involved political issues that did not directly impact their workplace. Yet, the Court held that this activity had a legitimate purpose and, thus, was protected under Section 7. This, in turn, means that the NLRA prohibits an employer from retaliating against an employee who is engaged in such conduct. In particular, the Court held that activities for "mutual aid or protection" include activities outside the direct employer-employee relationship if the purpose of the activity can be viewed as furthering employees' interests as employees more generally. Opposing a right-to-work constitutional amendment met this requirement of furthering employees' interests as employees, and thus was considered an appropriate purpose. One commentator has suggested that although these legitimate ends cases are decided on a case-by-case basis:

> The current decisions seem to suggest that if placed on a continuum, those activities that would be deemed not within the scope of section

> 7 would be those that merely tout a political candidate or party in an election. At the other end of the spectrum activity that would seem to almost always garner section 7 coverage are direct appeals by unions and employees to legislators over issues of general workplace concern.

Paul E. Bateman, *Concerted Activity: The Intersection Between Political Activity and Section 7 Rights*, 23 LAB. LAW. 41, 56 (2007). Recent examples of cases that straddle the line between protected Section 7 conduct and unprotected political activity include Google employees protesting their employer's contracts with the Chinese government and U.S. Customs and Border Protection agency (this case settled before an NLRB decision) and employees wearing Black Lives Matter (BLM) insignia at work (based largely on different facts in each case, three ALJs have split on this question, while the NLRB in *Home Depot USA, Inc.*, 373 N.L.R.B No. 25 (Feb. 21, 2024), found—contrary to the ALJ in the case—that wearing BLM insignia was Section 7 protected activity).

Another crucial part of "mutual aid and protection" is the right of union-represented employees to have a union representative at employer investigatory interviews where the employee reasonably believes the interview may result in disciplinary action against them. This right has come to be known as the *Weingarten* right, based on *NLRB v. J. Weingarten, Inc.*, 420 U.S. 251 (1975). As the Court observed in *Weingarten*:

> [E]ven though the employee alone may have an immediate stake in the outcome; he seeks "aid or protection" against a perceived threat to his employment security. The union representative whose participation he seeks is, however, safeguarding not only the particular employee's interest, but also the interests of the entire bargaining unit by exercising vigilance to make certain that the employer does not initiate or continue a practice of imposing punishment unjustly.

Id. at 260–61.

Notwithstanding the potential breadth of these rights, *Weingarten* rights extend only to investigatory interviews that could potentially lead to discipline. If discipline is not a possibility, or the decision to terminate has already been made, then a worker does not have the right to union representation during the employer meeting. An employer is under no obligation to inform employees of their *Weingarten* rights, and if an employee does not assert them, they are waived. Moreover, when an employee requests a co-worker's presence, the employer can avoid the *Weingarten* issue by opting to continue its investigation without interviewing the employee.

The question of whether *Weingarten* rights should apply in the nonunion context has been contentious. The NLRB has flip-flopped on this issue, most recently deciding in *IBM Corp.*, 341 N.L.R.B. 1288 (2004), that nonunion employees do not have the right to have a fellow employee present during an employer's disciplinary investigatory interview. In coming to this conclusion, the Board (3–2) found, among other things, that in a nonunion context: (1) co-workers do not represent the interests of the entire work force like union representatives; (2) co-workers cannot redress the imbalance of power between employers and employees like unions do through their presence in such a meeting; (3) co-workers do not have the same skills as union representatives; and (4) the presence of a co-worker may compromise the confidentiality of information. The Board in *IBM* expressly overturned the Clinton Board decision, *Epilepsy Foundation*, 331 N.L.R.B. 676 (2000), which had extended *Weingarten* rights to nonunion workplaces. In overturning *Epilepsy Foundation*, the Board controversially cited the growing number of investigatory interviews necessitated by security concerns over the terrorist attacks of 9/11 as part of the reason for returning to its prior position that nonunion employees are not entitled to representation during investigatory interviews. In dissent, Member Liebman wrote: "Workers without unions can and do successfully stand up for each other on the job—and they have the legal right to try, whether or not they succeed." *IBM Corp.*, 341 N.L.R.B. at 1305.

3. Legitimate Means and the Disloyalty Standard

An employee may be engaged in "concerted" activity for "mutual aid or protection," but the activity may still be deemed unprotected if the employee has engaged in "illegitimate means" for accomplishing their purpose or ends. The Board and courts have placed illegitimate means into the following four categories: conflict with another federal law; contrary to state law; in breach of contract; and disloyal or otherwise indefensible.

The first three categories involve concerted conduct that violates some other law. First, the question of whether Section 7 protects conduct that conflicts with another federal statute typically involves judicial analysis of the statutory language, history, and purposes of both statutes. For example, in *Southern S.S. Co. v. NLRB*, 316 U.S. 31, 38–49 (1942), the Court held that

Section 7 did not protect seamen whose concerted activity—a work stoppage in protest of working conditions aboard a ship that was away from its home port—constituted a mutiny in violation of a federal criminal statute. This is a question for which the Board receives no deference. Second, the question of whether Section 7 protects conduct that conflicts with a state statute involves a preemption analysis. *See infra* Chapter 18. However, even without doing a preemption analysis, it is safe to say that concerted activity that violates state criminal or property law, or conduct that constitutes an intentional tort will typically lose its protective cover. *See Glacier Northwest, Inc. v. Int'l Bhd. Of Teamsters*, 598 U.S. 771 (2023) (holding that, assuming the employer's factual claims were true, striking unionized truck drivers did not take reasonable precautions to protect employer's property from imminent danger and that the NLRA did not preempt the employer's state law tort claims against the union). For example, employers can lawfully discharge employees who engage in strike violence, blow up a factory, or slash the boss's tires, even if those employees concertedly planned such attacks to exert economic pressure on their employer. A "sit down" strike, in which strikers occupy the employer's property and refuse to work or leave, is also unprotected. Third, employees who engage in concerted activity in breach of their collective bargaining agreement typically lose the Act's protection. For example, employers may lawfully discharge union employees who go on strike in violation of their collective bargaining agreement's no-strike clause.

The disloyalty line of cases constitutes the fourth and final category of illegitimate means. The seminal case in this area is *NLRB v. Local 1229, IBEW (Jefferson Standard Broadcasting Co.)*, 346 U.S. 464 (1953). *Jefferson Standard* presented the question whether discharging employees engaged in concerted activity constitutes a ULP, where that activity results in disparagement of a TV-station-employer's business product—television programming. The fired employees, as part of a labor dispute, used picket signs that disparaged the TV station's programming without reference to the underlying labor dispute. The Supreme Court found the employee's conduct disloyal and, as a result, the employees were lawfully discharged for cause. Significantly, the employees' disparaging activity did not clearly relate to any given employment practice of the employer, or otherwise address wages, hours, or working conditions. The Court concluded that the only purpose of the activity was to harm the employer's business, and therefore, it was an illegitimate means for achieving the workers' ends of winning concessions from the employer.

Dissenting, Justice Frankfurter observed that, "[m]any of the legally recognized tactics and weapons of labor would readily be condemned for 'disloyalty' were they employed between man and man in friendly personal relations.... Furthermore, it ... disregard[s] the rough and tumble of strikes, in the course of which loose and even reckless language is properly discounted." *Id.* at 480. Professor Finkin, for his part, has commented: "'Disloyalty' is a shorthand expression, a catchphrase, and as such incapable of supplying a clear guide to decision, that, at least, being the near universal judgment of contemporaneous and later students of *Jefferson Standard*." Matthew W. Finkin, *Disloyalty! Does* Jefferson Standard *Stalk Still?*, 28 BERKELEY J. EMP. & LAB. L. 541, 547 (2007).

The Board has recently re-articulated its test, grounded in *Jefferson Standard*, for determining whether concerted activity is so disloyal that it loses the Act's protection. Under that test, "employee communications to third parties in an effort to obtain their support are protected where the communication indicated it is related to an ongoing dispute between employees and the employer, and the communication is not so disloyal, reckless or maliciously untrue as to lose the Act's protection." *MasTec Advanced Technologies*, 357 N.L.R.B. No. 17 (2011) (case and internal quotation mark omitted).

Although these four categories help delineate the line between protected and unprotected concerted activity, there is still much disagreement over which union conduct loses its protected status based on the use of illegitimate means. For instance, in *Elk Lumber Co.*, 91 N.L.R.B. 333 (1950), the Board held that an employee work slowdown, where employees purposefully slow down their work to place economic pressure on their employer, is an unprotected concerted activity. To be clear, this does not mean that slowdowns are illegal under the NLRA, but only that disciplining employees who engage in such tactics is not a ULP. Under the *Elk Lumber* rationale, although employees are free to go on strike or quit work, they are not protected from employer discipline when they continue to go to work, receive wages, and select how they want to work. The Board reasoned that allowing otherwise would be equivalent to permitting employees to prescribe all the terms and conditions of their employment. Similarly, a partial work stoppage would be unprotected activity under Section 7.

Another example of the unclear line between protected and unprotected conduct under the illegitimate means test can be found in *Five Star Transportation*, 349 N.L.R.B. 42 (2007). There, school bus drivers tried to convince the school board not to hire a nonunion competitor for a contract because that company had hired a sex offender in previous years. When the nonunion company won the contract, it refused to hire those union employees who had signed the letter to the school board. The employees in question were found to have failed the disparagement/disloyalty test of *Jefferson Standard* because they had called the nonunion bus company "sub-standard" and "reckless," among other things. Although the majority found the school bus drivers' conduct disloyal and unprotected, Member Liebman, dissenting, wondered whether employees such as these owe any duty of loyalty to an employer for whom they previously did not work when the activity in question occurred.

Even when employee behavior isn't strictly disloyal under *Jefferson Standard*, it could lose protection under Section 7. For instance, employees' use of offensive speech during what is otherwise Section 7 protected conduct has caused the NLRB to flip-flop in recent years. Under its current approach, the Board determines whether employees' conduct towards management was offensive enough to lose Section 7 protection based on a four-factor test: "(1) the place of the discussion; (2) the subject matter of the discussion; (3) the nature of the employee's outburst; and (4) whether the outburst was, in any way, provoked by an employer's unfair labor practice." *See Atlantic Steel*, 245 N.L.R.B. 814 (1979); *see also Lion Elastomers, LLC*, 372 N.L.R.B. No. 83 (2023) (reversing prior rule and reimplementing *Atlantic Steel*).

In the end, there is still much debate over these tricky questions. Perhaps, Professor Sharpe has come up with the best possible standard: "Employees who engage in lawful concerted activity for a Section 7 purpose should not be deprived of protection unless the activity itself (the means) unreasonably threatens the long-term viability of the enterprise, labor-management relationship, or the employment relationship." Calvin William Sharpe, *"By Any Means Necessary"—Unprotected Conduct and Decisional Discretion Under the National Labor Relations Act*, 20 BERKELEY J. EMP. & LAB. L. 203, 233 (1999). That standard has not yet been adopted.

CHECKPOINTS

- The heart of the NLRA, which contains employee statutory rights, is Section 7.
- Section 7 gives all employees the right to self-organization, the right to organize into a labor organization, the right to engage in collective

bargaining through such a labor organization, and the right to engage in concerted activities for mutual aid or protection.

- To be protected by Section 7, employees must act in a concerted manner for legitimate ends and through legitimate means.
- Employers are only considered to have committed an unfair labor practice (ULP) under Section 8 of the Act if they have interfered with employee Section 7 rights. Thus, if the employee is not engaged in Section 7 protected conduct, the employer is free to take disciplinary action without committing a ULP.
- Not only do employees act in a concerted manner when two or more employees act together to achieve a workplace goal, but individual employees can act in a concerted manner when they are speaking as a spokesperson for a group of employees or trying to persuade other employees to take group action.
- Under *City Disposal System*, an employee's honest and reasonable assertion of their right under a collective bargaining agreement to refuse to follow an employer's instruction constitutes concerted activity under the NLRA.
- Legitimate ends or purposes under Section 7 must be directed toward "mutual aid and protection." Activities for "mutual aid and protection" include activities outside of the employer-employee relationship if the purpose of the activity can be viewed as furthering an employee's interest as an employee.
- Although union employees are permitted to have union representation during employer disciplinary investigatory interviews under *Weingarten* as a type of mutual aid and protection, nonunion employees do not have such rights.
- Concerted activity typically loses its protection under Section 7 if it conflicts with federal law; is contrary to state law (typically, property law, criminal law, or intentionally tortious activity); breaches a collective bargaining agreement (typically, a no-strike clause); or is disloyal or otherwise indefensible.
- Under *Jefferson Standard* and its progeny, employees' conduct that is disloyal and/or disparages its employer's products, without clearly relating to the underlying labor dispute, is considered unprotected conduct.

- The Board's most recent articulation of the disloyalty test holds that "employee communications to third parties in an effort to obtain their support are protected where the communication indicated it is related to an ongoing dispute between employees and the employer and the communication is not so disloyal, reckless or maliciously untrue as to lose the Act's protection."
- Other illegitimate means for Section 7 purposes include work slowdowns, partial strikes, certain offensive conduct, and situations where employees have derided an employers' business, even when they did not work for the employer at the time of the labor dispute but came to work for them after a business transition.

CHAPTER 6

Section 7 Rights to Engage in Protected Conduct: Nonunion Employees

---

ROADMAP

- Protecting nonunion employee protests and complaints
- Individual action classified as concerted action
- Employer's ability to restrict employees' use of social media
- The bar on employer pay secrecy rules
- The NLRA's interaction with other laws

As noted in the previous chapter, Section 7 protects all employees, whether or not a union represents them. It is true that most cases before the NLRB involve unionized employees. A major reason for this is that most nonunion employees are unaware that the NLRA protects them in certain instances, even if they are aware of the NLRA at all. This lack of knowledge creates a self-perpetuating problem; the NLRB cannot initiate cases on its own, but the lack of nonunion cases limits employees' ability to learn about the NLRA and bring disputes to the NLRB.

Despite the limits on the NLRA's application to nonunion employees, the Act can supply important protections to these workers. Traditionally, nonunion employees have relied on the NLRA to protect collective complaints or protests against their employers, and to strike down unlawful bans on workplace communications. More recently, employer attempts to control employees' use of social media have put more focus on the NLRA's relevance in nonunion workplaces. This chapter discusses several common examples of nonunion Section 7 activity. Note, however, that these examples are not exclusive. Moreover, for those engaged in these activities to enjoy Section 7 protection, they must meet the same concerted and protected activity tests as described in the previous chapter.

A. Nonunion Protests and Complaints

Unionized employees are not the only workers who object to their working conditions. Indeed, because they lack representation, nonunion employees often face more serious workplace problems. When nonunion employees act together to improve their situation—even if they are not attempting to unionize—the NLRA protects them just as it would their unionized counterparts. For instance, as noted in Chapter 5, the NLRB recently concluded that Section 7 protected employees who wore Black Lives Matter insignia as part of a protest that was partially related to workplace concerns. *See Home Depot USA, Inc.*, 373 N.L.R.B No. 25 (Feb. 21, 2024).

Section 7 describes those protected by its provisions generically as "employees." Although the typical Section 7 case involves two or more employees acting together, at times, individual employees can engage in conduct that the NLRB will classify as concerted under Section 7. Those instances are less common, but they are often key precursors to action by a larger group of employees.

1. Concerted Action by a Group of Employees

The classic nonunion Section 7 decision is *NLRB v. Washington Aluminum Co.*, 370 U.S. 9 (1962). That case involved employees of a machine shop who walked out of work on a very cold day. The shop's furnace was broken, and one of the employees complained to the foreman, who stated—while looking at a group of employees huddled together—that "[i]f those fellows had any guts at all, they would go home." *Id.* at 11. The employee repeated the foreman's comments to his co-workers and said that he was going to leave. After some discussion, the rest of the employees decided to leave as well. The foreman convinced one employee to stay, but the employees who left were fired.

The NLRB concluded that the terminations violated Section 8(a)(1), but the circuit court disagreed. According to the court, Section 7 did not protect the employees' spontaneous walkout because the employees failed to give the employer an opportunity to grant a concession; therefore, the employer lawfully terminated the employees for cause.

The Supreme Court agreed with the NLRB and rejected the argument that employees lose Section 7 protection if they do not present a specific demand to their employer. The Court explained that, "[t]he language of [Section] 7 is broad enough to protect concerted activities whether they take place before, after, or at the same time such a demand is made." *Id.* at 14. The Court also stressed that the employees did not receive less protection because they were not represented by a union. On the contrary, because they lacked a bargaining representative, the employees "had to speak for themselves as best they could." *Id.* Given their complaints about the cold, the employer's lack of a response, and the lack of a company complaint procedure, the employees' concerted decision to walk off the job to "spotlight" their complaint was entitled to Section 7 protection.

Although it is rarely mentioned in the press, the NLRA's protection of nonunion employee protests and complaints remains highly relevant in modern workplace disputes. For instance, two widely publicized protest movements represent classic Section 7 concerted and protected action. One movement involves fast food workers—almost all of whom are nonunion—engaging in protests and walk-outs at fast food restaurants in major cities. Similarly, for many years employees had protested Walmart's low pay and poor working conditions during the company's post-Thanksgiving "Black Friday" sales. Unions assisted with the Black Friday protests, but nonunion employees were at the forefront in collectively demanding better working conditions. These employees, like their fast-food counterparts, engaged in Section 7 activity that protects them against terminations and other retaliation, assuming they did not lose protection because of misconduct. In fact, the NLRB's General Counsel filed several unfair labor practice charges against Walmart for disciplining and terminating employees who engaged in various Black Friday strikes and protests, as well as for threatening employees with reprisals if they engaged in such conduct. Although in one case the administrative law judge found that Walmart violated the employees' Section 7 rights, the Board reversed, concluding that the employees' conduct amounted to intermittent strikes, which are unprotected by the Act. *See Walmart Stores, Inc.*, 368 N.L.R.B. No. 24 (2019) (dissenting Board Member arguing that employees' action was protected under *Washington Aluminum* majority had improperly expanded the intermittent strikes doctrine).

2. An Individual Employee's Concerted Action

As noted in the previous chapter, in certain situations, individual employees can also engage in what counts as concerted activity. This situation can be particularly relevant in the nonunion context. As *Washington Aluminum* illustrates, often a single employee is behind what eventually becomes a group effort. Imagine if a manager had overheard the employees' discussion in *Washington Aluminum* and, before the group decided what to do, fired the employee who was urging his co-workers to join him in walking off the job. Would the terminated employee be protected by Section 7? The answer is probably "yes."

The NLRB classifies an individual employee's activity as concerted if it had the "object of initiating or inducing or preparing for group action or . . . had some relation to group action in the interest of employees." *Mushroom Transp. Co. v. NLRB*, 330 F.2d 683, 685 (3d Cir. 1964). When an individual employee is not trying to prompt group action but is instead engaging in conduct that is beneficial to the larger group, the analysis is more complicated. After much back and forth over the years, the NLRB stated its current position in *Meyers Industries*, 281 N.L.R.B. 882 (1986), *enf'd sub nom. Prill v. NLRB*, 835 F.2d 1481 (D.C. Cir. 1987), which involved the termination of an employee because he reported unsafe truck brakes to government authorities. In *Meyers*, the NLRB reaffirmed the *Mushroom Transportation* doctrine but concluded that "[i]n general, to find an employee's activity to be 'concerted,' we shall require that it be engaged in with or on the authority of other employees, and not solely by and on behalf of the employee himself." *Id.* at 885. *Meyers* represents a more limited interpretation of "concerted" than previous NLRB decisions. However, along with *Mushroom Transportation*, it still allows significant leeway for individual employees to enjoy Section 7 protection. Indeed, in *Parexel International*, 356 N.L.R.B. 516 (2011), the NLRB found that Section 7 protected an employee who had not engaged in concerted activity, but was fired because the employer suspected that he might do so later.

B. Employee Use of Social Media

One of the more recent phenomena in the workplace is employees' use of social media. As personal use of social media has grown, employees have also turned to social media to air complaints about their employers. Not surprisingly, employers do not like this trend, and some of them retaliate against their employees for postings that they view as disparaging to their business. The main question in many of these disputes is whether the conduct of the employees—who are often unorganized—is concerted and protected under Section 7.

One of the NLRB's first decisions on social media was *Knauz BMW*, 358 N.L.R.B. 1754 (2012). In *Knauz*, a BMW salesman posted on his Facebook page on the same day, two sets of photos and comments that criticized his employer. One set of postings involved a customer appreciation event that the employee felt was not befitting a luxury car brand, especially because of the low quality of food. The other set of postings addressed an incident at another of the employer's dealerships in which a salesman allowed a customer's thirteen-year-old child to sit in the driver's seat of a Land Rover, which he then drove into a pond. The NLRB found that the employee was fired solely for his Land Rover postings, which included, among other things, pictures of the accident with the caption: "This is your car. This is your car on drugs." *Id.* at 1758. Section 7 did not protect this post because it was not made on behalf of other employees and was not connected to employees' working conditions.

If the NLRB had made a different causation finding that included the customer event postings, this case might have come out differently. The ALJ found that the postings about the customer event were protected by Section 7 because the employee had earlier discussed the inadequate food at the event with other employees and because the event's quality arguably affected the employees' commission-based compensation. This finding was based on employees' Section 7 right to bring group concerns to management, as recognized in *Mushroom Transportation* and *Myers.* The ALJ also rejected the employer's argument that the posting was so disparaging that it lost Section 7 protection. (Chapter 5 discusses the loss of Section 7 protection under *Jefferson Standard.*)

Finally, in *Knauz,* the NLRB also concluded that the employer violated Section 8(a)(1) by implementing a "Courtesy" rule that prohibited employees from being "disrespectful" or from using any "language which injures the image or reputation of the" employer. *Id.* According to the NLRB, this rule was overbroad because employees would reasonably interpret it as prohibiting protests, criticisms, and other Section 7 activity. (Chapter 7 discusses the NLRB's current approach to work rules under its *Stericycle* decision.)

Knauz illustrates three general points about social media disputes. First, employers can violate the NLRA not only by punishing employees who use social media, but also by having overly broad policies that restrict the use of social media and other forms of concerted and protected activity. Second, there is nothing unusual about social media as far as NLRA doctrine is concerned. Although it is a newer form of protest and criticism, social media is merely one of many ways in which employees can express their workplace concerns.

A third point, which is related to the second, is that determining whether Section 7 protects employees' use of social media falls under the traditional test for concerted and protected activity. In *Knauz*, the Land Rover posts were not protected because they did not relate to the terms and conditions of work. In addition, the Land Rover posts were not concerted, which can often be an issue in social media cases. However, in *Hispanics United of Buffalo, Inc.*, 359 N.L.R.B. 368 (2012), the NLRB ordered the reinstatement of nonunion employees who were fired for Facebook postings that objected to another employee's criticism to management about their work. The target of the postings brought the exchange to the attention of the employer, which then fired the employees for "bullying and harassment." The NLRB concluded that there was no harassment and that the terminations were unlawful. Key to this latter finding was that several employees had made comments on the original post, meaning that the employees acted in concert to raise concerns about a protected matter—criticisms of their work—which could have resulted in disciplinary action against them.

C. Pay Secrecy Rules

Perhaps one of the most common, albeit infrequently reported, nonunion labor issues involves pay secrecy rules. Many employers prohibit employees from discussing their salaries with co-workers. There are many reasons why employers might have such policies, including the desire to avoid conflict among employees once they realize others receive higher compensation. There is also the reality that employees are better able to bargain for increased compensation if they know what their employer is paying others. Like social media policies, employers can violate the NLRA both by applying a pay secrecy rule against an employee and by simply having a rule on the books. What many employees (and employers) do not know is that most pay secrecy rules are unlawful under the NLRA if applied to statutory employees. Indeed, during the Obama administration, the President announced that he would implement an executive order banning federal contractors from having pay secrecy rules. Little attention was paid to the NLRA's already existing prohibition, which reflects the fact that most nonunion employees are unaware that the NLRA can protect their collective activity.

The NLRB has long concluded that pay secrecy rules violate Section 8(a)(1) because employees' discussion of their compensation is a concerted and protected activity. For example, in *Fredericksburg Glass and Mirror, Inc.*, 323 N.L.R.B. 165 (1997), the employer promulgated—although never enforced—a rule stating that "[a]n employee's earnings are a confidential matter between the employee and his earnings supervisor. Earnings may not be discussed among fellow employees and any such discussion will result in dismissal and/or disciplinary action at the supervisor's discretion." *Id.* at 168. The NLRB found that this rule was unlawful, quoting a court's observation that "dissatisfaction due to low wages is the grist on which concerted activity feeds. Discord generated by what employees view as unjustified wage differentials also provides the sinew for persistent concerted action." *Id.* at 174 (quoting *Jeannette Corp. v. NLRB*, 532 F.2d 916, 919 (3d Cir. 1976)). The NLRB noted further that the possibility of jealousy or strife among employees is generally insufficient to outweigh the Section 7 interests at stake. Thus, pay secrecy rules will almost always be unlawful under Section 8(a)(1).

D. Section 7's Interaction with Other Laws

Employees' Section 7 rights, at times, can relate—and even conflict with—other areas of law. When courts perceive a true conflict, especially the Supreme Court, the NLRA interests at stake are usually forced to take a back seat to the other legal interests at stake. For instance, in *Hoffman Plastics Compounds, Inc. v. NLRB*, 535 U.S. 137 (2002), the Court held that the NLRB could not order backpay to undocumented employees who were unlawfully fired because of conflicts that the majority perceived between this remedy and federal immigration law.

Another example involves employers' use of mandatory arbitration clauses. For many years, the Supreme Court has expanded companies' ability to insist that customers and employees arbitrate disputes—an ability that a large percentage of employers now take advantage of. More recently, the Court has permitted these arbitration agreements to bar class disputes, which unsurprisingly has led more employers to include such prohibitions in their mandatory arbitration clauses. However, in 2012, the NLRB cast doubt on the lawfulness of these anti-class action clauses. In *D.R. Horton, Inc.*, 357 N.L.R.B. 2277 (2012), the NLRB concluded that the prohibition against class arbitration violated Section 8(a)(1). It has long been held that one of employees' Section 7 rights is to use administrative, judicial, or arbitral forums to seek improvements in their working conditions. *See, e.g., NLRB v. City Disposal Systems, Inc.*, 465 U.S. 822, 836 (1984); *Eastex, Inc. v. NLRB*, 437 U.S. 556, 565–66 (1978). The NLRB has also concluded that bringing collective grievances is a protected activity. *See, e.g., NLRB v. Washington Aluminum Co.*, 370 U.S. 9 (1962). Combining these principles with the *Meyers* requirement that an individual employee's concerted activity must be made with the authority of other employees, or to induce group action, the NLRB in *D.R. Horton* stated that a named plaintiff in an employment class action is engaging in Section 7 concerted and protected activity. Because the agreement requires employees to waive their right to bring a class claim in either a judicial or arbitral forum, the NLRB concluded that it "clearly and expressly bars employees from exercising substantive rights that have long been held protected by Section 7 of the NLRA."

In *Epic Systems Corp. v. Lewis*, 138 S. Ct. 1612 (2018), the Supreme Court reversed the Board in a 5–4 decision. The majority held that the Federal Arbitration Act (FAA) "instructed federal courts to enforce arbitration agreements according to their terms" and that the NLRA "does not mention class or collection action procedures"; therefore, the NLRA cannot be read to displace the FAA. The dissent stressed the substantial imbalance of power between employers and employees and the fact that the NLRA was explicitly intended to address this imbalance. Thus, according to the dissent, the FAA should not shrink the NLRA's "protective sphere."

Another instance of Section 7's potential reach into areas usually regulated elsewhere involves non-compete clauses, which prevent an employee from working for certain other employers. These employment provisions are governed primarily by state laws. Yet, in 2023, the NLRB's General Counsel argued that most non-compete provisions violate Section 8(a)(1). *See* NLRB Office of General Counsel, *Non-Compete Agreements that Violate the National Labor Relations Act*, Memorandum GD 23-08 (May 30, 2023). The Federal Trade Commission followed suit in early 2024, issuing a rule banning non-compete agreements, although a district court enjoined the rule, finding that it exceeded the agency's authority. *See Ryan, LLC v. FTC*, Case No. 3:24-CV-00986 (N.D. Tex., July 3, 2024). Soon thereafter, an NLRB ALJ issued a decision that struck down a non-compete agreement as overly broad because it "would deter a reasonable employee from engaging in protected activity by barring employees from directly or indirectly, and in any capacity, engaging in, being employed by, or becoming interested in any enterprise that is 'similar or competitive' to the employer's business." *J.O. Mory, Inc.*, No. CA-309577, slip op. at 19–20 (2024). The NLRB has not ruled on the issue yet, but in what ways do you think that non-compete provisions might violate employees' concerted Section 7 rights?

CHECKPOINTS

- Section 7 protects nonunion employees' concerted action to try to improve working conditions.
- Individual nonunion employees can enjoy protection under Section 7 if they are trying to initiate group action or are acting with the authority of other employees.
- Nonunion employees' use of social media can be considered Section 7 activity if it meets the traditional concerted and protected requirements.
- Pay secrecy rules usually violate Section 8(a)(1) because employees' discussion of their compensation is a concerted and protected activity.
- Section 7 protects employees' collective use of administrative, arbitral, or judicial forums to improve their working conditions.
- In *Epic Systems*, the Supreme Court overruled the NLRB and concluded that the FAA prevented a finding that employers violate employees' Section 7 rights by using mandatory arbitration agreements that ban class arbitration.

- The NLRB's General Counsel has argued that employers violate employees' Section 7 rights by requiring non-compete agreements. Whether the NLRB adopts this position, and if so whether courts agree, is an open question at the time of this book's publication.

CHAPTER 7

Organizing a Union: Section 8(a)(1) Unfair Labor Practices

ROADMAP

- Overly broad work rules
- Employees' Section 7 right to communicate versus employers' property rights
- Employer speech: lawful predictions or unlawful threats?
- Factual misrepresentations in union campaigns
- Unlawful promises or provisions of benefits to employees
- Employer surveillance
- Interrogating and polling employees

The previous two chapters discussed protected conduct under Section 7 as applied to both union and nonunion employees. This chapter, and the two that follow, examine various unfair labor practices (ULPs) that commonly occur during a representation campaign, although they can occur at other times as well.

In general, when there is a question whether employer conduct infringes employees' Section 7 rights, the NLRB will find that conduct to violate Section 8(a)(1) if it has a "reasonable tendency to interfere with, restrain or coerce union or protected activities." *Farm Fresh Co., Target One, LLC*, 361 N.L.R.B.

848, 860 (2014). This inquiry typically hinges on whether employees would "reasonably construe" the employer's conduct as interfering, restraining, or coercing their ability to engage in Section 7 activity. In other words, the focus is on *employees'* reasonable perception of an employer's conduct, not the employer's intent. Moreover, this objective standard does not require evidence that any employees actually felt this way. However, such evidence can help support a finding that employer conduct has a reasonable tendency to interfere, restrain, or coerce Section 7 rights.

A finding that employees would reasonably construe the employer's conduct as interfering with Section 7 rights is not the end of the story. An employer can still avoid a Section 8(a)(1) ULP in many instances if it can show that it had a legitimate justification that outweighs the impact on employees' Section 7 rights. We'll see an example of this in Chapter 9, which discusses the *Darlington* case in which the Supreme Court agreed with the Board that an employer's interest in being able to decide whether to remain in business will always outweigh the impact on employees' Section 7 rights following a total plant closure, even when motivated by an attempt to avoid a union (although we will also see that there may still be another ULP in this situation and that a different rule applies to partial plant closures).

The NLRB will often modify the general "reasonably construe" Section 8(a)(1) balancing test to tailor its analysis to the particular factual scenarios and policies involved in a given situation. This Chapter highlights the most prevalent of these types of special Section 8(a)(1) cases, particularly those that commonly arise in union organizing campaigns. Improper conduct occurring during a representation campaign can have two effects. As discussed in the previous chapter, violations can be classified as a typical ULP and result in remedies that might include a cease-and-desist order, backpay, and reinstatement. However, as discussed in Chapter 10, if improper conduct occurs during a representation campaign, it may not only result in a ULP finding, but also serve as a basis to overturn the results of the union election. Therefore, although the ULPs discussed in this chapter can happen at any point in time, they are most common—and are especially impactful—during a representation campaign. These ULPs involve overly broad workplace rules; employer attempts to ban employee communications; employer threats; factual misrepresentations by both employers and unions; improper promises or provision of benefits by employers and unions; and employers' surveilling, interrogating, and polling employees.

A. Work Rules

At most workplaces, there is a set of rules that govern various types of employee conduct. Although many of these rules present no labor law issues, some have the potential to conflict with employees' Section 7 rights, even when they are facially neutral. For instance, as Chapter 6 noted, the NLRB has long found that "pay secrecy" or "pay gag" rules that prohibit employees from discussing their pay with each other violate Section 8(a)(1). The reason is that these rules interfere with employees' Section 7 right to provide "mutual aid or protection" by discussing each other's wages and using that information to improve their pay.

Because of the prevalence of work rules and their potential to impact Section 7 rights, the NLRB has paid close attention to the issue in recent years. Unsurprisingly, this has also meant that the NLRB has flip-flopped on its analysis of work rules. Following more aggressive challenges to work rules by the Obama-era General Counsel, the Trump Board issued two cases—*Boeing Co.*, 365 N.L.R.B. No. 154 (2017), and *LA Specialty Produce Co.*, 368 N.L.R.B. No. 93 (2019)—that gave employers more leeway to issue facially neutral work rules without violating Section 8(a)(1). The Biden Board, however, reversed these cases in *Stericycle, Inc.*, 372 N.L.R.B. No. 1113 (2023).

Stericycle involved work rules prohibiting certain types of personal conduct, forbidding conflicts of interest, and requiring confidentiality for harassment complaints. In evaluating these rules, the Board abandoned the *Boeing/LA Specialty* analysis, which required balancing a rule's impact on Section 7 rights against an employer's legitimate interests in promulgating the rule (and established a classification system for rules that were always lawful, always unlawful, or a middle category that required additional scrutiny). Moreover, the *Boeing/LA Specialty* analysis required the General Counsel to prove that a facially neutral rule would, in context, be viewed by a reasonable employee as chilling their Section 7 rights.

In *Stericycle*, the NLRB reversed *Boeing* and *LA Specialty* in favor of a revised version of the prior analysis under *Lutheran Heritage Village-Livonia*, 343 N.L.R.B. 646 (2004). Under the new *Stericycle/Lutheran Heritage* analysis, the General Counsel must first prove that a neutral work rule has "a reasonable tendency to chill employees from exercising their Section 7 rights." The Board will examine the rule "from the perspective of an employee who is subject to the rule and economically dependent on the employer, and who also contemplates engaging in protected concerted activity." The employer's intent in promulgating the rule is not a factor at this stage of the analysis. If the General Counsel meets their burden, the rule is presumptively unlawful under Section 8(a)(1). The employer, however, can rebut the presumption by proving that the rule "advances a legitimate and substantial business interest and that the employer is unable to advance that interest with a more narrowly tailored rule." If the employer meets this burden, the rule is lawful.

B. Employees' Section 7 Right to Communicate vs. Employers' Property Rights

Since the NLRA was enacted, there has been tension between employees' attempts to talk to each other about unions and other workplace matters, and employers' attempts to squelch such discussions. These disputes involve two basic interests. The first is employees' right to communicate with each other at work about working conditions. The second is the employers' right to control their property. Neither right is absolute, and the struggle to find an appropriate balance between the two has been contentious.

1. Employees' Right to Communicate with Each Other at Work

Cases involving employees' right to communicate with each other at work are often called *Republic Aviation* cases. In *Republic Aviation Corp. v. NLRB*, 324 U.S. 793 (1945), the Supreme Court addressed a consolidated group of cases in which employers implemented workplace solicitation bans. The employers implemented these bans before a union arrived on the scene, although they began enforcing them once union organizing commenced. One employer fired an employee for passing out union authorization cards to employees during the lunch period, another employer fired several employees for wearing union buttons, and a third employer suspended employees for distributing union literature in the company parking lot. Although the NLRB found Section 8(a)(3) violations in some instances, in others there was no finding that the employers were motivated by the union animus such ULPs require (Chapter 9 discusses that point in more detail). Thus, for the purposes of this section, it is best to think of *Republic Aviation* purely as an independent

Section 8(a)(1) case (an "independent Section 8(a)(1)" case is one in which the primary ULP is based on Section 8(a)(1); in contrast, a "derivative Section 8(a)(1)" case is one in which the primary ULP is based on another section and the Section 8(a)(1) violation is merely derivative of the other ULP).

The Supreme Court in *Republic Aviation* upheld the NLRB's finding that employers' solicitation bans were unlawful and emphasized that employer property rights were not absolute in NLRA cases. Rather, an employer's property right must be balanced against the "right of employees to organize for mutual aid without employer interference." *Id.* at 798. The Court also rejected the employers' argument that preventing pro-union communications at the worksite was necessary to maintain the employers' appearance of neutrality. The key aspect of *Republic Aviation* was the Court's adoption of the NLRB's theory that the solicitation bans deprived employees of their Section 7 right to "full freedom of association" at work during their own time. According to the Board's "*Peyton Packing* presumption," which the Court upheld in *Republic Aviation*, employers can implement solicitation bans during working hours, but not outside of that time, even while employees are on company property:

> The Act, of course, does not prevent an employer from making and enforcing reasonable rules covering the conduct of employees on company time. Working time is for work. It is therefore within the province of an employer to promulgate and enforce a rule prohibiting union solicitation during working hours. Such a rule must be presumed to be valid in the absence of evidence that it was adopted for a discriminatory purpose. It is no less true that time outside working hours, whether before or after work, or during luncheon or rest periods, is an employee's time to use as he wishes without unreasonable restraint, although the employee is on company property. It is therefore not within the province of an employer to promulgate and enforce a rule prohibiting union solicitation by an employee outside of working hours, although on company property. Such a rule must be presumed to be an unreasonable impediment to self-organization and therefore discriminatory in the absence of evidence that special circumstances make the rule necessary in order to maintain production or discipline.

Matter of Peyton Packing Co., 49 N.L.R.B. 828, 843 (1943), *enf'd*, 142 F.2d 1009 (5th Cir. 1943). This rule applies not only to the enforcement of bans but also to an employer's implementation of a policy, which can chill employees' freedom to engage in protected solicitations.

In the years since *Republic Aviation*, the NLRB has fleshed out the rules that apply to workplace communication disputes. The analysis begins with a presumption that an employer cannot lawfully prohibit oral employee solicitations that occur outside of work areas and during non-work time. Similarly, an employer cannot prohibit solicitations in work areas during periods of time when work is not being performed. The NLRB defines "work time" as a period during which employees are actually working and not on break or other types of downtime. The corollary presumption is that employers can generally prohibit employee solicitations in work areas during work time because such bans will typically serve a valid production concern. In a more traditional workplace, like a factory, determining what is "work time" and a "work area" is usually not difficult. However, in more modern workplaces, particularly for white-collar jobs, there may not be designated non-work areas or breaks. As a result, application of the *Republic Aviation* presumption can be more complicated.

Like other presumptions, parties can argue that special circumstances warrant an exception. Examples of special circumstances that might justify more restrictive solicitation bans include security concerns or significant interference with customers or patients. *See, e.g.*, *NLRB v. Baptist Hosp.*, 442 U.S. 773, 786 (1979) (permitting solicitation ban in hospital's immediate patient care areas, sitting rooms, and corridors). On the other hand, as discussed in the subsection below on electronic communications, solicitation bans that might otherwise be permissible will violate Section 8(a)(1) if they are enforced discriminatorily.

Yet another wrinkle in the *Republic Aviation* presumption is that it applies only to oral solicitations. When a ban on written distributions—such as fliers or handbills—is involved, the presumption is different. In *Stoddard-Quirk Manufacturing Co.*, 138 N.L.R.B. 615 (1962), the NLRB concluded that employers are presumptively allowed to restrict written distributions from all working areas, even if the distribution occurs during non-work time, so long as "employees have access to nonworking areas of the [employer's] premises." *Id.* at 621. According to the NLRB, written distributions risk creating litter that could interfere with production. Moreover, unlike bilateral oral solicitations, the purpose of a written distribution is satisfied once the employees receive it and have an opportunity to read it at some later point. As a result, the employer can ban most written distributions, as long as employees have some opportunity to pass out literature, such as in the company parking lot, break room, or other areas where work is not being performed.

At times, the distinction between oral solicitations and written distributions can be difficult. For instance, emails share attributes of both categories (although, as discussed below, electronic communications are analyzed under a separate rule). The distribution of union authorization cards also does not fit neatly into either category, although the NLRB has treated them as solicitations under the *Stoddard-Quirk* rule. *See Rose Co.*, 154 N.L.R.B. 228, 229 n.1 (1965). Other examples of hard-to-classify communications include union buttons, shirts, and other types of insignia. *See, e.g.*, *Meijer, Inc. v. NLRB*, 130 F.3d 1209, 1217 (6th Cir. 1997) (noting "employee's near-absolute right to wear union insignia"). Typically, union insignia is treated like an oral solicitation under the *Republic Aviation* test. *See Serv-Air, Inc. v. NLRB*, 395 F.2d 557 (10th Cir. 1968). But, like other solicitations, there might be special production, disciplinary, or customer concerns that warrant some restrictions *See, e.g.*, *NLRB v. Baptist Hosp.*, 442 U.S. 773, 786 (1979) (approving solicitation bans in "immediate patient care" areas, sitting rooms, and corridors of hospitals); *Davison-Paxon Co. v. NLRB*, 462 F.2d 364 (5th Cir. 1972) (approving employer's ban against wearing of bright yellow campaign buttons in customer area of department store).

Off-duty or off-site employees are also difficult to categorize. However, because these employees usually have the same "direct" Section 7 interest in communicating as other employees (the distinction between direct and derivative Section 7 rights is described in the next section), the NLRB applies the *Republic Aviation* analysis to employer attempts to exclude employees who are off-duty or who work at one of the employer's other locations. *See Hillhaven Highland House*, 336 N.L.R.B. 646, 648 (2001), *enf'd*, 344 F.3d 523 (6th Cir. 2003). But the NLRB will allow employers to restrict off-duty employees' access to a worksite if valid business reasons justify the restriction, the restriction applies to all activities, and the rule is clearly disseminated to all employees. *See Tri-County Med. Ctr.*, 222 N.L.R.B. 1089, 1090 (1976).

2. Nonemployees' Ability to Communicate at a Worksite

The *Republic Aviation* line of cases discussed in the previous section all involve employees' ability to communicate with each other at work. However, before those communications occur, employees often talk first with union organizers to learn about collective representation. In contrast to employees' right to communicate under *Republic Aviation*, the ability of union organizers and other nonemployees to enter the worksite is extremely limited.

The key decision in this area is *Lechmere, Inc. v. NLRB*, 502 U.S. 527 (1992), which involved a common fact pattern for union organizer cases. A union tried to start a campaign at a store located in a shopping plaza. After newspaper ads were unsuccessful in spurring interest among employees, the union went into the parking lot co-owned by the employer and placed handbills on cars, most of which were owned by employees. The employer told the organizers to leave, citing its preexisting no-solicitation rule. The union returned several times and was always asked to leave. Eventually, the union organizers went to a public grassy strip that separated the parking lot and a four-lane highway to try to distribute handbills to cars entering the lot before and after the store was open. This effort, in addition to others like the license plate numbers of cars in the parking lot to find employees' home addresses (which, while legal at the time, is now unlawful), failed to garner any significant employee support for the union.

The NLRB found that the employer violated Section 8(a)(1) by prohibiting the organizers from communicating with workers on the employer's property. The basis of the NLRB's finding was a test that it developed in reaction to an earlier Supreme Court decision. In *NLRB v. Babcock & Wilcox Co.*, 351 U.S. 105, 113 (1956), the Court recognized that there was some Section 7 right for nonemployee organizers to access an employer's property to contact employees, whose "right of self-organization depends in some measure on [their] ability ... to learn the advantages of self-organization from others." However, the Court described this right as a "derivative" one—that is, nonemployees' right to access employer property is derivative of employees' right to be informed about unionization. According to the Court, this derivative right is much weaker than employees' direct right to communicate at work, as was the case in *Republic Aviation*. Thus, the default under *Babcock* was that employers can ban nonemployees from its property, although the Court recognized that exceptions might exist, such as where the worksite is "beyond the reach of reasonable union efforts to communicate" with employees. *Id.* at 113.

The NLRB's response to *Babcock* was *Jean Country*, 291 N.L.R.B. 11 (1988), in which it created a three-factor test that balanced the strength of employees' right to communicate against the degree of infringement on the employer's property interest. In *Lechmere*, the Court struck down the *Jean Country* test as inconsistent with *Babcock*. In particular, the *Lechmere* Court held that a balancing of interests was appropriate only for direct employee communications;

when nonemployees are involved, the employer's property interests will usually take precedence. This is because, according to the Court, Section 7 "simply does not protect nonemployee union organizers except in the rare case where 'the inaccessibility of employees makes ineffective the reasonable attempts by nonemployees to communicate with them through the usual channels.'" *Lechmere*, 502 U.S. at 537.

When the Court says that the inaccessibility exception is "rare," it means it. As explained in *Lechmere*, the exception does not apply where access is difficult or ineffective. Rather, the worksite and employees' living space must be so isolated that company property is the unions' only realistic option to access employees. This means that the exception will only apply in unusual situations where employees live and work in places such as an offshore oil rig, remote logging camp, or isolated mountain resort.

Under *Lechmere*, an employer is almost always free to exclude nonemployees from its property. The only exceptions are the rare inaccessibility scenario, when an employer's exclusion of nonemployees is discriminatory, and when the NLRB orders the employer to remedy misconduct by giving the union access to the worksite. The following section discusses, in addition to electronic communications, how the NLRB recently made the discriminatory-exclusion exception significantly narrower than it used to be.

3. Electronic Communications and Discriminatory Exclusions

As noted in the discussion above, e-mail and other electronic communications do not fit well under the *Republic Aviation* analysis. This eventually led the NLRB to address employers' ability to restrict use of its electronic communication systems. Since then, the Board has flip-flopped on the issue. In its first analysis of the issue, the NLRB concluded that employees' use of company email to make Section 7 related communications should be treated differently from employees' in-person communications. *See Guard Publishing Co. (Register-Guard)*, 351 N.L.R.B. 1110 (2007), *rev'd in part*, 571 F.3d 53 (D.C. Cir. 2009). Comparing employees' use of company email to use of other personal property, like bulletin boards and copy machines, the Board in *Register-Guard* held that employees lacked a Section 7 right to use an employer's email systems in most instances. The NLRB denied that it was extending its *Lechmere* analysis to email communications, but that was the practical effect of *Register-Guard*.

In 2014, the NLRB reversed *Register-Guard* in *Purple Communications, Inc.*, 361 N.L.R.B. 1050 (2014). *Purple Communication* rejected the idea that personal property should be treated differently than the real property; therefore, employees' electronic solicitations would fall under the *Republic Aviation* analysis, providing a presumptive right to use company email for Section 7 communications. In 2019, the NLRB changed course again by reversing *Purple Communications* and reinstating the *Register-Guard* rule. *See Rio All-Suites Hotel & Casino*, 368 N.L.R.B. No. 143 (2019). Thus, the current rule is that "employees have no statutory right to use employer equipment, including IT resources, for Section 7 purposes." There is a limited exception, however, "in those rare cases where an employer's email system furnishes the only reasonable means for employees to communicate with one another."

There was a second issue in *Register-Guard* that has remained in place since 2007: whether an employer violates Section 8(a)(1) because it exercised its right to prohibit communications in a discriminatory fashion. Under this exception, a ban on communications that would normally be lawful will violate Section 8(a)(1) if it is "discriminatory" on its face or in its application. The NLRB and courts have struggled to define discrimination, setting forth definitions that included policies that allow access to the worksite for all groups except for unions; that allow access for work-related or isolated charitable solicitations, but not unions; that allow all charitable solicitations, but not union and other non-work-related communications; that favor one union over another; that allow distributions by the employer, but not unions; and that ban union and other Section 7 communications, but allow other types of communications that are of a similar character. In *Register-Guard*, the NLRB adopted this last, most narrow definition. Under that definition, an employer could, for instance, ban all solicitations for "membership" organizations from soliciting at the worksite, even if it is well aware that this policy would prohibit union communications. As long as the ban does not facially single out Section 7 communications, the NLRB will not classify it as discriminatory. This definition seems to apply in *Republic Aviation*, *Lechmere*, and *Register-Guard* cases—that is, cases in which the employer can prohibit employee solicitations, nonemployee solicitations, and employee electronic solicitations as long as it doesn't do so in a "discriminatory" way. Also, consider whether the rule regarding employee use of employer equipment to send and receive union-related emails is of diminishing importance in a world in which people increasingly communicate with personal cell phones, as opposed to employer equipment.

C. Employer Speech

1. Captive-Audience Meetings

During most representation elections, supporters and opponents of the union frequently communicate with employees in an attempt to sway votes. For employers, one of the most common and successful tactics is the "captive-audience meeting." These meetings are mandatory sessions during which an employer tries to convince employees not to vote for the union. Typically, employees are not only ordered to attend such meetings, but they also cannot question the employer representative. Moreover, the employer need not allow the union to present opposing views at the workplace. Most employers faced with an election use captive-audience meetings, which studies have shown to be very effective in reducing support for the union.

By and large, for the last 70 years, captive-audience meetings were lawful under the NLRA. This was not always true (nor is it true at the time of this book's publication), as the NLRB used to find that an employer violated Section 8(a)(1), and would provide grounds for overturning an election, if it gave a captive-audience speech without giving the union an equal opportunity to address employees. However, in *Livingston Shirt Co.*, 107 N.L.R.B. 400 (1953), the NLRB changed course. Key to this decision was the Taft-Hartley Act's new Section 8(c), which stated that the "expressing of any views, argument, or opinion, or the dissemination thereof ... shall not constitute or be evidence of an unfair labor practice ... if such expression contains no threat of reprisal or force or promise of benefit." According to *Livingston Shirt*, Section 8(c)'s prohibition against finding a ULP based on an employer's noncoercive speech would be negated if an employer were required to give a union access to the worksite simply because it engaged in such speech. In sum, although the NLRB in *Livingston Shirt* recognized that both the union and employer have a right to communicate with employees, it concluded that an employer that gives captive-audience speeches has no duty to give the union access to employees at the worksite. This means that an employer could order all employees—even ones who have already made up their mind—to attend a meeting where the employer disparages the union without allowing the union to rebut at the worksite. The one significant exception is that, under the *Peerless Plywood* rule, an employer is not allowed to give a captive-audience speech within 24 hours of an election. Violation of this rule can result in the NLRB ordering a new election if the union loses.

The idea that unions have no equal right to access employees at the worksite was extended by the Supreme Court in *NLRB v. United Steelworkers of America (Nutone Inc. & Avondale Mills)*, 357 U.S. 357 (1958). In that case, the Court held that an employer may exempt itself from its own, lawful anti-solicitation rule. Thus, even employers that are openly hostile to a union can engage in anti-union communications that, if conducted by employees, would violate a lawful anti-solicitation rule.

In 2024, the NLRB changed its position on captive-audience meetings. In *Amazon.com Services LLC*, 373 N.L.R.B. No. 136 (2024), the Board reversed *Livingston Shirt* and concluded that captive-audience meetings violate Section 8(a)(1). The Board argued that Section 8(c) only protects employers' noncoercive speech and that captive-audience meetings were coercive because they intruded on employees' privacy and autonomy to exercise their Section 7 rights. This intrusion occurs because captive-audience meetings impinge on employees' right to choose how much to participate in the debate over unionization without employer coercion, can provide a mechanism for employers to observe employees' exercise of Section 7 rights, and makes the employer's anti-union message coercive because failure to attend comes with the threat of discharge or discipline. As a result, employers that want to express their union views in a meeting with employees must take advantage of *Amazon.com*'s "safe harbor" by informing employees (and following through on) the following three requirements: 1) that the employer intends to express its views on unionization at a meeting and attendance is voluntary; 2) that employees will not be subject to discipline, discharge, or other adverse consequences if they fail to attend the meeting or leave the meeting; and 3) that the employer will not keep records of which employees attend, fail to attend, or leave the meeting.

Amazon.com is a significant change, as captive-audience meetings are extremely effective and, as a result, employers use them frequently during union campaigns. Because of the importance of captive-audience meetings, this is another issue that will likely fluctuate over time. Finally, several states have banned various types of captive-audience meetings. Any state laws that limit employers' ability to give labor-related captive-audience speeches raise potential NLRA preemption questions, which Chapter 18 explores.

2. Unlawful Threats versus Lawful Predictions

One issue that frequently arises with captive-audience meetings and other types of employer communications is whether some of the employer's anti-union statements constitute an unlawful threat. This issue is particularly difficult to litigate because it requires a careful balancing of employers' right to communicate with employees' right to freely choose whether to seek collective representation.

As noted above, in the Taft-Hartley Act Congress codified employer free speech rights in Section 8(c). One difficulty presented by this new section was how to define employer speech that loses protection because it contains a "threat of reprisal or force." The Supreme Court addressed this question in *NLRB v. Gissel Packing Co.*, 395 U.S. 575 (1969), which will also be discussed in a different context, dealing with bargaining orders, in Chapter 10.

In *Gissel*, the employer frequently verbally attacked the union before an election. Among other comments, the employer stressed that the company was on "thin ice" financially and that the union would likely strike, which "could lead to the closing of the plant." *Id.* at 588. According to the employer, if the plant closed, the employees would be unlikely to find new employment. The employer made many other similar comments, in addition to numerous ULPs.

The Court reemphasized employers' free speech rights under Section 8(c), particularly to provide their opinions about unionization, but noted the limits against threatening employees' Section 7 rights. In weighing these two concerns, the Court held that an assessment of the lawfulness of employer expression "must be made in the context of its labor relations setting." *Id.* at 617. In particular, "any balancing of those rights must take into account the economic dependence of the employees on their employers, and the necessary tendency of the former, because of that relationship, to pick up intended implications of the latter that might be more readily dismissed by a more disinterested ear." *Id.*

This balancing of interests is necessary to distinguish unlawful threats from lawful employer predictions about the effect of unionism. Under what is often referred to as the *Gissel* test, a lawful prediction "must be carefully phrased on the basis of objective fact to convey an employer's belief as to demonstrably probable consequences beyond his control or to convey a management decision already arrived at to close the plant in case of unionization." More generally, the employer must avoid implying that the negative consequences of unionization will be the result of economic reprisal rather than an outcome that is outside of its control. If the employer fails to meet these requirements, the statements are unlawful under Section 8(a)(1). *Compare Crown Cork & Seal Co. v. NLRB*, 36 F.3d 1130 (D.C. Cir. 1994) (employer statements such as noting that job preservation is based on the plant's ability to produce a competitive product at competitive prices was lawful prediction), *with TRW-United Greenfield Div. v. NLRB*, 637 F.2d 410, 415 (5th Cir. 1981) (statements that one company plant closed after a union was chosen and another closed because of union demands, which could happen again if the union won the campaign at issue, were unlawful).

In *Gissel*, the Court agreed with the NLRB that the employer lacked objective evidence to support its claims that the union would likely strike and close the plant. Indeed, the Court emphasized that predictions of a plant closure will usually be difficult to establish as an objective fact. Accordingly, although employers may lawfully close their business in response to a union organizing campaign, *see Textile Workers v. Darlington Mfg. Co.*, 380 U.S. 263 (1965), employers may not threaten to close their business in response to an organizing campaign.

D. Misrepresentations

As the previous section illustrates, there are numerous communications during a union campaign. Like political campaigns, some of this communication may stretch the truth, or worse. The NLRB has long struggled with its approach to handling parties' misrepresentations to employees.

Over the years, the NLRB has oscillated on the significance it will give to misrepresentations before an election. Much of the debate has centered on how to treat employees: as individuals who need to be protected from misinformation or individuals who can easily recognize propaganda for what it is. For a time, the NLRB leaned toward protecting employees by examining on a case-by-case basis whether a misrepresentation warranted setting aside an election. However, in *Midland National Life Insurance Co.*, 263 N.L.R.B. 127 (1982), the NLRB shifted to the opposite approach. *Midland* established a rule under which most misrepresentations will not trigger a new election under the *General Shoe* laboratory conditions test (Chapter 10 discusses both *General Shoe* and *Midland* in more detail). The exception is when a misrepresentation threatens employees' ability to recognize it as propaganda. Usually, this involves some type of forgery.

E. The Promise or Provision of Benefits

Perhaps one of the more curious aspects of NLRB representational misconduct—at least at first blush—is the doctrine of unlawful benefits. In general, both employers and unions can act improperly by either giving, or promising to give, employees a benefit. That is, a party can violate the NLRA by providing employees exactly what they want.

To understand why the promise or provision of benefits is a problem, it is important to remember that the NLRA protects employees' right to freely choose whether or not to seek collective representation. When either the employer or union acts in a way that tends to threaten or coerce that right, an election will be set aside and there may well be a Section 8(a)(1) ULP finding. (Chapter 10 explores how the NLRB decides whether to set aside an election—this usually coincides with significant ULPs during the campaign, but does not necessarily require an ULP, such as when the Board itself has made a mistake that interferes with the vote.)

1. Employer Provision of Benefits

The Supreme Court addressed an employer's provision of benefits in *NLRB v. Exchange Parts Co.*, 375 U.S. 405 (1964). Before a representation election, the employer in *Exchange Parts* gave employees an additional paid holiday and, among other things, informed employees that "[t]he Union can't put any [previously discussed benefits] in your envelope—*only the Company can do that.*" *Id.* at 407. The Court, agreeing with the NLRB, held that the announcement and grant of a new paid holiday violated Section 8(a)(1).

The crux of this holding was that benefits—like threats—can interfere with employees' right to choose whether or not to unionize. As the Court explained:

> The danger inherent in well-timed increases in benefits is the suggestion of a fist inside the velvet glove. Employees are not likely to miss the inference that the source of benefits now conferred is also the source from which future benefits must flow and which may dry up if it is not obliged.

Id. at 409. Because of the inference of improper employer interference, an employer's unilateral promise or grant of benefits during a representation campaign will almost always be considered unlawful. Relatedly, an employer may not lawfully solicit and remedy grievances during an election campaign, which the NLRB views as a promise to address the problems. *See, e.g.*, *NLRB v. V & S Schuler Engineering, Inc.*, 309 F.3d 362, 372 (6th Cir. 2002); *The Register Guard*, 344 N.L.R.B. 1142, 1142 (2005). There are some exceptions to these rules, such as when the employer has a valid business reason unrelated to the union or when the employer decided to grant the benefit before the union began organizing the workplace.

One common struggle for employers is how to deal with a regular benefit, such as an annual raise, when there is a union campaign. In these instances, an employer risks violating Section 8(a)(1) both for granting a benefit and for withholding a benefit that is expected. The best way for an employer to navigate these two possibilities is to maintain the status quo. In other words, if the employer gives a raise every year based on a fixed formula (for instance, based on firm profits and individuals' workload), it should do the same thing it would normally do if there was not a union campaign. In contrast, if raises are more discretionary, the employer is usually advised to hold off during a campaign. However, in practice, an employer in this position will often work with the union to find a solution—often by informing the employees that the employer and union have agreed to delay the determination of raises until after the election.

2. Union Provision of Benefits

Employers are not the only parties that get into trouble for promising or granting benefits. Although they have fewer opportunities to give benefits to employees, unions can also run afoul of this doctrine. One example occurred in *NLRB v. Savair Manufacturing Co.*, 414 U.S. 270 (1973), where the union promised to waive initiation fees for employees who signed authorization cards prior to the election. The union won the election, and the NLRB certified the union, concluding that the promise did not interfere with the election because employees were free to sign the cards but still vote against the union during the secret-ballot election. The Supreme Court, adopting the NLRB's previous approach to this question, disagreed.

The Court held that the NLRB's decision in *Savair* ignored the realities surrounding a union election. In particular, the Court stressed that employees' outward showing of support for a union helps to shape other employees' opinions; thus, the union was essentially "buy[ing] endorsements" and "paint[ing] a false portrait of employee support." *Id.* at 277. Moreover, even with a secret-ballot election, an employee may feel obligated to vote for the union after signing a card. Although the dissent complained that with union benefits, "the fist is missing" and "the union glove is not very velvet," the majority analogized the situation in *Savair* to the employer's actions in *Exchange Parts*. *Id.* at 285 (White, J., dissenting). The Court concluded that, as is the case with employer-provided benefits, employees are likely to infer that the refusal to sign cards could incur the union's wrath if it won the election. Another example of an improper union benefit during the critical period leading up to an election is a union funding employment law litigation on behalf of employees. In *Stericycle, Inc.*, 357 N.L.R.B. 582 (2011), the Board held that the union-funded suit, which alleged wage and hour violations under the Fair Labor Standards Act, was an improper benefit that warranted rerunning the election the union had won. However, the Board clarified that union-funded employment law litigation on behalf of employees is permitted outside of the critical period—i.e., before an election petition is filed or after the election. *Id.* (stressing that employees' joining with a union to file suit over unlawful employment practices "lies at the core of conduct protected by the" NLRA).

As a result of the *Exchange Parts* and *Savair* line of cases, both employers and unions must be careful what they promise or provide to employees. Some de minimis benefits may be lawful, such as the typical T-shirts, hats, and buttons that unions give to supporters. Benefits greater than this level run the risk of a Section 8(a)(1) or 8(b)(1) violation and a new election. When determining whether a benefit warrants a new election, the NLRB will consider the size of the benefit as compared to the parties' claimed reason for providing it, the number of employees who received the benefit, whether employees reasonably would view the benefit as threatening or interfering with their free choice, and the timing of the benefit (the closer to the election, the more likely the NLRB will overturn the election).

F. Surveillance

A common issue in union organizing campaigns involves employers' desire to learn more about the campaign's progress. Information such as the identity of employees who are working with or supporting the union can be particularly valuable to an employer that is trying to avoid unionization. The problem is that employer attempts to gather information can interfere with employees' Section 7 rights. The next section will discuss employer interrogation and polling of employees, and it will also address a related issue: employer surveillance.

An employer can gain valuable insights about a union campaign simply by observing the actions of its employees. For instance, by videotaping employees in the break room, an employer may learn which employees are soliciting for the union. Similarly, if the employer is aware of an off-site union meeting with its employees, it might drive by the location to see which employees are attending. The NLRB has long concluded that the surveillance of employees who are engaged in Section 7 activities can have the tendency to threaten or intimidate employees. Thus, absent a legitimate business reason for the surveillance, such activity will violate Section 8(a)(1) and may warrant a new election.

The NLRB's approach establishes a presumption that surveillance of Section 7 activity is unlawful. Establishing such surveillance is usually straightforward—most litigation centers on the employer's attempt to rebut the presumption. For instance, in *F.W. Woolworth Co.*, 310 N.L.R.B. 1197 (1993), the employer argued that it had a valid reason to photograph and videotape employees who were passing out handbills to customers at the store entrances. Although it recognized that an employer can merely observe employees who are openly and publicly engaged in Section 7 activity, the NLRB stated that recording such activity is more likely to intimidate employees and therefore requires justification. The NLRB rejected the employer's argument that the photographing was necessary to combat employee misconduct. According to the NLRB, the employees had not blocked entrances or engaged in other improper conduct; therefore, the employer lacked a valid reason to record their protected activity. In particular, the NLRB stressed that although a well-supported likelihood of misconduct could justify recording Section 7 activity, the mere possibility of misconduct did not. Additional justifications for surveillance may also include legitimate security concerns, obtaining evidence for a legal proceeding, and combatting theft problems.

In *Randell Warehouse of Arizona, Inc.*, 347 N.L.R.B. 591 (2006), the NLRB extended its analysis of employer photographing and videotaping to unions. However, under *Randell Warehouse*, a union can rebut the presumption that such activity is likely to intimidate employees if it timely gives employees a legitimate reason for the surveillance.

Finally, the NLRB also has a rule that the mere impression of surveillance is unlawful. In other words, if an employer makes employees think that they are being observed while engaging in Section 7 activity, even if they are not, the employer has presumptively violated Section 8(a)(1). For instance, a manager could untruthfully tell a pro-union employee that the employer knows everything about a union meeting the night before. Although actual surveillance is absent in this scenario, creating an impression that it occurred is just as likely to chill Section 7 activity. In deciding whether an impression of surveillance exists, the NLRB will look at all the relevant circumstances to determine whether reasonable employees would assume from the employer's actions that it was observing Section 7 activity.

G. Interrogation and Polling

Surveillance is not the only way that employers and unions can try to obtain information about employees' activities. Especially during union campaigns, parties may also try to elicit information directly from employees. This type of information gathering is usually classified as either interrogation or polling.

1. Interrogation

An interrogation typically involves an employer official talking to one or more employees about Section 7 activity. A common example includes questions about the identity and numbers of union supporters. Like surveillance, these types of questions carry the possibility of threatening or intimidating employees' willingness to exercise their Section 7 rights.

The NLRB analyzes interrogation allegations under its *Rossmore House* test. *See Rossmore House*, 269 N.L.R.B. 1176 (1984), *enf'd*, *Hotel Employees & Restaurant Employees Union, Local 11 v. NLRB*, 760 F.2d 1006 (9th Cir. 1985). Under this test, the NLRB considers several factors to determine whether the interrogation would reasonably tend to interfere with employees' Section 7 rights. Among the factors, which are viewed in totality, are the background of employer hostility to unionization; the type of information sought; the identity of the questioner; the place and method of interrogation; whether the employee was an open union supporter; and the truthfulness of the employee's responses (if the employee was not truthful, that tends to indicate that he or she felt threatened). *See also Bourne v. NLRB*, 332 F.2d 47 (2d Cir. 1964). These factors are not exclusive. For instance, in *Timsco, Inc. v. NLRB*, 819 F.2d 1173 (D.C. Cir. 1987), the D.C. Circuit upheld the NLRB's finding of unlawful interrogation. In addition to many of the above factors, the court and NLRB also noted the cumulative effect of several interrogations and, particularly with regard to the decision to overturn an election, the small size of the unit of employees and the closeness of the vote.

The Board's decision in *Sunnyvale Medical Clinic*, 277 N.L.R.B. 1217 (1985), illustrates how these interrogation factors can be interpreted differently. In *Sunnyvale*, the employer's personnel director asked a pro-union employee to remain after an unrelated meeting. The director asked why the employee had joined the union, asked whether it had anything to do with the director personally, said that she wanted the union out, emphasized that employees who joined the union may not get everything they want, and asked why the employees had not gone to her for help. The employee responded that employees had gone to the director, but nothing happened. The NLRB majority found that the interrogation was not unlawful, stressing the friendly nature of the conversation, that the interrogation was isolated, the employee's lack of interest in hiding her support of the union, lack of employer hostility toward union supporters, and the general and nonthreatening questions. However, there was a dissent which emphasized that the employee was not an open union supporter, that the director had stated that she wanted the union out, that the questioning was quite blunt, and that the questioner was the personnel director. The dissent also stated that the friendliness of the conversation placed more pressure on the employee because the director suggested that joining the union was a personal affront to her.

2. Polling

Another potentially unlawful means of eliciting information from employees is a poll. As Chapter 10 explains, employers may have legitimate reasons to use a poll to test whether a union still has majority support. An employer may also legitimately want to gauge employees' views on other topics. But no matter the reason, an employer's polling of its employees carries the risk of chilling Section 7 activity. Indeed, older NLRB cases held that all employer polling was unlawful. However, the NLRB has since allowed polling under certain circumstances.

The NLRB has developed safeguards to limit the possibility that a poll will interfere with employees' Section 7 rights. Under the *Struksnes* test, there is a presumption that employer polling of employees violates Section 8(a)(1). In the typical polling context—when the employer wants to test a union's claim of majority support—the employer can avoid a ULP only if: (1) the purpose of the poll is to determine if the union's claim of majority support is accurate; (2) the employer communicates this purpose to employees; (3) the employer assures employees that there will be no reprisals based on the polling results;

(4) the poll is conducted by secret ballot; and (5) the employer has not committed ULPs or created a coercive atmosphere in other ways. *See Struksnes Construction Co.*, 165 N.L.R.B. 1062 (1967).

In the less common instance when polling occurs in other contexts, the NLRB will usually apply a modified *Struksnes* test. For instance, the NLRB considers employer requests for employees to appear in anti-union campaign videos as a poll. Under its *Allegheny Ludlum* test, such a request is classified as an unlawful poll unless: (1) the solicitation is a general announcement that discloses the purpose of the video and gives assurances that participation is voluntary, participation will not lead to rewards, and refusals to participate will not lead to punishment; (2) employees are not pressured to participate in the presence of a supervisor; (3) the employer has not engaged in threats or other coercive conduct related to the announcement; (4) the employer has not created a coercive atmosphere; and (5) the employer does not seek any information exceeding the purpose of obtaining employees' consent to participate in the video. *See Allegheny Ludlum Corp. v. NLRB*, 301 F.3d 167, 176 (3d Cir. 2002).

Finally, although unions are held to a similar standard in surveillance cases, the same is not true for polling. Union polling is presumed lawful, in part because unions must poll employees to obtain enough interest to file an election petition with the NLRB (see Chapter 10 for more discussion of representation elections).

CHECKPOINTS

- A facially neutral work rule will violate Section 8(a)(1) if it has a reasonable tendency to chill employees' exercise of their Section 7 rights and the employer is unable to show that the rule advances a legitimate and substantial business interest that cannot be addressed with a more narrowly tailored rule.
- Employers cannot prevent employees from discussing Section 7 topics in non-work areas during non-work time, except under special circumstances.
- Employers can prevent employees from distributing written Section 7 materials at work, as long as employees have some way of giving the materials to other employees.

- Employers can prevent nonemployees (usually meaning paid union organizers) from contacting employees at the worksite, except when the nonemployees have virtually no other means of contacting employees.
- Employers can prevent both employees and nonemployees from using the company's electronic communication systems.
- Employers violate Section 8(a)(1) if they implement or apply a facially neutral non-solicitation policy in a discriminatory fashion.
- "Discrimination" means singling out union and other Section 7 communications; it does not apply to more general bans on communications that are of a similar character, even if the result is that Section 7 communications are prohibited.
- Employers used to be allowed to give captive audience speeches, as long as they occurred more than 24 hours before an election. However, at the time of publication, captive-audience meetings violate Section 8(a)(1) under *Amazon.com*, which allows employer campaign speeches about unionization only if the employer tells employees that it intends to express its views on the union, that attendance is voluntary and failure to attend will not result in adverse consequences, and that the employer will not keep records of which employees attend or leave the meeting.
- Under Section 8(c), an employer may disparage the union and predict that unionization will result in negative consequences for employees, but the employer will violate Section 8(a)(1) if its statements constitute a threat.
- To avoid a finding that its statements are threatening economic reprisal if employees unionize, an employer's prediction must be based on objective fact to show probable consequences that are beyond its control.
- A campaign misrepresentation will not warrant a new election unless it is a forgery or otherwise prevents employees from recognizing it as propaganda.
- Both employers and unions can violate Section 8(a)(1) by promising or providing benefits during an organizational campaign, although unions are less likely to engage in this type of violation because they generally do not have benefits to give.

- Employers will violate Section 8(a)(1) by surveilling their employees' Section 7 activity, unless they have a valid business justification for the surveillance.
- Employers will violate Section 8(a)(1) by creating an impression of surveillance, even if there was no actual surveillance.
- The NLRB uses the multifactor *Rossmore House* analysis to determine whether an employer's interrogation of an employee violates Section 8(a)(1).
- To avoid a Section 8(a)(1) violation, an employer's polling of employees must comply with the *Struksnes* safeguards.

CHAPTER 8

Employer Domination or Interference of a Labor Organization: Section 8(a)(2) Unfair Labor Practices

ROADMAP

- Section 8(a)(2)'s prohibition against employer domination or interference of a labor organization
- Section 2(5)'s definition of a "labor organization"
- Distinction between "domination" and "interference"
- Section 8(a)(2)'s prohibition against improper recognition of a labor organization

Among the many concerns that prompted Congress to enact the NLRA was employers' practice of establishing what are referred to as "company unions." These are not unions in the typical sense, but rather sham unions controlled by employers. The purpose of the traditional company union is to prevent legitimate, independent unions from organizing by making employees believe that they already have representation. Thus, Congress enacted what is now Section 8(a)(2) of the NLRA to ban these company unions. The importance of this issue at the time is illustrated by the fact that the NLRB's first unfair labor practice (ULP) case was a company union dispute.

Because of the seriousness and prevalence of the company union problem, the NLRA broadly prohibits employer interference or domination of a labor organization. As explained below, however, the prohibition is so broad that it has prompted much criticism for banning not only company unions, but also employer attempts to encourage employee input and participation at work. *See generally* Samuel Estreicher, *Employee Involvement and the "Company Union" Prohibition: The Case for Partial Repeal of Section 8(a)(2) of the NLRA*, 69 N.Y.U. L. Rev. 125, 135–39 (1994).

A. Overview of Section 8(a)(2): Prohibiting Employer Domination or Interference of a Labor Organization

Under Section 8(a)(2), it is a ULP for an employer to "dominate or interfere with the formation or administration of any labor organization or contribute financial or other support to it." Often, litigation in Section 8(a)(2) cases centers on whether a particular entity qualifies as a "labor organization." The broad scope of this term—which covers many entities that cannot fairly be described as sham unions—is responsible for most criticisms of the NLRA's company union ban. However, supporters of the current rule fear that any changes will interfere with employees' ability to seek truly independent collective representation.

1. Section 2(5)'s Definition of "Labor Organization"

The first step in any Section 8(a)(2) case is to examine whether the organization allegedly subject to unlawful domination or interference is a "labor organization." Section 2(5) defines this term as applying to:

> any organization of any kind, or any agency or employee representation committee or plan, in which employees participate and which exists for the purpose, in whole or in part, of dealing with employers concerning grievances, labor disputes, wages, rates of pay, hours of employment, or conditions of work.

Note how broad this language is, particularly its description of "any organization of any kind." This means that a labor organization does not need to have any formal structure, officers, offices, constitution or bylaws, regular meetings, or other elements that one might typically expect in a union. Given this broad coverage, disputes under Section 2(5) usually center on whether an organization is "dealing with" an employer over grievances, wages, and other terms and conditions of work.

In *Electromation, Inc.*, 309 N.L.R.B. 990 (1992), *enf'd*, 35 F.3d 1148 (7th Cir. 1994), the NLRB interpreted the statutory term, "labor organization," and, as discussed below, other aspects of Section 8(a)(2). The NLRB in *Electromation* emphasized that Congress intentionally defined "labor organization" broadly to eliminate improper employer support and domination of unions, which had previously "robbed" employees of their ability to freely choose an independent collective bargaining representative. Thus, any organization meets Section 2(5)'s definition of a labor organization if: "(1) employees participate, (2) the organization exists, at least in part, for the purpose of 'dealing with' employers, and (3) these dealings concern 'conditions of work' or concern other statutory subjects, such as grievances, labor disputes, wages, rates of pay, or hours of employment." *Id.* at 994. The NLRB added that if an "employee representation committee or plan" is at issue, it would look for evidence that the entity is representing employees in some fashion.

Embedded in the Section 2(5) definition of "labor organization" is the requirement that employees participate in that organization. The analysis here is typically a straightforward factual question. Litigation over that requirement in a Section 8(a)(2) ULP case is unusual, although this issue could arise in cases where, for example, workers' classification as statutory employees is a question, or if the employees involved are all arguably excluded from the NLRA's coverage as supervisors.

The subject-matter requirement—the need for the organization to deal with the employer over "grievances, labor disputes, wages, rates of pay, hours of employment, or conditions of work"—can be more difficult to judge at times, as its scope has more gray areas. For more on how to interpret the "conditions of work" language, see the discussion in Chapter 12 on unions' and employers' duty to bargain in good faith, which has a virtually identical subject-matter requirement (that is, a duty to bargain over "mandatory topics").

Most litigation over Section 2(5)'s application involves the vague term "dealing with." Long ago, the Supreme Court examined the term in *NLRB v. Cabot Carbon Co.*, 360 U.S. 203 (1959), in which it held that "dealing with" covered more actions than the negotiation of a collective bargaining agreement. However, the term does not cover all functions. As the NLRB stressed in *Electromation*, the hallmark of "dealing with" is that it involves bilateral discussions with an employer. That is, there must be some back and forth between the employer and the organization. A key fact to look for is evidence that the employer and organization are adjusting their proposals or positions in response to the other. Thus, "dealing with" requires a labor organization to interact with an employer and will not cover an organization that merely conveys information or proposals to the employer. These types of unilateral suggestions are usually considered more like a suggestion box than "dealing with."

Another issue that can arise in "dealing with" disputes is an employee-participation group that has independent decision-making authority. For example, an employer may create a group of employees that can make some decisions on its own regarding safety and production quality. In *Crown Cork & Seal Co.*, 334 N.L.R.B. 699 (2001), the NLRB addressed an employee team that could, among other things, independently stop production because of a safety concern. The NLRB concluded that if an organization has the same level of authority as a front-line supervisor, it is better classified as part of management rather than a Section 2(5) labor organization. In other words, these groups are not "dealing with" the employer because the groups *are* the employer.

Among the other issues that the NLRB clarified in *Electromation* was the role of intent and employees' subjective view of a challenged organization. Some circuit courts had required either that the employer intended to block an independent union or that employees view the organization as a union-like entity for Section 2(5) to apply. However, the NLRB rejected these holdings. Accordingly, even if an employer did not create an organization with the intent of thwarting a union, if the organization meets Section 2(5)'s elements, it is a labor organization. Similarly, an entity can be classified as a labor organization even if the employees do not view it as their representative.

The wide scope of Section 2(5) has prompted many calls for reform to allow employers more leeway to create employee-participation groups that could arguably give employees increased voice and make the business more productive. Reform proponents came close in 1995, when Congress passed the Teamwork for Employees and Managers Act of 1995, H.R. 743, 104th Cong. (1996) (TEAM Act), which would have allowed employers to create or assist organizations that addressed issues of quality, productivity, efficiency, and safety and health, and that do not seek to negotiate collective bargaining agreements or claim exclusive representative status. However, President Clinton vetoed the TEAM Act, largely based on unions' opposition to a measure that they believed would undermine employees' ability to freely choose independent representation.

2. Section 8(a)(2)'s Prohibition against Employer Domination and Interference

Once a group is classified as a labor organization under Section 2(5), the NLRB must determine whether the employer dominated or interfered with the organization before it can find a Section 8(a)(2) ULP. In particular, Section 8(a)(2) makes it a ULP for an employer "to dominate or interfere with the formation or administration of any labor organization or contribute financial or other support to it."

Domination is the more serious type of unlawful action under Section 8(a)(2) and, if found, will lead the NLRB to order a permanent dismantling of the dominated labor organization. As the Supreme Court noted in *NLRB v. Newport News Shipbuilding Co.*, 308 U.S. 241, 250 (1939), dominated labor organizations are so tainted that their continued existence should not be allowed. In contrast, if the NLRB finds only unlawful interference, it will allow the labor organization to continue and merely order the employer to cease its unlawful interference with the group. Note that in either of these cases, there is no financial penalty for a Section 8(a)(2) violation.

In both domination and interference cases, the NLRB typically looks for instances in which the employer's involvement with a labor organization is likely to create an impression for employees that they are resolving disputes bilaterally with their employer, when in reality the employer is engaging in some form of unilateral dealing. This inquiry is based on a totality-of-circumstances test that looks at a multitude of factors. Among the most common factors indicating domination or interference are an employer: creating a labor organization, establishing an organization's structure and functions, presenting the organization as the employees' sole means of revolving workplace disputes, having its officials preside over the organization's meetings, controlling the organization's agenda, and making the organization's continued existence dependent on the employer. Certain financial support can also be relevant, such as paying employees for their time working on organization activities, providing space for meetings, and providing the organization with supplies. These types of financial assistance are not always unlawful but, in combination with other factors, can be indicative of domination or interference.

The presence of these factors can support either a domination or interference finding, and the line between the two can be a thin one. Usually, the difference is one of degree, in which substantial levels of employer involvement indicate domination while mere employer "support" or "assistance" are more typical of interference. Although it is not a quantitative analysis, often interference cases are those in which a small number of factors are present, while domination is found when several factors—particularly an employer creating an organization and establishing its structure and purpose—are present.

One other important aspect of Section 8(a)(2) is that it does not require an employer's bad faith or employees' dislike of the organization. The Supreme Court held in *International Ladies' Garment Workers v. NLRB (Bernhard-Altmann)*, 366 U.S. 731, 739 (1961), that there is no scienter requirement under Section 8(a)(2), therefore "prohibited conduct cannot be excused by a showing of good faith." Much later, in *Electromation*, the NLRB concluded that although employees' subjective views on a challenged labor organization can be relevant to whether the employer's domination or interference is likely to create a false impression of bilateral dealing, a Section 8(a)(2) violation does not require that employees dislike the organization or how it is run.

Finally, Section 8(a)(2) contains the following proviso: "an employer shall not be prohibited from permitting employees to confer with him during working hours without loss of time or pay." This proviso ensures that employers can engage in some contact or cooperation with its employees, but this is still limited by Section 8(a)(2)'s prohibition against interactions that amount to "domination" or "interference."

B. Section 8(a)(2)'s Prohibition against Improper Recognition of a Union

In addition to the more traditional company union concern, Section 8(a)(2) also limits an employer's ability to voluntarily recognize an independent union in certain instances. The underlying issue in these cases is that voluntary recognition of a union that lacks support from a majority of unit employees amounts to unlawful assistance to that union.

For instance, in *International Ladies' Garment Workers v. NLRB (Bernhard-Altmann)*, 366 U.S. 731 (1961), an employer erroneously believed that a union had majority support and, because of this belief, recognized the union as its employees' representative and entered into a collective bargaining agreement with the union. The Supreme Court held that these actions violated Section 8(a)(2) because the union lacked majority support—even though the employer had a good-faith belief that such support existed. Like other Section 8(a)(2) ULPs however, there was no fine for the employer. Instead, the employer was merely ordered not to recognize the union or follow the collective bargaining agreement until the union won a representation election.

A similar issue can arise when two different unions seek to represent the same unit of employees. For many years, the NLRB concluded under its *Midwest Piping* doctrine that to avoid a Section 8(a)(2) violation, the employer must remain neutral and cannot recognize a union that shows support from a majority of employees if the other union has a "colorable claim" of majority support. Under *Midwest Piping*, the disagreement would have to be resolved by an election, not the employer. *Midwest Piping & Supply Co.*, 63 N.L.R.B. 1060 (1945). However, in 1982, the NLRB changed course and will now allow employers to continue negotiating with the first union unless the rival union files a valid election petition with the NLRB. *See Bruckner Nursing Home*, 262 N.L.R.B. 955 (1982). Note that if one of the unions is an incumbent, the employer can continue to recognize and negotiate with the union even if a rival union files an election petition (and it is a Section 8(a)(5) violation—a failure of the employer's duty to bargain—if the employer stops recognizing or bargaining with the incumbent union). Resolution of the dispute is left for an election. If the incumbent wins, any signed collective bargaining agreement will become effective; if the rival wins, the agreement will be void. *See RCA del Caribe, Inc.*, 262 N.L.R.B. 963 (1982).

Employers can also run afoul of Section 8(a)(2) by bargaining with a union in the expectation that it will receive support from a majority of employees. In *Majestic Weaving Co.*, 147 N.L.R.B. 859 (1964), *enf'd denied*, 355 F.2d 854 (2d Cir. 1966) (holding that critical issue was not timely raised during NLRB proceedings), the employer and union negotiated a collective bargaining agreement that would go into effect only when the union obtained majority support. The NLRB concluded that this violated Section 8(a)(2) because the employer's actions were essentially the same as the employer in *Bernard-Altmann*. In both cases, an employer infringed on employees' free choice by granting representation status to a union that lacked majority support.

One interesting limit to *Majestic Weaving* arose with the NLRB's decision in *Dana Corp.*, 356 N.L.R.B. No. 49 (2010), *enf'd sub nom. Montague v. NLRB*, 698 F.3d 307 (6th Cir. 2012), which involved an emerging practice known as a "pre-recognition framework agreement." These agreements between an employer and a union that lacks majority support attempt to outline basic principles that would govern their relationship if the union obtains majority support in the future. For instance, these agreements might state that the parties will emphasize team-based production approaches, commit to allowing the employer discretion in certain general areas, or maintain opportunities for employees to present ideas to the employer. The agreements might also include a promise by the employer to remain neutral in the organizing campaign or voluntarily recognize the union if it can show majority support. Employers may consider entering into such agreements because they can reduce some of the uncertainty and risk regarding what potential unionization might look like. In *Dana Corp.*, the NLRB concluded that, under certain conditions, pre-recognition framework agreements can be distinguished from unlawful *Majestic Weaving* agreements in which the union was presented to employees as an inevitable outcome.

To be lawful, an employer must negotiate the pre-recognition framework agreement without showing the union too much favoritism. Factors that the NLRB has used in pre-*Dana Corp.* cases that could help determine whether the employer's actions have gone too far include whether: the employer, especially through a high-ranking official, initiated negotiations with the union; the employer set up, or was present at, meetings between the union and employees; and the employer coerced employees to support the union. The NLRB also stressed in *Dana Corp.* that the substance of the agreement must be cabined to avoid the appearance of the employer giving the union exclusive representative status. In general, this means that a pre-recognition framework agreement cannot be as specific and complete as a collective bargaining agreement. For example, the agreement cannot alter the employees' existing terms and conditions—such changes must result from "substantive negotiations" that occur after the union has obtained majority support.

The Sixth Circuit upheld *Dana Corp.* as a reasonable interpretation of Section 8(a)(2). The court found particularly persuasive the fact that, unlike *Bernhard-Altmann*, the agreement here explicitly noted that it would not have any effect unless and until the union obtained support from a majority of employees. The court also agreed with the NLRB that the agreement was not like a completed collective bargaining agreement and, instead, "required substantial negotiations, post-recognition, before it could become the employees' terms and conditions of employment." *Montague*, 698 F.3d at 315.

An issue related to improper recognition is the legality of certain neutrality and voluntary recognition agreements. There have been several challenges to these agreements under Section 302 of the Taft-Hartley Act, which makes it a crime for an employer "to pay, lend, or deliver, or agree to pay, lend, or deliver, any money or other thing of value" to a union. 29 U.S.C. § 186(a)(2). One issue is whether an employer's promise to the union to remain neutral in an organizing campaign or to voluntarily recognize the union if it achieves majority support is a "thing of value" under Section 302. Most appellate courts that have addressed the issue have held that Section 302 does not apply to such promises. *See, e.g., Adcock v. Freightliner LLC*, 550 F.3d 369 (4th Cir. 2008); *Hotel & Restaurant Employees Local 57 v. Sage Hospitality Resources, LLC*, 390 F.3d 206 (3d Cir. 2004). However, the Eleventh Circuit held that Section 302 may apply if an employer makes such a promise with the intent to corrupt the union or because of union extortion. *See Mulhall v. Unite Here Local 355*, 667 F.3d 1211, 1215 (11th Cir. 2012) ("Employers and unions may set ground rules for an organizing campaign, even if the employer and union benefit from the agreement. But innocuous ground rules can become illegal payments if used as valuable consideration in a scheme to corrupt a union or to extort a benefit from an employer.").

The Supreme Court granted certiorari in *Mulhall*, but ultimately dismissed the case as improvidently granted, likely because of questions about whether the case was moot (the agreement had already expired) and whether the plaintiff-employee had standing (the case occurred in a right-to-work state; thus, the employee did not have to pay any union dues and may not have been able to show any harm). *See Unite Here Local 355 v. Mulhall*, 571 U.S. 83 (2013). Three Justices dissented from the order, arguing that the Court should have addressed these jurisdictional issues—in addition to the question whether Section 302 allowed private rights of action—and, if any applied, vacate the Eleventh Circuit's decision to remove any precedential effect.

CHECKPOINTS

- Section 8(a)(2) prohibits employer interference or domination of a "labor organization."
- Section 2(5)'s definition of "labor organization" requires: employee participation and the purpose of "dealing with" employers over con-

ditions of work and other statutory subjects. If an "employee representation committee or plan" is at issue, representation of employees may also be required.

- "Dealing with" requires some sort of bilateral discussions between the labor organization and the employer.
- If an employer dominates a labor organization in violation of Section 8(a)(2), the organization will be disbanded.
- If an employer interferes with a labor organization in violation of Section 8(a)(2), the organization will be allowed to exist, but the employer will be ordered to cease its interference.
- In both domination and interference cases, the NLRB will apply a totality-of-the-circumstances test, based on various factors that explore an employer's role in creating and maintaining an organization, controlling the organization's activities, and providing financial and other support.
- The difference between domination and interference is a matter of degree and usually depends on the number and seriousness of the above factors.
- A Section 8(a)(2) violation does not depend on an employer's bad faith or employees' dislike of the organization.
- Section 8(a)(2) prohibits an employer from recognizing a union that lacks majority support, even if the employer erroneously believes it has such support.
- An employer can bargain with a union that has majority support when a rival union seeks to represent employees. If the union with majority support is the current exclusive bargaining representative, the employer must continue to recognize and bargain with it until an election resolves the dispute.
- Under Section 8(a)(2), an employer cannot negotiate a collective bargaining agreement with a union that lacks majority support, even if the agreement is contingent on the union obtaining such support.
- In some circumstances, an employer can enter into a pre-recognition framework agreement with a union that lacks majority support.

CHAPTER 9

Employer Discrimination: Section 8(a)(3) Unfair Labor Practices

ROADMAP

- Section 8(a)(3)'s prohibition against an employer's union-based discrimination
- Employer intent as a central aspect of discrimination ULP
- Distinction between Section 8(a)(1) and 8(a)(3) cases
- Distinction between individual and group discrimination cases
- Distinction between dual motive and pretext cases
- The *Wright-Line* test for dual-motive, union-based discrimination
- Special issues concerning refusal to hire cases and salts
- Runaway shops, complete shutdowns, and partial shutdowns under *Darlington*
- Remedies available under Section 8(a)(3)

A. Overview of Section 8(a)(3) ULPs: The Importance of Intent

As discussed in previous Chapters, to protect Section 7 rights, Congress prohibited certain employer practices as unfair labor practices (ULPs) under Section 8(a) of the Act (union ULPs are found in Section 8(b)). The purpose of all employer ULPs is to prevent employers from unfairly restraining, coercing, or interfering with employees' organizational efforts or their right to union representation. Section 8(a)(3) specifically bars discrimination based on union conduct or sympathies. It provides: "It shall be an unfair labor practice for an employer ... by discrimination in regard to hire or tenure of employment or any term or condition of employment to encourage or discourage membership in any labor organization...." (There is a further part of Section 8(a)(3), and its union ULP counterpart, Section 8(b)(2), that goes to union security clauses, but those provisions are discussed in Chapter 19.)

The U.S. Supreme Court has made clear that the statutory phrase "to encourage or discourage membership in any labor organization" also encompasses discouraging or encouraging participation in union activities. There is a similar, less-utilized provision under Section 8(b)(2) prohibiting discrimination by unions. In cases involving encouragement of participation in union activities, one will more typically see a union being charged under Section 8(b)(2).

Employer intent or motivation to discriminate is central to the discrimination provisions under Section 8(a)(3). By contrast, Section 8(a)(1) ULPs do not require the employer's bad intent and use instead a balancing of employer and employee interests. In Section 8(a)(3) cases, the NLRB is required to find that anti-union intent motivated an act of employer discrimination, which has a foreseeable effect of either encouraging or discouraging union membership.

For example, in the classic case of *Edward G. Budd Manufacturing Co. v. NLRB*, 138 F.2d 86 (3d Cir. 1943), the employer established a company union that purportedly gave employees a voice in the workplace. Management treated the employee representatives better than the rest of the workforce, including one representative who was allowed to come and go as he pleased, to show up drunk for work, and to bring women (including one referred to as the "Duchess") to work for illicit purposes. When supervisors initially complained to management about this employee representative's behavior, management failed to take any disciplinary action. However, once management learned of this employee's involvement with an independent union, it discharged him for bad service. Both the NLRB and the Third Circuit found that the employer violated Section 8(a)(3) when it discharged the employee. The court stated that the key to finding an 8(a)(3) violation was a showing of anti-union animus or motive on the part of the employer. Although an employer under the rule of at-will employment may generally discharge an employee for a good reason, a bad reason, or no reason at all, it may not discharge them for a reason that violates the NLRA. Discharging the employee representative for their association with an independent union constituted such an unlawful reason, even though the employee's work performance was poor. The essential fact in *Edward G. Budd Manufacturing*, then, was the employer's unwillingness to act on the supervisors' complaints until learning of the employee's connection to an opposing union. This fact established anti-union animus on the part of the employer.

In other cases where the employer never expressly states its motivation for firing or not hiring an employee, among the significant factors that can play into a circumstantial determination that anti-union motivation existed are: (1) the employer's knowledge of and hostility to its employees' union activity; (2) the presence of other ULPs; (3) the timing of the adverse action compared to the protected activity; (4) the implausibility of the employer's nondiscriminatory explanation; (5) the disparate treatment of alleged victims compared to others or the employer's past practices; (6) the proportionality of adverse action to employer's explanation; and (7) the failure to investigate misconduct alleged by the victim.

B. Distinguishing Section 8(a)(1) and 8(a)(3) Discrimination Cases

There can sometimes be confusion over whether employer conduct violates Section 8(a)(1), Section 8(a)(3), or both. The main distinction between the two types of violations is that the employer's intent to encourage or discourage *union* activity is an element of a Section 8(a)(3) violation, whereas the employer's intent to discriminate against nonunion concerted activity is an element of a Section 8(a)(1) violation. Consider a typical case under both Section 8(a)(1) and 8(a)(3) involving an employer firing an employee who engaged in concerted activity. Determining which ULP is more appropriate turns on whether the employer acted with the intent to discourage/encourage union activity or whether the employer's actions discriminated against or otherwise interfered with nonunion concerted activity. For example, if an employer fires an employee because that employee is a member of a union, then the employer has violated Section 8(a)(3). If the employer fires an employee because that employee is trying to organize a union, then the employer has also violated Section 8(a)(3). But imagine an employer discharges an employee because that employee organized a spontaneous walkout in protest of unsafe work conditions in a nonunion work setting. In that case, the employer has violated Section 8(a)(1) but has not violated Section 8(a)(3).

Suppose the Board or courts find a Section 8(a)(3) violation because the requisite anti-union intent was present. Then, there will also be a derivative Section 8(a)(1) violation (as opposed to an independent Section 8(a)(1) violation, which was discussed in Chapter 7, and stands on its own). A "derivative Section 8(a)(1) violation" piggybacks off another ULP, such as Section 8(a)(3). This makes sense because Section 8(a)(3) discrimination claims, like other enumerated ULPs in Section 8(a), are just one specific type of interference with Section 7 rights covered more generically under Section 8(a)(1).

C. Individual vs. Group Section 8(a)(3) ULPs

Not all cases involve situations, as in *Edward G. Budd Manufacturing*, where the employer is alleged to have taken an adverse action against an employee based on their association with the union. Indeed, the General Counsel may establish anti-union intent in Section 8(a)(3) cases in one of two ways: either through specific direct or inferential evidence of unlawful intent in individual employee cases or intent inferred from the very nature of the employer's conduct in group cases. This Chapter focuses primarily on individual discrimination cases under the *Wright Line* standard and other related cases. Inferential cases of discrimination under the *Great Dane* framework involving an employer's conduct in response to concerted union activity (i.e., strikes, pickets, and boycotts) will be discussed in Chapter 14 (involving private sector strikes and lockouts). Importantly, under either method, unlawful intent must be established to make out a Section 8(a)(3) claim.

D. *Wright Line*: Specific Evidence of Anti-Union Intent

There are two lines of individual Section 8(a)(3) cases: (1) pretext cases and (2) dual-motive cases. In a pretext case, the employer will attempt to justify the employee discharge based on a "business reason," which the union or employee alleges is merely a subterfuge for the employer's anti-union motive. For instance, in *NLRB v. Transportation Management*, 462 U.S. 393 (1983), the U.S. Supreme Court observed that, "it is undisputed that if the employer fires an employee for having engaged in union activities and has no other basis for the discharge, or if the reasons that he proffers are pretextual, the employer commits an unfair labor practice."

In a dual-motive case (sometimes referred to as a "mixed-motive case"), by contrast, the employer has legitimate business reasons for discharging the employee but also evinces anti-union animus in doing so. In such cases, intent is often difficult to prove, just as it is in the context of employment discrimination law or criminal law. To determine whether the necessary intent for a finding of a Section 8(a)(3) violation is present, the Board—with Supreme Court approval—has adopted the *Wright Line* test. The *Wright Line* analysis creates a two-step process for Section 8(a)(3) "mixed-motive" cases. In practice, the NLRB uses *Wright Line* for most Section 8(a)(3) cases, as the employer almost always alleges a lawful reason for an adverse action.

1. Dual-Motive Cases

Originally, the Board held that an employer violated Section 8(a)(3) when the General Counsel (acting on behalf of the union or employee filing the complaint) could prove that the employer acted with anti-union intent in any manner. Courts, however, consistently held that anti-union intent must be a substantial or motivating factor in the discharge. As a result, the Board clarified the burden of proof in *Wright Line*, 251 N.L.R.B. 1083 (1980), *enf'd*, 662 F.2d 899 (1st Cir. 1981).

In *Wright Line*, the Board, relying on Section 10(c), required the General Counsel to prove by a "preponderance of the evidence" that the employee's protected Section 7 activity was a substantial or motivating factor in the discharge. There are three parts to the General Counsel's "prima facie" case: (1) the employee was engaged in protected activity, (2) the employer was aware of the activity, and (3) the protected activity was a substantial or motivating factor for the employer's action. If the General Counsel fails to establish the *prima facie* case, the employer need not take any action to prevail.

Suppose the General Counsel establishes these three factors. Then, the employer has the burden of persuasion (i.e., like having the burden to prove an affirmative defense) under the second part of the analysis to establish that the employer would have made the same decision, in any event, even in the absence of protected Section 7 activity. In these cases, the employer can argue that the employee had poor work performance, had broken workplace rules, or would have been discharged anyway as part of a reduction-in-force. If the employer is successful in proving that the "same decision" would have been taken against an employee, the employer is absolved from a finding of liability.

The U.S. Supreme Court upheld the *Wright Line* approach in *NLRB v. Transportation Management*, 462 U.S. 393 (1983). In agreeing with the Board that the employer bears the burden of persuasion on the "same decision" test, the Court observed:

> The employer is a wrongdoer; he has acted out of a motive that is declared illegitimate by the statute. It is fair that he bear the risk that the influence of legal and illegal motives cannot be separated, because he knowingly created the risk and because the risk was created not by innocent activity but by his own wrongdoing.

Id. at 403.

E. Refusal to Hire Cases

Although many Section 8(a)(3) cases involve adverse actions, such as termination, that occur to current employees, Section 8(a)(3) applies to job applicants as well. *See Phelps Dodge Corporation v. NLRB*, 313 U.S. 177, 184–85 (1941). In *FES (A Division of Thermo Power)*, 331 N.L.R.B. 9, 12–13 (2000), *enf'd* 301 F.3d 83 (3d Cir. 2002), the Board held that to prove that an employer engaged in Section 8(a)(3) hiring discrimination, the General Counsel had to demonstrate a prima facie case that (1) the employer was hiring; (2) the applicant had experience or training relevant to the announced or generally known requirements; and (3) anti-union animus contributed to the employer's decision not to hire the applicant. Hiring cases can pose special problems, including the fact that the General Counsel cannot rely on a job applicant's past performance and history with an employer to demonstrate discrimination.

A recurring issue in this area also concerns a union's use of "salts" to organize a targeted employer. The term "salts" refers to individuals employed by unions to apply for jobs with nonunion employers with the intent of organizing (or "salting") the workers. Union salts have become especially important to union organizing efforts since the Supreme Court expanded the employers' privilege to exclude individuals who are not employees from their property under *Lechmere*, as discussed in Chapter 7. In the face of these salting attempts, employers argued that salts should not be classified as their employees under the NLRA because the salts' primary aim was to organize the workforce, and their primary employer was the union (this employee classification issue is also discussed in Chapter 4 as part of the jurisdiction discussion). Unions responded that salts, like any other moonlighter, can be an employee of more than one employer.

In *NLRB v. Town & Country Electric, Inc.*, 516 U.S. 85 (1995), the Supreme Court resolved the issue by holding, in agreement with the NLRB, that salts are employees under the NLRA. The Court justified its conclusion by emphasizing the NLRA's general aim of protecting employees' opportunity to organize and the broad language of Section 2(3), which includes "any employee, and shall not be limited to the employees of a particular employer." The Court also rejected the employer's reliance on the salts' association with their union employer, holding that as long as the salts perform satisfactorily for the employer involved in the dispute, they are employees.

Salts also present employee classification issues before they are hired. At times, union employees may apply for jobs not to organize a workplace, but rather to test whether the employer is discriminating against union applicants. Traditionally, the NLRB considered salts, like other applicants, to be employees unless the employer could show evidence why this presumption should not apply. However, in *Toering Electric Company*, 351 N.L.R.B. 225 (2007), the NLRB changed this rule by creating a new test for determining whether the NLRA protects a salt as a job applicant in a discriminatory refusal to hire case. Under this rule, the General Counsel must show that the salt submitted a bona fide application for employment and is "genuinely interested in seeking to establish an employment relationship with the employer" before they can be considered an employee. While this test is broadly worded, the *Toering* decision appears to apply only in the salting context. Thus, post-*Toering*, although the *FES* burden-shifting framework still applies in refusal-to-hire cases, proof of an applicant's genuine job interest is now also an element of the General Counsel's prima facie case. Although the Democratic-appointed General

Counsel asked the Board to overturn *Toering* in 2023, the Board never acted on that request.

F. Runaway Shops, Complete Shutdowns, and Partial Shutdowns

A recurring situation in discrimination cases is that of the "runaway shop." A "runaway shop" occurs when a company, because of the election or continuing presence of a union, decides to close its plant and relocate elsewhere (typically in areas with low union density). If the company's decision is substantially motivated by anti-union animus, then the company violates Section 8(a)(3). However, courts have been willing to permit employers to relocate their facilities where the prospect of higher union wages would substantially worsen the company's economic outlook. Two older examples of this line of reasoning are *NLRB v. Rapid Bindery, Inc.*, 293 F.2d 170 (2d Cir. 1961), and *NLRB v. Lassing*, 284 F.2d 781 (6th Cir. 1960), where the courts determined that the employer was permitted to relocate based on a host of factors, one of which being the anticipated rise in the cost of labor due to the union's higher wage scale. The court in *Rapid Bindery* emphasized that the union is just one factor that the Board must evaluate when looking at the broad economic outlook of the company, and the court in *Lassing* stated that it is reasonable to anticipate higher labor costs when employees organize. But what is anti-union animus, if not a resistance to the union because of the economic burdens it will impose? These cases also appear inconsistent with the D.C. Circuit's later well-known and widely adopted statement in *Local 57, ILGWU v. NLRB (Garwin Corp.)*, 374 F.2d 295 (D.C. Cir. 1967), that an employer acts with anti-union animus if it decides to relocate or close shop to violate its employees' Section 7 union rights.

The runaway shop issue received national publicity in 2011 when the NLRB filed a complaint against Boeing for moving some union work to South Carolina in retaliation for workers previously engaging in strike activity in Washington State. Assuming that the General Counsel was able to prove all facts alleged, the Boeing case is easily distinguishable from *Lassing* and *Rapid Bindery*, because Boeing officials admitted that they were moving to avoid protected activity—as opposed to lowering business costs. That complaint led congressional Republicans to seek (unsuccessfully) to pass legislation and to hold the NLRB General Counsel in contempt for his role in the case. The parties settled the case when Boeing agreed to build another new airplane in Washington State before the Board issued its decision.

A related issue involves the so-called complete or partial shutdown scenario. Consider the Supreme Court case of *Textile Workers Union v. Darlington Manufacturing Co.*, 380 U.S. 263 (1965), in this regard. The first issue addressed by this case is whether an employer can go completely out of business if it loses a union election. The second related issue is whether an employer can partially close its operation by shutting down a facility that has chosen to unionize. Darlington Manufacturing Co. closed after its employees unionized. Central to the facts in this case is that Darlington was but one company owned by a larger enterprise, Deering Milliken, and operated by Deering's president, Roger Milliken. After liquidating Darlington, Deering still operated sixteen other textile manufacturing facilities and twenty-six other mills.

The union claimed that Deering, through Darlington, violated Section 8(a)(3) under a single integrated employer theory—that is, that Darlington and Deering Milliken were really one company. The Board found that anti-union animus on the part of the president, Roger Milliken, played a significant role in closing the Darlington plant. As a result, the Board found a Section 8(a)(3) violation and, under the single integrated employer theory, ordered Deering to compensate the terminated employees by providing backpay until the employees obtained equivalent work or reinstatement at another of Deering's still-operational mills.

Justice Harlan, writing for the Supreme Court majority, issued two foundational holdings that continue to shape labor law under the NLRA. First, the Court held that an employer has the absolute right to terminate its entire business for any reason it chooses. However, it rejected the idea that this right extends to partial closures regardless of motive. The Court emphasized that decisions such as closing a plant or shutting down a company are typically managerial prerogatives and do not, in themselves, violate Section 8(a)(1). In such cases, the employer's interests are heavily favored. But when only part of a business is closed, the employer's motive becomes central to the analysis, potentially implicating Section 8(a)(3) if the action is intended to suppress union activity.

Second, the Court held that a partial closing violates Section 8(a)(3) if the employer is motivated by a purpose to chill unionism in any of the remaining plants of the single employer and if the employer could reasonably have foreseen that the closure would likely have that effect. To establish a violation under this framework, the General Counsel must demonstrate three elements: (1) the individual or entity controlling the closed facility holds a substantial interest in another business that could benefit from reduced union activity; (2) the closure was executed with the intent to discourage unionization in the remaining enterprise; and (3) the relationship between the businesses was such that the chilling effect on union activity was reasonably foreseeable. To prove foreseeability, it must generally be shown that the employer's actions were motivated by a desire to achieve this prohibited effect.

This focus on whether the employer stands to gain a future advantage in dealings with the union is commonly referred to as the "future benefit" test. The Court in *Darlington* clarified that the NLRA prohibits the discriminatory use of economic weapons—such as plant closures—to secure future benefits in labor relations. If an employer shuts down a facility without an ulterior motive or strategic gain, no violation occurs. However, if the business remains viable after the closure—as in *Darlington*—the action may resemble a runaway shop, where work is relocated to avoid unionization. In such cases, the potential for a chilling effect on organizing efforts in affiliated businesses is substantial and, if foreseeable, may constitute a ULP. The NLRB has since clarified that it is sufficient to show foreseeability of the chilling effect; actual evidence of its occurrence is not required.

On remand, the Board found that Deering Milliken closed the plant to chill union organization throughout the conglomerate. It, thus, reaffirmed its Section 8(a)(3) violation finding.

G. Remedies in Individual Section 8(a)(3) Cases

1. Remedial Authority under Section 10(c)

Remedial authority under the NLRA is granted to the Board under Section 10(c). Section 10(c) states in pertinent part:

> If upon the preponderance of the testimony taken the Board shall be of the opinion that any person named in the complaint has engaged in ... any such unfair labor practices, then the Board ... shall issue ... an order requiring such person to cease and desist from such unfair labor practice,

> and to take such affirmative action including reinstatement of employees with or without backpay, as will effectuate the policies of this Act.

29 U.S.C. § 160(c).

Courts have held that this section does not permit the NLRB to levy fines or to issue awards for pain or suffering, punitive damages, or attorney's fees. *See Republic Steel Corp. v. NLRB*, 311 U.S. 7, 10 (1940). Instead, the NLRB's remedial options are limited to "make-whole relief," which can consist of a cease-and-desist order and appropriate affirmative relief such as reinstatement with backpay. *See Phelps Dodge Corp. v. NLRB*, 313 U.S. 177, 194 (1941). Typically, the regional office will hold a subsequent "compliance hearing" to determine remedial issues after the Board has determined the violations in the ULP proceeding.

Section 10(c) states that the NLRB "shall" issue a cease-and-desist order. Accordingly, in every case in which the NLRB finds a ULP, there is a cease-and-desist order. This order is essentially an injunction, instructing the employer or union to stop doing whatever the NLRB found to be unlawful. This order serves multiple purposes. First, if an appellate court enforces the NLRB's order, then the cease-and-desist order becomes the equivalent of a judicial injunction. Failure to comply with that injunction could lead to contempt of court charges. The NLRB has a separate department called the Contempt, Compliance, and Special Litigation Branch, whose duties include seeking compliance with these orders—which at times has involved asking the courts to jail officials of recalcitrant parties for contempt. Second, the cease-and-desist order dovetails with another consistent practice of a Board order: the notice posting. Once the Board finds a ULP, it will simultaneously order the employer or union to post a notice stating its unlawful actions and its duty to comply with the detailed cease-and-desist order. This ensures that all employees are aware of both the NLRB's findings and the employer's or union's duty to comply.

In addition to the cease-and-desist order, in a run-of-the-mill Section 8(a)(3) violation case, the usual remedy is reinstatement with backpay to place the employee in the same position they would have been, had the discrimination not taken place. Backpay represents the compensation that the employee would have earned had the unlawful adverse action not occurred, minus any subsequent earnings (called "mitigation," which is discussed in more detail below). An award of monetary damages typically requires a jury trial under the Seventh Amendment. However, the Supreme Court has ruled that the Seventh Amendment extends only to remedies that were available at English common law, which did not include equitable remedies. Therefore, according to the Court, a jury trial is not necessary in NLRB backpay cases because the relief is incidental to the equitable relief—the cease-and-desist order. However, when in *Thryv, Inc.*, 372 N.L.R.B. No. 22 (Dec. 13, 2022), the Board changed its make-whole remedy to expressly compensate employees "for all direct or foreseeable pecuniary harms that these employees suffer as a result of the [employer's] unfair labor practice," some employers challenged the expansion of the make-whole remedy as violating the Seventh Amendment because such remedies looked "legal" and not equitable. Although the Fifth Circuit did not reach this issue in *Thryv*, a similar argument has been successful in other cases. *See, e.g., NLRB v. Starbucks Corp.*, 125 F.4th 78, 96 (3d Cir. 2024) (holding that the Board exceeded its authority by ordering *Thryv* remedies).

Another special issue arises when a backpay award is sought for undocumented workers in a Section 8(a)(3) case. Under *Hoffman Plastic Compounds, Inc. v. NLRB*, 535 U.S. 137 (2002), the Supreme Court ruled that, although employers could be found in violation of Section 8(a)(3) for engaging in union-based discrimination against undocumented workers and a cease-and-desist order should issue, undocumented workers are not entitled to backpay or reinstatement. Such relief, the Supreme Court majority held, is foreclosed by federal immigration policy, as expressed by Congress in the Immigration Reform and Control Act of 1986 (IRCA).

Although it has always been assumed that *reinstatement* was a permissible remedy in most discriminatory discharge cases, initially, there was some question centered on the permissibility of *instatement* in a discriminatory hiring case. In *Phelps Dodge Corp. v. NLRB*, 313 U.S. 177 (1941), the Court found that the literal reading of Section 10(c) with Section 2(3) (defining "employee") only addressed private injuries and thwarted the central purpose of the Act to promote organization on the group level. Therefore, the Court concluded that the broad remedial power afforded to the Board permitted it to order an employer to hire an employee, even if that employee has already found another job. Sometimes, instatement or reinstatement is not possible because the job no longer exists or the relationship between the employee and employer is irretrievably broken. In such instances, the NLRB can award front pay. For example, if the unlawfully terminated employee's former department no longer exists, and there is no job to reinstate them to, then the NLRB may award front pay for a reasonable period of time (usually no more than two years) to offset the lack of reinstatement and to compensate the employee until they can obtain a substantially similar job.

Section 10(c) also states that the Board may award reinstatement "with or without backpay." The Court held in *Phelps Dodge* that the Board must consider principles of mitigation when ordering backpay. An employee who has been discriminatorily discharged must exercise reasonable diligence in finding a comparable job in the meantime. The backpay award will be reduced by the amount earned in the interim or by the amount that could have been earned during the interim period.

In *St. George Warehouse*, 351 N.L.R.B. 961 (2007), the Board considered the issue of who has the burden to prove the employee made reasonable efforts to mitigate their damages. The Board reaffirmed that the employer had the ultimate burden of persuasion to demonstrate that an employee had not properly mitigated. However, the Board reversed forty-five years of precedent on the burden of production. The Board concluded that although the employer still has the initial burden of showing evidence that substantially equivalent jobs existed in the geographical area, the General Counsel would now have the burden of producing evidence that the employee took reasonable steps to find other jobs. In *Grosvenor Resort*, 350 N.L.R.B. 1197 (2007), the Board also found that age, lack of skills and education, and limited transportation did not excuse an employee from looking for work for the initial two weeks after being unlawfully fired. Finally, in *Oil Capitol Sheet Metal, Inc.*, 349 N.L.R.B. 1348 (2007), reversing another longstanding rule, the NLRB placed the burden on the General Counsel to prove, after a successful adjudication, that salts unlawfully discharged from employment had a continuing entitlement to backpay. The NLRB reasoned that most salts stay on the job only until their organizing efforts at that particular company end. Thus, the Board will award damages only for periods that the General Counsel could show that the salt would have remained on the job.

Since 1947, the NLRA has explicitly given employers the authority to terminate employees where appropriate. In this regard, Section 10(c) also provides that the Board shall not "require the reinstatement of any individual as an employee who has been suspended or discharged, or the payment to him of any backpay, if such individual was suspended or discharged for cause." This "for cause" provision has been interpreted to allow the Board to find a ULP against an employer without requiring the employer to reinstate the discharged employee or award them backpay if the employee is found to have engaged in misconduct.

2. Remedial Authority under Section 10(j)

Finally, in addition to the remedies available under Section 10(c), parties may ask the General Counsel to seek interim injunctive relief as well. Section 10(j) permits the Board to seek injunctive relief in federal district court, but the Board in Washington, D.C., must first agree. Usually, the General Counsel seeks the injunction after the Regional Director issues the complaint and while the ULP proceeding is before the ALJ. Although the Act permits the Board to seek injunctive relief whenever there is reasonable cause to believe the Act has been violated, the courts generally require more, and historically, very few 10(j) injunctions have been sought on behalf of employees and unions (perhaps because of the extensive resources required for such adjudications). In *Starbucks Corp. v. McKinney*, 602 U.S. 339, 345 (2024), the Court held that "district courts must use the traditional four-part test [likelihood of success on merits, irreparable harm, balance of equities, and public interest] when evaluating the Board's request for a preliminary injunction under § 10(j)."

3. Criticisms of Section 8(a)(3) Remedial Scheme

Many have criticized the ineffectiveness of the NLRA's remedial scheme. This critique focuses on the fact that the remedial philosophy espoused by the Board and courts has emphasized the reparable harm done to individual victims of discrimination, rather than deterring employers from taking further discriminatory actions against the union organizing campaign itself. Scholars and practitioners note that employers consistently discharge union activists or supporters to break the momentum of an organizational campaign. Due to lengthy procedural delays in processing unfair labor charges, by the time the employee is reinstated, the union has already lost the campaign. There is also concern that backpay amounts alone are too small to provide a significant deterrent effect, and that the duty to mitigate removes much of what deterrent effect there might be by substantially shrinking the size of backpay awards. Even reinstatement may not always be a viable or effective remedy, as the employee may be subject to further discipline once reemployed and therefore may not feel comfortable returning to the workplace.

To overcome these criticisms of the remedial scheme, the Board has attempted to fashion creative remedies on rare occasions and on a case-by-case basis to further the purposes of the Act. (Section 10(c) provides that the Board can "take such affirmative action ... as will effectuate the policies of th[e] Act".) Board remedies under this provision of Section 10(c) have included: 1) posting the usual notice not only in the plant where the ULP was committed, but also at all of the employer's plants; 2) mailing the notice of the violation to each employee of the company; 3) having a company official read the notice to the employees during working time; 4) giving the union access to every plant within the company to provide the union officials access to company bulletin boards; and 5) reimbursing union attorneys for litigation expenses.

CHECKPOINTS

- Section 8(a)(3) prohibits discrimination against employees based on union activities. Employer intent is central to the discrimination inquiry.
- NLRB's General Counsel must show an act of employer discrimination that has been motivated by anti-union animus and has a foreseeable effect of either encouraging or discouraging union activities.
- The key distinction between Section 8(a)(1) and Section 8(a)(3) cases is that while employer intent may be relevant in Section 8(a)(1) cases, it is a necessary element in Section 8(a)(3) cases.
- This Chapter focuses on Section 8(a)(3) cases involving specific evidence of anti-union intent in individual discrimination cases. Discriminatory intent can also be inferred from the very nature of the employer's conduct itself. These group inferential cases involving discrimination are discussed in Chapter 14.
- In pretext cases, the union or employee seeks to show the employer's business reason for taking adverse action is a pretext for discrimination.
- In a dual motive case, the vast majority of Section 8(a)(3) cases involving both legitimate and illegitimate reasons for employer action, the *Wright Line* test is utilized to establish that anti-union intent was the substantial or motivating factor, and that the employer cannot show that it would have taken the same action absent its unlawful union intent.

- Section 8(a)(3) applies to refusal-to-hire cases, especially those with union salts.
- Runaway shops, where a company closes down a plant and relocates elsewhere, are generally prohibited if undertaken for anti-union purposes.
- Under *Darlington*, although an employer can always completely shut down its operation in the face of unionization, it cannot partially shut down a segment of its operation to chill Section 7 rights of employees in other parts of the company.
- Section 10(c) provides remedial authority for cease-and-desist orders, reinstatement with or without backpay, and other actions to effectuate the purposes of the Act. Section 10(j) permits an injunction, under appropriate circumstances, to immediately enjoin the employer's discriminatory conduct. District courts must use the traditional four-part test when evaluating the Board's request for injunctive relief.
- Under *Hoffman Plastics*, backpay for undocumented workers is prohibited because the Court viewed that remedy as inconsistent with federal immigration policy.
- Critics believe that the NLRA's remedial scheme is ineffectual and inadequate.

CHAPTER 10

The Representation Election

ROADMAP

- Questions concerning representation and election petitions
- Preconditions for having a Board-conducted secret-ballot election
- The bars to conducting an election—the certification-year bar, the election bar, the voluntary-recognition bar, the contract bar, and the successor bar
- Blocking charges
- Types of election petitions
- Showing of interest—the authorization card
- Bargaining-unit determinations
- Election objections
- Material misrepresentations
- *Gissel* bargaining orders
- *Cemex* bargaining orders
- Testing the incumbent union's majority status
- Public-sector election rules

Chapter 3 outlines the basic election procedures under the NLRA. This chapter provides more depth to that discussion.

A. Question Concerning Representation

The question whether a union enjoys majority support, known as a question concerning representation (QCR), is generally triggered where (1) an employer has refused a union's request for recognition and bargaining, or (2) a party has filed an election petition. A QCR alone does not automatically trigger an election. *See Linden Lumber Div., Summer & Co. v. NLRB*, 419 U.S. 301 (1974) (holding that employers may lawfully refuse to recognize unions even when presented with evidence of majority support and may also refuse to petition for an election in such cases). *But see Cemex Construction Material, Pacific, LLC*, 372 N.L.R.B. 130 (2023) (discussed below). To obtain a Board-conducted secret-ballot election, a party, typically the union seeking to represent a unit of employees, must file an election petition alleging a QCR. [Note, as discussed below, *Cemex* modifies this rule: when a union shows majority support, the employer must file the election petition if the union has not.] Section 9(c) provides: "Whenever a petition shall have been filed, in accordance with [the Board's rules and regulations] ... the Board shall investigate such petition and if it has reasonable cause to believe that a question of representation affecting commerce exists shall provide for an appropriate hearing upon due notice."

B. The Three Necessary Conditions for a Board-Conducted Secret-Ballot Representation Election

Notwithstanding a petition filing, the Board will only conduct a representation election if three conditions are met. First, it must determine that it has jurisdiction. Second, it must conclude that the union is qualified. Third, it must conclude that there is no bar to conducting the election.

1. Jurisdiction

The NLRB's jurisdiction—both to prevent unfair labor practices (ULPs) and to conduct secret-ballot elections—extends to firms whose business affects interstate commerce. Congress intended the Board "to exercise whatever power is constitutionally given to it to regulate commerce by the adoption of measures for the prevention or control of certain specified acts—unfair labor practices—which provoke or tend to provoke strikes or labor disturbances affecting interstate commerce." *NLRB v. Fainblatt*, 306 U.S. 601, 607 (1939). Chapter 4 discusses the Board's jurisdiction in more detail.

2. Qualified Union

Section 9(c)(1)(A) provides that employees may be represented "by any employee or group of employees or any individual or labor organization." Accordingly, the Board will conduct an election to certify the employee representative "unless the proposed bargaining representative fails to qualify as a bona fide representative of the employees." NLRB, An Outline of Law and Procedure in Representation Cases § 6-100 (updated Aug. 2012). Whether an entity qualifies as a bona fide employee representative depends primarily on the following definition of labor organization found in NLRA Section 2(5): "any organization of any kind, or any agency or employee representation committee or plan, in which employees participate and which exists for the purpose, in whole or in part, of dealing with employers concerning grievances, labor disputes, wages, rates of pay, hours of employment, or conditions of work." 29 U.S.C. § 152(5). Interpreting that language, the Board has determined that Section 2(5) requires two findings to meet the statutory definition of labor organization: (1) "it must be an organization in which employees participate;" and (2) "it must exist for the purpose, in whole or in part, of dealing with employers concerning wages, hours, and other terms and conditions of employment." *Alto Plastics Mfg. Corp.*, 136 N.L.R.B. 850, 851–52 (1962).

Once an organization meets these requirements, it is exceedingly unlikely that the Board will find the organization disqualified from representing employees for some collateral reason. As the Board observed:

> If an organization fulfills these two requirements, the fact that it is an ineffectual representative, that its contracts do not secure the same gains that other employees in the area enjoy, that certain of its officers or representatives may have criminal records, that there are betrayals of the trust and confidence of the membership, or that its funds are stolen or misused, cannot affect the conclusion which the Act then compels us to reach, namely, that the organization is a labor organization within the meaning of the Act.

Id. at 852.

There are a few situations that will disqualify a union. For example, Section 9(b)(3) prohibits the Board from certifying a union "as the representative of employees in a bargaining unit of guards if such organization admits to membership, or is affiliated directly or indirectly with an organization which admits to membership, employees other than guards." 29 U.S.C. § 159(b)(3). In other words, a union that represents guards cannot represent other employees who are not guards. *See* Section F.2. for other limitations on bargaining-unit determinations.

The question whether an organization meets the definition of "labor organization" under the NLRA arises more often in the context of Section 8(a)(2) violations. Accordingly, it is treated in greater depth in Chapter 8. *See Electromation, Inc.*, 309 N.L.R.B. 990 (1992), *enforced*, 35 F.3d 1148 (7th Cir. 1994) (upholding the Board's construction of the statutory phrase "dealing with").

3. Bars to Conducting an Election

Suppose the Board has jurisdiction over the employer, and the labor organization is a qualified union. Four main bars could still block an election: the certification-year bar, the voluntary-recognition bar, the contract bar, and the successor bar. While the bar is in place, the union enjoys an irrebuttable presumption of majority status. The primary purpose of these bars is to promote industrial stability during a period when the bargaining relationship is most vulnerable.

Under the certification-year bar doctrine, absent unusual circumstances, the Board's certification of a union bars another election petition for the next twelve months. *See* 29 U.S.C. § 159(c)(3); *see generally Brooks v. NLRB*, 348 U.S. 96 (1954) (explaining the certification-year bar). This bar would block any election including a union decertification election, 29 U.S.C. § 159(c)(1)(A)(ii); an employer petitioned election to substantiate the union's majority status, 29 U.S.C. § 159(c)(1)(B); or a certification election for a rival union. This bar runs from the election date, not the certification date. Unusual circumstances will be found in the following three situations: (1) where the certified union dissolves or becomes defunct; (2) where there is a union schism that substantially changes all the officers in the certified union; or (3) the size of the bargaining unit has changed within a short period.

The certification-year bar should not be confused with the election bar. Under the election bar, if a union loses an election, no election in the same bargaining unit may be held for one year following that election.

In cases where the employer recognizes the union upon a majority card check in place of a Board-conducted election, the voluntary recognition bar affords the parties "a reasonable time to bargain and to execute the contracts resulting from such bargaining." *Keller Plastics Eastern, Inc.*, 157 N.L.R.B. 583, 587 (1966). In *Dana Corp.*, 351 N.L.R.B. 434 (2007), the Bush II Board temporarily removed the voluntary recognition bar for the first 45 days following employer recognition—time sufficient for employees to file a decertification petition. In *Lamons Gasket Co.*, 357 N.L.R.B. 739 (2011), the Obama Board returned to the *Keller Plastics* rule. The first Trump Board returned to the *Dana Corp.* rule when it overturned *Lamons Gasket* by regulation in 2020. The Biden Board then returned to *Lamons Gasket* as of September 2024. *See* 29 C.F.R. § 103.21(a).

Voluntary bargaining relationships, those bargaining relationships that arise by agreement, usually based on majority card check rather than by election, result in noncertified unions. The primary difference between the two unions is that a certification-year bar protects the certified union, while a voluntary-recognition bar protects the noncertified union. The Employee Free Choice Act (EFCA) would have changed this arrangement. EFCA Section 2 would have required the Board to certify unions, without requiring an election, where the union could present to the Board valid authorization cards signed by a majority of employees in an appropriate unit. EFCA Section 2 would have essentially removed the employer's right, as established in *Linden Lumber*, to refuse to recognize a union based on a majority card check.

The primary bar to holding an election is the contract bar, whereby a collective bargaining agreement (CBA) serves to block an election for the duration of the contract up to three years. A contract must meet the following formal requirements before it can serve as a bar to an election: (1) it must be a collective agreement; (2) it must be written and signed by all parties (i.e., the employer and union); (3) it must contain terms and conditions of employment sufficient to establish a stable bargaining relationship; (4) it must cover an appropriate bargaining unit; and (5) it must clearly and expressly cover those employees involved in any rival petition. Although the contract must be reduced to writing to serve as a contract bar, it does not need to constitute a formal CBA. For example, a series of written documents between the parties will suffice to establish the contract bar. By contrast, some contracts are insufficient either as a matter of law or as a matter of fact to serve as a bar. For example, a CBA will not serve as a bar to an election if the union representing the employees is defunct.

The Board has recognized that the contract bar could potentially suspend indefinitely the employees' right to decertify an unpopular union. To create a finer balance between industrial stability and employee free choice, the Board has developed, through adjudication, the following rules. First, a CBA serves as a bar to an election only for the duration of the contract, up to three years. To illustrate, a CBA with a four-year term will be treated like a three-year CBA for contract bar purposes. Second, the Board permits employees to file a decertification petition during the window period—between 60 and 90 days before expiration of a CBA with a term of three years or less, or before the three-year mark for a longer CBA. This 30-day window is the insulation period during which the Board will not entertain a petition to decertify the union. In the healthcare industry, the insulation period is 90 to 120 days, with a 90-day window to file for a decertification election. These periods are non-waivable. For an authoritative statement of these rules, see NLRB, OFFICE OF THE GENERAL COUNSEL, AN OUTLINE OF LAW AND PROCEDURE IN REPRESENTATION CASES, §§ 9-540–9-550 (updated Jan. 2025) (collecting cases).

Finally, the Board oscillates on the question whether the predecessor's CBA in a successorship situation will or will not serve as a bar to an election. Under the successor bar doctrine, a successor employer must bargain with its predecessor's union for a reasonable period, typically for a minimum of six months up to one year. In *Southern Moldings, Inc.*, 219 N.L.R.B. 119 (1975), the Board held that recognition of a successor union will not serve as a bar. The Board reversed position in *St. Elizabeth Manor, Inc.*, 329 N.L.R.B. 341 (1999). The Board reversed course once again in *MV Transportation*, 337 N.L.R.B. 770 (2002), but then reinstated the successor bar in *UGL-UNICCO Service Co.*, 357 N.L.R.B. 801 (2011), and defined a reasonable period as ranging from a minimum of 6 months to 1 year. *See* Chapter 20 for additional discussion on successorship.

C. Blocking Charges

Although either a union or an employer may petition for an election, the Region may decline to proceed under certain conditions. The most frequent scenario involves the filing of ULP charges during the election campaign. If these charges allege conduct that could compromise employees' ability to freely choose representation, the Board may suspend the election process—these are known as "blocking charges." Both unions and employers can use blocking charges strategically to delay representation or decertification elections. Importantly, filing such a charge does not automatically halt the election; the Board retains discretion to move forward if the alleged violations are considered minor. In 2020, the first Trump-era Board issued a rule that significantly curtailed the use of blocking charges to delay elections. However, in 2024, the Biden-era Board reversed course, reinstating the traditional doctrine that allows blocking charges to pause election proceedings.

D. Types of Petitions

There are four types of representation petitions used to initiate an election: RC, RD, RM, and UD petitions. In each case, the petitioner seeks a Board-conducted secret-ballot election.

1. RC Petition—Representation Petition Seeking Certification

Under Section 9(c)(1)(A)(i), an "employee or group of employees or any individual or labor organization acting in their behalf" may petition for an election to certify a union as bargaining agent, where that petition alleges that "a substantial number of employees wish to be represented for collective bargaining and that their employer declines to recognize their representative." Unions typically file this RC petition.

2. RD Petition—Representation Petition Seeking Decertification

Under Section 9(c)(1)(A)(ii), "an employee, group of employees, individual, or labor organization" may file a decertification petition alleging that the currently certified or recognized union no longer represents the employees in the bargaining unit. An employee, not the employer, typically files this RD petition.

3. RM Petition—Employer Representation Petition

Under Section 9(c)(1)(B), an employer may petition for an election "alleging that one or more individuals or labor organizations have presented ... a claim to be recognized as the representative" of employees. The employer generally must show that the union has requested recognition. An employer may also file an RM petition if it "has a good faith uncertainty" about majority support for an existing representative. That is, the RM petition allows an employer to seek a decertification election for an incumbent union if the employer can show that it has a good-faith uncertainty about the union's majority status. *See Levitz Furniture Co.*, 333 N.L.R.B. 717 (2001), *overruled on other grounds*, *Johnson Controls*, 368 N.L.R.B. No. 20 (2019) (modifying the anticipatory withdrawal of recognition doctrine).

4. UD Petition—Union-Security Deauthorization Petition

A union-security clause, also known as a Section 8(a)(3) agreement, between labor and management, makes the payment of union dues a condition of employment. (Union security provisions are discussed in further detail in Chapter 19). Under Section 9(e), upon a petition supported by 30 percent or more of the employees alleging a desire to rescind the union-security provisions, the Board must conduct a secret-ballot vote of bargaining-unit employees covered by the agreement. Unlike the RC, RD, and RM petitions, this petition does not affect the union's status as the majority bargaining representative; it only affects the authorization of union security.

5. Petitions That Do Not Culminate in an Election

The Board also has the authority to act on two other petitions—the petition for clarification (UC) and the petition for amendment of certification (AC). The Board's authority to clarify and amend union certification flows from its Section 9(c)(1) power to issue certifications. Any party may file a petition for clarification where there is currently a certified or recognized union and no QCR exists. *See* NLRB Rules and Regulations, § 102.60(b). A petition to amend certification "reflect[s] changed circumstances, such as changes in the name or application of the labor organization or in the site or location of the employer, when there is a unit covered by a certification and no [QCR] exists." NLRB, An Outline of Law and Procedure in Representation Cases § 4-600 (updated Aug. 2012).

E. Showing of Interest: The Authorization Card

As stated above, unions must support a petition for election with at least a 30-percent showing of interest. The authorization card is the most common type of evidence to support a showing of interest. Although only a 30-percent showing of interest is required to obtain an election, unions try to obtain 70 percent or more valid authorization cards before requesting an election because they know that interest in having a union often wanes during the election campaign. The date by which the Board calculates this ratio is usually during the payroll period immediately preceding the petition date.

In *NLRB v. Gissel Packing Co.*, 395 U.S. 575 (1969), the Supreme Court held that authorization cards are not inherently unreliable indicators of employee interest in unionization. The Board has, nonetheless, established rules to ensure the validity of the cards for counting purposes. To be valid, and thus counted, an authorization card must be signed, dated, and current. Signatures may be authenticated in several ways, including comparing card signatures to payroll records. Dating may be shown by affidavit. *See Metal Sales Mfg.*, 310 N.L.R.B. 597 (1993). The Board has held that cards dated more than a year earlier can be sufficiently current to be valid. *See Covenant Aviation Security, LLC*, 349 N.L.R.B. 699 (2007) (citing *Carey Mfg. Co.*, 69 N.L.R.B. 224, n. 4 (1946)). Cards found to be obtained by fraud, duress, coercion, or supervisory involvement will not be counted.

There are two main types of cards that can serve as evidence of employee interest: single-purpose and dual-purpose cards. The single-purpose card authorizes the union to act as the undersigned's bargaining representative: "The undersigned authorizes the Union to represent me in collective bargaining." By contrast, the dual-purpose card authorizes the union to act as the undersigned's bargaining representative and to request a Board-conducted secret-ballot election: "The undersigned authorizes the Union to represent me in collective bargaining and wants the Board to conduct an election." Unions prefer single-purpose cards because such cards may be used not only for a showing of interest but also for a showing of majority status. Single-purpose cards may be used to show majority status even if the one soliciting union support told the signatory that the card could be used to obtain an election. *See Cumberland Shoe Corp.*, 144 N.L.R.B. 1268, 1269 (1963) (cards counted where cards, "on their face, explicitly authorized the Union only to act as bargaining agent of the employees" even though the union solicitors told the employees that the cards could be used to obtain an election). The Board has also held that cards that only request an election may be used to demonstrate majority status where the card explains that the purpose of seeking an election was to certify the union as the bargaining representative. *Potomac Electric Co.*, 111 N.L.R.B. 553, 554–55 (1955).

F. Bargaining-Unit Determinations

1. The Board Has Broad Discretion to Decide What Constitutes an Appropriate Unit

NLRA Section 9(b) empowers the Board to "decide in each case the unit appropriate for the purposes of collective bargaining." As the Supreme Court has observed, "[t]he selection of an appropriate bargaining unit lies largely within the discretion of the Board whose decision, if not final, is rarely to be disturbed." *So. Prairie Construction v. Operating Engineers Local 627*, 425 U.S. 800, 805 (1976). To that end, the Board's determination of the bargaining unit need not be the only appropriate unit or the most appropriate unit; it need only be *an* appropriate unit. Nevertheless, in keeping with the statute's mandate of "assur[ing] to employees the fullest freedom in exercising the rights guaranteed by this Act," 29 U.S.C. § 159(b), "the Board generally attempts to select a unit that is the smallest appropriate unit encompassing the petitioned-for employees." *Bartlett Collins Co.*, 334 N.L.R.B. 484, 484 (2001). The Board will not, however, select a unit of one employee.

2. Statutory Limitations on the Board's Discretion

There are some statutory limits on the Board's discretion. The Board may not create a bargaining unit comprising professional and nonprofessional employees unless the majority of professional employees vote for inclusion in that unit, 29 U.S.C. § 159(b)(1). The Board may not conclude that a craft unit is inappropriate merely because a different unit had been previously established, 29 U.S.C. § 159(b)(2). The Board may not create a unit consisting of guards and other employees who are not guards, 29 U.S.C. § 159(b)(3). The Board may not use the extent of organization as the controlling factor in its determination whether a unit is appropriate, 29 U.S.C. § 159(c)(5). Bargaining units may not include workers who are not statutory employees.

3. The Community-of-Interest Test

In determining an appropriate unit, the Board uses the community-of-interest test. The idea behind this rule is that, if employees' interests are too dissimilar, then it becomes inappropriate to place those employees into a single unit for purposes of collective bargaining. The Board uses the following factors to determine whether a bargaining unit has a sufficient community of interest to be appropriate: (1) degree of functional integration; (2) common supervision; (3) nature of employee skills and functions; (4) interchangeability and contact among employees; (5) work situs; (6) general working conditions; (7) fringe benefits; and (8) collective bargaining history. No one factor is determinative. The Board need not find commonality within all factors to find a unit appropriate. However, bargaining history is given substantial weight because the Board, to promote industrial stability, is reluctant to disturb bargaining relationships that have worked and are not repugnant to national labor policy.

4. The Board's Rule Governing Acute-Care Hospitals

Generally, the Board determines bargaining units by adjudication. The Board has, however, issued one rule in this area. In *American Hospital Association v. NLRB*, 499 U.S. 606 (1991), the Supreme Court upheld the Board's rule that, absent extraordinary circumstances, the Board would presume the following eight and only eight bargaining units in acute-care hospitals: (1) all registered nurses; (2) all physicians; (3) all professionals except for registered nurses and physicians; (4) all technical employees; (5) all skilled maintenance employees; (6) all business office clerical employees; (7) all guards; and (8) all other nonprofessional employees.

5. Multi-Facility Employers

In cases involving multi-facility employers, the Board applies a single-store presumption as an appropriate unit for bargaining. The party favoring the multi-facility bargaining unit bears the burden of rebutting the single-store presumption. This presumption is inapplicable, however, where the union seeks a multi-facility unit. In *Friendly Ice Cream v. NLRB*, 705 F.2d 570, 576 (1st Cir. 1983), the Board applied this presumption in the context of a union seeking a bargaining unit of employees who worked at the Weymouth, Massachusetts, restaurant that was part of a chain of 605 restaurants in 16 states owned and operated by a central corporation. Applying both the community-of-interest test and the single-store presumption, the court upheld the Board's determination that the Weymouth, Massachusetts, restaurant constituted an appropriate unit. The court, in reviewing that determination, found that the contrary evidence—that each store's management "was bound by central management's specification of curriculum, wages and benefits"—was insufficient to rebut the single-store presumption.

6. Court Review of Bargaining-Unit Determinations

Court review of the Board's determination of a bargaining unit is limited. For an employer to challenge the Board's determination of an appropriate unit, the employer must wait for the union to win the election and request bargaining. The employer then must refuse the union's request and wait for the union to file ULP charges based on the employer's refusal to bargain. In responding to those charges, the employer will admit that it refused the union's bargaining request but contend that it was privileged to do so because the bargaining unit was inappropriate. These types of cases are called "technical 8(a)(5)s" because the employer must technically violate its duty to bargain under Section 8(a)(5) to obtain court review of the Board's determination of the appropriateness of the underlying bargaining unit. Technical 8(a)(5)'s are not available to unions.

There is, theoretically, one other way for an employer to obtain court review of the appropriateness of the Board's bargaining-unit determination. In *Leedom v. Kyne*, 358 U.S. 184 (1958), the Supreme Court permitted direct court review of the Board's determination permitting a mixed professional-nonprofessional employee bargaining unit, which was in direct violation of Section 9(b)(2). The professional employees sued the Board in district court, arguing that the Board was acting outside its delegated authority. The Supreme Court has reiterated that the "*Kyne* exception is a narrow one, not to be extended to permit plenary District Court review of Board orders in certification proceedings whenever it can be said that an erroneous assessment of the particular facts before the Board has led it to a conclusion which does not comport with the law." *Boire v. Greyhound Corp.*, 376 U.S. 473, 481 (1964).

7. Multi-Employer Bargaining

The Board also applies a single-employer presumption when a multi-employer association is involved: "A single employer unit is presumptively appropriate and a party urging a multiemployer unit must demonstrate a controlling history of bargaining on a multiemployer basis and an unequivocal intent by the employer to participate in and be bound by the results of group bargaining." *Central Transport, Inc.*, 328 N.L.R.B. 407, 408 (1999). The most prominent illustration of multi-employer bargaining can be seen in sports, where professional sports club owners participate in collective bargaining and bind themselves to a league agreement, such as the Agreement Between 30 Major League Clubs and the Major League Baseball Players Association. *See* 2022–26 Basic Agreement, available at https://www.mlbplayers.com/cba.

The primary legal argument that arises in the context of multi-employer association bargaining is whether and when a member can lawfully withdraw from the multi-employer unit. In *Retail Associates, Inc.*, 120 N.L.R.B. 388, 395 (1958), the Board announced guidelines for such withdrawals. The Board explained that it would permit withdrawal from an established multiemployer bargaining unit only "upon adequate written notice given prior to the date set by the contract for modification, or to the agreed-upon date to begin the multiemployer negotiations." The Board further explained that "[w]here actual bargaining negotiations based on the existing multiemployer unit have begun, [it] would not permit, except on mutual consent, an abandonment of the unit upon which each side has committed itself to the other, absent unusual circumstances."

In *Charles D. Bonanno Linen Service, Inc. v. NLRB*, 454 U.S. 404 (1982), the Board fleshed out answers to the question of what constitutes unusual circumstances. There, a member of a multi-employer association notified the association that it was withdrawing after ten bargaining sessions, union rejection of a completed agreement, impasse, and a lockout. The Court upheld the Board's finding that this series of events, culminating in an impasse and lockout, does not constitute unusual circumstances sufficient to permit withdrawal. The Supreme Court accepted the Board's explanation for its policy of not permitting withdrawal from a multiemployer bargaining group at impasse:

> If withdrawal were permitted at impasses, the parties would bargain under the threat of withdrawal by any party who was not completely satisfied with the results of negotiations ... [P]arties could precipitate an impasse in order to escape any agreement less favorable than the one expected. In addition, it is precisely at and during impasse, when bargaining is temporarily replaced by economic warfare, that the need for a stable, predictable bargaining unit becomes acute in order that the parties can weigh the costs and possible benefits of their conduct.

Id. at 412, n.8.

Relatedly, unions have for years responded to large industries and to multi-employer bargaining by creating industry-wide standards, sometimes through master agreements and sometimes through coordinated bargaining efforts amongst themselves. The steel industry, mining industries, and professional sports are examples of some of these efforts.

G. Interference with Elections

1. The Election Objection

The Region, an employer, or a union can question the validity of an election by filing objections to the conduct of an election or to conduct affecting the results of an election. Objections must be filed within seven days after the Region tallies the ballots, typically the same day that the election was held. Objections to pre-election campaign interference may be filed under the *General Shoe* doctrine. In that case, the Board famously articulated its role in ensuring the integrity of the election process and protecting employee free choice:

> In election proceedings, it is the Board's function to provide a laboratory in which an experiment may be conducted, under conditions as nearly ideal as possible, to determine the uninhibited desires of the employees. It is our duty to establish those conditions; it is also our duty to determine whether they have been fulfilled. When, in the rare extreme case, the standard drops too low, because of our fault or that of others, *the requisite laboratory conditions are not present and the experiment must be conducted over again.*

General Shoe Corp., 77 N.L.R.B. 124, 127 (1948) (emphasis added), *enf'd* 192 F.2d 504 (6th Cir. 1951). Here, the Board imposed a stringent benchmark: elections must approximate laboratory conditions. When the election falls short of that standard, the experiment must be repeated—meaning the Board will mandate a rerun election.

The *General Shoe* doctrine also clarifies that conduct does not necessarily have to constitute a ULP to upset laboratory conditions:

> Conduct that creates an atmosphere which renders improbable a free choice will sometimes warrant invalidating an election, even though that conduct may not constitute an unfair labor practice. An election can serve its true purpose only if the surrounding conditions enable employees to register a free and untrammeled choice for or against a bargaining representative. *For this reason the Board has sometimes set elections aside in unconsolidated representation cases, in the absence of any charges or proof of unfair labor practice.* When a record reveals conduct so glaring that it is almost certain to have impaired employees' freedom of choice, we have set an election aside and directed a new one.

Id. at 126 (emphasis added). The most common example of conduct, which might render free choice improbable, thereby upsetting laboratory conditions, but which does not constitute a ULP, is employer (or sometimes union) free speech protected by Section 8(c), discussed further at Chapter 7. A famous example of such conduct involved the United Auto Workers' allegations that third parties—namely government officials—disrupted the laboratory conditions during their 2014 organizing campaign of the Volkswagen Plant in Chattanooga, Tennessee. However, allegations that third parties have disturbed the laboratory conditions are much rarer and more difficult to prove than allegations that the employer has disturbed those conditions.

2. Material Misrepresentations

The Board has struggled with the question whether campaign propaganda during an election campaign should justify holding a re-run election, even though such propaganda might be protected speech under Section 8(c) and therefore could not form the basis of a ULP. The Board has changed its position on this question several times in the past half-century. In *Hollywood Ceramics Co.*, 140 N.L.R.B. 221, 224 (1962), the Board held that it would set aside an election where "a misrepresentation or other similar campaign trickery, which involves a substantial departure from the truth, at a time which prevents the other party or parties from making an effective reply, so that the misrepresentation, whether deliberate or not, may reasonably be expected to have a significant impact on the election." The Board abandoned that position in *Shopping Kart Food Market, Inc.*, 228 N.L.R.B. 1311, 1313 (1977), explaining that employees do not need the Board's "'protection' from campaign misrepresentations,'" and holding that it would "no longer set elections aside on the basis of misleading campaign statements" except in cases involving the Board's processes or "the use of forged documents which render the voters unable to recognize the propaganda for what it is." The following year, the Board returned to its rule in *Hollywood Ceramics. See General Knit of California*, 239 N.L.R.B. 619 (1978) (holding that, in cases of material misrepresentation, the re-run election is necessary to "preserve[] the integrity of [its] electoral processes").

In *Midland National Life Insurance Co.*, 263 N.L.R.B. 127 (1982), the Board returned to the view that, absent cases involving the integrity of the Board's processes, forgery, or inflammatory appeals to prejudice, it would not set aside elections based on misleading campaign statements. In *Midland*, the union lost a secret-ballot election in 1978. Applying *General Knit*, the Board initially ordered a re-run election.

In that second election of approximately 239 eligible voters, 107 voted for the union, 107 voted against the union, one ballot was void, and 20 ballots were challenged—enough to affect the results of the election. During a post-election hearing, the parties agreed that the 20 challenged ballots were cast by ineligible voters, rendering them void. The Hearing Officer then ordered a third re-run election, again relying on the Board's material misrepresentation doctrine from *General Knit*. The employer's campaign propaganda included a photograph of a deserted facility accompanied by the caption: "They too employed between 200 and 300 employees. This Local 304A struck this plant—violence ensued. *Now all of the workers are gone*! What did Local 304A do for them? Where is the 304A union job security?" This statement was misleading as the union had not been on strike when this plant closed. Other campaign documents were similarly deceptive, including a manipulated version of the union's financial disclosure form that omitted key sections to falsely imply the union was not allocating funds to the unit.

After reviewing the evidence, the Board rejected the Hearing Officer's recommendations for a third election. Instead, it certified the results of the election, declaring that "after painstaking evaluation and careful consideration," it was returning to the "sound rule" established in *Shopping Kart* and formally overruling *General Knit* and *Hollywood Ceramics.*

The Board's decision in *Midland* rested on several key policy considerations. Chief among them was the importance of promoting the finality of election results and discouraging tactics that delay resolution. The Board also concluded that a bright-line rule—declining to assess the accuracy of campaign statements—would be more efficient and predictable than attempting to determine whether a particular statement constituted a substantial misrepresentation. Drawing on its experience under *Hollywood Ceramics*, the Board announced a significant shift: it would no longer scrutinize the truth or falsity of campaign statements, nor set aside elections based solely on misleading content. However, it carved out an exception for cases involving forged documents that prevent voters from recognizing propaganda as such. In those instances, the Board emphasized that its concern lies not with the substance of the message, but with the deceptive method of delivery—specifically, conduct that impairs employees' ability to critically evaluate the material presented.

Simply put, the Board will not set aside elections based on campaign propaganda except in cases of forgery, *see Formco, Inc.*, 233 N.L.R.B. 61 (1977) (articulating the forgery exception), and inflammatory appeals to prejudice, *see, e.g., Sewell Mfg. Co.*, 138 N.L.R.B. 66 (1962) (setting aside an election where the employer linked the union to racial integration and distributed pictures of a black man dancing with a white woman). *But see Van Dorn Plastic Machine Co. v. NLRB*, 736 F.2d 343 (6th Cir. 1984) (refusing to endorse the Board's *Midland* doctrine and suggesting that it would carve out greater exceptions for misrepresentation than in cases where forgery can be proven).

3. Remedy for Employer Misconduct That Undermines a Free Election: The Affirmative Bargaining Order

In some cases, a regional NLRB office may refuse to hold an election due to pending blocking charges (see Section C above), or an election may proceed, but the union loses—allegedly because of the employer's ULPs. In other instances, even when an election is held, the employer's misconduct may have so thoroughly undermined laboratory conditions that a re-run election would be insufficient to remedy the situation. Under such circumstances, the Board has historically issued a *Gissel* bargaining order, which compels the employer to recognize and bargain with the union as a remedy for its unlawful conduct.

However, in *Cemex Construction Materials Pacific, LLC*, 372 N.L.R.B. 130 (2023), the Board criticized the *Gissel* framework as insufficient to protect employees' Section 7 rights. Rather than overruling *Gissel* outright, the Board introduced a new doctrine—discussed below—that aims to strengthen remedies in cases of employer interference. At the time of this book's publication, the Board was applying both *Gissel* and *Cemex* standards as alternative analyses. That said, the Interim General Counsel has since rescinded prior guidance on seeking relief under *Cemex*, signaling a shift in enforcement priorities. With the likely appointment of a Republican-majority Board under President Trump, further doctrinal changes are expected. Considering this uncertainty, students of labor law must be conversant with both approaches until the Board provides clearer direction.

4. *Gissel* Bargaining Order

In *NLRB v. Gissel Packing Co.*, 395 U.S. 575 (1969), the Board was confronted with four cases consolidated for appeal. In each of these cases, the union had gathered a significant majority of support through valid authorization cards (see Section E above); the employer refused to recognize the union based on a card check; the union petitioned for an election; and throughout the election campaign, the employer committed numerous ULPs including coercive interrogations, promise of benefits in exchange for voting against the union, threats of discharge, and discharge. In two cases, the union lost the election; in the other two cases, the election was never held because the employer's misconduct formed the basis of blocking charges. The Board issued not only the normal remedies to redress the ULPs—cease-and-desist orders and other affirmative relief—but also an extraordinary remedy. The Board ordered the employer, in each case, to bargain with the union.

The Board, with the Supreme Court's approval, explained that it would issue what has come to be known as *Gissel* bargaining orders in cases that meet the following criteria:

- The union had previously enjoyed majority card support;
- The employer refused the union's request for bargaining;
- The employer has committed ULPs that "have the tendency to undermine majority strength and impede the election processes," *id.* at 614; and

- The Board "finds that the possibility of erasing the effects of past practices and of ensuring a fair election (or a fair rerun) by the use of traditional remedies, though present, is slight and that employee sentiment once expressed through cards would, on balance, be better protected by a bargaining order," *id.* at 614–15.

The cases are known as *Gissel II* cases. They are contrasted with *Gissel III* cases, which are cases where the ULPs have only a minimal impact on the election and therefore no bargaining order is issued. The Court never passed on the propriety of imposing a *Gissel I* bargaining order, that is ordering bargaining "without need of inquiry into majority status ... in 'exceptional' cases marked by 'outrageous' and 'pervasive' unfair labor practices ... [that] are of 'such a nature that their coercive effects cannot be eliminated by the application of traditional remedies, with the result that a fair and reliable election cannot be had." *Id.* at 613–14. Ultimately, the Board decided that it would not issue *Gissel I* orders, where the union had never established majority support; accordingly, the standard for issuing a *Gissel* bargaining order is the *Gissel II* standard. *See Gourmet Foods, Inc.*, 270 N.L.R.B. 578 (1984) (announcing that the Board will not issue remedial bargaining orders unless the union has, at some point, demonstrated majority support).

Gissel and its progeny demonstrate that employer coercion can be a substantial obstacle to employee free choice. Unions have responded to this coercion by attempting to pair card check with neutrality agreements—voluntary agreements with employers "establish[ing] a code of conduct that prohibits each party from disparaging the other or using intimidating, coercive tactics on employees." Adrienne Eaton & Jill Krieskyon, *Fact Over Fiction: Opposition to Card Check Doesn't Add Up* (2006). Congress also attempted to address this problem by introducing EFCA, discussed above, which would have, among other things, required the Board to establish procedures for certifying unions based on a card check. That bill has repeatedly failed to pass.

5. *Cemex* Bargaining Orders

The Board infrequently issued *Gissel* bargaining orders. Moreover, courts frequently refused to enforce these orders, for three reasons: (1) the courts view them as extraordinary remedies because the union had lost the election or the election was never held; (2) the courts are concerned about employee turnover and therefore the Section 7 rights of those employees who never signed authorization cards; and (3) the passage of time makes a union's claim of majority support less certain. Unions grew increasingly frustrated with the problem of obtaining and enforcing *Gissel* bargaining orders, thereby allowing employers to engage in egregious election misconduct with near impunity.

To remedy these problems, Biden-appointed General Counsel Jennifer Abruzzo asked the Board to restore an old precedent: the *Joy Silk* doctrine. Under *Joy Silk*, the Board would find an employer to have violated Section 8(a)(5) if the union presented the employer with evidence of the union's majority support and the employer refused to recognize and bargain with the union, absent a good-faith doubt of the union's majority support. *See Joy Silk Mills, Inc.*, 85 N.L.R.B. 1263 (1949), *enforced*, 185 F.2d 732 (D.C. Cir. 1950). The remedy for this ULP was an order for the employer to bargain with the union, even though there had not been an election.

The Board had a chance to review its *Joy Silk* doctrine in *Cemex Construction Materials Pacific, LLC*, 372 N.L.R.B. No. 130 (2023), a case involving numerous hallmark ULPs committed by the employer during a union organizing campaign. In *Cemex*, the Board adopted a modified version of the *Joy Silk* doctrine, which had long been dormant. Under this revised standard, when a union demands recognition and presents evidence of majority support—typically in the form of employee-signed authorization cards—the employer must either voluntarily recognize the union or file an RM petition for a representation election within two weeks, unless the union has already initiated the election process. This modification overrules *Linden Lumber Division, Summer & Co.*, 190 N.L.R.B. 718 (1971), which had placed the burden entirely on the union to petition for an election, even when majority support had been demonstrated.

The remedy under this framework—the *Cemex* bargaining order—represents a significant departure from prior Board practice. Suppose the employer commits any ULP that would ordinarily justify setting aside an election, such as coercion, retaliation, interference, or discriminatory discipline. In that case, although the Board has not fleshed out precisely which conduct would justify the Cemex bargaining order, the Board would likely dismiss the election petition and issue a bargaining order compelling the employer to recognize and bargain with the union. This approach stands in contrast to the traditional *Gissel* bargaining order, which requires a more substantial showing of employer misconduct and a breakdown of laboratory conditions to bypass the election process. The *Cemex* standard lowers that threshold, permitting bargaining orders even in cases involving less severe or isolated ULPs, provided they compromise the fairness of the election.

The Board's decision in *Cemex* reflects a broader intent to deter employer interference, reinforce employees' Section 7 rights, and streamline the path to union recognition. By shifting procedural burdens and enhancing remedies, the Board aimed to reduce delays and obstacles that have historically favored employers. As discussed above, the future of the *Cemex* doctrine remains uncertain. A newly constituted Board under President Trump may revisit or dismantle the framework.

H. Testing an Incumbent Union's Majority Status

As explained above in Section B.3., unions enjoy an irrebuttable presumption of majority status during the certification year, for the duration of a CBA up to three years, or for a reasonable period of time after voluntary recognition. Where these circumstances do not hold, the union enjoys a rebuttable presumption of majority status. In those cases, if an employer has some doubt about the incumbent union's majority support, it has three ways to test the union's majority status: (1) poll employees; (2) file an RM decertification petition; or (3) withdraw recognition.

The degree of doubt needed to lawfully test the union's majority status varies depending on which test the employer uses. An employer may poll its employees if it has a good-faith doubt of the union's majority status. *See Allentown Mack Sales & Serv., Inc. v. NLRB*, 522 U.S. 359 (1998) (upholding Board's unitary good-faith doubt standard but reversing the Board on substantial evidence grounds); *Levitz Furniture Co.*, 333 N.L.R.B. 717, 723 (2001) (retaining by silent implication good-faith doubt standard for polling). The employer may file an RM decertification petition if it has a good-faith reasonable uncertainty about the union's continuing majority status. *See Levitz*, 333 N.L.R.B. at 717. The employer may withdraw recognition only if it can show through objective evidence that the union has actually lost majority support. *See id.*

In *Levitz*, the Board replaced its previous unitary good-faith standard that it had applied to all three methods of testing an incumbent union's majority status. The Board concluded that it made more sense to apply a higher standard to withdrawing recognition than to requesting an RM election. The Board explained its heightened standard for permitting employers to withdraw recognition:

> Allowing employers to withdraw recognition from majority unions ... wrongfully destroys the parties' bargaining relationship and, as a result, frustrates the exercise of employee free choice. It deprives employees of their chosen representative and disrupts the bargaining relationship until the union reestablishes its majority status in an election. Even if and when the union wins an election, its attention has been diverted from its representational functions and its stature as the employees' representative has been weakened.

Id. at 724. The Board proceeded to explain the type of evidence that would suffice to show good-faith uncertainty:

> In RM cases, then, the regional offices should determine whether good-faith uncertainty exists on the basis of evidence that is objective and that reliably indicates employee opposition to incumbent unions—i.e., evidence that is not merely speculative. The specific types of evidence that are probative of such uncertainty, and the weight to be afforded each type under the circumstances, will be decided on a case-by-case basis.

Id. at 729.

Allentown Mack illustrates the type of evidence that might suffice for showing good-faith reasonable uncertainty or even good-faith doubt, but which would not suffice for showing actual loss of majority status (at the time of *Allentown Mack*, the Board used its unitary standard of good-faith reasonable doubt). In that case, shortly after Allentown Mack purchased a business whose employees were unionized, it claimed to have a good-faith doubt as to the union's majority status. It asked a Roman Catholic priest to conduct a secret-ballot poll, following the Board's standards, to verify majority support. Allentown Mack based its alleged good-faith doubt on statements made by six of its thirty-two employees, which conveyed the message that those employees did not want a union shop. These statements amounted to 20 percent first-hand confirmed opposition to the union. After the union lost the poll, it filed ULP charges. The questions presented to the Court were (1) could the Board use one standard for all three tests, and (2) did the evidence that the employer used as the basis for conducting the poll meet the Board's good-faith doubt standard. The Court concluded not only that this evidence was sufficient to meet the Board's good-faith doubt standard but also that the evidence compelled that conclusion. This included statements from some employees that they believed that other employees did not support the union—statements that could provide the employer with good-faith reasonable doubt but would not, on their own, show objective evidence of the union's lack of majority support.

The Board will remedy an employer's unlawful withdrawal of recognition by issuing an affirmative bargaining order. *See Vincent Industrial Plastics, Inc. v. NLRB*, 209 F.3d 727, 738 (D.C. Cir. 2000). However, the D.C. Circuit will not enforce that bargaining order absent "a reasoned analysis that includes an explicit balancing of three considerations: (1) the employees' § 7 rights; (2) whether other purposes of the Act override the rights of employees to choose their bargaining representatives; and (3) whether alternative remedies are adequate to remedy the violations of the Act." The Board now provides that explanation in every affirmative bargaining order case. *See Vincent Indus. Plastics, Inc.*, 336 N.L.R.B. 697, 697–98 (2001); *Caterair Int'l*, 322 N.L.R.B. 64 (1996).

I. Public-Sector Election Rules

1. Elections in the Public Sector

Most public-sector jurisdictions use rules similar to the NLRA rules for governing union elections. For example, public-sector jurisdictions usually require a 30 percent showing of interest to support a representation petition for obtaining an election. Most public-sector jurisdictions follow the current NLRA rule on material misrepresentations. However, such misrepresentations are grounds to overturn an election under Iowa's public-sector law. *See, e.g., Broadlawns Medical Center and AFSCME Iowa Council 61*, Case No. 5944 (Iowa Public Relations Board 2000). Public-sector labor laws generally adopt the same criteria for "community of interest" as under the NLRA, although many explicitly adopt a policy against "over-fragmentation" of bargaining units. This means that, at least at the margins, public-sector labor laws often prefer fewer but larger bargaining units, as opposed to more but smaller units. Public-sector jurisdictions also typically utilize certification-year and contract bars. The most significant difference arises in how the contract bar functions in the public sector, where contract execution is often held up by the need for higher levels of approval even after the parties have agreed. A few important variations exist. In Ohio, employers cannot file decertification petitions or refuse to deal with a previously certified union on the grounds that the employer believes the union no longer enjoys majority support. *See State Emp. Relations Bd. v. Miami University*, 643 N.E.2d 1113 (Oh. 1994). In Wisconsin, under Act 10 (enacted in 2011), most public-sector unions must undergo a mandatory "recertification" election each year, and if the union does not receive support from 51 percent of the *entire bargaining unit*, not just of those voting in the election, the union is decertified.

2. Card-Check Recognition in the Public Sector

Almost all public-sector laws allow voluntary card check recognition. Significantly, though, six public-sector jurisdictions, including New York, Illinois, California, New Jersey, New Hampshire, Massachusetts, and Oregon, have *mandatory* card-check recognition rules: employers must recognize a union if it produces cards from a majority of bargaining-unit members and those cards were not obtained through fraud or coercion.

New York has had a mandatory card check rule since 1967. The relevant statutes state that the New York state labor board may "ascertain the public employees' choice of employee organization as their representative choice ... on the basis of dues deduction authorization and other evidences...." N.Y. Civil Service Law § 207(2). In fact, in New York, certification based on dues deduction cards and similar evidence, rather than election, is the preferred method for determining employee choice. *See Town of Islip*, 8 N.Y.P.E.R.B. ¶ 3049 (N.Y.P.E.R.B. 1975).

More recently, Illinois, California, New Jersey, New Hampshire, Massachusetts, and Oregon added rules that provide for mandatory card check recognition (although New Hampshire later revoked that rule). *See, e.g., County of Du Page v. Illinois Labor Relations Board*, 900 N.E.2d 593 (Ill. 2008) (holding, among other things, that under the mandatory card-check recognition rule of the Illinois Public Labor Relations Act, § 9(a-5), the employer has no right to see the cards).

In contrast, the public-sector statute in Kansas does not permit even voluntary recognition based on cards. Instead, it requires a secret ballot election before a public employer may recognize a union. Kan. Stat. Ann. § 75-4327(d). Ohio's statute permits voluntary recognition based on cards but adds more procedural steps. Specifically, Oh. Rev. Code § 4117.05(a) requires that before an employer may voluntarily recognize a union, the employer must first post notice of the proposed recognition and allow other unions to intervene and oppose the voluntary recognition.

CHECKPOINTS

- To initiate a representation case, a party must file an election petition alleging a QCR.
- Absent coercion, employers may lawfully refuse to recognize and bargain with a union based solely on a card check.
- The Board's jurisdiction to conduct a representation election is coextensive with the federal government's power to regulate interstate commerce.
- Under the certification-year bar doctrine, absent unusual circumstances, the Board's certification of a union bars another election for twelve months.
- The voluntary recognition bar affords the parties a reasonable time in which to bargain and to execute a CBA.
- Under the contract bar, a CBA blocks an election for the contract's duration up to three years.
- Even in cases where there is no bar, the Region may refuse to hold an election where a party has filed blocking charges.
- Unions can use authorization cards to make a showing of interest. At least 30 percent is needed to obtain an election.
- The Board has broad discretion to decide an appropriate unit. That unit need not be the most appropriate unit—it need only be an appropriate unit.
- The Board may not create a bargaining unit comprising professional and nonprofessional employees unless the majority of professional employees vote for inclusion into that unit. Nor may the Board create a unit consisting of guards and non-guards.
- The Board uses the multi-factored community of interest test to determine whether a bargaining unit is appropriate.
- In *American Hospital Association v. NLRB*, the Supreme Court upheld the Board's rule that, absent extraordinary circumstances, it would presume only eight bargaining units in acute-care hospitals.
- In cases involving multi-facility employers, the Board applies a single-store presumption as an appropriate unit for bargaining.

- There are two ways that an employer can challenge in court the Board's bargaining unit determination: a technical 8(a)(5) refusal to bargain or, in extremely limited circumstances, direct court review under *Leedom v. Kyne.*
- The Board applies the single-employer presumption to its bargaining unit determinations involving multi-employer associations.
- The Board permits withdrawal from an established multi-employer bargaining unit only on adequate written notice given prior to the date set by the contract for modification, or to the agreed-upon date to begin the multiemployer negotiations. Where negotiations have begun, the Board does not permit withdrawal, absent mutual consent or unusual circumstances. Impasse does not constitute unusual circumstances.
- Under the Board's *General Shoe* doctrine, the Board will order a re-run election where laboratory conditions during an election campaign are not met.
- Under the Board's *Midland* doctrine, except in cases involving the integrity of the Board's processes, forgery, or inflammatory appeals to prejudice, the Board will not set aside elections and order a re-run election based on misleading campaign statements.
- In *Cemex,* when confronted with a card majority, an employer must bargain with the union or file a petition for election to test the union's majority support. This doctrine overturns the Board's prior rule that the union has the duty to file the election petition if the employer refuses to voluntarily recognize it when confronted with a card majority.
- An affirmative bargaining order may be an appropriate remedy where the employer engages in misconduct during an organizing campaign. There are two types of bargaining orders in such cases: *Gissel* bargaining orders and *Cemex* bargaining orders.
- A *Gissel* bargaining order may be appropriate where the union had previously enjoyed majority card support; the employer refused the union's request for bargaining; the employer has committed numerous ULPs that tend to undermine majority strength and impede the election processes; and the possibility of erasing the effects of past practices and of ensuring a fair election by the use of traditional remedies is slight.

- Under *Cemex*, if the union had majority support from employees and the employer commits ULPs during the campaign that warrants setting aside an election, the Board will order the employer to bargain with the union, without re-running the election.
- At time of publication of this book, the Board issues both *Gissel* bargaining orders and uses *Cemex* bargaining orders instead. However, the future of the *Cemex* doctrine remains uncertain. The Interim General Counsel has rescinded prior guidance on seeking relief under *Cemex*, and a newly constituted Board under President Trump may revisit or dismantle the framework.
- To poll employees, the employer must have a good-faith doubt of the union's majority support.
- The employer may file an RM decertification petition if it has a good-faith reasonable uncertainty about the union's continuing majority status.
- The employer may withdraw recognition only if it can show that the union has actually lost majority support. The remedy for an honest but mistaken belief that the union has lost majority support is an affirmative bargaining order.
- Most public-sector jurisdictions follow the same or similar rules to the NLRA rules for governing union elections.
- Most public-sector laws allow voluntary card check recognition. Some public-sector jurisdictions have *mandatory* card-check recognition rules.

CHAPTER 11

The Duty to Bargain: Exclusivity and Good Faith Bargaining

ROADMAP

- The prohibition against employers dealing directly with represented employees
- What bargaining tactics are considered to be "bad faith"?
- Parties' duty to provide information to each other
- What is an impasse, and what does it allow employers to do?
- What are the similarities and differences between the NLRA and public-sector duty-to-bargain rules?

The previous chapters explored the difficulties that employees face in attempting to unionize. However, employees who elect a union in an NLRB-run election or persuade an employer to voluntarily recognize the union have won only half the battle. The decision to unionize means little unless the union can provide benefits to the employees. But the extent to which the union is able to help the employees depends on the outcome of discussions with the employer. These discussions can involve everything from negotiating a formal collective bargaining agreement to resolving a dispute about an individual employee's work performance. For the union to have an impact, it must be able to talk and bargain with the employer.

The NLRA recognizes the importance of bargaining between employers and unions. It also recognizes the problems that can occur if one of those parties does not want to talk to the other. Such a failure threatens to undermine one of the central goals of the NLRA, which Section 1 describes as "promot[ing] the flow of commerce by removing certain recognized sources of industrial strife." 29 U.S.C. § 151. The primary means of reducing industrial strife is to encourage "practices fundamental to the friendly adjustment of industrial disputes arising out of differences as to wages, hours, or other working conditions, and by restoring equality of bargaining power between employers and employees." A critical component of the "friendly adjustment of industrial disputes" is ensuring that employers and unions talk to each other, rather than always using work stoppages or other types of labor unrest.

The NLRA promotes discussion between employers and unions by establishing for both parties a "duty to bargain." Under Section 8(a)(5), an employer commits an unfair labor practice (ULP) if it refuses "to bargain collectively with the representatives of his employees." Unions face a similar ULP under Section 8(b)(3) if they fail "to bargain collectively with an employer." Although there can be questions whether a party's duty to bargain has been triggered at all—primarily due to a representational dispute—the more frequently litigated issue is what "bargaining" means. The NLRA defines the duty "to bargain collectively" in Section 8(d) as "the mutual obligation of the employer and the representative to meet at reasonable times and confer in good faith with respect to wages, hours, and other terms and conditions of employment." As a result of Section 8(d), you will usually see references to parties' "duty to bargain in good faith." Yet, what this duty entails can be quite complicated. For instance, the next chapter will discuss the substantive topics that parties must bargain over. But first, this chapter examines a more process-oriented issue: whether the parties' actions meet the standard of "good faith" bargaining.

A. The Prohibition against Direct Dealing

Before exploring the process through which parties must bargain with each other, it is essential to address what "parties" we are referring to. The answer may seem obvious, but as the company union discussion in Chapter 8 shows, some significant nuances exist.

Both Sections 8(a)(5) and 8(d) require employers to bargain with the employees' "representative"—not the employees themselves. This requirement reflects the collective nature of labor law and the idea that employees as a whole will be better served by banding together when dealing with their employer rather than splitting up into factions or cutting deals individually.

As part of this system, NLRA Section 9(a) requires that unions act as "the exclusive representative of all employees ... for the purposes of collective bargaining in respect to rates of pay, wages, hours of employment, or other conditions of employment." This exclusivity means that when an employer is discussing terms or conditions of employment that affect a group of employees, it must bargain with the union only—not employees or any other entity claiming to act on the employees' behalf. That said, Section 9(a) does allow employees to present grievances to the employer and, if the employer chooses, have those grievances addressed without the union's agreement (although the union has a right to be present at these discussions), as long as the solution is not inconsistent with a collective bargaining agreement.

The Supreme Court addressed the exclusivity requirement in *Emporium Capwell Co. v. Western Addition Community Organization*, 420 U.S. 50 (1975), which involved several African-American employees who were upset about what they believed were serious racial discrimination problems and did not feel that their union was doing enough to address the issue. Because of their dissatisfaction, the employees repeatedly demanded that the employer's president meet with them to work out a broad agreement to address discrimination. The president refused and told the employees that they should use the grievance procedures that were part of their collective bargaining agreement, which prohibited discriminatory employment practices. The employees kept insisting on working out a deal themselves and began picketing to bring attention to the issue. The employer then fired them.

The Supreme Court held in *Emporium Capwell* that the terminations were not unlawful because the employees were not engaged in protected activity. Underlying this holding was the principle that "[c]entral to the policy of fostering collective bargaining, where the employees elect that course, is the principle of majority rule." *Id.* at 62. Then, quoting its decision in *NLRB v. Allis-Chalmers Manufacturing Co.*, 388 U.S. 175, 180 (1967), the Court explained the significance of this majority rule principle:

> National labor policy has been built on the premise that by pooling their economic strength and acting through a labor organization freely chosen by the majority, the employees of an appropriate unit have the most effective means of bargaining for improvements in wages, hours, and

> working conditions. The policy therefore extinguishes the individual employee's power to order his own relations with his employer and creates a power vested in the chosen representative to act in the interests of all employees.... Thus only the union may contract the employee's terms and conditions of employment, and provisions for processing his grievances; the union may even bargain away his right to strike during the contract term....

According to the Court, the union's exclusive representative status was so strong that an exception for an issue even as serious as racial discrimination was not justified. The Court noted the risk that the employer's solution with the employees could create problems for other employees—for instance, reassigning or promoting some employees to a limited number of positions could divide employees and lead to industrial strife.

Emporium Capwell stressed that under the NLRA, it is the union alone that is able to consider all employees' preferences and negotiate with the employer. The union may still leave some employees unsatisfied, but there are ways of dealing with that result. If the union's actions are far out of bounds, it could face a charge that it violated its duty of fair representation, which Chapter 19 discusses. Short of that, dissatisfied employees can use the democratic process, including voting for different union officials or trying to decertify the union. Unlike a union, individual employees are not subject to these processes and, under the NLRA, are not proper representatives of a larger group of employees who have chosen to be represented by a union.

Another similar exclusivity issue arose in *J.I. Case Co. v. NLRB*, 321 U.S. 332 (1944). In that case, the employer had individual employment contracts in force with most of its employees before they elected a union. The employer relied on these contracts in an attempt to avoid bargaining with the union. The Court rejected that argument and held that individual employees or employment agreements cannot waive or block the negotiation of a broader, collective bargaining agreement. Similarly, employees cannot individually negotiate terms that conflict with a collective bargaining agreement, even if such terms are better for the employees involved. Again, the NLRA puts the group's welfare above that of an individual employee, if a majority of employees have chosen collective representation.

The unlawful situations in *J.I. Case* and *Emporium Capwell* are called "direct dealing." When employees have chosen a union, their employer must respect that choice and avoid bargaining with individual employees, especially over matters that affect the entire unit. *See, e.g.*, *Medo Photo Supply Corp. v. NLRB*, 321 U.S. 678, 684 (1944) (finding Section 8(a)(5) violation for direct dealing). However, there are ways in which unionized employees can obtain more individualized terms and conditions of employment. In fact, in some industries—such as professional sports and entertainment—individual bargaining is the norm. The way in which this individualization is allowed is that the union's collective bargaining agreement permits it. *See Toledo Typographical Union No. 63 v. NLRB*, 907 F.2d 1220, 1222 (D.C. Cir. 1990) (stating that although "[a]n employer may deal directly with its employees ... if it ... obtains the consent of their union," it may not negotiate directly with an employee before bargaining with the union first). Typically, these agreements will set a minimum level of compensation and other terms for all represented employees but allow employees to negotiate better deals (sometimes through retained agents) as long as they do not violate any of the base guarantees.

B. "Good Faith" Bargaining Tactics

This section will explore the distinction between "good faith" and "bad faith" bargaining. In other words, if the parties are technically meeting and discussing issues with each other, is that enough? Or must they be more proactive in trying to reach an agreement?

The line between good faith and bad faith bargaining can be a blurry one. The next subsection reviews the difficulties presented by a party that is bargaining but remains hostile to or aggressive against the other party—usually through economic means. The following subsection will address what is referred to as "surface bargaining." Unlike the open hostility of economic pressure, surface bargaining may be better described as a lack of meaningful bargaining, in which a party goes through the motions of bargaining but has no genuine interest in reaching an agreement.

1. Economic Pressure

Although the NLRA's aim is to reduce industrial strife, it is not intended to eliminate strikes, lockouts, or other forms of economic pressure. Such tactics will always be a part of labor relations. Indeed, Section 13 of the NLRA expressly protects unions' right to engage in the most extreme form of economic pressure: the strike (discussed in more detail in Chapter 14). Therefore, the goal of the NLRA is merely to force parties into constructive negotiations that will hopefully reduce the need for economic pressure.

One example of the role economic pressure can play in negotiations occurred in *NLRB v. Insurance Agents' Union*, 361 U.S. 477 (1960). In *Insurance Agents*, a union was bargaining with an employer for a new collective bargaining agreement. During the negotiations, the union made good on a threat that, if a new agreement was not reached by the time the old one expired, the insurance agency employees would engage in tactics that included refusing to solicit new business, reporting late to work, engaging in "sit ins" at work, picketing outside company offices, and soliciting policyholder signatures on petitions to the company. The employer alleged that these tactics violated the union's duty to bargain in good faith under Section 8(b)(3), and the NLRB agreed, concluding that the tactics were a per se violation.

The Court disagreed with the NLRB and held that economic pressure during negotiations did not necessarily violate the duty to bargain in good faith. This is true even for permissible tactics that are not protected by Section 7, yet not prohibited by Section 8, as was the case in *Insurance Agents*. The Court acknowledged that at the heart of the duty to bargain is the requirement that a party make a good faith effort to reach an agreement. However, the Court also stressed that the NLRA was not intended to regulate how parties make such an effort. Rather, "Congress intended that the parties should have wide latitude in their negotiations, unrestricted by any governmental power to regulate the substantive solution of their differences." *Id.* at 488. In the Court's view, the NLRB was wrong to find that economic pressure during bargaining will always violate the duty to bargain in good faith. Certain types of economic pressure in certain situations might evidence a lack of a desire to reach an agreement—a topic that the next subsection will address—but economic pressure in general does not mean that a party is not bargaining in good faith. Indeed, economic pressure is "part and parcel of the system that the Wagner and Taft-Hartley Acts have recognized." *Id.* at 489. The Court found this to be especially true in *Insurance Agents*, where it viewed the union's tactics as an attempt to push the employer into reaching an agreement. That said, although the union's tactics did not violate Section 8(a)(5), they were not protected by Section 7. Thus, the employer could lawfully punish or terminate employees for engaging in such unprotected conduct.

As the Court recognized in *Insurance Agents*, although the NLRA permits economic pressure in general, parties can go too far. Chapter 17 discusses some examples of this possibility regarding specific statutorily prohibited union actions. However, the next subsection will address a different problem that occurs when a party acts like it is bargaining, but is not really doing so in good faith.

2. Surface Bargaining

As the Court held in *Insurance Agents*, the concept of good faith bargaining equates to a "mutual duty upon the parties to confer in good faith with a desire to reach agreement." Although parties sometimes make their lack of a desire to reach an agreement obvious, they are frequently well-versed enough in the law to know how to look like they are bargaining. Complicating matters is the fact that parties are allowed to engage in hard bargaining to reach what they view as a good outcome. It can therefore be challenging to determine when one party has moved from good faith, hard bargaining to unlawful, "surface bargaining."

The Supreme Court first recognized the concept of unlawful surface bargaining in *NLRB v. American National Insurance Co.*, 343 U.S. 395 (1952). In that case, a newly certified union met several times with the employer to negotiate a collective bargaining agreement. Among the sticking points was a union proposal to implement a grievance-arbitration system for resolving disputes. Although such systems are common, the employer rejected having unlimited arbitration and made a counter-proposal with a broad "management rights clause," which would have given the employer unilateral control over topics such as promotions, discipline, and work scheduling. The parties agreed on other topics, but the union repeatedly rejected the management rights clause. The employer responded by proposing an even broader clause, prompting the union to file a Section 8(a)(5) charge that the employer was violating its duty to bargain in good faith. Ultimately, however, the parties reached an agreement that included a slightly narrower management rights clause that exempted from arbitration topics such as discipline and work schedules.

The NLRB found that by insisting on a clause that would waive the union's right to bargain over "mandatory subjects of bargaining" (topics that parties must bargain about, which is discussed in the next chapter), the employer violated its duty to bargain in good faith. However, the Supreme Court disagreed, emphasizing that the NLRA does not compel parties either to agree to certain substantive terms or to reach an agreement at all. The Court also noted that management rights clauses are legal and, in fact, relatively common. Therefore, as long as the parties are bargaining in good faith, it is up to them to determine whether to allow the employer more or less flexibility in certain situations. Crucially, the determination of whether a party is engaged in good faith bargaining "is to be enforced by application of the ... standards of Section 8(d) to the facts of each case." *Id.* at 409. In subsequent cases, the NLRB established several factors to help it determine, on a case-by-case basis, whether a party is engaged in lawful, good-faith bargaining or unlawful, surface bargaining.

One example of the NLRB's approach is found in *NLRB v. A-1 King Size Sandwich*, 732 F.2d 872 (11th Cir. 1984), in which an employer virtually performed a how-to guide on surface bargaining. In some cases, such as the *Garden Ridge* decision discussed below, an employer violates its duty to bargain in good faith by meeting infrequently with the union, but that was not the case in *A-1 King Size*. Rather, the NLRB and court found surface bargaining based primarily on the substance of the employer's proposals.

In *A-1 King Size*, the employer insisted on language that gave it total control over wages, evaluations, promotions, discharge, discipline, layoffs, recalls, and other terms and conditions of work. It also proposed a no-strike clause that was so broad that it applied to ULP strikes and rejected the union's proposals for an anti-discrimination policy and dues checkoff, even though those provisions would not cost the employer anything of significance. Moreover, the employer proposed both a strong management rights clause that applied to any decision that the employer had controlled in the past, to subcontracting, and to the effects of any decision under its control. This clause was to be paired with a zipper clause, which stated that the union waives the right to bargain over any topics that are not part of the collective bargaining agreement.

The NLRB and court both agreed that the employer had engaged in surface bargaining. Of particular concern was the employer's insistence on controlling virtually all aspects of the workplace—eliminating the union's right to bargain in most cases—without offering the union or employees anything in return. Combining the management rights and zipper clauses was a related red flag because, together, those clauses dramatically narrow a union's ability to represent employees. In addition, the employer engaged in "regressive bargaining," which occurs when a party pulls back on its earlier proposals; this type of bargaining is likely to lead to a surface bargaining finding if there is not a good reason for the change. However, neither regressive bargaining, nor any particular proposal, guarantees a surface bargaining finding. Instead, the combination of all these proposals showed that the employer lacked a genuine interest in reaching an agreement with the union.

Garden Ridge Management, Inc., 347 N.L.R.B. 131 (2006), is a case in which a bad-faith bargaining finding was based on an employer's refusal to meet enough times with the union. The parties had 20 negotiating sessions over an 11-month period, during which they agreed to numerous provisions for a collective bargaining agreement. However, the employer rejected approximately eight requests by the union to meet more often, and the union subsequently lost majority support. The NLRB found that these repeated refusals, for which the employer offered no reasons, violated the employer's duty under Section 8(d) "to meet at reasonable times."

Although the NLRB found that the employer engaged in bad-faith bargaining, it rejected the argument that the employer engaged in surface bargaining, contrary to the views of a dissenting Board member and the ALJ. The argument for surface bargaining was based on the content and timing of the employer's proposals, the low number of bargaining sessions, the lack of progress on significant issues, and pre-negotiation statements by the employer that it would not give the union anything. The majority admitted that this was a close case but found that the employer did show a willingness to bargain by, for instance, making concessions to reach an agreement on a management rights clause. The majority also refused to assume that the employer's unwillingness to meet more often implied an unwillingness to reach an agreement.

One helpful aspect of *Garden Ridge* is the dissent's reiteration of some of the NLRB's surface bargaining factors. Quoting the NLRB decision in *Regency Service Carts, Inc.*, 345 N.L.R.B. 671, 671 (2005), the dissent noted that a non-exclusive list of surface bargaining factors includes:

> delaying tactics, the nature of the bargaining demands, unilateral changes in mandatory subjects of bargaining, efforts to bypass the union, failure to designate an agent with sufficient bargaining authority, withdrawal of already-agreed-upon provisions, and arbitrary scheduling of meetings. It has never been required that a respondent must have engaged in each of those enumerated activities before it can be concluded that bargaining has not been conducted in good faith.... [R]ather, a respondent will be found to have violated the Act when its conduct in its entirety reflects an intention on its part to avoid reaching an agreement.

347 N.L.R.B. at 135. The dissent in *Garden Ridge* believed that these factors, particularly the delaying tactics, evidenced "an intention on its part to avoid reaching an agreement." *Id.* But the case illustrates how NLRB members and courts can interpret the same set of facts differently.

C. The Duty to Provide Information

In addition to the general failures to bargain in good faith discussed above, parties can engage in more specific actions that can result in a Section 8(a)(5) violation. This section will address a party's failure to provide information to the other party during bargaining. Although there is no general duty to provide whatever information the other side requests, certain types of information are viewed as so important to the collective bargaining process that the duty to bargain in good faith includes giving the information to the other party. The following subsection examines the specific case of employers' claiming an inability to afford a union demand; the next subsection then examines the duty to provide information more generally.

1. Inability-to-Pay Claims

In a typical negotiation, the union seeks more compensation for employees, and the employer resists. Often, this resistance is based in part on the employer's claim that giving the union what it wants will create economic difficulties for the business. In response, the union will frequently ask for company financial data that might support or counter that claim. Not surprisingly, employers are loath to give out such information, not only because it might improve the union's bargaining position but also because of concerns about the information leaking to competitors.

In *NLRB v. Truitt Manufacturing Co.*, 351 U.S. 149 (1956), the Supreme Court held that, under certain circumstances, an employer has a duty to provide financial information to a union. The employer in *Truitt* rejected union demands for higher wages by saying that it could not afford to pay them. But the employer also denied the union's request for evidence to support that claim, including having an accountant look at the company's books. The NLRB found that, given the circumstances, the refusal violated Section 8(a)(5).

The employer argued that the information was not relevant to the bargaining process and was solely under its authority; it did not argue that providing the information would overly burden or injure the business, which is an exception to providing information that the Board has long recognized. The Court rejected the employer's position and held that it violated its duty to bargain in good faith. Noting that both parties treated the employer's ability to increase pay as highly relevant to negotiations, the Court held that a mechanical repetition of an inability to pay without support for that claim shows a lack of good faith bargaining. Yet, the Court also stressed that not every inability-to-pay claim will trigger a duty to provide information. Instead, the NLRB must consider the circumstances of each case to determine whether good faith bargaining was present.

In the years following *Truitt*, the NLRB modified its inability-to-pay analysis in the face of appellate courts' frequent insistence on a narrow application of the decision. As a result, the NLRB currently uses what amounts to a "magic words" test, under which the *Truitt* duty to provide information will only apply when an employer states that it is unable to pay for the union's demands during the life of the collective bargaining agreement. The NLRB explained this rule in *Nielsen Lithographing Co.*, 305 N.L.R.B. 697, 700 (1991), *enf'd sub nom. Graphic Communications Int'l Union, Local 508 O-K-I, AFL-CIO v. NLRB*, 977 F.2d 1168 (7th Cir. 1992):

> The employer who claims a present inability to pay, or a prospective inability to pay during the life of the contract being negotiated, is claiming essentially that it cannot pay. By contrast, the employer who claims only economic difficulties or business losses or the prospect of layoffs is simply saying that it does not want to pay.

In the latter scenario, when the employer is stating that it is only unwilling to pay, there is no duty to provide information because the employer is simply taking a bargaining position. In contrast, a specific claim of an inability to pay over the term of the contract implicates an objective barrier to an agreement that warrants more evidence.

2. The General Duty to Provide Information

Aside from the specific inability-to-pay duty under *Truitt*, the NLRB and courts have recognized a more general duty to provide information in certain circumstances. This duty arises from the fact that some information is relevant to a party's ability to engage in collective bargaining. Although the duty can apply to either party, it is most common in cases involving union information demands. This is because unions' ability to adequately represent employees will often depend on their access to company information. For example, if there are allegations that managers are discriminatorily applying sick leave policies against union supporters, a union would legitimately want access to relevant records.

When analyzing whether a party has a duty to provide information, the NLRB first determines whether the information is relevant to the union's ability to represent employees. The Supreme Court has described this question as a relatively low standard under which the union must show that "desired information was relevant, and that it would be of use to the union in carrying out its statutory duties and responsibilities." *NLRB v. Acme Indus. Co.*, 385 U.S. 432, 437 (1977). When the roles are switched, an employer must show that the information it has requested is needed to comply with its duties, or monitor the union's compliance, under a collective bargaining agreement. If the union (or employer) makes such a showing, the employer (or union) is presumed to have a duty to provide the information. However, a party can rebut that presumptive duty by showing "special circumstances" that outweigh the other party's need for the information.

An example of this analysis—especially the special circumstances exception—is *Detroit Edison Co. v. NLRB*, 440 U.S. 301 (1979). In that case, the union challenged the employer's use of aptitude tests for employees interested in filling certain open positions. The union filed grievances alleging that the tests violated the collective bargaining agreement's seniority provisions. After the grievances were denied, the union sought arbitration and requested from the employer the tests, as well as the applicants' answers and scores. The employer refused and supplied only validation studies of the test. Later, during the arbitration, the employer provided applicants' raw scores and sample questions, and it offered to supply the scores of any applicant who signed a waiver. The union declined the offer. The NLRB concluded that the employer's refusal to turn over the requested information violated Section 8(a)(5), although it ordered the union to keep the tests confidential. The Supreme Court reversed.

In *Detroit Edison*, there was no serious disagreement that the requested information was relevant to the union's grievance, although the employer insisted throughout the litigation that the union did not need applicants' test scores. Instead, the dispute centered on whether the employer had shown special circumstances to rebut its presumptive duty to provide the information. Among the employer's reasons was the time and expense of creating the tests, which could be leaked if the union had access to them, and the applicants' confidentiality. The Court stressed that the duty to provide information is based on the circumstances of a given case and, emphasizing the reasonableness of the employer's secrecy concerns, the Court held that the NLRB's attempt to protect the tests' confidentiality while ordering their disclosure was inadequate. In particular, the NLRB lacked effective means to enforce its order against the union, especially given the risk of inadvertent leaks. The Court also thought it relevant that the employer had, in good faith, promised applicants that their scores would remain confidential and that in previous situations, there had been harassment of employees with low scores that had been made public. Thus, the Court concluded that "[i]n light of the sensitive nature of testing information [and] the minimal burden that compliance with the Company's offer would have placed on the [u]nion," the employer did not have a duty to turn over the requested information for employees who did not waive their confidentiality. *Id.* at 319–20.

Other instances where confidential information might rebut the duty to provide information include the sick leave dispute mentioned earlier. In such a dispute, the employer might be justified in refusing to provide employees' sick leave requests that included medical information, but it could be required to fulfill those requests with that confidential information redacted. *See Norris, a Dover Resources Co. v. NLRB*, 417 F.3d 1161 (10th Cir. 2005) (holding that the employer unlawfully refused to provide sick leave slips with medical information redacted). Relatedly, suppose an initial request for information is too broad or creates some other legitimate problem. In that case, the party with the information must try to propose an alternative that would both provide the needed information and address the problems with the initial request. *See United States Testing Co. v. NLRB*, 160 F.3d 14, 21 (D.C. Cir. 1998).

Another issue that can arise in these cases is the cost of gathering information. In general, the NLRB will not consider the cost of providing information as a special circumstance justifying an employer's refusal. However, if the union makes a precise request that would create substantial costs, the NLRB requires the parties to bargain over who is responsible for the costs. *See Tower Books*, 273 N.L.R.B. 671 (1984), *enf'd sub nom. Queen Anne Record Sales, Inc. v. NLRB*, 772 F.2d 913 (9th Cir. 1985).

D. Impasse and the Duty to Bargain

Although one of the central tenets of the NLRA is the belief that good faith bargaining between employers and employees will lead to more agreements and less industrial strife, that is not always the result. Even when parties are bargaining in good faith, there are times when they cannot reach a final agreement. This reality, combined with the rule that the NLRB cannot force parties to enter into a collective bargaining agreement or agree to specific terms, means that there will be instances when negotiations are deadlocked or at an "impasse."

The occurrence of an impasse is a significant turning point in negotiations. Before that point, an employer is prohibited from changing mandatory terms of employment without reaching an agreement with the union. But once an impasse occurs, the rules change drastically and the employer, in most instances, will be able to unilaterally implement changes.

The seminal case on impasse is *NLRB v. Katz*, 369 U.S. 736 (1962), which involved an employer's implementation of changes without first negotiating with the recently elected union. While the parties were negotiating a collective bargaining agreement, the employer granted merit pay increases, announced a new sick leave policy, and implemented a new system of automatic pay raises—all without first discussing the changes with the union. The employer defended its unilateral changes to these mandatory subjects by arguing that the negotiations were at an impasse. The NLRB, however, found that the employer implemented those changes before any possible impasse could have occurred.

The Supreme Court upheld the NLRB's finding of a Section 8(a)(5) violation. First, the Court emphasized the general rule that unilateral changes in a mandatory subject of bargaining violate the requirement that the employer "meet ... and confer in good faith," even if the employer was not acting in bad faith. As the Court held, "[a] refusal to negotiate *in fact* as to any [mandatory subject], and about which the union seeks to negotiate, violates [Section] 8(a)(5) though the employer has every desire to reach agreement with the union upon an over-all collective agreement and earnestly and in all good faith bargains to that end." *Id.* at 743.

Because the employer in *Katz* acted unilaterally without first discussing the mandatory issues with the union, it committed a per se violation of Section 8(a)(5). The corollary to this rule is that if the employer and union have discussed the issue and the negotiations are truly at an impasse, the employer can usually take unilateral action. This is because post-impasse unilateral implementation not only allows the employer to make necessary changes once negotiations are at a standstill but also represents an economic weapon that may spur further negotiations. *See McClatchy Newspapers, Inc. v. NLRB*, 131 F.3d 1026, 1032 & n.4 (D.C. Cir. 1997)

When addressing a dispute involving an employer's unilateral action, the first step is to determine that the action involves a mandatory subject of bargaining (Chapter 12 discusses this question in depth). If it does, the next step is to examine whether an impasse exists. The NLRB determines impasse based on the circumstances of each case, but typically looks for factors showing that "good-faith negotiations have exhausted the prospects of concluding an agreement":

> The bargaining history, the good faith of the parties in negotiations, the length of the negotiations, the importance of the issue or issues as to which there is disagreement, the contemporaneous understanding of the parties as to the state of negotiations are all relevant factors to be considered in deciding whether an impasse in bargaining existed.

Taft Broadcasting Co., 163 N.L.R.B. 475, 478, (1967), *enf'd sub nom. American Federation of Television & Radio Artists, AFL-CIO, Kansas City Local v. NLRB*, 395 F.2d 622 (D.C. Cir. 1968).

Suppose the NLRB finds that an impasse exists. In that case, most unilateral employer actions are lawful. The Fifth Circuit, alone, permits an employer to implement a unilateral action even without an impasse, if the employer notifies the union that it intends to institute the change and gives the union the opportunity to respond. *See, e.g., NLRB v. Pinkston-Hollar Construction Services, Inc.*, 954 F.2d 306, 311–12 (5th Cir. 1992). Other circuits share the view of Judge Posner, who emphasized that the Fifth Circuit's "partial impasse" rule "would empty the duty to bargain of meaning" because "(1) by removing issues from the bargaining agenda early in the bargaining process, it would make it less likely for the parties to find common ground" and "(2) by enabling the employer to paint the union as impotent, it would embolden him to hold out for a deal so unfavorable to the union as to preclude agreement." *Duffy Tool & Stamping, L.L.C. v. NLRB*, 233 F.3d 995, 998 (7th Cir. 2000).

The next step involves determining whether an exception to the unilateral implementation rule exists. For instance, during an impasse, an employer cannot implement a change that is significantly worse than what it proposed to the union. *See Thryv, Inc. v. NLRB*, 102 F.4th 727, 733 (5th Cir. 2024) ("Once the employer declares an impasse, it does not violate the NLRA by making unilateral changes so long as the 'changes [it makes] are reasonably comprehended within [the employer's] pre-impasse proposals.'") (internal quotation omitted). The employer also cannot implement a change that is significantly better than an earlier proposal because, as the Court held in *Katz*, "such action is necessarily inconsistent with a sincere desire to conclude an agreement with the union." 369 U.S. at 745. On the other hand, an employer can implement a change that the parties have discussed and that the union has rejected. Accordingly, if an employer wants to reserve the right to make changes after impasse has occurred, it will make sure that it first proposes those changes to the union—often making what is called a "best and final offer" before declaring an impasse.

Finally, an employer faces a potential problem when it typically grants annual wage increases because a failure to implement the raise could be considered retaliatory while implementation of the raise could violate the duty to bargain. Much like the issue of promising or granting benefits during a union campaign, which was discussed in Chapter 7, an employer should strive to maintain the status quo. Accordingly, as the Court noted in *Katz*, if the raises are "automatic increases to which the employer has already committed himself" then it should grant them even if there is no impasse. *Id.* at 746. In contrast, if the raises "were in no sense automatic, but were informed by a large measure of discretion," then an employer cannot implement them before impasse. *Id.*

E. Good Faith Bargaining in the Public Sector

In the public sector, rules regarding the duty to bargain in good faith are often similar or identical to NLRA rules. Some important variations exist, however.

1. "Meet and Confer" Bargaining

One variation from the NLRA is that a few public-sector laws impose only a more limited duty to "meet and confer." This duty merely requires employers to meet with the union and listen to its proposals; there are no obligations to negotiate to agreement or impasse, and no procedures to resolve impasses. For example, the Missouri statute, V.A.M.S. § 105.520, provides:

> Whenever such proposals are presented by the exclusive bargaining representative to a public body, the public body or its designated representative or representatives shall meet, confer and discuss such proposals relative to salaries and other conditions of employment of the employees of the public body with the labor organization which is the exclusive bargaining representative of its employees in a unit appropriate. Upon

> the completion of discussions, the results shall be reduced to writing and be presented to the appropriate administrative, legislative or other governing body in the form of an ordinance, resolution, bill or other form required for adoption, modification or rejection.

In *Sumpter v. City of Moberly*, 645 S.W.2d 359, 363 (Mo. 1982), the court explained the obligation under this statute as follows: "The public employer is not required to agree but is required only to 'meet, confer and discuss.'... The act provides only a procedure for communication between the organization selected by public employees and their employer without requiring adoption of any agreement reached." *Sumpter* continued:

> The Law gives public employees the vehicle for petitioning their employer through a designated representative. When this representative submits proposals and grievances relative to salaries and other conditions of employment, the public body or its designated representative must acknowledge such proposals and grievances and must discuss them with the bargaining representative.... The public body must then give them its consideration in the form of an ordinance, resolution, bill or other form required for adoption, modification or rejection.

645 S.W.2d at 362; *see also City & Borough of Sitka v. Int'l B'hood of Elect. Workers, Local Union 1547*, 653 P.2d 332 (Alaska 1982) ("meet and confer" system for the city of Sitka).

This type of system is relatively uncommon today. Indeed, in 2012, the Missouri Supreme Court held that the Missouri state constitution contained a "good faith" bargaining requirement for the public sector. It further stated, however, that "good faith" would be defined by Missouri state law, not federal law. *American Federation of Teachers v. Ledbetter*, 387 S.W.3d 360, 367–68 (2012). But the term can cause confusion, as some public-sector statutes that use the term "meet and confer" actually require more traditional "collective bargaining" (e.g., California and Arizona, *see City of Phoenix v. Phoenix Relations Bd. ex rel. AFSCME Local 2384*, 699 P.2d 1323 (Ariz. App. 1985)). For example, in *Kansas Board of Regents v. Pittsburg State University Chapter of Kansas-National Education Association*, 233 Kan. 801, 804 (1983), the court described the Kansas Act, K.S.A. §§75-4321, *et seq.*, as "a hybrid containing some characteristics of pure 'meet and confer' acts with other characteristics of 'collective bargaining.' It imposes upon both employer and employee representatives the obligation to meet, confer and negotiate in good faith with affirmative willingness to resolve grievances and disputes, and to endeavor to reach agreement on conditions of employment."

Minnesota has a statute that requires public employers to "meet and confer" with their employees, who are defined as "professionals," on subjects that relate to employment but are outside the scope of mandatory bargaining. There is no duty under this statute to bargain in good faith to impasse. Minn. Stat. Ann. §§ 179.63, 179.65, 179.73.

2. Statutory Limits on Public-Sector Bargaining

Another public-sector variation from NLRA bargaining jurisprudence results from statutory limits on specific terms and conditions of work. For example, suppose a legislature sets limits on compensation for certain public employees during a certain period (e.g., capping raises in a given year). In that case, it is not a failure to bargain in good faith for an employer to refuse to negotiate on compensation beyond the statutory limits. *See Ass'n of Oregon Corrections Employees v. State of Oregon, Dept. of Corrections*, 164 P.3d 291 (Or. App. 2007).

Political action by employers can also raise bargaining in good faith issues unique to the public sector. For example, *City of Akron v. SERB*, 195 LRRM (BNA) 2582 (Oh. App. 2013), upheld the state labor board's finding that a city failed to bargain in good faith with its police union on the following facts. The city had refused to negotiate layoffs with the union. Instead, it argued that layoff policies could only be altered by amending the city's civil service rules. The city then stated it would only propose new civil service rules on layoffs if the union withdrew its proposal on this issue from the ongoing contract negotiations. The city then proposed amending the relevant civil service rules without giving any notice to the union. The Ohio labor board found that this violated the objective standard of good faith bargaining. The trial and appellate courts agreed with the labor board, using a "totality of the circumstances" approach. *See also Boling v. Public Employees Rel. Bd.*, 5 Cal. 5th 898 (2018). In *Boling*, San Diego's mayor sponsored a citizens' initiative to eliminate pensions for new municipal employees, then refused union demands to bargain over the measure. The labor agency held that San Diego had to bargain with the union before it could place this initiative on the ballot. An appellate court reversed, holding that the initiative was not officially from the employer; the mayor's support of the initiative could not be imputed to the city council. Reversing the appellate court, the California Supreme Court held that this matter had to be negotiated. The Court held that the appellate court had given insufficient deference to the state agency, and that it had read the statutory obligation to bargain too narrowly.

Lobbying the public during negotiations can also raise bargaining in good faith issues. *Compare Reno Police Protective Ass'n v. City of Reno*, Item No. 52 (Nev. LGE-MRB 1976) (employer placing a misleading newspaper advertisement concerning negotiations violates its duty to bargain in good faith), *with Inter-Lakes Educ. Ass'n/NEA-New Hampshire*, 1988–90 PBC ¶ 54,522 (NH PELRB Case No. T-0237, 1989) (no breach of the duty to bargain in good faith where employer placed advertisements publicizing its views about a fact-finder's report).

3. Parity Clauses

"Parity clauses," much more common in the public sector than in the private, also raise bargaining in good faith issues. A "parity" clause is a provision in a collective bargaining agreement that requires an employer to agree to the same terms with one union as it does with another. For example, a city agrees with a firefighters' union that salary increases for firefighters will be the same percentage as the city negotiates with its police union. These clauses help prevent competition among various types of employees and provide some predictability. But in some public-sector jurisdictions, labor boards and courts have found that such clauses may, or do, violate the duty to bargain in good faith. Such decisions reason that the union used as the parity comparison (e.g., the police union in the above example) is, or could be, unfairly burdened in its bargaining because the employer is aware that giving, say, a significant raise to the police union means that it must also give the same raise to the firefighters' union.

Using that rationale, *Local 1650, IAFF v. City of Augusta*, No. 04-14 (Maine Labor Relations Board Aug. 10, 2004), held that the city violated its duty to bargain in good faith with one union, Local 1650, because the city had entered into parity agreements with other unions that were based on the terms of Local 1650's contracts. Local 1650 was thus unfairly burdened in a manner that subverted the bargaining process. The decision concluded that "parity agreements are inherently destructive of collective bargaining rights and are therefore a per se violation of [the statute]." Other jurisdictions take a case-by-case approach with parity clauses. *See, e.g., Whatcom County Deputy Sheriff's*

Guild v. Whatcom County, Decision 8512-A (Wash. Pub. Emp. Rel. Comm. 2005) (parity clauses are not per se violations of the duty to bargain in good faith; rather, the charging party has the burden of proving that the parity clause(s) did in fact burden its negotiations); *TWU Local 106 & New York City Transit Auth.*, 39 NY PERB ¶ 3021 (2006) (parity agreements are illegal if they trespass on the negotiation rights of a union that is not a party to the agreement, but there was no illegal burden in case under review).

4. Privacy Rules and the Duty to Provide Information

Some public-sector jurisdictions have special privacy rules that can limit the type of information that unions have a right to obtain pursuant to the duty to bargain in good faith. Notably, in the federal sector, unions do not have a right to demand that employers provide the home addresses of bargaining unit members. In *Department of Defense v. FLRA*, 510 U.S. 487 (1994), the Supreme Court held that Section 552 of the Freedom of Information Act, 5 U.S.C. § 552a(b)(2), shielded this information.

Similarly, in *Michigan Federation of Teachers v. University of Michigan*, 481 Mich. 687 (2008), the Michigan Supreme Court, citing *Department of Defense v. FLRA*, held that the home addresses and telephone numbers of employees of a state university were not subject to disclosure under the Michigan Freedom of Information Act. Most public-sector jurisdictions, however, follow the private-sector rule in this area. *See, e.g.*, *Morris County v. Morris Council No. 6*, 30 NJPER 93 (N.J. Sup. Ct., App. Div. 2004) (under the New Jersey Employer-Employee Relations Act, employers must provide unions with requested information that is needed to fulfill unions' statutory obligation to represent bargaining unit members, including the type of information denied in *Department of Defense v. FLRA*); *California Sch. Emp. Ass'n v. Bakersfield City Sch. Dist.*, 22 PERC ¶ 29089 (Cal. PERB 1998) (school district violated its duty to bargain by refusing to provide union with an updated list of employee home addresses and phone numbers); *County of Los Angeles v. Los Angeles County Employee Relations Commission*, 301 P.3d 1102 (Cal. 2013) (rejecting a constitutional privacy defense to a union obtaining this type of data on the grounds that the union had a legitimate business need for it).

5. Impasse Procedures

Unlike the NLRA, many public-sector statutes bar or limit strikes and instead have specific alternative procedures to resolve impasses (e.g., mediation, fact-finding, and interest arbitration). Chapter 15 discusses this topic in detail, but for present purposes, these statutes create some important issues and variations in private-sector rules regarding the duty to bargain in good faith.

As Chapter 15 explains, in most jurisdictions, strikes by public employees are illegal. What does an illegal strike do to the duty to bargain in good faith? A Michigan case has held that employers have no duty to bargain during illegal strikes. *Melvindale-Northern Allen Park Fed. of Teachers Local 1051 v. Melvindale-Northern Allen Park Public Schools*, 9 MPER ¶ 27046 (Mich. Ct. App. 1996). A New York case has strongly implied the same. *In the Matter of Town of South Hampton v. New York State PERB*, 37 PERB ¶ 7001 (N.Y. Ct. App. 2004) ("[A]s long as an employee organization does not engage in an illegal strike, the duty to negotiate in good faith prohibits an employer from 'unilaterally alter[ing] existing mandatory subjects of negotiations.'").

Is an illegal strike a violation of the *union's* duty to bargain in good faith (if such a strike is not specifically a separate ULP)? *Teamsters State, County & Municipal Workers and Ann Arbor Public Schools*, 16 MPER ¶ 8 (Mich. Pub. Rel. Comm. 2003), held that it was not necessarily a per se violation, but it could be evidence of the union's failure to bargain in good faith.

Similarly, jurisdictions that allow some public employees to strike often require unions of such employees to engage in certain impasse resolution procedures before striking. It is usually a failure to bargain in good faith or another ULP to refuse to participate in these procedures. *See, e.g.*, Cal. Gov. Code §§ 3543.5(e), 3543.6(d). Also, striking before engaging in such procedures, in cases where there is not an independent ULP itself, may well amount to a failure to bargain in good faith. *See, e.g.*, *Fresno Unified School Dist. v. Fresno Teachers Ass'n*, CTA/NEA, 6 PERC ¶ 13110 (Cal. P.E.R.C. 1982)

Further, these alternative procedures to resolve impasses create interesting questions as to when an "impasse" exists, which allows an employer to unilaterally impose its final offer. Public-sector laws generally adopt the *Katz* rule from the private sector, permitting such actions. *See, e.g.*, *Detroit Transp. Corp. & Teamsters Local 214*, 20 MPER ¶ 112 (Mich. Emp. Rel. Comm. 2007); *Union of American Physicians & Dentists v. State of California*, 30 PERC ¶ 142 (Cal. PERB ALJ 2006); *Rockford Educ. Ass'n & Rockford School Dist. 205*, 21 PERI ¶ 179 (Ill. ELRB ALJ 2005).

In jurisdictions where the parties are required to go through impasse resolution procedures, when may an employer unilaterally impose its final offers? In *Moreno Valley Unified School District v. Public Employment Relations Board*, 142 Cal. App. 3d 191 (Cal. App. 1983), the court held that it was a *per se* violation of the duty to bargain in good faith for an employer to unilaterally impose its final offer before the statutory impasse resolution procedures had been completed. (In this case, the employer imposed its offers during a mandatory mediation process.) This approach, which is typical in the public sector, means that where the law mandates impasse procedures, which ultimately set contract terms (by ending in mandatory binding interest arbitration, common in the public sector), the employer may never be allowed to implement its final offer unilaterally. That is because the union and employer are obliged to use impasse resolution procedures until use of those procedures resolves the impasse. *See, e.g., Green County*, 7 NPER 51-16028, Dec. No. 20308-B (Wisc. Emp. Rel. Comm., 1984).

However, not all public-sector employees are governed by rules that require impasse procedures that are both mandatory and binding. Again, some employees may legally strike, and others have impasse procedures that are minimal, not binding, and/or not mandatory. In Alaska alone, employees are divided into three classes. "Class I" employees may never strike. "Class II" employees have a limited right to strike: after an impasse, they must submit to mediation, but if mediation fails, they may strike as long as the strike does not endanger the public's health, safety, or welfare. "Class III" employees may legally strike after an impasse in negotiations, without such limitations. *See Alaska Public Emp. Ass'n v. State of Alaska*, 776 P.2d 1030, 1030 (Alaska 1989). The Alaska Supreme Court has held that "[f]or Class II employees, an impasse is reached when the parties have reached a good faith impasse, and the mediation process has been exhausted. For Class III employees, an impasse is reached when negotiations are deadlocked." *Id.* at 1033.

Pennsylvania uses an interesting variation on the *Katz* rule. For employees who are allowed to strike, even if the parties are at impasse, the employer cannot implement unilaterally so long as the union does not strike. *See Philadelphia Housing Auth. v. Penn. Labor Rel. Bd.*, 620 A.2d 594 (PA 1993). This approach does not seem to apply, however, to public employees in Pennsylvania who have no right to strike. *See Central Dauphin Educ. Ass'n v. Central Dauphin Sch. Dist.*, 792 A.2d 691 (Pa. Cmmw. 2001).

Also, as noted in the previous section, the *Katz* rule requires employers to maintain the status quo until agreement or impasse. But jurisdictions are split as to exactly what sort of status quo the employer must maintain before then. This is often a critical issue in the public sector because many, and possibly most, public-sector contracts have some provision for "step increases," and also because negotiating contracts in the public sector often takes a considerable amount of time. So, for example, in the period after one contract has expired and before the next has been completed, is the employer obligated to continue to pay step increases as described in the expired contract?

There are two approaches in the public sector: the "dynamic status quo" model and the "static status quo" model. The majority approach in the public sector is to use the dynamic status quo, which is also the approach used under the NLRA. Under the dynamic status quo, the employer must "pay wages according to the wage plan of the expired agreement, including any scheduled step increases." *See* Steven Scott, *The Status Quo Doctrine: An Application to Salary Step Increases for Teachers*, Note, 83 CORNELL L. REV. 194, 216 (1997); *see also Bd. of Trustees of the University of Maine System v. Associated Colt Staff*, 659 A.2d 842, 847 & n. 1 (1995).

A minority of jurisdictions use the static status quo. The static status quo rule requires or at least permits public employers to pay only the wages specified and in effect when the contract expired, unless the contract provides otherwise. For cases using this rule, *see, e.g.*, *Pennsylvania State Park Officers Ass'n v. Pennsylvania Labor Rel. Bd.*, 854 A.2d 674 (Pa. Commw. 2004), and *Bd. of Trustees of the University of Maine System*, *supra*. New Jersey is atypical in that it uses the dynamic status quo rule for most public employees, but the static status quo rule for teachers. *See In re County of Atlantic and PBA Local 243*, 445 N.J. Super. 1 (N.J. App. 2016), *aff'd*, 230 N.J. 237 (2017).

Finally, the alternative impasse procedures in the public sector raise an interesting issue regarding mid-term bargaining (which is discussed, with regard to the private sector, in the next chapter). Are the parties obliged, or even allowed, to use the full range of such procedures—mediation, fact-finding, and/or interest arbitration—when engaged in mid-term bargaining? The majority approach is that they must use such statutory procedures. *See, e.g.*, *Teamsters Local 764 v. Snyder County*, 36 PPER ¶ 96 (Penn. Lab. Rel. Bd. 2005) (stressing that these procedures are the quid pro quo for the bar on strikes). On the other hand, *SERB v. Toledo District Board of Education*, 18 OPER ¶ 1645 (Ohio SERB 2001), held that statutory impasse procedures under the Ohio statute are not required in mid-term bargaining; rather, the parties should specify the procedures they wished to use in their contracts.

Absent such contractual specification, the employer may implement its last best offer at impasse.

For a while, it was unclear whether mid-term bargaining was even permitted in the federal sector. But in *National Federation of Federal Employees v. Department of Interior*, 526 U.S. 86 (1999), the Supreme Court held that the federal sector labor statute, 5 U.S.C. §§7101, *et seq*., delegated to the Federal Labor Relations Authority (FLRA) the power to decide this issue. The FLRA then held that "agencies are obligated to bargain during the term of a collective bargaining agreement on negotiable union proposals concerning matters that are not 'contained in or covered by' the term agreement, unless the union has waived its right to bargain about the subject matter involved." *U.S. Dept. of the Interior & U.S. Geological Survey, Reston, VA*, 56 F.L.R.A. 45, 50 (2000). Then in 2020, the FLRA held both that the federal-sector statute did not require mid-term bargaining, but proposals for mid-term bargaining were mandatory subjects of negotiation. *United States Office of Personnel Management*, 71 F.L.R.A. 977 (2020).

CHECKPOINTS

- Under Section 8(d), as enforced by Section 8(a)(5) and 8(b)(3), parties have a "mutual obligation ... to meet at reasonable times and confer in good faith with respect to wages, hours, and other terms and conditions of employment."
- Duly selected unions are the exclusive bargaining representative of a unit of employees.
- Employers violate Section 8(a)(5) if they engage in "direct dealing" with employees who are represented by a union.
- Economic pressure and hard bargaining are generally lawful bargaining tactics, as long as the parties act with a good-faith desire to reach an agreement. Bargaining without a good-faith desire to reach an agreement is called "surface bargaining" and violates Section 8(a)(5).
- The NLRB looks to many factors to determine surface bargaining, including—but not limited to—delaying tactics, the substance of the demands, unilateral changes in mandatory subjects, and regressive bargaining.

- The NLRB will not require parties to enter into an agreement or agree to any given substantive position.
- An employer that claims an inability to pay a union's demands during the life of a contract under negotiation has a Section 8(a)(5) duty to provide financial information supporting that claim, if requested.
- There is a presumptive Section 8(a)(5) duty for an employer to provide information that is relevant to a union's duties and responsibilities to employees.
- There is also a presumptive Section 8(b)(3) duty for a union to provide information that is relevant to an employer's compliance with, or monitoring of a union's compliance with, duties under a collective bargaining agreement.
- Parties can rebut the presumptive duty to provide information by showing special circumstances, such as confidentiality concerns.
- Generally, an employer violates Section 8(a)(5) by making unilateral changes to mandatory terms and conditions of employment.
- Employers can make unilateral changes to mandatory terms if the parties are at an impasse and the change is not substantially better or worse than what the employer offered the union in negotiations.
- To determine whether an impasse existed, the NLRB looks at all the circumstances, including the bargaining history, the parties' good faith during negotiations, the length of the negotiations, the importance of issues that the parties disagree over, and the parties' understanding of the state of negotiations.
- Some public-sector laws do not require the parties to bargain in good faith, but rather only to "meet and confer."
- If a relevant legislative body passes a law restricting what otherwise would have been a mandatory topic of bargaining, the parties will not have a duty to bargain in good faith over the topic.
- "Parity clauses," in which terms reached with one union are incorporated into contracts between the same employer and other unions, are legal in some public-sector jurisdictions; in other jurisdictions, however, they will always or sometimes violate the duty to bargain in good faith.

- Some public-sector jurisdictions limit the type of requested information that employers are required to give to unions, particularly the home addresses of bargaining unit employees.
- In jurisdictions that prohibit strikes, an illegal strike may be, but is not always, considered a failure to bargain in good faith. Similarly, employers likely have no duty to bargain in good faith during an illegal strike.
- Refusing to participate in mandatory impasse resolution procedures is generally considered a failure to bargain in good faith.
- In jurisdictions that use mandatory, binding procedures to resolve impasses, employers may not ever be able to implement their final proposals as *Katz* allows under the NLRA.
- Most public-sector jurisdictions use the NLRA "dynamic status quo" rule, under which the employer must pay wages according to the plan of an expired contract, including any scheduled step increases.
- A minority of public-sector jurisdictions use the "static status quo" rule, under which employers need only pay the wages specified in an expired contract in the period before a new contract is agreed to (e.g., employers need not pay step increases under the old contract).
- Most public-sector jurisdictions require the parties to use statutory impasse procedures for mid-term bargaining, but not all jurisdictions follow that approach.

CHAPTER 12

The Duty to Bargain in the Private Sector: Subjects of Bargaining

ROADMAP

- The scope of the duty to bargain in good faith: subjects of bargaining
- The nature of the bargaining duty under Sections 8(d) and 9(a)
- Mandatory subjects of bargaining and management rights clauses
- Distinctions between mandatory and permissive subjects of bargaining
- Bargaining over subcontracting, partial closures, and runaway shops
- Distinctions between decision bargaining and effects bargaining
- Bargaining over the rights of retired workers under *Pittsburgh Plate Glass*
- Section 8(d) bargaining procedures and the duty to bargain during strikes
- The scope of bargaining remedies under *H.K. Porter* and *Thryv*

A. The Scope of Bargaining in the Private Sector

As discussed in the previous chapter, the duty to bargain in both the private and public sectors includes the qualitative manner in which the employer and the union must bargain in good faith, consistent with their obligations under the NLRA or parallel state public sector collective-bargaining laws. Additionally, the duty to bargain in good faith in the private and public sectors also includes a quantitative component concerning the scope of bargaining. In other words, what topics must be included as subjects of bargaining that the parties must discuss, may discuss, or may not discuss at all? This Chapter focuses on the scope of bargaining consistent with the employer's duty outlined in Section 8(a)(5) and the union's duty to bargain outlined in Section 8(b)(3). The next chapter will consider the same issues in the public sector.

As an initial matter, Section 8(a)(5) for employers and Section 8(b)(3) for unions establish that it is an unfair labor practice (ULP) for either party to refuse to bargain collectively with the other. In turn, Section 8(d), added by the Taft-Hartley Amendments of 1947, provides: "[T]o bargain collectively is the performance of the mutual obligation of the employer and the representatives of the employees to meet at reasonable times and confer in good faith with respect to wages, hours, and other terms and condition of employment." Additionally, Section 9(a) states that unions "are the exclusive representative of all employees ... for the purposes of collective bargaining in respect to rates of pay, wages, hours of employment, or other conditions of employment." Thus, the duty to bargain typically extends to the subjects listed in Sections 8(d) and 9(a), and it is a ULP for either the employer or union to refuse to bargain about these "mandatory" subjects—unless an exception applies, such as the "core of entrepreneurial control" issue discussed later in this Chapter. As to potential subjects of bargaining that fall outside the statutory language, there is no mandatory duty to bargain, and such topics are either considered permissive or illegal. Permissive subjects of bargaining may be bargained over, and the parties are allowed to enter enforceable contract clauses over permissive issues. However, the parties do not have to bargain over or enter into agreements if they do not want. Illegal subjects of bargaining are not negotiable, even if the parties agree—any resulting agreement is void. As discussed further below, insisting upon bargaining over permissive subjects is a per se violation of Section 8(a)(5) or 8(b)(3).

1. Duty to Bargain over Mandatory Subjects of Bargaining and Management Rights Clauses

The Supreme Court case of *NLRB v. American National Insurance Co.*, 343 U.S. 395 (1952), provides some insight into the scope of the duty to bargain over mandatory subjects of bargaining. In that case, as described in the prior chapter's discussion of surface bargaining, the union proposed an unlimited arbitration clause, while the employer's counter-proposal contained a management rights clause that excluded some decisions the employer felt were strictly for management and should be free from arbitration. The parties were unable to come to an agreement, and the union filed a Section 8(a)(5) charge, arguing that the employer's demand amounted to an insistence that it not have to discuss mandatory subjects of bargaining with the union.

Although the Board found that the employer's insistence on the management rights clause was a per se violation of 8(a)(5) because it manifested bad faith, the Supreme Court refused to enforce the Board's order. The Court pointed to the fact that Congress added 8(d) through the Taft-Hartley Amendments to promote industrial peace through *voluntary* agreements. Section 8(d), according to the Court, was not meant to allow the Board to compel agreements between the parties, but only to require that the parties bargain in a good-faith attempt to reach agreement. The Court concluded that bargaining for management rights clauses is empirically a common collective-bargaining practice. Therefore, whether such a clause should be included in an agreement is left for negotiations at the bargaining table between parties and not to be decided by the Board. Under this reasoning, the Court found that the employer bargained in good faith and that there was no ULP. In dissent, Justice Minton expressed the view that the employer's demand essentially forced the union to agree to the management rights clause to make the employer bargain over other working conditions. By doing so, the union was forced to give up bargaining over mandatory subjects that it had the right to bargain over.

American National Insurance also appears to stand for the proposition that an important distinction exists between not engaging in the bargaining process at all and engaging in the process but standing firm on one's proposal. The idea is that by bringing the parties to the bargaining table, even when one side does not believe that it could accept any changes proposed by the other side, the possibility for some negotiated settlement at least still exists. Further, as we shall see when we discuss the use of economic weapons in Chapters 14 and

15, if a compromise on the contested issues is not possible, then parties can use economic weapons like strikes, lockouts, pickets, and boycotts to break the negotiating stalemate.

Finally, the Supreme Court seems to have made a fateful choice on how to interpret the obligation to bargain in good faith on mandatory subjects of bargaining going forward after *American National Insurance*. Then, there were at least two ways Section 8(a)(5) could have been interpreted in this context: (1) an employer must bargain with respect to each Section 8(d) and 9(a) subject, and a refusal to discuss a covered subject is a ULP; or (2) an employer who insists upon unilateral control of any condition of employment under the statutory language is not guilty of a ULP as long as the employer can back its position with legitimate arguments and engages in good faith negotiations. *American National Insurance* adopted the second approach, drawing the line between the area of exclusive management rights on the one side and the sphere of joint management-union responsibility on the other.

B. The Distinction between Mandatory and Permissible Subjects of Bargaining

Sometimes it is not apparent whether the subject of bargaining falls within the NLRA's mandatory bargaining language. Whether the bargaining subject is mandatory or not has many potential consequences, including whether those topics must be discussed at the bargaining table and, perhaps more importantly, whether a party can insist that a topic be discussed under threat of economic pressure or holding up discussion of other topics.

The case of *NLRB v. Wooster Division of Borg-Warner Corp.*, 356 U.S. 342 (1958), divides the universe of subjects of bargaining into three categories: (1) mandatory; (2) permissive; and (3) illegal. To be clear, these distinctions are not in the NLRA but were created by the courts. The issue in *Borg-Warner* was whether specific contract clauses should be considered mandatory bargaining subjects under Section 8(d). The employer insisted on a "ballot" clause and a "recognition" clause. The "ballot" clause would have required a pre-strike secret vote of employees on the employer's last collective bargaining agreement offer. The "recognition" clause would have recognized only the local affiliate union, without recognizing the international union that, unlike the local union, was the certified bargaining representative.

The Board found that the employer violated Section 8(a)(5) by insisting on bargaining to impasse over both clauses. The court of appeals enforced the Board's order as to the "recognition" clause, but it reversed the Board on the "ballot" clause. For its part, the Supreme Court found that neither clause fell within the scope of Section 8(d), and therefore, the clauses were not mandatory subjects of bargaining. First, the Court held that the "ballot" clause was not a mandatory subject of bargaining because it related only to procedures among the employees themselves before the union could call a strike, as opposed to procedures that involve the joint employer-employee relationship. In other words, the "ballot" clause settled no "terms or conditions of employment," but merely provided for an advisory vote. (Justice Harlan dissented, finding that the clause did affect the employer-union relationship because it impacted the union's ability to go on strike.) Second, the Court held that the "recognition" clause was also not a mandatory subject of bargaining because it contravened a statutory provision. The NLRA requires the employer to bargain with a certified representative, which was the international union in this case. The fact that the Act did not permit such a clause led Justice Harlan to concur with this point and find the "recognition" clause to be an illegal subject of bargaining (i.e., one that even if the parties agreed to bargain over, they could not).

Moreover, because neither of these clauses were found to be mandatory subjects of bargaining under the statute, the employer could not insist on bargaining over these clauses before agreeing to a contract. To so insist amounted to a per se violation of the duty to bargain in good faith under Section 8(a)(5). Justice Harlan, commenting on the "ballot" clause, differed from the majority because he disagreed with the concept that a party could propose a term as a permissive subject of bargaining, yet could not insist upon its inclusion in the collective bargaining agreement. He said that this dynamic resulted in a watered-down notion of bargaining.

The result following *Borg-Warner* is that a party's insistence on a permissive subject of bargaining amounts to the same thing as an overall refusal to bargain. The *Borg-Warner* Court stressed that insistence on permissive topics is dilatory and detracts from bargaining over mandatory issues. However, others have argued that this approach ignores the importance of the typical "give-and-take" involved in negotiations that helps the parties to agree on a variety of topics. By unilaterally allowing one party to remove subjects from bargaining, through a refusal to bargain over permissive subjects, the argument goes that the Court has frustrated the overall purpose of getting the parties to negotiate through their disagreements. Of course, a sophisticated attorney negotiating for their client may be able to get around this obstacle by attempting to include a permissive topic of bargaining through other means. For instance, a party could insist on very favorable terms on mandatory subjects, while at the same time signaling that they may be willing to reduce these demands if the other party agrees to discuss and consent to the desired permissive terms. In any event, the consensus view now is that insisting on a permissive subject of bargaining is a per se violation of Section 8(a)(5) or 8(b)(3). *See Borg-Warner*, 356 U.S. at 349.

The distinction between mandatory and permissive subjects of bargaining also affects other essential matters in the bargaining relationship. Four such issues discussed in this Chapter and elsewhere include: (1) Whether a party must bargain in good faith if requested; (2) Whether a party must disclose pertinent information; (3) Whether a party may take unilateral action only after bargaining to impasse; and (4) Whether a party may use economic force as a means of insisting on a topic. If the topic at issue is a mandatory subject of bargaining, the answer to all these questions is "yes."

C. Recurring Scope of Bargaining Issues

1. Bargaining over Subcontracting

A question that frequently arises is whether an employer may subcontract work that was at one time done by a union's bargaining unit members without first bargaining over the decision to subcontract with the union. The Supreme Court addressed this issue in *Fibreboard Paper Products Corp. v. NLRB*, 379 U.S. 203 (1964). In that case, the company had a contract with a union that represented maintenance employees. Shortly before the collective bargaining agreement expired, the union approached the company to negotiate a new contract, but the company first delayed, then refused to bargain, because it had decided to subcontract the maintenance work to a third party. The union filed charges with the Board, which found that the company had violated Section 8(a)(5) and ordered reinstatement and backpay. The court of appeals enforced the Board's order.

The Supreme Court affirmed the appellate court's enforcement of the Board's order, finding that contracting out work previously performed by bargaining unit employees is a mandatory subject of bargaining. The Court reasoned that contracting out work was of immediate concern to both parties and it was amenable to being successfully resolved through collective bargaining without intruding on the employer's freedom to manage the business. The Court, however, limited the holding to the facts of the case by stating that, "the type of 'contracting out' involved in this case—the replacement of employees in the existing bargaining unit with those of an independent contractor to do the same work under similar conditions of employment—is a statutory subject of collective bargaining." *Id.* at 215. Thus, if the employer is merely substituting one group of employees for another group of employees through the subcontracting arrangement, it is treated like a termination decision, which directly impacts a term and condition of employment and must be mandatorily bargained under Sections 8(d) and 9(a).

Justice Stewart concurred in the decision, but he made some critical observations, which the Supreme Court would later adopt in *First National Maintenance.* Specifically, Justice Stewart narrowed the scope of Section 8(d) by seeking to clarify that the Court's holding was not meant to encroach into areas that are considered exclusively within management's prerogative (think of the subject of bargaining continuum above). Based on the notion that Section 8(d) was added by the Taft-Hartley Amendments to limit the areas subject to the mandatory duty of collective bargaining, Justice Stewart developed three categories of managerial decisions:

(1) Decisions that have a *direct impact on employment*, such as hours of work, layoffs, discharges, retirement and seniority, *which have little to no entrepreneurial implications* and are therefore mandatory subjects of bargaining;

(2) Decisions having an impact on job security that are "*extremely indirect and uncertain*," such as advertising expenditures, product design, manner of financing, and sales programs and are therefore permissive subjects of bargaining; and

(3) Decisions that directly "*imperil job security*" of the employees or "terminate employment entirely," *but* because they "*lie at the core of entrepreneurial control*" are permissive subjects of bargaining. Examples include investing in labor-saving machinery, changing product lines, or going out of business (much like the employer in the Section 8(a)(3) *Darlington* case in Chapter 9).

Justice Stewart concurred in *Fibreboard* because he concluded that this type of subcontracting involved a mandatory subject of bargaining under category one. This was because the nature of the subcontract made it no different than a layoff or discharge that had a direct impact on employment, and "[t]his kind of subcontracting falls short of such larger entrepreneurial questions as what shall be produced, how capital shall be invested in fixed assets, or what the basic scope of the enterprise shall be." *Fibreboard*, 379 U.S. at 225 (Stewart, J., concurring). Note, however, that this does not mean that a subcontract will always be a mandatory subject of bargaining. Rather, a subcontract will be mandatory where it is tantamount to replacing an existing group of union employees with a group of nonunion employees to do essentially the same job. If the subcontract is entered into because a different product is being produced and differently skilled employees are needed, then this would be a permissive subject of bargaining under category three, because it lies at the core of entrepreneurial control.

While subcontracting is usually a mandatory subject of bargaining, the union may waive its statutory right to bargain over the issue by negotiating it away in the collective bargaining agreement, usually through agreeing to a management rights clause that states that management has the unilateral right (or something close to it) to subcontract bargaining unit work. Another form of waiver involves the employer's past practice, sometimes called the "safe-harbor exception." In *Westinghouse Electric Corp.*, 150 N.L.R.B. 1574 (1965), the Board reviewed several factors to determine whether this exception applied. One factor was whether the employer followed the status quo in subcontracting work. Another factor was whether the union had an opportunity to bargain over the practice.

Finally, one more way to understand the mandatory-permissive subject of bargaining issue is by considering a continuum between subjects that concern the internal affairs of the union on one side, and subjects that involve managerial prerogative on the other side. On either side of this spectrum, the subject is a permissive one because it is within the discretion of either the union or the employer. Those topics in the center of the continuum involve terms and conditions of employment that are suitable for joint management-employee negotiations and are, therefore, mandatory subjects of bargaining.

Subjects of Bargaining Continuum

←	↔	→
Internal Union Affairs Permissive	Joint Management-Employee Issue Mandatory	Management Prerogative Permissive

Examples of subjects that courts or the Board have concluded were permissive or illegal include: (1) the determination of the appropriate bargaining unit (illegal to bargain over because Board has this power under Section 9(c)); and (2) the formation of an industry promotion fund that related primarily to the employer's relationship with other employers (permissive because within the realm of managerial prerogative). On the other hand, in *Ford Motor Co. (Chicago Stamping Plant) v. NLRB*, 441 U.S. 488 (1979), the Supreme Court held that in-plant food and beverage services are a mandatory subject of bargaining because they were a "condition of employment" and "germane to the working environment." Similarly, in *Johnson-Bateman Co. v. International Association of Machinists*, 295 N.L.R.B. 180 (1989), the Board found that a provision that required drug and alcohol tests any time an employee was injured and required treatment was a mandatory subject of bargaining because it was "germane to the working environment" and a "condition of employment." In particular, the Board stressed that the testing could result in disciplinary action against an employee.

2. Bargaining over Partial Closings

In addition to subcontracting, duty to bargain disputes also concern whether employers must bargain over partial plant closings. In *First National Maintenance Corp. v. NLRB*, 452 U.S. 666 (1981), the employer was a contractor that performed cleaning and maintenance services for commercial customers in New York City. The employer terminated a contract with a nursing home because the fee paid to the employer was too low. While the employer and the nursing home were discussing the fee issue, the union won a representation election and became the bargaining agent of the employees who worked for the employer at the nursing home. Despite the union's victory, the employer unilaterally terminated its contract with the nursing home without ever bargaining with the union, maintaining that the fee paid by the nursing home was not worth continuing the contract. The Board found that the employer violated its duty to bargain over both *the decision* to partially close its operations (decisional bargaining) and *the effect* of the partial closing on the employees (effects bargaining).

The Supreme Court reversed the Board on the question whether it was necessary to bargain over the decision to close its operations at the nursing home but affirmed the Board's finding that the employer had the duty to bargain over the effects of the partial closing on the employees. Although the

Court found that the union had the right to participate in the decision to cease operations at the nursing home to protect the job security of its members by offering concessions and other information to the employer, the Court believed that this right could be protected adequately in two ways: (1) Section 8(a)(3) discrimination rules (remember that under *Darlington Manufacturing*, an employer is prohibited in some cases from partially closing the business based on anti-union motive), and (2) the union's right to effects bargain. As to effects bargaining, the record in *First National Maintenance* indicated that the employer did in fact bargain with the union over the effect of the closing, and the parties reached an agreement on severance pay for those employees.

A significant aspect of the decision is that the majority in *First National Maintenance* adopted, with slight modification, Justice Stewart's analytical approach in his *Fibreboard* concurrence. Under this framework, the Court found that this case fell within the third category of management decisions that directly imperil job security of the employees but, because they "lie at the core of entrepreneurial control," are permissive subjects of bargaining. The modification to the Stewart *Fibreboard* approach took the form of a new balancing test to discern when entrepreneurial decisions are mandatory—as opposed to permissive—subjects of bargaining. The Court stated that, "bargaining over management decisions that have a substantial impact on the continued availability of employment should be required only if the benefit, for labor-management relations and the collective bargaining process, outweigh the burden placed on the conduct of the business." *Id.* at 679. This test appears to favor management sovereignty, as an employer's ability to make decisions without having to bargain with the union seems to win out in close cases. This is curious because the NLRA says very little about the interests of management and is focused on the interests of employees under Section 7.

3. Bargaining over Runaway Shops/Plant Relocations

Along with subcontracting and partial closing, there is also an issue whether an employer must bargain over a "runaway shop" decision (i.e., an employer who relocates to avoid bargaining with a union). In *United Food & Commercial Workers, Local 150-A v. NLRB (Dubuque Packing Co.)*, 1 F.3d 24 (D.C. Cir. 1993), the court considered whether the relocation of a plant constituted a mandatory subject of bargaining. Another way of characterizing this issue is whether a plant relocation is more like the subcontracting in

Fibreboard (and therefore a mandatory subject of bargaining) or more like the partial closing in *First National Maintenance* (and thus a permissive subject of bargaining). The Board concluded that the plant relocation was more like *Fibreboard* because the runaway shop scenario similarly involved the replacement of union workers with nonunion workers who were performing basically the same work. In so finding, the Board held that the decision to relocate did not fall entirely within managerial prerogative because the union had the ability to make concessions that could have lessened labor costs and perhaps convinced the employer not to relocate.

In *Dubuque Packing*, the D.C. Circuit affirmed and approved the Board's new test for these plant relocation scenarios. Under this test, the burden is placed initially on the General Counsel (prosecuting the Section 8(a)(5) complaint) to establish that the employer's decision involved a relocation of unit work unaccompanied by a basic change in the nature of the employer's operation. If the General Counsel successfully carries this prima facie burden, there is a presumption that the relocation decision is a mandatory subject of bargaining. However, the employer can rebut this presumption by establishing that: (1) the work performed at the new location varied significantly from the work performed at the former plant, (2) the work performed at the former plant was to be discontinued entirely and not moved to the new location, or (3) the employer's decision involved a change in the scope and direction of the enterprise. In the alternative, the employer can prove an affirmative defense by showing that: (1) it did not consider labor costs, including indirect, as a factor in the decision, or (2) even if the employer considered labor costs as a factor in the decision, the union could not have offered concessions that could have changed the employer's decision to relocate.

The purpose of this test is both to heed the employer's entrepreneurial control concerns and to preserve a place for the collective-bargaining process to work. The key question is whether the dispute is amenable to being resolved through the collective-bargaining process. If the union can grant concessions that would allow the employer not to relocate, then the bargaining process should be given a chance to work. In such situations, it is mandatory that the employer bargain over its decision to relocate with the union.

Not all federal circuit courts have adopted the *Dubuque Packing* test. The Fourth Circuit, for instance, in *Dorsey Trailers, Inc. v. NLRB*, 233 F.3d 831 (4th Cir. 2000), found that an employer that closed one of its facilities and moved the work to another nonunion facility was not required to bargain with the union. The court's rationale was that the relocation involved a decision about the withdrawal and location of capital resources, a decision that the court felt lay at the core of entrepreneurial control (i.e., a category three case). The *Dorsey* court went even further, stating that it did not believe that a plant relocation could be based on factors wholly separate from labor costs.

D. Scope of Bargaining Issues for Retirees

One of the common mandatory subjects of bargaining under the NLRA's scheme is retirement benefits, including pensions and retiree health benefits. There is no dispute that unions must engage in mandatory bargaining with employers over these benefits on behalf of active employees because they fall under the statutory language of the Act. However, there are questions surrounding the union's obligation to bargain on behalf of former employees who are now retired.

In *Allied Chemical & Alkali Workers v. Pittsburgh Plate Glass Co.*, 404 U.S. 157 (1971), the Supreme Court considered several issues surrounding the union's continuing obligation to bargain on behalf of retired workers who are no longer members of the bargaining unit. The more specific issue was whether an employer's mid-term (i.e., during the term of the existing collective bargaining agreement) unilateral modification of retired employees' benefits constituted a ULP because there had been no bargaining over the modification. Such a mid-term modification without bargaining over mandatory topics would have been a ULP if active employees' pension and insurance benefits were at issue. But the Court held that retirees were not statutory employees under Section 2(3) of the Act and, therefore, were not part of the certified bargaining unit. As a result, the employer had no obligation to bargain with the union over the mid-term modification of retiree benefits because such benefits did not concern the employer-employee relationship. To be clear, although the retirees do not have a viable Section 8(a)(5) ULP here, other laws, including the Employee Retirement Income Security Act of 1974 (ERISA) (which had not been enacted at the time of this case), may provide retirees with legal protection if the employer modification interfered with already vested retirement benefits. Moreover, the retirement benefits of future retirees who are currently working for the employer are mandatory subjects of bargaining. *See Pittsburgh Plate Glass,* 404 U.S. at 180.

Although this treatment of retired employees under the NLRA might seem unfair to some, issues surrounding benefits owed to current retirees are a permissive subject of bargaining because not only are retirees not members of bargaining units (or even union members for that matter), but also including these retiree issues as mandatory subjects could prevent the employer and current employees from otherwise reaching an agreement on topics strictly germane to them. However, a union may still represent retirees in certain situations where the retirees consent, and there is no conflict of interest with current members.

E. Section 8(d) and the Duty to Bargain during Strikes

Another related issue in this area of law is whether the duty to bargain over mandatory subjects of bargaining still operates when a union goes on strike. In discussing the process of collective bargaining, it is inevitable that the necessity and the utility of strikes arise.

Although peaceful work stoppages are protected under Section 13 of the Act (as will be discussed in more detail in Chapter 14), Congress has expressed its preference that disagreements at the bargaining table be resolved without a strike (when employees refuse to work) or lockout (when an employer refuses to let employees work). Congress fosters voluntary settlements by enshrining notification and cooling-off periods in Section 8(d). Section 8(d)(1) requires written notice 60 days before a contract's expiration if a party wants to terminate or modify the contract. Section 8(d)(2) requires a party to meet and confer with the other party to negotiate a new contract or modify the current contract. Section 8(d)(3) next requires that 30 days after the initial termination or modification notice, the parties must notify the Federal Mediation and Conciliation Service (FMCS) of the pending dispute. However, the parties are not required to mediate with the FMCS. Finally, Section 8(d)(4) states that parties must keep the current contract in place and not engage in a strike or lockout for 60 days after notification. Failure to comply with this rule violates the duty to bargain in good faith under Sections 8(a)(5) or 8(b)(3). Additionally, the 1974 amendments to the NLRA added special rules under Section 8(g) for strike activity at health care institutions. These institutions, because of patient health concerns, must notify the health care institution and the

FMCS of their intent to strike not less than ten days prior to such action. The FMCS has the power to appoint an impartial Board of Inquiry to investigate and make settlement recommendations.

With these procedural explanations out of the way, the question remains whether a strike modifies the employer's duty to bargain in good faith (or vice versa in the case of a lockout). The answer is that a strike generally does not relieve the employer of the duty to bargain in good faith. *See NLRB v. J.H. Rutter-Rex Mfg. Co.*, 245 F.2d 594 (5th Cir. 1957).

A related case, *Land Air Delivery, Inc. v. NLRB*, 862 F.2d 354 (D.C. Cir. 1988), addresses whether employers can permanently contract out work in response to a strike without bargaining with the striking union over the subcontract. In *Land Air Delivery*, the union authorized a strike for thirteen truck drivers because of a dispute with the company. In response, the company first hired replacement workers (permanent replacements will be discussed in more detail in Chapter 15) but thereafter contracted out all the bargaining unit work to a third party. The company never bargained with the union over the subcontracting arrangement. Normally, under *Fibreboard*, there would be no question that this type of subcontracting is a mandatory subject of bargaining because it amounts to nothing more than a replacement of current bargaining unit employees. In *Land Air Delivery* the court found that the same duty to bargain with the union existed, even when the union was on strike.

However, in *Hawaii Meat Co. v. NLRB*, 321 F.2d 397 (9th Cir. 1963), the Ninth Circuit held that an employer's unilateral decision to subcontract work permanently during a strike did not violate Section 8(a)(5). The difference in treatment of the subcontract in *Hawaii Meat* was that the use of the permanent subcontract in that case was *defensive*, in that its purpose was to keep the plant operating during the strike. To make the company bargain under these circumstances, the *Hawaii Meat* court reasoned, would give the union a practical veto over the decision to subcontract. In *Land Air Delivery*, on the other hand, no evidence existed that Land Air needed to subcontract the work to stay in business. In fact, the company was able to survive the strike even before it decided to use the subcontract by hiring replacement workers. Thus, the emphasis in *Land Air Delivery* was whether the company was able to maintain operations during the strike without the subcontract. Because the court determined it could have, the company had a mandatory duty to bargain over the subcontracting even though the union was out on strike.

F. Bargaining Remedies

The remedies available under Sections 8(a)(5) and 8(b)(3) for failure to bargain in good faith are generally different in nature than the reinstatement and backpay remedies discussed in conjunction with Section 8(a)(3) discrimination violations in Chapter 9. *H.K. Porter Co. v. NLRB*, 397 U.S. 99 (1970), is the watershed case in this area. *H.K. Porter* involved a company's unwillingness to agree to a dues checkoff provision (taking union dues out of paychecks like payroll taxes, which Chapter 19 discusses) as part of a bargaining dispute with the union. Indeed, over an eight-year period, the company appeared to use every avenue for delay available to it to avoid agreeing to a first contract with the union. Based on this conduct, the Board found a Section 8(a)(5) violation.

Although the ULP finding was straightforward, the interesting part of the case was the Board's remedy. The Board ordered the company to grant the union a contract clause providing for the checkoff of union dues, stating that it was within the Board's discretion to grant this remedy under Section 10(c), which includes "affirmative relief ... to effectuate the policies of the Act." The Supreme Court reversed, holding that although the Board has power to make parties negotiate over terms of employment, Section 8(d) does not give the Board the power to compel a company to agree to any substantive provisions, no matter how egregious the employer's conduct. Although Section 8(d) does not go expressly to remedies (Section 10(c) does), the *H.K. Porter* Court maintained that the same considerations that free parties from making any concessions at the bargaining table under Section 8(d) also lead to the conclusion that the Board does not have the remedial power to compel contract provisions between the parties.

Justice Douglas dissented on the grounds that under Section 10(c), where one party does not bargain in good faith, the Board has the power to take such affirmative action as will effectuate the policies of the Act. According to Douglas, the policy of the Act is to endorse collective bargaining and the formation of an agreement, and here, the employer resolved not to reach an agreement with the union. The only outcome that would promote collective bargaining in this type of case would be the issuance of an order requiring the company to accept the disputed contract clause. Indeed, the question remains after *H.K. Porter*: what is to prevent a company from negotiating in bad faith as long as it keeps up the pretense of wanting to come to an agreement? Also, because the bargaining remedies available after *H.K. Porter* are so minimal (i.e., only a cease-and-desist order, notice posting, and an affirmative bargaining order), perhaps it does not even make sense for employers to challenge a Section 8(a)(5) finding against them.

On the other hand, proponents of the holding in *H.K. Porter* suggest that the case is consistent with the overarching structure of the Act, which is to keep the government out of the parties' substantive discussions and let them come to mutually agreeable terms. Opponents respond by saying that in a case like *H.K. Porter*, the issue is no longer the substantive duty to bargain in good faith, but rather a question of what the appropriate equitable remedies should be, given the egregiousness of the employer's bargaining stance.

Another major bargaining remedies case, also showing the limited nature of remedies available for Section 8(a)(5) violations, is *Ex-Cell-O Corp.*, 185 N.L.R.B. 107 (1970). In that case, the United Auto Workers (UAW) demanded recognition, the company refused, the union petitioned for an election and won, and the company refused to bargain for six years. Not surprisingly, a Section 8(a)(5) violation was proved against the employer. The Trial Examiner (the precursor to the current-day Administrative Law Judge (ALJ)) entered a compensatory order, awarding back pay to employees impacted by the employer's unlawful refusal to bargain. The Trial Examiner (and the dissent in *Ex-Cell-O*) would have calculated the damages by estimating what the employer would have agreed to had the employer been bargaining in good faith.

The Board majority in *Ex-Cell-O*, however, reluctantly concluded that the Trial Examiner overstepped his authority in issuing the remedial order, even though the Board agreed that the current remedies available under Section 8(a)(5) were inadequate. Remedial orders like the one in *Ex-Cell-O* are not allowed because they impermissibly impose a penalty (and punitive damages are not provided by Act). Also, it was impossible to determine what terms the union and employer would have agreed to had they bargained in good faith. The Board majority found the compensatory order akin to punitive damages because it imposed a significant financial obligation on an employer based on a debatable issue over whether the company should be required to bargain. The company was thus being punished for pursuing the election dispute beyond the Board and to the courts. In the end, the Board was not comfortable distinguishing between debatable and frivolous refusal-to-bargain cases.

Also, similar to *H.K. Porter*, the Board concluded in *Ex-Cell-O* that, although it had discretion in exercising power to effectuate purposes of the Act under Section 10(c), the remedial order could not compel agreements between parties under Section 8(d). Indeed, the Board reasoned that if it required contractual terms, it would be operating retroactively to impose financial liability on an employer flowing from a presumed contractual agreement. This would be problematic because it is for Congress to provide for such additional remedies in the first instance, not for the Board.

The *Ex-Cell-O* dissent believed that the compensatory order did not involve punitive damages at all, but only compensatory damages for a legal wrong. And although such compensatory damages could not be precisely measured, the Trial Examiner should not have been barred from awarding such remedies. The dissent also concluded that the order did not violate Section 8(d) because the order did not propose contractual terms but only sought to approximate the damages caused by the employer's unlawful conduct. According to the dissent, such remedies are within the broad scheme of Section 10(c)'s grant of authority to the Board to take affirmative action to effectuate the policies of the Act.

In 2022, the NLRB expanded relief in certain cases, including ones involving an unlawful refusal to bargain. Under *Thryv, Inc.*, 372 N.L.R.B. No. 22 (Dec. 31, 2022), *rev'd on other grounds*, 102 F.4th 727 (5th Cir. 2024), the Board will order make-whole relief in cases where the General Counsel can show that a financial harm was the "direct or foreseeable" result of a ULP. For instance, if an employer's refusal to bargain led to out-of-pocket medical costs or penalties on credit card bills, the Board could order monetary damages to make employees whole for such losses. At the time of this book's publication, litigation over *Thryv* relief was pending.

Because of the lack of inadequate bargaining remedies under current law, Congress has considered amending the NLRA to permit more financial remedies (e.g., the Employee Free Choice Act (EFCA) and Protecting the Right to Organize Act (PRO Act)). In addition to other labor reforms, these laws would expand NLRB remedies by, for example, allowing for monetary fines or permitting the parties to proceed to interest arbitration if they are unable to come to a first contract after a specified number of days of impasse. Under interest arbitration, the parties would submit their bargaining proposals to a board of arbitrators who, after taking evidence, would establish the first contract (and only the first contract) between the parties for a limited number of years. As described in Chapter 15, this interest arbitration process has proven successful in the public sector for various groups of employees, including but not limited to police, firefighters in many states, and Postal Service employees. In the private sector, however, these laws have not been enacted.

CHECKPOINTS

- The quantitative component of the duty to bargain in good faith concerns the scope of the subjects over which the parties must bargain.
- It is a ULP for employers (under Section 8(a)(5)) or for unions (under Section 8(b)(3)) to refuse to bargain collectively with the other.
- Sections 8(d) and 9(a) identify the topics over which the parties must bargain: wages, hours, and terms and conditions of employment. These are known as mandatory subjects of bargaining.
- If topics of bargaining fall outside of this statutory language, they are either permissive subjects of bargaining (which parties may bargain over) or illegal subjects of bargaining (which parties may not bargain over).
- Bargaining in good faith for a management rights clause, which takes away a union's ability to bargain over mandatory subjects, does not constitute a violation of Section 8(a)(5).
- Mandatory subjects of bargaining are conditions of employment that are germane to the working environment. Permissive subjects of bargaining generally concern internal union affairs or matters of managerial prerogative.
- Three categories of managerial decisions exist: (1) decisions directly impacting employment with relatively few entrepreneurial implications (mandatory); (2) decisions that indirectly affect job security (permissive); and (3) decisions that impact job security but lie at the core of entrepreneurial control (permissive).
- Subcontracting is a mandatory subject if employees are merely being replaced without any substantial business reasons.
- Partial closing of an employer's business lies at the core of entrepreneurial control. The decision to close does not need to be bargained, but the effects of decision do.
- Plant relocations are subject to a burden-shifting test to determine whether a decision to relocate is amenable to collective bargaining. If so, the decision is mandatory.

- Retirees are not statutory employees who are members of the bargaining unit and thus, unions have no right to demand bargaining over modifications to retiree benefits.
- Section 8(d) sets out procedures to conciliate bargaining disputes without a work stoppage, but the duty to bargain over subcontracting and other mandatory subjects of bargaining applies even when a union is out on strike or there is a lockout.
- Bargaining remedies generally include cease-and-desist orders, but do not include compelling a party to accept unwanted provisions, compensatory orders for damages (except for make-whole relief under *Thryv*), or first contract interest arbitration.

CHAPTER 13

Subjects of Bargaining in the Public Sector

ROADMAP

- Policy concerns: why the scope of bargaining is often narrower in the public sector than in the private sector
- The broad statutory language/balancing test approach to public-sector bargaining
- The "laundry list" approach to public-sector bargaining
- Restrictions on the scope of bargaining from external laws (e.g., civil service laws)
- Use of effects bargaining in the public-sector context
- Remedies for the failure to bargain in good faith in the public sector

The scope of bargaining is one of the most important issues in public-sector labor law. It has tremendous practical consequences, determining what topics unions have a right to negotiate. It presents critical policy questions regarding what subjects primarily involve the working lives of public employees and what subjects involve broader public policy determinations that should be controlled entirely by democratically accountable officials. This is one of the areas in which public-sector labor laws can deviate most sharply from private-sector law, and one of the areas in which public-sector laws differ the most among themselves.

A. Special Policy Considerations in Public-Sector Scope of Bargaining

Many public-sector statutes contain language regarding the scope of bargaining, or the subjects of bargaining, that is the same, or substantively the same, as in the NLRA: the parties must bargain over "wages, hours, and other terms and working conditions of employment." But those same statutes usually also set out management/government rights that are not negotiable, or at least not mandatory subjects of bargaining, in equally broad language. This approach leads to "balancing tests" to determine what is and is not a mandatory topic of bargaining. In a minority of jurisdictions, statutes use a "laundry list" approach: specifically listing in detail what topics are and/or are not negotiable. Some of these jurisdictions have a much narrower scope of bargaining than in the private sector or most public-sector jurisdictions. There are significant variations within each approach. But generally, the scope of bargaining in the public sector is often narrower than that in the private sector. Even where statutory language in the public-sector statute is similar to that of the NLRA, the scope of bargaining in the public sector is often more restricted because of interpretations of labor boards and courts, and because other statutes that govern public employment make certain topics non-negotiable. This is one of the most important areas of public-sector labor law.

Why the differences from private-sector law? From the employee's perspective, bargaining looks much the same as it does in the private sector: employees are concerned about compensation, hours of work, and working conditions. But from the employer's perspective, and in some sense from the public's perspective, there are differences. Public-sector collective bargaining raises questions about what sorts of decisions that affect the jobs of public employees could or should be negotiated with unions, as opposed to what decisions involve the public policy considerations that should be left to the unilateral discretion of democratically accountable public officials. While noting those concerns, Professor Clyde Summers, in an influential article, defended public-sector collective bargaining on the grounds that, in its absence, the legitimate workplace concerns of public employees would be overwhelmed by political forces seeking both lower taxes and more public services. Also, Summers argued, many issues of great importance to employees simply do not matter to voters (e.g., most discipline and discharge cases, seniority rules, and job-bidding rules). Still, Summers stressed, some decisions should be left to the normal political process. Clyde Summers, *Bargaining in the Government's Business: Principles and Politics*, 18 U. Tol. L. Rev. 265 (1987). Balancing these factors is central to determining the proper scope of bargaining in the public sector.

In making this balance, public-sector jurisdictions vary considerably. In the majority of states that authorize public-sector collective bargaining—for example, Ohio, Pennsylvania, and New York—most topics that are mandatory under the NLRA are mandatory under the state labor law. A significant exception are pension benefit formulas, which are almost never negotiable in the public sector as they are set by an external statute. At the other end of the spectrum, some jurisdictions severely limit the scope of bargaining. For example, under the labor law that covers most federal employees outside the postal service, compensation is not negotiable. *See* § 7103(a)(14)(c) (exempting from the scope of bargaining matters covered by other federal statutes). In Wisconsin, after Act 10 nearly eliminated collective bargaining for most public employees in 2011, the *only* issue that is negotiable is pay, and then only up to the rise in the cost of living. Iowa adopted a similar approach in 2017. Notably, both states exempted public safety employees from these limits.

Broadly speaking, restrictions on the scope of bargaining come from three sources. First, some public-sector statutes state explicitly (in ways that the NLRA does not) that certain topics are either not negotiable or not mandatory subjects of negotiation. These include, but are not limited to, "laundry list" statutes that specifically note which topics are and are not mandatory. Second, state labor agencies and courts sometimes more narrowly interpret statutory language similar to the NLRA for policy reasons. Finally, non-labor legal rules that govern public employment often cover topics that overlap with topics that may be negotiable, and sometimes collective bargaining cannot alter the specific employment rules these laws set. Most important here are civil service rules, public pension statutes, tenure laws, and in some instances, federal and state constitutional law.

B. Balancing Tests: Public-Sector Statutes Containing Language Similar to the NLRA and Broad "Management Rights" Clauses

Many public-sector statutes provide that unions and employers have a duty to bargain over "wages, hours, and other terms and conditions of employment." These statutes often also state that certain "management rights" or "government rights" are either not negotiable or are not mandatory topics and describe such rights with similarly broad language. Labor boards and courts typically develop "balancing tests" to resolve competing interests in close cases.

In re State Employment Relations Board v. Youngstown City School District Board of Education, 12 Ohio Pub. Employee Rep. 1543 (OH SERB 1995), is a typical example of the balancing test approach. In this case, the Ohio Labor Board noted the following tension in the statutory language. First, O.R.C. § 4117.08(A) seems to indicate that the scope of bargaining should be broad. Using language similar to that of the NLRA, this section states: "All matters pertaining to wages, hours, or terms and other conditions of employment … are subject to collective bargaining between the public employer and the exclusive representative, except as otherwise specified in this section…." Second, however, O.R.C. § 4117.08(C) sets out a broad statement of management rights:

> Unless a public employer agrees otherwise in a collective bargaining agreement, nothing in Chapter 4117 … impairs the right and responsibility of each public employer to:
>
> (1) Determine matters of inherent managerial policy which include, but are not limited to areas of discretion or policy such as the functions and programs of the public employer, standards of services, its overall budget, utilization of technology and organizational structure;
>
> (2) Direct, supervise, evaluate, or hire employees;
>
> (3) Maintain and improve the efficiency and effectiveness of governmental operations;
>
> (4) Determine the overall methods, process, means, or personnel by which governmental operations are to be conducted;
>
> (5) Suspend, discipline, demote, or discharge for just cause, or lay off, transfer, assign, schedule, promote, or retain employees;
>
> (6) Determine the adequacy of the work force;

(7) Determine the overall mission of the employer as a unit of government;

(8) Effectively manage the work force;

(9) Take actions to carry out the mission of the public employer as a governmental unit.

The employer is not required to bargain on subjects reserved to the management and direction of the governmental unit except as affect wages, hours, terms and conditions of employment, and the continuation, modification, or deletion of an existing provision of a collective bargaining agreement.

These provisions are noticeably in tension: a significant number of issues that involve wages, hours, and working conditions under the former section would at least arguably also come under one of the restrictions in the latter section.

In *Youngstown City School District*, the Ohio Labor Board resolved, or at least mitigated, this tension. The state labor board announced that in determining whether a topic was negotiable, it would balance the following factors:

1) The extent to which the subject is logically and reasonably related to wages, hours, terms and conditions of employment;

2) The extent to which the employer's obligation to negotiate may significantly abridge its freedom to exercise those managerial prerogatives set forth in and anticipated by O.R.C. 4117.08(C), including an examination of the type of employer involved and whether inherent discretion on the subject matter at issue is necessary to achieve the employer's essential mission and its obligations to the general public; and

3) The extent to which the mediatory influence of collective bargaining and, when necessary, any impasse resolution mechanisms available to the parties are the appropriate means of resolving conflicts over the subject matter.

A significant number of other jurisdictions have adopted the same, or similar, type of balancing test. Indeed, this is the majority approach. *See, e.g., San Mateo City School Dist. v. PERB*, 33 Cal.3d 850 (1983), *Penn. Labor Relations Bd. v. State College Area School Dist.*, 90 L.R.R.M. 2081 (1975), and *Central City Education Assn. v. Ill. Educational Labor Relations Bd.*, 599 N.E.2d 892 (1992).

The first two prongs of these tests balance employee and employer interests. *Youngstown City School District*, and several similar decisions from other jurisdictions, add a third prong concerning the extent to which collective bargaining is an "appropriate means" to resolve the conflict. What does that mean? *Chicago Park District v. Illinois Labor Relations Board*, 354 Ill. App. 3d 595 (2004), applying a similar three-prong test, held that a reduction in hours was a mandatory topic. After noting that the employees had obvious interests in hours worked but also that the financial constraints driving the reduction implicated management rights involving the overall budget and standards of service, the court looked at the third factor. It explained: "the benefits of bargaining an economically-motivated reduction in hours could be substantial," because the union "could offer concessions in other areas to achieve the financial savings which the employer seeks or identify employees who wish to work reduced hours." Further, employees "may be able to identify cost-saving measures of which the employer is unaware." 354 Ill. App. 3d 595, 602–04.

In these "balancing test" jurisdictions, boards and courts have found mandatory many topics that are also mandatory under the NLRA: wages, hours of work, and many conditions of employment, including but not limited to discipline rules, grievance and arbitration procedures, and anti-discrimination rules. Some issues, however, raise concerns about inherent government authority sufficiently serious that they are often or always found to be non-mandatory topics even when they indisputably affect the jobs of the employees, and even where the issue would be mandatory in the private sector.

For example, *San Jose Peace Officers Association v. City of San Jose*, 78 Cal. App. 3d 935, 947 (1978), held that a new city policy that added additional limits on when police officers could use deadly force was not a mandatory subject. Even though officer safety was involved, the court explained, the conditions under which police officers could use deadly force against members of the public was a policy decision that accountable officials should make without being subject to the "trade-offs" of collective bargaining. In *Matter of Sergeants Benevolent Association of the City of New York, Inc. v. City of New York*, 6 N.Y.S.3d 474 (2015), the court upheld the labor board's ruling that a police department policy requiring alcohol testing for police officers when their discharge of a firearm had resulted in an injury or death was not a mandatory subject. On the other hand, *International Brotherhood of Teamsters Local 700 v. Illinois Labor Relations Board*, 73 N.E.3d 108 (2017), held that a sheriff department's order stating that its employees may not associate with gang members was a mandatory subject of bargaining.

Further complicating this issue is the rule (from the private sector, broadly adopted in the public sector) that even if a substantive decision is not a mandatory topic, unions may still have the right to negotiate the *effects* of such decisions. For example, in *Claremont Police Officers Association v. City of Claremont,* 139 P.3d 532 (Cal. 2006), the employer had unilaterally instituted a rule that police officers who made traffic stops must fill out a form that, among other things, listed the driver's race. The form was part of a study designed to garner information about, and inhibit, racial profiling. In this case, both sides agreed that the employer's decision to require the form as part of a study of profiling was a non-negotiable management right. Yet, the union argued that the city should be required to negotiate about the effects of the study, e.g., on the discipline of officers. Although the court rejected the union's argument, it stressed that this was because the study had only just been implemented. The decision strongly implied that a duty to bargain effects would exist if the city's use of the study had an impact on officer discipline or privacy.

Generally, bargaining over "effects" of decisions that are not themselves negotiable is a much more significant issue, practically and legally, in the public sector than in the private. This is because fewer substantive decisions by employers are mandatory under public-sector laws, and unions may only demand to bargain over the "effects" of those decisions. Further, in some situations, employers may not implement the substantive (non-mandatory) decision before they have negotiated the (mandatory) effects.

The most complicated and vexing "effects" bargaining cases come from the federal sector. Under the Federal Service Labor-Management Relations Statute (FSLMRS), which governs most federal employees, covered employees have the right to bargain over "conditions of employment" (5 U.S.C. § 7102), which is later defined to include "personnel policies, practices, and matters ... affecting working conditions." 5 U.S.C. § 7103(a)(14).

But, under this statute, many important subjects, including wages and benefits, are not negotiable because they are set by external statute and/or regulation. Also, Section 7106(a)(2) limits negotiability by listing a significant set of management rights. These include the rights:

> (A) to hire, assign, direct, layoff, and retain employees in the agency, or to suspend, remove, reduce in grade or pay, or take other disciplinary action against such employees;
>
> (B) to assign work, to make determinations with respect to contracting out, and to determine the personnel by which agency operations shall be conducted; ... [or]

(D) to take whatever actions may be necessary to carry out the agency mission during emergencies.

Additionally, Section 7106(b)(1) lists topics over which bargaining may take place "at the election of the agency." Such topics include decisions concerning "the technology, methods, and means of performing work."

This means that the federal sector has an exceedingly limited scope of negotiability on the *substance* of management decisions affecting employees, but federal sector unions have broad rights to negotiate about the *effects* of employer actions. Specifically, unions have a right to negotiate the "impact and implementation" of management decisions that have more than a *de minimis* adverse effect on conditions of employment. Unions also have the right to negotiate "procedures" and "appropriate arrangements" under Section 7106(b)(2) and (3) for the exercise of management rights. So, for example, although federal employers have the right to "remove" employees, "just cause" discipline rules in contracts enforceable through negotiated grievance and arbitration procedures are mandatory topics.

Scope of bargaining rules in the federal sector are among the most difficult to grasp, in large part because the question often is whether certain union proposals go primarily to the substantive exercise of a management right, or whether they are an attempt to bargain a procedure or appropriate arrangement for employees. For example, in *National Treasury Employees Union v. FLRA*, 404 F.3d 454 (D.C. Cir. 2005), a union at the Customs Service proposed, in response to Customs rules requiring employees to store their firearms safely at all times, that the employer ensure that a lockbox or other safe storage would be available at the workplace. The employer, relying on the statutory management right to determine the "internal security practices of the agency," argued that this proposal was not negotiable. The union responded that its proposal was a "procedure" or "appropriate arrangement" and thus was negotiable under the statute. The Federal Labor Relations Authority (FLRA) ruled for the employer because the proposal involved a security practice. The D.C. Circuit agreed that it was a security practice, but the court then held that the FLRA had not adequately addressed whether the union's proposal was a negotiable procedure or not. The question in such cases, the court explained, is whether the proposal "excessively interferes with the exercise of management's rights." Thus, it remanded the case to the FLRA to follow the agency's precedent on that issue.

In jurisdictions using balancing tests, there are certain recurring areas in which boards and courts often find proposals non-mandatory that would be mandatory in the private sector. Many of these cases involve police officers, firefighters, and teachers, likely because policies regarding schools and public safety often raise public policy concerns. Other cases involve the type of proposal rather than the type of employee: staffing and subcontracting issues, for example. Again, these cases are further complicated by the possibility of effects bargaining.

For example, as to police and fire employees, *Oak Park Public Safety Officers Association v. City of Oak Park*, 277 Mich. App. 317 (2007), held not mandatory a proposal requiring that, as long as the employer continued to operate a public safety department providing joint fire and police protection, it would maintain certain minimum staffing levels of employees who had law enforcement and fire-fighting certifications. It also held not mandatory the union's proposal requiring at least specified minimum staffing when responding to fires. 277 Mich. App. 317, 319–20. Notably, the relevant Michigan statute stated that "wages, hours, and other terms and conditions of employment" were mandatory subjects. MCL § 423.215(1). Still, the court held that to be mandatory, the "impact of a staffing decision on working conditions, including safety, must be proven to be significant." The court reasoned that adopting the union's position "would be tantamount to requiring that most, if not all, minimum staffing proposals ... be subject to mandatory bargaining" and that this "would have the effect of invading the city's prerogative to determine the size and scope of its business, including the services it will provide." 277 Mich. App. at 329–30.

Nonetheless, bargaining over the effects of such decisions may well be mandatory. Even when "manpower issues are not mandatory subjects of bargaining ... there is a duty to bargain over the impact of manpower decisions to the extent that they related to workload and safety." *City of Sault Ste. Marie v. Fraternal Order of Police Labor Council*, 163 Mich. App. 350 (1987); *see also Philadelphia Fire Fighters' Union, Local 22, IAFF v. City of Philadelphia*, 37 Penn. Pub. Emp. Rep. ¶ 67 (Cmwlth.Ct. 2006) (decision to reorganize the fire department was not a mandatory topic, but the city had to engage in effects bargaining because of the impact of the reorganization on terms and conditions of employment). What might such mandatory effects bargaining cover? *City of Niagara Falls & Niagara Falls Uniformed Firefighters Association, AFL-CIO, Local 714*, 37 PERB ¶ 4520 (NY PERB ALJ Decision, Feb. 9, 2004), found a proposal to increase compensation after a staffing cut to be mandatory effects bargaining.

Public schools also raise issues of inherent government policy. For example, *Racine Education Association v. Racine Unified School District*, Dec. No. 27972-C (Wisconsin Emp. Rel. Comm. 1996), held that the decision to change a year-round school calendar was not a mandatory topic. The Wisconsin statute in effect at that time required employers to bargain over "wages, hours, and conditions of employment," but also stated that employers "shall not be required to bargain on subjects reserved to management and direction of the governmental unit" except for effects bargaining. *Id.* The Wisconsin Commission held that the decision was based on educational policy judgments about potentially improved learning opportunities, and thus the topic was substantially related to educational policy, an area reserved to management.

Jurisdictions are split over whether the school calendar, meaning the starting and ending dates of the school year, is a mandatory topic. *Compare Clark County Sch. Dist. v Local Government Employee Management Rel. Bd.*, 90 Nev. 442 (1974) (school calendar is mandatory as it is significantly related to working conditions), *with Eastbrook Community Schools Corp. v. Indiana Education Employment Rel. Bd.*, 446 N.E.2d 1007, *reh. den.* 450 N.E.2d 1006 (Ind. App. 1983) (changes in school calendar not mandatory, issue is within school board's exclusive managerial prerogative); *see also Mars Area Educational Support Personnel Ass'n v. Mars Area Sch. Dist.*, 32 PPER ¶ 32023 (Pa. Lab. Rel. Bd., Hearing Examiner, 2000) (employer's proposal to change the length of the school year from 188 to 205 days was a mandatory subject).

Jurisdictions are also divided over the topic of class size. *See* Martin Malin & Charles Kerchner, *Charter Schools and Collective Bargaining: Compatible Marriage or Illegitimate Relationship?*, 30 Harv. J. L. & Pub. Pol'y 885, 915 (2007). A number of cases have held that class size is not a mandatory subject because, although it does affect conditions for teachers, it is a matter of education policy. *See, e.g., Hillsborough Classroom Teachers Ass'n, Inc. v. School Bd. of Hillsborough County*, 423 So. 2d 969 (Fla. App. 1982); *Kenai Peninsula Dist. v. Kenai Peninsula Educ. Ass'n*, 557 P.2d 416 (Alaska 1977); *West Irondequoit Bd. of Educ.*, 4 PERB ¶ 3070 (1971), *aff'd sub nom. Matter of West Irondequoit Teachers' Ass'n v. Helsby*, 35 N.Y.2d 46 (1974). In these jurisdictions, class size usually remains a permissive subject on which the parties are permitted to agree. *See, e.g., Bd. of Educ. v Greenburgh Teachers Fed.*, 381, N.Y.S.2d 517 (1976). Meanwhile, class size is a mandatory topic in a number of other jurisdictions. *See, e.g., Oroville Union High Sch. Dist. v. Oroville Secondary Teacher's Ass'n*, 26 PERC ¶ 33083 (Cal. PERB ALJ, 2002); *Decatur Bd. of Educ. Dist. No. 61 v. IELRB*, 180 Ill. App. 3d 770 (1989).

Subcontracting also raises concerns about inherent government power. In most jurisdictions, subcontracting is at least usually a mandatory subject of bargaining. *See, e.g., Rialto Police Benefit Ass'n v. City of Rialto*, 66 Cal. Rptr. 3d 714 (Cal. App. 2007) (subcontracting police services is mandatory); *Interurban Transit Partnership*, 17 MPER ¶ 40 (Mich. Emp. Rel. Comm. 2004) (subcontracting "on demand" transportation system is mandatory). Some jurisdictions, however, view subcontracting as a management right. For example, *Amalgamated Transit Union Local 1593 v. Hillsborough Area Regional Transit Authority*, 742 So. 2d 380 (Fla. App. 1999), held that subcontracting is not a mandatory topic, distinguishing *Fibreboard* (discussed in Chapter 13) on the grounds that "there are critical distinctions between private and public sector bargaining." 742 So. 2d at 381.

Many of these cases found that a topic was not mandatory or implied that a topic was permissive. Notably, though, one of the main public-sector statutes in New Jersey uses an interesting variation: only mandatory and illegal subjects of bargaining exist; there is no "permissive" category. *See Local 195, IFPTE, AFL-CIO v. State of New Jersey*, 443 A.2d 187 (N.J. 1982) (no "permissive" category under the New Jersey Employer-Employee Relations Act, N.J.S.A. 34:13A-1 to -21, and subcontracting is an illegal topic of bargaining). The theory is that "the very foundation of representative democracy would be endangered if decisions on significant matters of governmental policy were left to the process of collective negotiations.... Our democratic system demands that governmental bodies retain their accountability to the citizenry." *Ridgefield Park Ed. Ass'n v. Ridgefield Park Bd. of Ed.*, 78 N.J. 144, 163 (1978). In other words, if a subject should truly be under unilateral control of democratically accountable officials, unions should not even be allowed to negotiate about it, even if the employer agrees to do so. *Local 195* did hold that unions could propose that the employer discuss decisions to contract or subcontract whenever it becomes apparent that a layoff or job displacement will result, if the proposed subcontracting is based solely on fiscal considerations.

This case represents both the minority rule on subcontracting and an almost unique approach in rejecting the permissive category. *See also Montgomery City Educ. Ass'n v. Bd. of Educ.*, 534 A.2d 980 (Md. App. 1987) (no "permissive" category exists under the Maryland statute covering teachers). Indeed, even in New Jersey, a separate public-sector statute governing police and firefighters explicitly provides for permissive topics. *Ridgefield*, 78 N.J. at 158, *citing* C. 85, N.J.S.A. 34:13A-14 to 21.

C. "Laundry List" Statutes

The second and minority approach to subjects of bargaining in the public sector is the "laundry list" model. In these jurisdictions, the labor statute itself lists most or all of the specific topics that are or are not negotiable. There is no "balancing": the statute either explicitly makes a given topic of bargaining mandatory, or it does not.

Sometimes such specific restrictions only apply to a particular set of employees and employers, most commonly, schools and teachers. For example, Michigan's law generally provides that public-sector unions and employers must bargain over "wages, hours and other ... conditions of employment." But in the 1990s, this law was amended to restrict the scope of bargaining for public school employers, adding specific topics that these employers and unions of their employees may not negotiate. These included (but were not limited to) the starting day of the school year, the amount of pupil contact time required, whether to contract with a third party for non-instructional support services, and the use of experimental or pilot programs. In 2012, Michigan enacted P.A. 53, which provides that "dues check-off" for employees of public schools may no longer be negotiated. These special rules for teachers were repealed in the early 2020s.

Oregon also has special rules for public schools in O.R.S. § 243.650(7) (e):

> For school district bargaining, "employment relations" excludes class size, the school or educational calendar, standards of performance or criteria for evaluation of teachers, the school curriculum, reasonable dress, grooming and at-work personal conduct requirements respecting smoking, gum chewing and similar matters of personal conduct, the standards and procedures for student discipline, the time between student classes, ... requirements for expressing milk under ORS 653.077, and any other subject proposed that is permissive under paragraphs (b), (c) and (d) of this subsection.

In these "laundry list" jurisdictions, teachers are often denied the right to negotiate over topics that are mandatory topics for other public employees in the jurisdiction. As noted above, in Michigan, one of the special rules for teachers made subcontracting a permissive topic. *See also Detroit Public Schools and Int'l Ass'n of Machinists and Aerospace Workers,* 17 MPER ¶ 14 (Mich. Emp. Rel. Comm. 2004). But in Michigan, subcontracting was and is generally mandatory for other public employees. *See, e.g.*, *Interurban Transit Partnership*, 17 MPER ¶ 40 (Mich. Emp. Rel. Comm. 2004).

In contrast, other "laundry list" statutes have applied to all covered public employees, not just teachers. For example, before 2017, Iowa Code § 20.9 required all unions and employers in the public sector generally

> to negotiate in good faith with respect to wages, hours, vacations, insurance, holidays, leaves of absence, shift differentials, overtime compensation, supplemental pay, seniority, transfer procedures, job classifications, health and safety matters, evaluation procedures, procedures for staff reduction, in-service training and other matters mutually agreed upon. Negotiations shall also include terms authorizing dues checkoff for members of the employee organization and grievance procedures for resolving any questions arising under the agreement, which shall be embodied in a written agreement and signed by the parties.
>
> ... All retirement systems shall be excluded from the scope of negotiations.

In 2017, the scope of bargaining for all public employees who were not "public safety" employees" was restricted much more dramatically (along the lines of Wisconsin Act 10).

One purported advantage to "laundry list" statutes is that unions and employers will understand more clearly what is and is not negotiable, and there will be less litigation over negotiability issues. But such statutes do not eliminate litigation. *Black Hawk County & Public Professional & Maintenance Employees Local 2003*, Case No. 7218 (Iowa Pub. Rel. Bd. 2006), decided after Iowa's statute had been in effect for decades, addressed whether seventeen separate proposals were negotiable. The union and employer each prevailed on some issues, and during the litigation, the Iowa Board reversed itself on one topic. The most obvious result of the "laundry list approach" is that it gives the state legislature, as opposed to labor boards and courts, much more power to decide what is and is not a mandatory topic.

D. Restrictions on the Scope of Bargaining from External Law

Public employees are governed by many laws that have no analogy in the private sector: civil service laws, pension statutes, teacher tenure laws, and the federal and relevant state constitutions are only the most important of these. Questions frequently arise as to when unions may negotiate rules that are different than the "default" rules set by such external laws.

Some labor statutes explicitly state how potential conflicts with other laws should be resolved. For example, the Ohio public-sector labor statute specifically provides that certain civil service rules cannot legally be altered by bargaining. "The conduct and grading of civil service examinations, the rating of candidates, the establishment of eligible lists from the examinations, and the original appointments from the eligible lists are not appropriate subjects for collective bargaining." Ohio Rev. Code. § 4117.08(B). Section 4117.10(A) of the Ohio public-sector labor law then lists various external laws governing public employment, placing them in one of three categories: (1) those that trump collectively bargained rules; (2) those which provide minimums that collectively bargained rules may exceed; and (3) those which may be superseded entirely by collective bargaining agreements. *See, e.g., Null v. Ohio Dept. of Mental Retardation & Developmental Disabilities*, 738 N.E.2d 105 (Oh. Ct. App. 2000) (holding that an Ohio wage and hour law was in the third category, and thus a collective bargaining agreement could set overtime rules that in some circumstances would be less generous than state law).

Often, though, state statutes are not clear as to the extent to which an external law governing public employment may limit the scope of bargaining. *Patrolmen's Benevolent Association of City of New York, Inc. v. New York State Public Employment Relations Board*, 848 N.E.2d 448 (N.Y. 2006), involved a topic arguably covered both by the collective-bargaining law and by external law where neither statute explicitly resolved the conflict. In this case, the employer refused to negotiate certain procedural protections for police officers in disciplinary proceedings. The New York Court of Appeals held that the proposal was not negotiable, despite what it labeled the "strong and sweeping policy of the State to support collective bargaining" and the strong presumption that terms and conditions of employment were mandatory subjects. The Court explained that some subjects were not negotiable simply as a matter of policy (e.g., limits on the power of the city's Department of Investigation to interrogate city employees in a criminal investigation). But, the court added, the issue in this case was "not so simple." The relevant civil service law had rules on discipline, yet prior cases had held that police discipline matters could be negotiable. On the other hand, part of the New York City Charter provided that the police commissioner had control of "discipline of the department," and part of the city Administrative Code said that in cases of police misconduct, the commissioner had the power to punish the offending party. The court held that this overrode the presumption in favor of negotiability. Also, the court stressed the importance of the policy of civilian control over police.

Even cases in this specific area are not consistent. For the opposite result on a similar issue, see *City of Taylorville and Policemen's Benevolent Labor Comm.*, 21 PERI ¶ 222 (Ill. Lab. Rel. Bd. Gen. Counsel 2005), which explained that the state law governing police discipline did not preempt bargaining on the topic, because the law exempted certain employers and unions that had negotiated discipline policies prior to the enactment of the law. The broader point is that when external laws governing public employment and relevant labor statutes are not clear on which controls, difficult issues regarding scope of bargaining often arise.

Civil service laws have been perhaps the largest single source for potential conflicts with public-sector labor laws. Civil service laws date back to the late 19th century, and these laws usually (although not always) pre-date public-sector labor statutes. Civil service laws arose in part to help combat corrupt patronage practices in hiring and firing by installing "merit" employment rules. Thus, civil service laws typically require certain procedures, including exams, before hiring and require "cause" for discharge. They also often set various terms and conditions of employment, including wage scales for various positions.

Courts have rejected claims that civil service systems entirely preempt public-sector labor laws. *See, e.g., Pacific Legal Foundation v. Brown*, 29 Cal. 3d 168 (1981) (California's State Employer Employee Relations Act (SEERA), which grants collective-bargaining rights to state employees, does not impermissibly conflict with the general "merit principles" of civil service employment in the state constitution). But claims of conflicts between labor laws and civil service laws continue. Sometimes those claims fail. *See, e.g., Abel v. City of Pittsburgh*, 890 A.2d 1 (Pa. Cmwlth. 2005) (rejecting a challenge to union contract provision on layoffs because it conflicted with a provision in the state's Civil Service Act providing that the last employee appointed should be the first to be laid off, regardless of job title or classification). Sometimes, these claims succeed. *See, e.g., Connecticut State Employees Ass'n & State of Connecticut*,

Dec. No. 4096 (Conn. State Bd. of Lab. Rel. 2005) (holding non-negotiable union proposal that would have required the employer to retain and make available for inspection description of the process for ranking and evaluating candidates who completed civil service merit exam because the public-sector labor statute expressly exempted "the establishment, conduct and grading of merit examinations, the rating of candidates and the establishment of lists from such examinations" from the collective-bargaining process).

Another recurring issue involving civil service laws concerns discipline and discharge rules. Unionized employees are often covered by both a just-cause discharge clause in their union contract that must be enforced through arbitration and similar protection under civil service rules that must be enforced through civil service hearings. States vary as to whether employees can be limited to using one or the other (and if so, which one). *See* Ann Hodges, *The Interplay of Civil Service Law and Collective Bargaining in Public Sector Employee Discipline Cases*, 32 B.C. L. Rev. 95 (1990).

Education laws also may remove a variety of issues from the scope of bargaining. *See, e.g., Bd. of Educ. of the Round Valley Unified Sch. District v. Round Valley Teachers Ass'n*, 20 PERC ¶ 27076 (Cal. 1996) (union and school employer cannot legally agree to grant probationary teachers who were not rehired greater procedural protections than they were entitled to under the state Education Code); *Matter of Cohoes City Sch. Dist. v. Cohoes Teachers Ass'n*, 40 N.Y.2d 774 (1976) (state Education Law implicitly bars the subject of tenure decisions from collective bargaining); *Ass'n of N.J. State College Faculties, Inc. v. Dungan*, 64 N.J. 338 (1974) (new, more stringent requirements for tenure are not negotiable, as New Jersey's Education Law gives the Board of Higher Education the right to set education policy).

Also, the federal constitution provides some protections to public employees, and these protections may affect the scope of bargaining. For example, certain searches of public employees by public employers, including drug tests, may violate the Fourth Amendment. Applying a balancing test, the Court in *National Treasury Employees Union v. Von Raab*, 489 U.S. 656 (1989), held that, under the Fourth Amendment, employees in certain jobs implicating public safety could be drug-tested without reasonable individualized suspicion of drug use. In *Von Raab*, the Court permitted such drug testing for employees who carried weapons and interdicted drugs. But it is unconstitutional for public employers to subject employees who are *not* "safety sensitive" to random drug tests as a condition of employment or requirement for promotion.

Safety sensitive employees commonly include: police (*Carroll v. City of Westminster*, 233 F.3d 208 (4th Cir. 2000)); firefighters (*Aguilera v. City of East Chicago, Fire Civil Service Comm.*, 768 N.E.2d 978 (Ind. App. 2002)); and those who operate public transportation (*Southwest Ohio Regional Trans. Auth. v. Amal. Trans. Union, Local 627*, 91 Ohio St. 3d 108 (Oh. 2001)). While this issue is in some ways independent of whether drug testing is or is not a mandatory topic under a state public-sector labor law, it is likely that a proposal by an employer to institute a drug testing program that would violate the Fourth Amendment rights of employees is an illegal subject of bargaining (although one case, *In the Matter of Buffalo Police Benev. Ass'n v. City of Buffalo*, 20 NYPER 3048 (NY PERB 1987), held that such a program could be a permissive topic).

In some states, unions representing certain types of public employees have a wider scope of bargaining than unions representing other types of public employees. This raises the issue of whether such differing rules violate the Equal Protection Clause. The Supreme Court rejected such a claim in *Central State University v. American Association of University Professors, Central State University Chapter*, 526 U.S. 124 (1999), holding that such distinctions need only satisfy the rational basis test. In this case, removing certain workload issues from the scope of bargaining for university faculty unions (and those unions only) only had to be rationally related to a legitimate government concern: the goal of increasing teacher time in classrooms.

E. Remedies for Failing to Bargain in Good Faith in the Public Sector

Public-sector laws generally track private-sector law regarding remedies for the failure to bargain in good faith. However, as elsewhere, the public-sector context can sometimes create an interesting variation.

In *City of Seattle v. Public Employment Relations Commission*, 826 P.2d 158 (Wash. 1992), the employer had repeatedly and flagrantly violated its duty to bargain in good faith. As a remedy, the state labor board ordered binding interest arbitration to set contract terms. As Chapter 15 explains, interest arbitration is a procedure used in many (but not all) public-sector labor statutes to resolve bargaining impasses. Notably, the employees and union involved in this case (unlike some other types of public employee unions in Washington state) would not otherwise have been entitled to binding interest arbitration, to resolve an impasse or otherwise. The Washington Supreme Court upheld this remedy. It balanced the considerations articulated in the private-sector case *H. K. Porter* (discussed in Chapter 12) with the need to remedy this type of abuse. The Court also explained that public-sector and private-sector bargaining were "radically different" (e.g., the employees here could not legally strike), and that "interest arbitration need not be specifically permitted or required by statute in order for it to be lawful."

While remedies are usually the same in the public sector and the private sector, the substance of the scope of bargaining is often different: sometimes significantly so. This issue remains one of the most important facets of public-sector labor law for practitioners to understand.

CHECKPOINTS

- Scope of bargaining rules in the public sector often are significantly different than rules under the NLRA, and public-sector jurisdictions vary widely among themselves in their approaches to these rules.
- One approach in public-sector statutes is using broad statutory language regarding the right to bargain and also regarding management rights. In these jurisdictions, labor boards and courts use balancing tests, weighing the impact on the wages, hours, and working conditions of employees, the extent of the infringement on management rights, and the utility of collective bargaining to resolve the issue.
- In public-sector jurisdictions using balancing tests, there are certain recurring areas in which proposals that would be mandatory in the private sector are often held not mandatory. Many such cases involve public safety officers and teachers; others involve staffing and subcontracting.
- Other public-sector jurisdictions use the "laundry list" approach in which the statute itself specifies in detail which topics are mandatory and which are not.
- Some laundry list statutes have specific limitations that apply only to certain types of employees, often teachers.

- At least two states, Wisconsin and Iowa, have greatly limited the scope of bargaining for all public employees *except* "public safety" employees.
- Even where the substance of an employer's decision is not mandatory, unions typically have the right to negotiate the "effects" of the decision; this is an especially significant issue in the public sector, where many decisions are otherwise not negotiable, but the effects of those decisions are negotiable.
- External laws governing public employment may also limit the scope of bargaining by setting rules that may not be altered by negotiations. These laws include civil service laws, teacher tenure and other education laws, and federal and state constitutional rules.
- In some cases, these external laws and/or the relevant public-sector labor statute specify how the two laws should interact; in other cases, they do not, leaving the issue up to labor boards and courts.
- Public-sector law generally tracks private-sector law regarding remedies for the failure to bargain in good faith, but occasional variations exist.

CHAPTER 14

Employer Responses to Concerted Union Activity: Private Sector Strikes and Lockouts

---

ROADMAP

- The right to strike under Section 13 of the NLRA
- Unprotected strike activity
- National emergencies and notice/cooling off provisions
- *Mackay Radio* and the use of permanent replacements
- Distinction between economic and ULP strikers
- Proving intent through inference: conduct that speaks for itself
- The inherently destructive nature of super-seniority provisions
- The general permissibility of bargaining lockouts
- The current inherently destructive framework under *Great Dane*
- *Laidlaw* rights of permanently replaced workers and treatment under *Great Dane*

A. The Right to Strike

Historically, unions and their members had no constitutionally protected right to engage in strikes to gain concessions in the workplace. In *Dorchy v. Kansas,* 272 U.S. 306 (1926), the Supreme Court held that neither the common law, nor the Fourteenth Amendment (under the Due Process Clause), confers the absolute right to strike. Indeed, strike activity was subject to both legal actions (under criminal conspiracy, civil conspiracy, and antitrust law) and non-legal actions (through the notorious use of Pinkerton agents and other company-hired private police forces). Eventually, however, there came more general acceptance of peaceful strikes (and associated picketing), and legal and non-legal interventions became less common as the law also formally changed in this area.

Before the 1930s, employers routinely used injunctions, often obtained *ex parte*, to defeat strikes. Then, in 1932, the Norris-LaGuardia Act outlawed most labor injunctions in the federal courts (followed by the outlawing of such injunctions under similar laws enacted in many states). Norris-LaGuardia was also read to shield most peaceful strike activity from antitrust liability. *See* Chapter 21. Although the Supreme Court has never recognized a federal constitutional right to engage in strikes as a type of associational activity, as other countries have done, Section 13 of the National Labor Relations Act of 1935 (NLRA) recognized at least some strike rights. Section 13 states in full: "Nothing in this Act, except as specifically provided for herein, shall be construed so either to interfere with or impede or diminish in any way the right to strike or to affect the limitations or qualification on that right."

The importance of the right of workers to engage in strikes to bring economic pressure to bear on their employers cannot be overstated. Under the Wagner model of labor relations, it is the parties—not the government—who determine wages and other terms and conditions of employment. Collective bargaining works, when it does, because negotiations narrow the issues between the parties, and the threat of a work stoppage looms over them. When push comes to shove, the union must decide whether to compromise or go on strike, and the employer must decide whether to compromise or lock out its employees. If a strike or lockout occurs, there will only be a settlement if the costs of not settling become greater than the costs of accepting the terms of the proposals.

Not all strikes, or strike-like activities, are protected by the NLRA. For example, "sit down strikes" (where the employees occupy the employer's property for at least a non-trivial amount of time) are not protected. Nor are strikes that feature destruction of the employer's property or other significant illegal acts. *NLRB v. Fansteel Metallurgical Corp.*, 306 U.S. 240 (1939). Also, the NLRA does not protect "partial" or "slowdown" strikes, work stoppages where the employees do some, but not all, their required work. *See NLRB v. Insurance Agents*, 361 U.S. 477 (1960).

In addition, otherwise legal strikes will lose protection if the union fails to take reasonable precautions to protect employer property from foreseeable, aggravated, imminent danger due to a sudden work stoppage. *See Glacier Northwest, Inc. v. International B'hood of Teamsters Local Union No. 174*, 598 U.S. 771 (2023). In *Glacier Northwest*, the Court held that assuming the facts the employer alleged were true, they were sufficient to remove protection for a strike by employees who, among other things, operated concrete-mixing trucks. The allegations were that the union intentionally called the strike when it knew that trucks were full of wet concrete that would harden and likely severely damage the trucks. Cases alleging harm to employers are very fact-dependent because it is also true that unions have no responsibility to time strikes in a way that minimizes economic harm to the employer.

Beyond the above, note that all, or almost all, labor contracts themselves contain "no strike/no lockout" clauses that bar such actions during the term of that contract. The NLRA does not protect strikes in breach of such clauses.

1. National Emergencies

The statute itself contains other limits on the strike right. Although national emergency provisions have only been used very rarely in the NLRA's history, challenging issues arise when dealing with industries where strikes become intolerable to the public long before they become intolerable to the parties. Sections 206 through 210 of the Labor Management Relations Act (Taft-Hartley Act) set forth detailed procedures that govern strikes that are deemed to constitute a national emergency. The President can impanel a Board of Inquiry if the strike would imperil the national health or safety. After investigation, the President can ask the Attorney General to petition the federal court for a 60-day injunction. The injunction must be dissolved after 80 days. A recent use of these procedures occurred in 2002, when the Bush II administration sought an injunction to stop a lockout of longshoremen. A court granted the injunction based on its finding that the lockout had caused a national emergency by delaying shipments of goods through the affected West Coast ports.

2. Notice and Cooling Off Provisions under Section 8(d)

Even when a work stoppage does not constitute a national emergency, the NLRA has some provisions designed to at least minimize the economic disruption caused by strikes and lockouts. This policy is meant to foster voluntary settlements of disputes through, among other things, Section 8(d)'s elaborate notification and cooling-off procedures.

Section 8(d)(1) requires written notice 60 days before expiration of a collective bargaining agreement (CBA) if a party wants to terminate or modify the CBA. Section 8(d)(2) requires the party to meet and confer with the other party to negotiate a new CBA or modify the current CBA. Section 8(d)(3) next requires that 30 days after the initial notice, the parties must notify the Federal Mediation and Conciliation Service (FMCS) of the pending dispute. The parties, however, are not required to mediate with the FMCS. Finally, 8(d)(4) states that parties must not strike for 60 days after notification under 8(d)(1), and failure to comply with this rule violates the duty to bargain in good faith under Section 8(a)(5). As a result of the 1974 amendments to the NLRA, special rules exist under Section 8(g) for health care institutions (which are discussed in more detail in Chapter 12).

B. *Mackay Radio* and Permanent Replacements

Although the text of Section 13 of the Act seems to provide robust protection for peaceful strike activity, the introduction of the permanent replacement doctrine by the Supreme Court a few years after the enactment of the Wagner Act significantly weakened this section.

At first blush, *NLRB v. Mackay Radio & Telegraph Co.*, 304 U.S. 333 (1938), appeared to be a relatively straightforward application of the Section 8(a)(3) unfair labor practice (ULP) to employer discriminatory actions against employees engaged in union activities. In *Mackay Radio*, the company responded to its employees' strike activity by replacing them during the strike with new employees and then refusing to displace those replacement workers once the strike had ended. The employer maintained that it had permanently replaced the strikers not for anti-union reasons, but for the legitimate reason of continuing its business operations during the strike. The uncontroversial holding of the case is that the employer violated Section 8(a)(3) because, in not bringing back certain workers who were the most active union members, the employer's true purpose was to discourage union membership.

The more controversial proposition for which this case has come to stand is that an employer may permanently replace striking workers. That is, the employer does not have to remove those replacement workers once the strike is over and does not have to offer employment to the strikers until suitable vacancies arise. Technically speaking, the employer is not discharging the striking workers for engaging in striking activity; therefore, they should be reinstated if their positions become open (if, for example, the replacements occupying their positions leave). However, the reality of the situation is hardly lost on workers who realize that they may lose their job permanently or for a very long time after the strike is over if their employer chooses to permanently replace them with replacement workers while they are out on strike.

While critics of *Mackay Radio* say that the doctrine chills employees' willingness to exercise their right to strike, proponents would argue that it limits unreasonable CBA demands, and that employers have the right to run their workplaces as they see fit, which includes the right to hire other employees (if they can find appropriate skilled labor) to keep their business running during a strike. Moreover, the argument against allowing only temporary replacement workers (such that striking employees could reacquire their jobs at the end of the strike) is that the training of such temporary replacements would be unduly burdensome on the employer, and many employees would not risk crossing a picket line to obtain employment for what could be a relatively short time. Thus, employers argued that they must offer permanent positions to replacement workers to secure the necessary employees during the strike.

For decades after *Maclay Radio*, employers did not regularly take advantage of the power of permanent replacements, so strikes continued to be part of the normal bounded economic struggle between employers and unions. Permanent replacements became a more regular part of industrial life in the United States in the 1980s. Many commentators believe that it was the firing of some 11,000 air traffic controllers (not even covered by the NLRA as they were federal employees) by President Reagan in 1981 that led to the more frequent use of this tactic in the private sector, and to the subsequent precipitous decline in the number of strikes by unions. That being said, the use of permanent replacements was already increasing by the time of the air traffic controllers' strike.

In any event, the employer's right to permanently replace workers remains controversial both because the NLRA's language does not expressly support this right, the Court's reasoning in *Mackay Radio* is cursory at best, and the practice has had a dramatic impact on the ability of employees to engage in strikes to exercise economic power against their employers. In addition to several failed pieces of legislation to overrule the *Mackay Radio* rule over the years, President Clinton sought by executive order to forbid the use of permanent replacements by federal contractors. That executive order was found invalid in *Chamber of Commerce of the U.S. v. Reich*, 74 F.3d 1322 (D.C. Cir. 1996), as the court held that an employer's right under the Act to hire permanent replacements during a labor strike preempted the executive order (preemption is discussed in more detail in Chapter 18).

Regardless of what side of the debate one falls on regarding the permanent replacement doctrine, the fact is that many employees will refuse to consider striking as an option if all that awaits them at the end of the strike is unemployment. Without the threat of a strike to give weight to their bargaining demands, many unions are at the employer's mercy because they have no effective way to exercise collective power in the face of employer intransigence.

1. Economic versus Unfair Labor Practice (ULP) Strikers

As a general rule, only workers who have struck to pressure their employers on bargaining demands may be permanently replaced. These strikers are referred to as "economic strikers," and the *Mackay Radio* rule only applies to them. By contrast, strikers motivated at least in part by significant ULPs are considered "ULP strikers," and they may only be temporarily replaced. Specifically, ULP strikers have a right to return to their jobs if the strikers make an unconditional offer to return to work. In the event of a strike caused or prolonged by the employer's ULP, the Board's preferred remedy is reinstatement of the strikers, even if reinstatement requires that replacement workers hired during the strike be discharged. The rationale is that strikers protesting their employers' illegal acts should have superior reinstatement rights.

There is not always a bright line between which employees are economic strikers and which are ULP strikers. Given the consequences for reinstatement rights, unions and employers often argue about the cause of the strike while the strike is ongoing. This is why, for example, union billboards and other appeals to the public during strikes often say that the employer has "failed to bargain in good faith." Adding to these difficulties surrounding the characterization of the strike is the fact that a strike might start from disagreements at the bargaining table (i.e., an economic strike) but might transform into a ULP strike if the employer committed a ULP, such as discriminating against or otherwise intimidating union members during the bargaining process while the strike continues. The union must prove that the strike has been transformed into a ULP strike. This can only be done by showing that the union was protesting against specific unlawful employer acts, the employer was found in fact to have committed such acts, and that the duration of the strike has been prolonged as a result of the commission of the ULP. Because it is not always clear whether a striker is a ULP striker until after the Board has determined the lawfulness of the employer conduct, the worker and the employer undertake a considerable risk that the Board will characterize the employer's conduct and, therefore, the strike in a way that is unfavorable to them. Consequently, their status as a striker is another consideration that employees must take into account before going out on strike.

Another important distinction between ULP and economic strikers is that, although both can vote in union decertification elections, economic strikers' right to vote expires if the election is held more than twelve months after the strike begins. Moreover, replacement workers hired during an economic strike may vote in such elections, while those hired during a ULP strike may not. Finally, a strike's characterization is also crucial in determining whether there has been compliance with the notice and cooling-off requirements of Section 8(d) (discussed above) or whether a strike violates a no-strike contract provision (discussed in Chapter 17). No-strike provisions in CBAs generally bar only economic strikes and less serious ULP strikes.

Distinctions concerning whether the strike is an economic strike or a ULP strike only apply when the strikers have not engaged in conduct that is outside Section 7's protection. However, even when strikers have engaged in unprotected activity, the Board has historically been open to the ULP strikers' right to reinstatement. The Board and some courts have reasoned that a ULP striker should not automatically be denied reinstatement as a result of unprotected activity that the employer's ULP may have provoked. Despite the striker's improper conduct, reinstatement may be the only way to prevent the employer from benefiting from its ULP. *See Local 833, UAW v. NLRB (Kohler Co.)*, 300 F.2d 699 (D.C. Cir. 1962). *But see Clear Pine Mouldings Inc.*, 268 N.L.R.B. 1044 (1984) (Board plurality disagreeing with *Kohler* and denying reinstatement to ULP strikers engaged in abusive threatening behavior).

C. Employer Responses to Union Concerted Activities and Group-Based, Inferential Section 8(a)(3) Cases

As discussed in Chapter 9, there are generally two recognized types of Section 8(a)(3) discrimination claims: (1) individual discrimination claims based on specific evidence that an employer engaged in anti-union discrimination by firing, refusing to hire, or otherwise taking adverse employment actions against employees in retaliation for union activity, and (2) group discrimination claims based on inferential evidence that an employer responded to concerted union activities for discriminatory unlawful purposes. The *Wright Line* analysis discussed in Chapter 9 applies to most individual discrimination claims. This Chapter discusses inferential discrimination claims under the *Great Dane* framework. In these cases, the ULP must be established based upon the impact of the employer's conduct on employee Section 7 rights, as there is no specific evidence of anti-union intent.

1. *Radio Officers* and Conduct That Speaks for Itself

Although employer anti-union intent or motive is always an essential feature of any Section 8(a)(3) charge, the Supreme Court held fairly early on that specific evidence of anti-union intent is not always required. In *Radio Officers Union v. NLRB (Gaynor News)*, 347 U.S. 17 (1954), in one of the three consolidated cases before the Court, a company had agreed under a CBA to grant retroactive wage increases and vacation payments to union members, but not to nonunion members. The Court found that specific evidence of intent to encourage or discourage unionism is not an indispensable element of proof under Section 8(a)(3), and the mere existence of certain types of discriminatory conduct can satisfy the intent requirement. Thus, the Court concluded that some employer conduct so inherently encourages or discourages union membership that specific proof of intent is unnecessary, and intent is presumed. In other words, the conduct speaks for itself. According to the Court, this was not a novel concept, but an application of the common law rule that "a man is held to intend the foreseeable consequences of his conduct." When the "natural" consequences of an employer's conduct are to discourage or encourage union activity, an employer's response that it was not its "true purpose" to interfere with its employees' Section 7 rights will be unavailing. In *Radio Officers*, the employer was found to have committed a ULP under Section 8(a)(3) because the employer's discriminatory action of granting better benefits to union members inevitably caused the encouragement of union membership; that is, unlawful intent could be inferred based on the foreseeable consequences of such conduct on employees' rights under the Act.

2. *Erie Resistor* and Super-Seniority

Nailing down the "natural" or "foreseeable" consequences of an employer's action is far from a straightforward exercise. Nowhere is that better seen than in *NLRB v. Erie Resistor Corp.*, 373 U.S. 221 (1963), in which the Supreme Court explored the relationship between an employer's business justifications and "conduct which speaks for itself" in the context of an employer's plan to extend a 20-year super-seniority credit to strike replacement workers and strike breakers. To lure replacement workers and encourage union employees to cross the picket line, the company offered a one-time "super" seniority credit to ensure the permanency of the replacement workers' and strike breakers' jobs and to provide them with continued seniority benefits after the strike ended.

In deciding whether the employer's conduct in using the super-seniority plan during the strike violated the discrimination provisions of Section 8(a)(3), the Court found that it was the Board's task to weigh the interest of employees in concerted activity against the interest of the employer in operating its business in a particular manner. This balancing of interests had previously been restricted to cases arising under Section 8(a)(1) concerning employer interference with employee concerted activities (discussed in Chapter 4), but *Erie Resistor* was the Court's first use of a similar balancing approach concerning Section 8(a)(3) intent-based cases.

Regarding the balancing of interests, the Court deferred to the Board's finding that the employees' interest won out because the super-seniority plan was inherently discriminatory or destructive of Section 7 rights as it favored non-strikers in the terms of their employment and had the effect of discouraging union membership far into the future. More specifically, the Court observed that the Board made a detailed assessment of super-seniority and the devastating consequences such plans visited on employees' right to engage in concerted strike activity, including the fact that such plans: (1) affect the tenure of all strikers; (2) treat non-strikers better than strikers; (3) induce individual strikers to abandon the strike; (4) deal a crippling blow to any strike effort; and (5) render future collective bargaining difficult because of the lasting effects of the super-seniority plan on different groups of employees. It can thus be argued, based on these attributes of super-seniority, that the practice is worse for union workers than hiring permanent replacements. Indeed, the *Erie Resistor* Court reexamined and reaffirmed the *Mackay Radio* rule concerning the use of permanent replacements, finding that the use of such replacements did not have an inherently destructive impact on the Section 7 rights of employees and thus did not violate Section 8(a)(3).

The *Erie Resistor* decision was arguably unclear as to whether it was holding that an "inherently destructive" employer tactic does not require direct proof of employer anti-union animus, unlike other types of 8(a)(3) cases, or an employer tactic that was "inherently destructive" of union rights was itself sufficient to demonstrate such animus. One could say the case utilized a balancing process for establishing motive through inferential means. Alternatively, because the super-seniority plan in *Erie Resistor* had such an inherently destructive impact on union members' right to engage in concerted activities, it was deemed to be the type of conduct that speaks for itself as far as establishing the employer's discriminatory purpose.

As to what type of activities constitute "inherently destructive" acts (given that permanently replacing strikers is not such an activity), one could look to acts that specifically reward or punish specific employees based on their level of union/strike support. Recall that *MacKay Radio* held that permanently replacing economic strikers was legal, but rehiring some (but not all) strikers on the basis that those strikers were the least loyal to the strike violated Section 8(a)(3).

3. *American Ship Building*, *Brown*, and Lockouts

In addition to unions striking to place economic pressure on employers to cede to their demands at the bargaining table, employers are free to preempt such activity by choosing to lock out their employees. A lockout means that the employees cannot come to work even if they are willing to do so, and the lockout will not be lifted until the employer agrees to let them back. Although lockouts are usually not permitted during organizational drives and when aimed specifically at union supporters, lockouts are permissible in specified circumstances. The question arises whether lockouts, even when permitted, are inherently destructive of employee Section 7 rights and, therefore, violate Section 8(a)(3).

The Supreme Court considered this question in *American Ship Building Co. v. NLRB*, 380 U.S. 300 (1965), in which it examined the legality of an employer's use of a bargaining lockout. Bargaining or offensive lockouts involve situations where an employer locks out its employees not in response to union pressure (a defensive lockout, such as the one in *NLRB v. Brown* discussed below), but to bring economic pressure to bear on the union during collective bargaining negotiations. In *American Ship Building*, the employer had a long history of collective bargaining with the union, but it had locked out its employees to exert economic pressure after extensive collective negotiations had proven fruitless. This time, the Court articulated the inherently destructive test as whether the employer practices "are inherently so prejudicial to union interests and so devoid of significant economic justification that no specific evidence of intent to discourage union membership or other antiunion animus is required." *Id.* at 311.

This formulation of the inherently destructive standard appeared to significantly limit the Board's ability to infer anti-union intent in most Section 8(a)(3) cases, as only those instances involving the most extreme forms of employer conduct would satisfy the Court's standard and permit an inference of unlawful intent. Given that the employer initiated the bargaining lockout to win the economic dispute at the bargaining table, and that the employer had a substantial reason for engaging in the lockout because of the highly seasonal nature of the employer's business (which made it crucial for the employer to determine the timing and duration of any work stoppage), the Court found that unlawful intent could not be inferred from the employer's conduct. In other words, the employer's conduct here did not bespeak discrimination.

Also, the *American Ship Building* Court chastised the Board for engaging in an improper balancing exercise. Although the Court appeared willing to permit the Board to intervene in labor disputes where employer conduct was inherently destructive of the collective-bargaining process, it was unwilling to condone the use of the inherently destructive standard where the employer was merely deploying its economic weapons within a given bargaining dispute to bring economic pressure to bear on the union. Because the Court believed the Board had ruled in favor of the union based on its view that the lockout weapon gave the employer too much power, the Court found that the Board had exceeded the scope of its authority by involving itself improperly in the substantive aspects of the bargaining process. As long as the employer had some economic justification for its actions, the Board was precluded from inferring unlawful intent based on the impact that the employer's actions had on employee rights.

In another lockout case decided on the same day as *American Ship Building—NLRB v. Brown*, 380 U.S. 278 (1965)—the Court considered whether an employer member of a multi-employer bargaining unit faced with a whipsaw strike could lockout its employees and temporarily hire replacement workers until the strike ended. A whipsaw strike occurs when the union attempts to undermine the cohesiveness of a multi-employer bargaining unit by striking individually each member of the unit consecutively. Because the other unstruck members of the multi-employer bargaining unit gain a resultant unfair advantage as a consequence of the union's tactic, the struck member is forced to give in to the union's terms in derogation of its commitment to the multi-employer bargaining unit. Lockouts that occur in reaction to union pressure, like the one in *Brown*, are referred to as defensive lockouts.

As in *American Ship Building*, there was no specific evidence of intent, and so the Court had to consider whether unlawful intent could be inferred from the impact of the employer's conduct on employee rights under the Act. The *Brown* Court set forth the applicable inherently destructive standard in the following manner: "[W]hen an employer practice is inherently destructive of employee rights and is not justified by the service of important business ends, no specific evidence of intent to discourage union membership is necessary to establish a violation of § 8(a)(3)." *Id.* at 287. In such instances, the Court found, inherently destructive conduct could not be saved from illegality by an overriding business reason pursued in good faith. However, where the tendency to discourage union membership is comparatively slight, and the employer's conduct is reasonably adopted to achieve legitimate business ends, the Court required the General Counsel to provide specific evidence of the employer's improper motivation.

Applying these standards in *Brown*, the Court found the use of a lockout with temporary replacements in the context of a whipsaw strike to have only a comparatively slight tendency to discourage union membership. In other words, the preservation of the multi-employer bargaining unit was a "legitimate business end" that was not unlawful under the Act because such actions only had a comparatively slight impact on employee rights under the Act. Under these circumstances, the Court required specific evidence of anti-union intent to find that the employer violated Section 8(a)(3). Because there was no such specific evidence in *Brown*, the Court concluded that the employer's lockout was lawful.

The *Brown* decision is important because it marks the first time the Supreme Court expressly divided employer conduct having a discriminatory effect on employee rights under the Act into two groups: (1) conduct that had an inherently destructive impact on employee rights and (2) conduct that had a comparatively slight impact on employee rights. Although the Court explained why in the case of a lockout with temporary replacements the conduct had a comparatively slight impact, there was no attempt by the Court to establish prospective rules for making this distinction in the future.

More recently, the D.C. Circuit held in *International Brotherhood of Boilermakers, Local 88 v. NLRB*, 858 F.2d 756 (D.C. Cir. 1988), that the employer did not violate the Act by staging a lockout and using temporary replacements during the lockout. According to the court, hiring temporary workers during a lockout was not a ULP because the Act does not guarantee employees a bargain, only the right to bargain. Therefore, it is not unlawful for an employer to strengthen its bargaining position by hiring temporary workers during a lockout. By contrast, the Board and courts have generally not allowed employers to hire *permanent* replacements during lockouts, on the grounds that this would give the employer too much power.

D. The Gradual Development of the *Great Dane* Framework

In *NLRB v. Great Dane Trailer, Inc.*, 388 U.S. 26 (1967), the Supreme Court sought to establish the definitive framework for inferential Section 8(a)(3) cases involving employer responses to union concerted activities. *Great Dane* embraced the inherently destructive/comparatively slight dichotomy set forth in *Brown*, but with an important twist.

Great Dane involved an employer's reaction to a strike. At the same time the employer refused to pay striking employees vacation benefits that had accrued under the terms of the expired CBA, it announced its intention to pay these same vacation benefits to striker replacements, returning strikers, and non-strikers who had been at work on a certain date during the strike. Because there was no specific evidence that the employer's actions against the strikers were motivated by anti-union intent, the Court considered whether such intent could be inferred based on the impact the conduct had on employee rights under the Act.

Synthesizing the holdings of previous inferential Section 8(a)(3) cases, the Court divided all such cases into two categories: (1) if it can reasonably be concluded that the employer's discriminatory conduct was "inherently destructive" of important employee rights, no proof of an anti-union motivation is needed, and the Board can find a ULP even if the employer introduces evidence that the conduct was motivated by business considerations; and (2) if the adverse effect of the discriminatory conduct on employee rights is "comparatively slight," an anti-union motivation must be proved to sustain the charge if the employer has come forward with evidence of legitimate and substantial business justifications for the conduct. Under either circumstance, "once it has been proved that the employer engaged in discriminatory conduct which could have adversely affected employee rights to *some* extent, the burden is upon the employer to establish that he was motivated by legitimate objectives since proof of motivation is most accessible to him." *Id.* at 34. Placing the initial burden on the employer to show a legitimate and substantial reason for its discriminatory conduct is arguably the most significant holding of *Great Dane.*

Because the Court concluded in *Great Dane* that the employer had not met its initial burden of proving that it had legitimate and substantial reasons for treating strikers in a discriminatory fashion as compared with other workers, it was not necessary to decide whether the employer's vacation benefits policy had an inherently destructive or comparatively slight impact on employee Section 7 rights. The employer violated 8(a)(3) because the necessary anti-union intent could be inferred from the fact that the employer's discriminatory conduct lacked a legitimate and substantial reason. Placing the initial burden on the employer to prove that it had legitimate and substantial justifications for its conduct made the inherently destructive/comparatively slight characterization unnecessary in some inferential cases, like *Great Dane* itself.

To this day, the Supreme Court has still not supplied clear rules for deciding when employer conduct has an inherently destructive impact versus a comparatively slight impact. In its first inferential Section 8(a)(3) case after *Great Dane*, *NLRB v. Fleetwood Trailer Co.*, 389 U.S. 375 (1967), the Court avoided the inherently destructive determination in much the same manner as the *Great Dane* Court did. Having found that refusing to reinstate replaced strikers had some discriminatory effect on employee rights, the *Fleetwood Trailer* Court searched the record in vain for legitimate and substantial reasons for the employer not to reinstate the former strikers. Finding none, the Court was able under the *Great Dane* framework to infer anti-union intent in violation of Section 8(a)(3) without needing to categorize the conduct as inherently destructive or comparatively slight.

1. Board's Application of *Great Dane*'s Inherently Destructive Standard

Where the employer is able to meet its initial burden and establish a legitimate and substantial reason for its discriminatory conduct, the Board has more frequently found conduct to be inherently destructive in cases where the employer distinguishes workers based on participation in protected activities and where an employer discourages the process of collective bargaining by making it appear to be a futile exercise. On the other hand, the Board has generally found employer conduct to have a comparatively slight impact on employee rights in cases in which the employers have locked out their employees and used temporary replacement workers. Additionally, many Board decisions mimic the *Great Dane* decision itself by not even reaching the inherently destructive determination. Such cases involve fact patterns where there have been changes in the workforce during a strike, where striker reinstatement rights are at issue (see discussion of *Laidlaw* below), and where there has been a withholding of accrued benefits from employees during a labor dispute.

The Board has established fundamental guiding principles based on past Supreme Court inferential Section 8(a)(3) cases. In *International Paper Co.*, 319 N.L.R.B. 1253 (1995), *enf. den.*, 115 F.3d 1045 (D.C. Cir. 1997), the Board considered whether permanently subcontracting out bargaining unit work during a lockout constituted inherently destructive conduct. The Board applied four "guiding principles" for making this determination: (1) the severity of the harm suffered by employees as well as the severity of the impact on the statutory right being exercised; (2) the temporal nature of the conduct in question; (3) whether the employer's conduct demonstrated hostility to the process of collective bargaining as opposed to a simple intention to support its bargaining position as to compensation and other matters; and (4) whether employer conduct discouraged collective bargaining in the sense of making it seem a futile exercise in the eyes of employees. Applying these four guiding principles to the permanent subcontracting scenario under review, the Board concluded that the conduct in question had an inherently destructive impact on employee rights because all four principles had been violated by the employer's conduct. As if to underline the unsatisfactory resolution of the inherently destructive standard conundrum by the Board in *International Paper*, the D.C. Circuit looked at the same conduct as the Board in *International Paper* but came to the opposite conclusion. Thus, there is still much uncertainty in this area of the law.

2. *Laidlaw* Rights: Applying the *Great Dane* Framework to the Rights of Replaced Workers

Interestingly, a sizable number of *Great Dane* decisions concern similar types of cases involving striker reinstatement rights. These cases concern the reinstatement of economic strikers after a vacancy has occurred and an unconditional offer to return to work has been made by the workers. The rights involved in these cases are referred to as *Laidlaw* rights based on the Board's decision in *Laidlaw Corp.*, 171 N.L.R.B. 1366 (1968). Under *Laidlaw, striking* employees are statutory employees under Section 2(3) of the Act, meaning that they retain their seniority, and upon an unconditional offer to return to work, they go to the front of the queue for any appropriate job vacancies. However, if striking employees find substantially equivalent work elsewhere, they no longer have these *Laidlaw* rights. *Laidlaw* is a typical *Great Dane*-type case, where the employer is found not to have legitimate and substantial reasons for not hiring back the strikers, and thus, discriminatory intent is permitted to be inferred and a Section 8(a)(3) violation found. The remedy for this type of violation is to reinstate the workers with backpay to the time when they should have been able to exercise their *Laidlaw* rights. A sizeable percentage of these types of cases are for the failure of employers to reinstate strikers.

As to the Board's inherently destructive finding in *Laidlaw*, the better understanding of *Great Dane* is that if the employer does not have a legitimate and substantial reason for its discriminatory conduct, discriminatory intent can be inferred without characterizing the impact of the conduct as inherently destructive or comparatively slight. And although some recognized situations meet the legitimate and substantial business reasons standard in the replacement worker reinstatement context (for instance, where the striking employee has found other substantially equivalent employment in the meantime), the Board will find that most employers who fail to reinstate such strikers according to their *Laidlaw* rights have violated Section 8(a)(3) without there being any need to establish specific evidence of anti-union intent.

3. Strike-Settlement Agreements and *Laidlaw* Rights

Different issues arise when an employer, under a strike-settlement agreement, decides to bring all striking employees back to work and discharges the permanent replacements. In *Belknap v. Hale*, 463 U.S. 491 (1983), the Supreme Court held that permanent replacements who lost their jobs because of a strike-settlement agreement between the company and the union could bring state tort and contract claims against the company. The company argued that the NLRA preempted any such state common law claims, but the Court disagreed (preemption is discussed in more detail in Chapter 18). In some cases, *Belknap* might make employers less likely to promise permanent positions to replacements unless they are certain that a subsequent strike settlement agreement will not require strikers to get their jobs back. In other cases, strikes might be harder to settle if employers have already made these promises and the union will not end the strike until it can ensure that strikers will get their jobs back.

CHECKPOINTS

- No federal constitutional right to strike exists.
- Section 13 of the NLRA statutorily recognizes employees' right to strike for private-sector employees. Not all strike activities are protected. For example, the NLRA does not protect "partial strikes," "sit-down strikes," and strikes involving significant illegal activity or intentional damage to employer property. Special provisions apply to national emergencies, and notice and cooling-off provisions also exist. Moreover, union contracts typically bar strikes (and lockouts) during the term of the contract.
- Under *Mackay Radio*, employers may permanently replace striking workers, do not have a duty to remove replacement workers once the strike ends, and do not have to offer employment to strikers until a suitable vacancy arises.
- Only economic strikers can be permanently replaced. In most circumstances, ULP strikers may only be temporarily replaced.

- Although anti-union intent must be established in Section 8(a)(3) cases, this can be done either through specific evidence of anti-union intent under *Wright Line* or through employer conduct that speaks-for-itself under *Radio Officers*.
- Super-seniority plans in response to strikes are considered inherently destructive of employee Section 7 rights, violating Section 8(a)(3). Permanently replacing economic strikers is not considered inherently destructive conduct.
- A bargaining lockout has a comparatively slight, as opposed to inherently destructive, impact on employees' Section 7 rights and does not violate 8(a)(3).
- The Board is not permitted to weigh the effectiveness of a party's economic weapons in bargaining disputes, but only whether a party's conduct undermines the collective-bargaining process.
- Under *Great Dane*, employer conduct that has some discriminatory effect on employees must be taken for legitimate and substantial business reasons. If not, the Board can infer discriminatory intent and find a Section 8(a)(3) violation.
- If legitimate and substantial business reasons exist, then the Board must decide, largely by relying on past cases, whether employer conduct had an inherently destructive or comparatively slight impact on the employees' Section 7 rights.
- Under *Laidlaw*, replaced striking employees have the right to be re-hired when they make an unconditional offer to return to work, a suitable vacancy arises, and they have not accepted substantially equivalent work elsewhere.
- When an employer refuses to honor employees' *Laidlaw* rights without legitimate and substantial business reasons, the Board can infer discriminatory intent and find a violation of Section 8(a)(3) under *Great Dane*.

CHAPTER 15

Resolving Bargaining Impasses in the Public Sector

ROADMAP

- Most public-sector labor laws prohibit strikes by public employees
- How "strike" is defined in the public sector
- The penalties and remedies for illegal strikes
- Alternative procedures for resolving bargaining impasses in the public sector: public-sector mediation, fact-finding, and interest arbitration
- Standards of court review of interest arbitration awards
- Rules for legal strikes in the public sector
- The lack of permanent replacement of strikers in the public sector

While some state laws permit some public employees to strike, the clear majority of public-sector labor laws bar strikes and also provide alternative methods to resolve bargaining impasses. Typically, these methods involve some combination of mediation, fact-finding, and interest arbitration. This is a very important part of public-sector labor law, both because of its practical significance and because public-sector rules in this area are quite different from NLRA rules. Public-sector jurisdictions also vary considerably among themselves, but there are important common elements and themes.

Early public-sector labor laws all barred strikes. By the year 2000, of the thirty-eight states that allowed at least some public employees to bargain collectively, only ten had statutes that permitted any public workers to strike. A few other states, notably California, allowed some such strikes under common law, but this remains a distinctly minority approach. All jurisdictions bar strikes by police and firefighters. Even where some strikes are permitted, public-sector laws usually place significantly more restrictions on the right to strike, by requiring unions to engage in various procedures before striking and by making it easier for courts to enjoin strikes that were legal when they began.

This chapter will first explore rules regarding illegal strikes; then turn to alternative methods of impasse resolution that have been developed in the public sector; then finally examine rules for legal strikes.

A. Illegal Strikes

As Chapter 2 described, the Boston police strike had a major, lasting impact in this area in the U.S., as judges and policy-makers long associated any strike by any public employees with that disastrous event. Other traditional arguments against strike rights in the public sector include claims that such strikes would prevent the government from providing important services, and that they are an affront to government sovereignty. In more modern times, Harry Wellington and Ralph Winter's influential book, THE UNION AND THE CITIES (1971), argued that public-sector strikes should be barred because government officials would give in to union demands due to popular cries to end the strike. Actual experience with public-sector strikes, however, shows a much more mixed record.

1. Bars on Public-Sector Strikes

a. Common Law

The overwhelming majority rule is that, in the absence of a specific statutory authorization or ban, the common law bars public sector strikes. *See, e.g., Anchorage Educ. Ass'n v. Anchorage Sch. Dist.*, 648 P.2d 993, 995–96. (Alaska 1982) (citing cases from fourteen states for the proposition that by 1972, not one case had found such strikes to be legal absent statutory authorization, and agreeing with this authority).

Thirteen years after that case, however, the California Supreme Court diverged from this path. *County Sanitation Dist. No. 2 of Los Angeles County Employees Ass'n Local 660, SEIU*, 699 P.2d 835 (Cal. 1985), held that a strike by sanitation employees *could* be legal under common law. The court majority noted that the U.S. is "virtually alone among Western industrial nations" in generally banning strikes by public employees. It added that while the relevant public-sector statute was silent on the right to strike, in general it "closely mirrors" the NLRA. The majority critiqued the traditional objections to public-sector strikes, arguing that the "government sovereignty" and non-delegation arguments were outdated, that not all government services are essential, and that strikes did not give unions too much power, citing examples of public officials defeating public-sector strikes (perhaps most famously the Professional Air Traffic Controllers PATCO strike of 1981). The majority agreed that public employees who perform essential services should not be allowed to strike. But it reasoned that absent some means of equalizing the parties' respective bargaining power, such as a credible strike threat, both sides would be less likely to bargain in good faith, which would lead to *more* strikes. Thus, the majority concluded, public-sector strikes "are not unlawful at common law unless or until it is clearly demonstrated that such a strike creates a substantial and imminent threat to the health or safety of the public." Applying this test to the facts in the instant case, the majority found that the strike was legal. A strong dissent argued that the legislature was the appropriate body to legalize strikes and determine how strike rules should work.

This case represents the minority approach, but a few other cases have found some public-sector strikes legal in the absence of explicit statutory authorization. *See, e.g., State of Montana v. Public Employees Craft Council of Mont.* 529 P.2d 785 (Mont. 1974) (strike permitted under the "right to engage in concerted activities" language of the statute); *Davis v. Henry*, 555 So.2d 457 (La. 1990) (public employees have the right to strike unless it clearly endangers public health and safety, the common law rule was inapplicable because Louisiana is not a common law state). For a case following the traditional and still majority approach that public-sector strikes are illegal under common law, *see Boston Housing Authority v. LRC*, 398 Mass. 715 (1986).

b. Statutory Prohibitions

A number of statutes barring public-sector strikes date back to the aftermath of the Boston police strike; more were passed in 1947 after a strike wave in 1946 included some public workers. By the early 21st century, thirty-eight states had passed no-strike laws for government employees (these include some states that do not authorize collective bargaining for public employees). After Act 10 in Wisconsin in 2011, only twelve states permitted any public employees to strike under any circumstances.

These bans, along with common law bans, raise two significant issues discussed below. First, what conduct by public employees covered by a strike ban constitutes a strike? Second, when illegal strikes occur, what remedies and penalties are available, and to whom?

c. *What Activities Constitute a Strike?*

One long-standing issue in jurisdictions that ban strikes is the "blue flu" or similar activities: employees engaging in coordinated job actions without calling them strikes. The term "blue flu" comes from a tactic used by some police unions in which their members would call in sick *en masse*. Boards and courts have long held that such tactics constitute strikes under statutes barring strikes. *See, e.g.*, *In re City of Youngstown and Fraternal Order of Police Lodge #28*, SERB 87-002 (Ohio State Emp. Rel. Bd. 1987) (finding that twenty-eight notices of illness from a total of thirty-three officers were an illegal strike, as "[e]ven a modicum of street sense will recognize the events in this case for ... symptoms of blue-flu—a euphemism for a badly camouflaged job action").

In reaction to these and related activities, a number of public-sector laws prohibit "job actions" as well as strikes. *See, e.g.*, N.H. REV. STAT. 273-A:13 (barring "strikes and other forms of job action by public employees"). Even under this law, however, not all concerted activities regarding work are strikes. *Appeal of City of Manchester*, 144 N.H. 320 (1999), held that a union campaign to discourage police officers from volunteering from overtime was not an illegal strike, in part because the city did have the power to order officers to work overtime, and the union did not contest that power or attempt to impede that process.

Other tactics may also be considered illegal strikes. In *Board of Education v. Shanker*, 283 N.Y.S.2d 432 (1967), *aff'd w/out opinion*, 286 N.Y.S.2d 453 (1967), a large number of teachers signed petitions stating they would resign if the employer did not reach a satisfactory contract agreement with their union. The court held that this threat was an illegal strike, because the purpose was not really to quit work but rather to affect negotiations. *Board of Education v. N.J. Education Association*, 53 N.J. 29 (1968), also held that a mass resignation was illegal. Some cases have also found that union "work to rule" campaigns are illegal strikes. *See, e.g.*, *Local 252, TWU v. N.Y. State Public Employment Relations Board*, 58 N.Y.2d 354 (1983) (illegal strike when bus drivers engaged in a concerted refusal to drive buses which violated the state Vehicle and Traffic Law in ways that did not pose imminent dangers to people or property).

If, during an illegal strike or job action, an employee misses work for a legitimate reason (because, for example, the employee was truly sick or on vacation), the employee will usually be required to rebut a presumption that they were striking illegally. *See, e.g., City of Pittsburgh v. Fraternal Ass'n of Professional Paramedics*, 592 A.2d 786 (Pa. 1991) (employees on vacation at the time of the strike were not illegal strikers).

Courts are split as to whether barring the mere advocacy of an illegal strike violates the First Amendment. *Compare Brown v. Department of Transp., F.A.A.*, 735 F.2d 543 (Fed. Cir. 1984) (supervisor could be fired for urging traffic controllers to "stay together" during PATCO strike, even though supervisor did not strike) *with Tygrett v. Barry*, 627 F.2d 1279 (D.C. Cir. 1980) (probationary police officer improperly fired for advocating a "blue flu" action).

d. Remedies and Penalties for Illegal Strikes

Issues of remedies and penalties for illegal strikes break down into four distinct sub-issues. First, penalties and remedies against individual employees who go on strike illegally. Second, penalties and remedies against unions in such situations. Third, whether the employer and/or private parties should be able to collect money damages for such unlawful activity. Fourth, if an employer's unfair labor practices (ULPs) provoked the strike, whether that fact should mitigate the penalties and remedies.

In some instances, the public-sector labor statute gives specific answers to these questions. Other statutes, however, leave many of these issues open to the general remedial powers of the relevant labor board. Usually, individual strikers may be discharged and fined, and limitations are often placed on their future public employment. Unions may also be fined, decertified, and/or lose the right to dues check-off (at least for a period). The federal sector makes illegal strikes a criminal offense. The injunctive remedy also arises frequently in this area, as do contempt sanctions for violations of such injunctions.

i. Remedies Against Individual Strikers

Public-sector laws typically authorize fines and discipline against illegal striking employees. For instance, New York's Taylor Act requires, among other things, fines equal to twice the strikers' daily rate of pay for each day on strike. N.Y-McKinney's Civ. Serv. L. § 210. Ohio, which allows many public workers to strike if their union complies with statutory requirements, has a similar sanction for illegal strikes. Further, Oh. Rev. Code § 4117.17.23(B) provides that if a strike is illegal, other common penalties are available. Under this provision, the public employer:

> (1) May remove or suspend those employees who one day after notification by the public employer of the board decision that a strike is not authorized continue to engage in the nonauthorized strike; and
>
> (2) If the employee is appointed or reappointed, employed, or reemployed, as a public employee, within the same appointing authority, may impose the following conditions:
>
> (a) The employee's compensation shall in no event exceed that received by him immediately prior to the time of the violation.
>
> (b) The employee's compensation is not increased until after the expiration of one year from the appointment or reappointment, employment, or reemployment.
>
> (3) Shall deduct from each striking employee's wages, if the board also determines that the public employer did not provoke the strike, the equivalent of two days' wages for each day the employee remains on strike commencing one day after receiving the notice called for in division (B)(1) of this section....

Note that under subsection (3), the two-day pay penalty can be avoided if the public employer provoked the strike.

If employees engage in an illegal strike, employers are generally permitted wide discretion in disciplining the employees. In *Hortonville Joint School District v. Hortonville Education Association*, 426 U.S. 482 (1976), the local school board fired a number of teachers who had illegally struck. The teachers argued they had been denied due process because the school board members who had presided over their discharge hearings had provoked the strike by engaging in ULPs. The U.S. Supreme Court rejected these arguments, holding that the employer had broad powers to run the schools.

ii. Remedies against Unions for Sanctioning Illegal Strikes

Unions as institutions will not be held responsible for truly "wildcat" strikes (job actions that the union did not encourage or condone). *See, e.g. Ann Arbor Public Schools and Teamsters State, County, and Municipal Workers Local 214*, 15 MPER ¶ 33037 (Mich. PER 2002). But more often in cases of concerted job actions, the union as an institution is involved. In such cases, they are subject to a number of penalties.

(A) Injunctions

The first priority of a public employer faced with an illegal strike is usually just to end the strike, and thus employers often seek injunctions. While injunctions have long been controversial in labor law in general (*see* Chapter 2 for a discussion of the Norris-LaGuardia Act), courts often grant them in cases involving illegal public-sector strikes. Still, such injunctions raise various issues.

For example, *Feaster v. Vance*, 832 A.2d 1277 (D.C. App. 2003), upheld an injunction issued after school employees struck illegally. The court first rejected the union's argument that, because an illegal strike was a ULP, the employer had to go to the D.C. labor board before going to court. The court explained that although ULP proceedings normally must first go to the labor board, a separate part of the D.C. Code made strikes illegal, and allegations of violations of that code section could be taken directly to court. Further, public policy favored employers being able to go directly to court to enjoin illegal strikes. Next, the court rejected the union's claim that the Norris-LaGuardia Act barred this injunction, noting that this Act did not apply to public employees and employers. Finally, the court upheld the lower court's ruling that the traditional equitable factors favored an injunction.

These equitable factors are: whether the plaintiff has demonstrated (1) that there is a substantial likelihood plaintiff will prevail on the merits; (2) that plaintiff is in danger of suffering irreparable harm during the pendency of the action; (3) that more harm will result to plaintiff from the denial of the injunction than will result to the defendant from its grant; and, where applicable, (4) that the public interest will not be disserved by the issuance of the requested order. Especially important here, *Feaster* rejected the union's equitable "unclean hands" defense, based on the union's allegation that the employer prompted the strike by bargaining in bad faith.

Notably, in some earlier cases, courts had accepted this "unclean hands" defense and had refused to issue injunctions if the employer had provoked the strike (typically by failing to bargain in good faith). *See, e.g., School Dist. No. 351 Oneida County v. Oneida Educ. Ass'n*, 98 Idaho 486 (1977); *School Dist. For City of Holland v. Holland Educ. Ass'n*, 380 Mich. 314 (1968). This is now a distinctly minority approach. In Michigan, a 1994 amendment to the relevant state statute essentially overruled the *Holland* case. MICH. COMP. LAWS § 423.202a(10). As shown above, the Ohio statute provides that if employer ULPs provoked a strike, illegal strikers are not subject to the normal fines of two days' pay for each day on strike. OH. REV. CODE § 4117.17.23(B). But

Ohio still follows the majority rule that the role of employer ULPs in provoking a strike is not a defense to an injunction for at least many illegal strikes. OH. REV. CODE § 4117.23 (for strikes by public safety and other personnel not permitted to strike in Ohio, employer ULPs are "not a defense" to injunction proceedings).

Some jurisdictions differ from *Feaster's* rule that claims involving illegal strikes may be brought directly to court without having to go to the labor agency first. *See, e.g., San Jose v. Operating Engineers Local 3*, 49 Cal.4th 597 (Cal. 2010) (in at least most cases where employers seek injunctions against a threatened illegal strike, the employer must first seek relief from PERB, the state labor agency).

(B) Contempt

Sometimes even after a court has issued an injunction against an illegal strike, the union continues to strike. In such cases, contempt sanctions are usually available. Contempt can be civil (resulting in fines), criminal (additional fines and possible jail sentences), or both. Criminal cases raise additional legal issues.

New York City Transit Authority v. Transport Workers Union of America (N.Y. Sup. Court, App. Div. 2006), involved criminal contempt charges arising out of a union's failure to obey an injunction against an illegal strike by transit workers in New York City in 2005. This decision explained that, given the facts in this case, the Sixth Amendment to the U.S. Constitution did not grant a right to a jury trial as a condition of imposing criminal sanctions. Civil contempt does not require a jury trial, but in criminal contempt cases a jury trial is required if the offense was "serious" (as opposed to "petty"). Here, the court held the fine was not sufficiently "serious" to trigger the right to a jury trial. In this case, the fine was $1 million initially, which was then scheduled to double each additional day the union ignored the injunction. This, the court held, was in part punitive and thus criminal (the $1 million for the acts already done), but part prospectively coercive, and thus civil. The issue, therefore, was whether the initial $1 million fine was sufficiently "serious" to trigger the Sixth Amendment right to a jury trial. The court held that it was not, given the Local's relatively robust assets and large membership. The court also rejected the union's claim that it was entitled to have a jury because of the "extreme provocation" of the employer's refusal to bargain in good faith.

Individual union officers responsible for encouraging or leading an illegal strike that continues after an injunction may be liable in civil contempt and guilty of criminal contempt as well. For example, a case arising out of the same illegal transit workers strike, *New York City Transit Authority v. Transport Workers Union of America*, 39 NYPER ¶7510 (N.Y. Supreme Ct., April 19, 2006), considered the contempt penalties for the President, Secretary-Treasurer, and Recording Secretary of the union that struck illegally. The maximum penalties under the relevant statute, Judiciary Law § 751(1), were $1,000 and imprisonment of up to thirty days. Given the "willful disobedience" of the union leaders, the Court ordered a fine of $1,000 for the union president and ten days incarceration, and $500 fines for two other union officers.

(C) Forfeiture of Dues Check-Off Clauses

Another penalty that a number of public-sector jurisdictions make available is revoking the right of unions to negotiate or enforce contract clauses in which the employer agrees to automatically deduct union dues from the pay of individual members and forward the dues to the union. First, distinguish "dues check-off" or "dues deduction" contract clauses from "union security" clauses. The latter, discussed Chapter 19, involves the amount of dues members of bargaining units are obliged to pay to the union. In contrast, dues check-off concerns how dues owed are conveyed to the union. For obvious reasons, unions prefer to have dues paid to them via dues check-off, as opposed to having to collect dues from individual members. Thus, revoking the right to check-off clauses is a significant penalty. Questions arise concerning this penalty, however, including when it is justified and how long it should last.

MTA Bus Company v. Transport Workers Union of America 820 N.Y.S.2d 479 (N.Y. Supreme Ct. 2006), another case arising out of the transit workers' strike discussed above, involved this penalty. The relevant New York public-sector labor law permits forfeiture of dues check-off provisions as a sanction for an illegal strike. Under this statute, courts must conduct hearings to decide first, if the penalty is appropriate and second, if it is, how long it will last. Here, the court first held that the sanction was appropriate because the union intentionally engaged in a serious, illegal strike. As to the duration of the forfeiture, the court explained that the law required it to consider the extent of the union's willful defiance of the law, the impact of the strike on public health, safety, and welfare, the financial resources of the union, and, if relevant, any "acts of extreme provocation" by the employer. The court noted the inconveniences of the 2005 strike, and the fact that the same union had struck illegally in 1980, 1999, and 2002, with preliminary injunctions issued against it in the latter two. On the other hand, the court also noted that the union had tried to mitigate the effect of the 2005 strike by safeguarding facilities and ensuring that operators finished their runs before striking. The court rejected the union's claim that the employer had engaged in "extreme provocation" by trying to bargain over pension benefits (an illegal topic). Weighing all the factors, the court ordered an "indefinite" suspension of dues check-off. The union would be allowed, no earlier than three months from the date of the order, to ask for the forfeiture to end based on representations that it would comply with the law.

The behavior of both parties is relevant to determining the duration of the sanction. For example, *In the Matter of City of New Rochelle and Uniformed Fire Fighters Association, Inc., Local 273 of the IAFF*, 35 NYPER ¶ 3005 (N.Y. PERB, 2002), found that six months was reasonable, because while the union had struck illegally, public inconvenience had been limited to the cost of additional overtime to non-striking workers, the union had not struck previously, and the parties were trying to repair their damaged relationship. As to employer behavior, *In the Matter of Buffalo Teachers Federation*, 16 NYPER ¶ 3018 (N.Y. PERB, 1983), held that because the employer engaged in acts of "extreme provocation" during contract negotiations that led to the strike (violating its duty to bargain in good faith in various ways), the dues deduction should be limited to six months. The PERB noted that the normal remedy would have been eighteen months because the union had struck illegally before.

Some decisions have struggled with this remedy, on the grounds that it actually hurts individual union bargaining unit members in a way that is too severe or unfair. For example, *United Federation of Teachers, Local 2, NYSUT, AFT*, 15 N.Y. PERB ¶ 3091 (1982), reduced the duration of the penalty because the union had lost so much income (30 percent of what was normal) it was no longer able to represent its members effectively. The types of remedies discussed in this section are common, albeit not universal, in public-sector laws.

(D) Decertification and Other Penalties

Some public-sector laws permit, but generally do not require, decertification of unions that strike illegally. One famous example of this, along with other penalties, came in response to the illegal strike by the Professional Air Traffic Controllers Organization (PATCO) in 1981. The relevant federal-sector law barred strikes. All the PATCO strikers were fired (a penalty permitted, but not required by the statute), and PATCO was decertified. Also, pursuant to a directive from then-President Ronald Reagan, all PATCO strikers were barred from employment with the Federal Aviation Administration (FAA). The FAA further insisted that private employers with which it had contracts not employ any former PATCO striker. These policies remained in place until 1993 when President Clinton repealed them. *See Clarry v. United States*, 85 F.3d 1041 (2d Cir. 1996) (upholding FAA's actions).

iii. May Private Parties Affected by Illegal Strikes Recover Damages?

Suppose a private party suffers, or allegedly suffers, damage because of an illegal public-sector strike. Jurisdictions are divided as to whether such a party may sue the union for those damages, but the majority does not allow such actions.

For example, *Burns, Jackson, Miller, Summit & Spitzer v. Lindner*, 451 N.E.2d 459 (N.Y. 1983), rejected such a claim. This case involved an earlier illegal strike by transit workers in New York City. Plaintiff, the Burns, Jackson management-side law firm, sought $50 million in damages for each day of the strike (apparently for loss of business and related costs, although because of the ruling the court did not address the calculation of damages). Plaintiff alleged various causes of action, including "*prima facie* tort," public nuisance, intentional interference with business, and breach of plaintiff's rights as a third-party beneficiary of the labor contract.

The first issue was whether the state labor law supported the concept of a private remedy. The court held that "the history and genesis" of the statute indicated it was "not intended to establish a new cause of action." This was partly because the relevant statute, the Taylor Act, had replaced a law that was even more punitive regarding illegal strikes, the Condon-Wadlin Act, and one purpose of the Taylor Act was "to defuse the tensions in public employer-employee relations by reducing the penalties and increasing reliance on negotiation and the newly created Public Employment Relations Board as a vehicle toward labor peace." A private action, the court reasoned, would upset the balance the legislature struck in this regard. Specifically, if private remedies were allowed, they could easily crush unions entirely. They could even be used against individual strikers.

The court then rejected the common law claims. "*Prima facie* tort" failed because it required that malevolence be the only motive for defendant's act. Public nuisance failed because that action required that plaintiff's harm must be different than that suffered by others. Here, economic losses because of the strike were not different than harms suffered by others in the community. Intentional interference with business failed because the effects on business were only an "incidental result" of the strike, and because the legislature had balanced the penalties in the labor statute. Finally, third-party beneficiary contract claims required a contract, and the relevant labor contract here expired before the strike. Even had the contract been in effect, plaintiff was only an "incidental" beneficiary to it.

For other cases following the majority rule that private parties may not sue for damages caused by illegal public-sector strikes, see *White v. International Association of Firefighters, Local 42*, 738 S.W.2d 933 (Mo. App. 1987) (private parties who suffered property damage from a fire during an illegal strike by firefighters strike did not state a valid claim because allowing private suits would disturb the balance of penalties the state legislature created in the labor statute and could inhibit effective firefighting, as the potential liability of individual firefighters would discourage people from joining the profession); and *Jackson v. Chicago Firefighters Union, Local No. 2*, 160 Ill. App. 3d 975 (1987) (similar). Still, a few cases have allowed private suits. *See, e.g., Boyle v. Anderson Firefighters Association Local 1262*, 497 N.E.2d 1073 (Ind. App. 1986) (because firefighters' strike was illegal, the strikers owed a duty to property owners either not to strike or to fight fires, so strikers could be held individually liable for damages proximately caused by their breach of that duty).

Distinguish these cases from those in which the struck *employer* sues the union to recover its damages from an illegal strike. For example, *White v. International Association of Firefighters, Local 42*, which, as noted above, rejected a suit by a private party, specifically distinguished and approved of *State v. Kansas City Firefights Local 42*, 672 S.W.2d 99 (Mo. App. 1984), which allowed the struck public employer to sue for damages. *White* reasoned that the employer, unlike private parties, was a member of the class for whose especial benefit the public-sector law was passed. *See also Koons by Koons v. Kaiser*, 567 N.E.2d 851 (Ind. App. 1991) (struck public employer could sue teachers for illegally striking, but an individual student could not); *Franklin Township Board of Education v. Quakertown Education Association*, 643 A.2d 34 (N.J. App. 1994) (allowing tort suit by the struck employer against striking teachers).

Some jurisdictions hold that a struck employer cannot sue the striking union in tort either. These cases generally use the argument above that the relevant legislature struck the proper balance of penalties in the labor statute to also exclude extra damages to employers. *See, e.g., City and County of San Francisco v. United Association of Journeyman & Apprentices of the Plumbing & Pipefitting Industry of the United States & Canada, Local 38*, 42 Cal. 3d 810 (1986).

B. Alternatives to Strikes: Public-Sector Impasse Resolution Procedures

This section discusses the main alternatives to strikes that have been developed in the public sector. While public-sector laws generally use some combination of mediation, fact-finding, and interest arbitration, there are significant variations in how the process works under different statutes.

1. Introduction and Mediation

As discussed above, a clear majority of states permit at least some public employees to bargain collectively, but a majority of those states do not permit any public employees to strike. Further, even states that permit some public employees to strike do not allow all unionized public employees to strike (again, police and firefighters are barred from striking in all jurisdictions). Thus, public-sector statutes usually provide procedures meant to resolve bargaining impasses that are alternatives to strikes. Most commonly, these procedures involve some form of mediation, fact-finding, and what is called interest arbitration. Also, as will be discussed in more detail below, even where public-sector employees are allowed to strike, they often must go through mediation and even fact-finding first. These alternative procedures are usually mandatory, and they often result in a binding contract. But there are variations, including but not limited to non-binding procedures.

In mediation, a neutral party with no power to impose a contract meets with the parties to try to work out a voluntary agreement. Sometimes the mediator is a private party chosen by the union and employer, sometimes the state labor agency supplies the mediator. Almost all states that permit public-sector employees to bargain collectively provide for some type of mediation when or even before bargaining reaches impasse. In most jurisdictions, either party may invoke mediation; in some, both must request it; in some, the state labor agency can trigger mediation on its own initiative.

Mediation is relatively inexpensive, and in some cases, it helps resolve impasses by informing the parties about the strengths and weaknesses of the positions of each side, or by inspiring new solutions. But it is non-binding, and it often does not resolve the impasse where the parties disagree on important issues or are reluctant to compromise voluntarily.

2. Fact-Finding

Most states that provide for public-sector collective bargaining use fact-finding for at least some public-sector impasses. Fact-finding uses a neutral party, or sometimes a panel, to hold hearings to determine facts relevant to the impasse. This usually involves presentations from both sides. Fact-finders typically issue reports that include non-binding recommendations, based on the facts and on statutory criteria that fact-finders are required to follow in forming their conclusions. These reports are often used as evidence in interest arbitration hearings (discussed below), if the parties reach that stage.

The goal of this process is, first, to give the parties more information and a more realistic view of their positions and their prospects at an interest arbitration. (Most, although not all, states that use fact-finding also use interest arbitration.) Also, many public-sector statutes provide that if the fact-finder's report does not resolve an impasse, the report will be made public. That rule is designed to help put public pressure on the parties to come to an agreement. For example, under the Ohio public-sector law, a fact-finder's report is only available to the union and the employer, unless and until the parties reject the recommendations in the report. OHIO REV. CODE §4117.14(C)(6)(a). If that happens, the report is made public.

What facts should be found in these hearings and how should they be analyzed? The public-sector statute itself generally provides guidance and criteria for fact-finders. Typically, the criteria fact-finders must use are the same as the criteria which interest arbitrators must use. While these criteria vary somewhat depending on the jurisdiction, it is standard to have criteria that include the employer's ability to pay, the pay and conditions of "comparable" employees, the interest of the public, and the effect of contract terms on other public services.

While fact-finding can and does resolve some impasses, it is not binding, and it does not resolve all impasses.

3. Interest Arbitration

a. Varying Types of Interest Arbitration

Interest arbitration is available to at least some public-sector unions in over half the states. First, be sure to distinguish *interest* arbitration from *grievance* arbitration. Grievance arbitration, used in both the public and private sectors, involves interpreting collective bargaining agreements. Interest arbitration involves setting the substantive terms of these agreements. Interest arbitration is common and often required by statute in the public sector, but it is generally not used (and is not required by statute) in the private sector.

Interest arbitration involves a neutral arbitrator, or panel of arbitrators, holding a hearing, evaluating sometimes voluminous documentary evidence, and making a binding decision typically based on criteria set by the relevant public-sector labor statute. The most common model is to use a single arbitrator, who in some systems is selected by the employer and union and in others is appointed by the state agency. Much of the evidence concerns information about the employer's budget, the wages, hours, and working conditions of "comparable" employees (a topic discussed in more detail below), cost-of-living numbers, and the more amorphous "interests of the public."

There are three main varieties of binding interest arbitration: (1) "conventional" interest arbitration; (2) "final offer, issue-by-issue" arbitration; and (3) "final offer, total package arbitration." In conventional arbitration, the arbitrator may pick from the final offers of the parties, or the arbitrator may compromise between them. For example, if the union's final offer regarding wages was $20 per hour, and the employer's final offer was $15 per hour, the arbitrator could choose $15, $20, any number in between (or, in theory, if not typically practice, higher or lower numbers).

In final offer, issue-by-issue arbitration, for each issue at impasse, the arbitrator may only choose the final offer of one party or the other. Thus, for example, suppose the parties were at impasse over wages as described above (the union's final offer at $20 per hour, the employer's final offer at $15 per hour) and also at impasse over how many personal days employees may receive, with the union's last offer at five and the employer's last offer at two. The arbitrator, in a final offer, issue-by-issue, jurisdiction could choose only $15 or $20 for wages (no other number), and could choose only two or five personal days, and no other number. In final offer, issue-by-issue arbitration, the arbitrator could choose the union's proposal on one issue and the employer's proposal on the other, or the arbitrator could choose the proposals of one party on both issues.

In final offer, total package arbitration, however, the arbitrator is limited to selecting either all the union's final offers on every issue at impasse, or all the employer's final offers on every issue at impasse. Thus, in the hypothetical above, the arbitrator could choose either the employer's offers on wages and personal days, or the union's offers on wages and personal days. The arbitrator could not choose one final offer from the union and one from the employer.

Some states use one model for all employees. Some states use different models for different employees. Some states use one model for some issues, and another model for other issues (e.g., final offer arbitration for economic issues but not for others). Michigan's police and firefighter statute provides for final offer, issue by issue arbitration for economic issues, but uses conventional arbitration for non-economic issues. New Jersey law uses the final offer, total package model for economic issues, but uses final offer, issue by issue arbitration for non-economic items. Arvid Anderson and Loren Krause, *Interest Arbitration: The Alternative to the Strike*, 56 FORDHAM L. REV. 153, 157–58 (1987). In Ohio (for employees not allowed to strike), the default model is final offer, issue by issue, but the parties can choose other alternatives, including but not limited to conventional and final offer total package arbitration. OHIO REV. CODE §§ 4117.14(C)(1), (D)(1), and (G)(7).

There are advantages and disadvantages, or at least arguments for and against, each of these models. Arbitrators often favor conventional arbitration. They criticize "final offer" rules, especially the total package variation, in part because it limits their ability to craft compromises. For example, in *In the Matter of Interest Arbitration Between Eastern Illinois University and IL FOP Labor Council*, Case No. S-MA-22-303 (Nov. 12, 2022), Arbitrator Marvin Hill lamented that the relevant Illinois statute "restricts an Arbitrator's discretion in resolving economic issues to the adoption of the final offer of one of the parties.... Thus ... there is no Solomon-like 'splitting of the child.'" Similarly, in a decision from Montana, Arbitrator Jeffrey Jacobs wrote that the final offer, total package requirement "makes it difficult ... as there are many times when one party's position is reasonable and justifiable in one respect while in some others another party's position may well also have considerable merit." Final offer, total package arbitration "removes any power ... to fashion an award that reflects the best of both arguments or conforms to the most appropriate evidence brought forth by either side." *City of Helena, Mont. v. Int'l Ass'n of Fire Fighters, Local 448*, BOPA CASE # 5-2010 (407-2010, April 19, 2010).

The traditional argument against conventional arbitration is that it discourages realistic, productive bargaining because the parties expect the arbitrator to come up with a compromise. Thus, the parties tend to cling to more extreme positions. *See, e.g.*, James Chelius and Marian Extejt, *The Narcotic Effect of Impasse-Resolution Procedures*, 38 INDUS. & LAB. REL. REV. 629, 630 (1985). On the other hand, some studies have found that arbitrators do not "split the baby" in most interest arbitrations done under the conventional model. *See*

Henry Farber, *Splitting-the-Difference in Interest Arbitration*, 35 INDUS. & LAB. REL. REV. 70, 76 (1981).

Final offer systems can have other disadvantages. In final offer, total package arbitrations, it is likely that the major cost items (usually compensation) will be the deciding factor, and proposals on other, less costly issues from the prevailing side on cost issues will be swept into the chosen package, even if they are less reasonable than the proposals on the less costly issues from the other side.

The arguably offsetting advantage of final offer, total package over final offer, issue by issue final offer is that total package rules at least tend to give the parties added incentive to resolve more issues themselves, leaving fewer issues at impasse. Also, in final offer issue by issue arbitration, a potential disadvantage is that parties sometimes litigate over what are or are not separate "issues." For example, in *Fairborn Professional Fire Fighters' Association, IAFF Local 1235 v. City of Fairborn*, 736 N.E.2d 5 (Oh. 2000), the union claimed that the employer had "improperly bundled" into a single "issue" proposals regarding hours of duty in a work week, vacations, and holidays. The court upheld the interest arbitrator's determination that these topics were properly combined into a single "issue" for the purposes of the final offer, issue by issue arbitration.

b. Statutory Criteria Interest Arbitrators Must Consider in More Detail

Statutes that provide for interest arbitration usually set out criteria that interest arbitrators must consider in making their awards. As noted above, when statutes also require fact-finding, the criteria are typically the same for fact-finders and arbitrators. For example, Ohio's statute provides that interest arbitrators and fact-finders must consider the same factors. Those factors include past collective bargaining agreements between the parties; comparable private and public employees; the interests of the public; the ability of the employer to finance and administer the issues proposed; the lawful authority of the public employer, and such "other factors ... which are normally or traditionally taken into consideration" in resolving bargaining impasses in the public service or in private employment. OH. REV. CODE § 4117.14(G)(7).

While statutory language varies, the criteria in other state statutes usually address similar concerns. For example, the Montana statute provides that interest arbitrators will look at comparable employees, the interest and welfare of the public; the employer's ability to pay; appropriate cost-of-living indicators; and "any other factors traditionally considered in the determination of wages, hours, and conditions of employment." MONT. CODE ANN. § 39-34-103.

Some statutes, however, make the criteria more detailed. For example, some statutes specify the types of comparable employees to be used, refer to particular cost-of-living numbers, list what financial data from the employer the arbitrator should examine, and/or instruct arbitrators to give more weight to some criteria than others. The following language from Oregon's statute, notable for its degree of detail, is an example of this approach. It begins by stating that arbitrators shall give "first priority" to "the interests and welfare of the public." It then states that arbitrators should give "secondary priority" to the following factors

> (b) The reasonable financial ability of the unit of government to meet the costs of the proposed contract giving due consideration and weight to the other services, provided by, and other priorities of, the unit of government as determined by the governing body. A reasonable operating reserve against future contingencies, which does not include funds in contemplation of settlement of the labor dispute, shall not be considered as available toward a settlement.
>
> (c) The ability of the unit of government to attract and retain qualified personnel at the wage and benefit levels provided.
>
> (d) The overall compensation presently received by the employees, including direct wage compensation, vacations, holidays and other paid excused time, pensions, insurance, benefits, and all other direct or indirect monetary benefits received.
>
> (e) Comparison of the overall compensation of other employees performing similar services with the same or other employees in comparable communities. As used in this paragraph, "comparable" is limited to communities of the same or nearest population range within Oregon. Notwithstanding the provisions of this paragraph, the following additional definitions of "comparable" apply in the situations described as follows:
>
> > (A) For any city with a population of more than 325,000, "comparable" includes comparison to out-of-state cities of the same or similar size;
> >
> > (B) For counties with a population of more than 400,000, "comparable" includes comparison to out-of-state counties of the same or similar size; and
> >
> > (C) For the State of Oregon, "comparable" includes comparison to other states.

> (f) The CPI-All Cities Index, commonly known as the cost of living....
>
> (h) Such other factors, consistent with paragraphs (a) to (g) of this subsection as are traditionally taken into consideration in the determination of wages, hours, and other terms and conditions of employment. However, the arbitrator shall not use such other factors, if in the judgment of the arbitrator, the factors in paragraphs (a) to (g) of this subsection provide sufficient evidence for an award. OR. REV. STAT. § 243.746.

In most interest arbitration cases, the most important factors are "comparable" employees and the ability of the employer to pay. The next section discusses this topic.

c. *"Comparable Employees"*

Interest arbitrators consider two kinds of comparable employees: external and internal. External comparables are employees of other public employers who do the same or similar work as the employees at issue in the arbitration. For example, in a case involving police officers in city A, external comparables would be police officers in city B, assuming city B is roughly the same size with a similar tax base, and (usually) in the same state. "Internal" comparables involve employees of the same employer. For example, in a case involving teachers, internal comparables could be other school employees. In a police arbitration, firefighters in the same city could be internal comparables. Some interest arbitration cases place more emphasis on external comparables than on internal comparables, while other cases take the opposite approach. *Compare, e.g., Hennepin County of Paramedics and Hennepin County Medical Center*, BMS No. 17PNO203 (Arb. Befort, 2017) (focusing on internal comparables), *with Capital City Labor Program Supervisory Division and Ingham County*, MERC Case No. L15H0958 (Arb. Stratton, 2016) (rejecting internal comparables, because the relevant employees "are not responsible for what the County does with respect to other employee groups"). The point of looking at external comparables is to determine the equivalent of the market rate for certain jobs, which again goes to recruitment and retention. The point of looking at internal comparables is to maintain a level of fairness (and avoid destructive jealousy and competition) among employees working for the same employer.

Many interest arbitrations involve disputes over which other employees and employers are appropriate "comparables." Most statutes give relatively little guidance as to how to make such determinations, so arbitrators have established factors to consider. For example, the arbitration decision in *White Lake Township and Police Officers Labor Council*, Mich. Emp. Rel. Comm., Case

No. D06 G-1698 (2008) first noted that the relevant Michigan statute did "not prescribe specific factors" for determining comparability, and then explained:

> Generally, factors commonly considered include size of the community to be served, form of government, SEV [property value] and taxing authority ... and other economic factors, scope of duties, the location of the comparable communities as they relate to the local labor market and population demographics....

Determining comparables can be a complicated issue. This is true even when the statute gives more specific guidance to arbitrators in how to determine comparables. As shown above, Oregon's statute gives, comparatively speaking, very specific guidance, yet one Oregon decision devoted twenty-eight pages solely to the issue of which cities were comparable to Roseburg, Oregon for the purposes of determining comparables for firefighters. *City of Roseburg, Oregon and Int'l Ass'n of Firefighters, Local 1110*, Case No. IA-09-06 (2007).

d. The Employer's Ability to Pay

The employer's ability to pay is also usually one of the most significant criteria in interest arbitrations. This factor was given even more prominence in the years following the recession that begin in 2008 and in the "COVID" years. For example, in a case arising in Illinois at the beginning of the 2008 recession, Arbitrator Edward Benn noted that during the arbitration hearings, "the economy went into free-fall." The relevant statute required interest arbitrators to consider changes in circumstances during the pendency of arbitration hearings, as well as cost-of-living numbers (which had declined sharply after the initial crash). For these and related reasons, the arbitrator held for the employer, rejecting a higher rank differential sought by the union. *State of Illinois, Dept. of Cent. Mgmt. Serv. and Int'l Brotherhood of Teamsters Local 726*, Case Nos.: S-MA-08-262, rb. Ref. 08.208 (Arb. Benn, 2009). Many arbitrators in that period took a similar approach. *See, e.g., State of Washington and SEIU Local 775 NW* (supplemental interest award) (Arb. Williams, 2009) Arb.) ("in the current tough economic times the State's ability to pay trumps all of the other statutory factors").

Even in more "normal" economic times, disputes arise over ability to pay. Predicting a city's overall budget over a period of several years, for example, is not a precise science (tax income and expenses, including pension and benefit liabilities, may fluctuate greatly). Also, even when a public employer can literally afford a proposed raise, a decision to grant that raise may mean committing the employer to reallocate resources from, say, one city department to another. "Comparables" play a role here, in that a showing that similar cities in similar areas pay a certain salary to similar employees can be persuasive evidence that the employer is able to pay that salary.

Also, absent significant changes in the economy or other relevant circumstances, arbitrators will often require a *quid pro quo* for any substantial change from previous contracts. Indeed, interest arbitration is sometimes critiqued for being too cautious a system in this regard. *See* David Bloom, *Arbitrator Behavior in Public Sector Wages* Disputes, *in* WHEN PUBLIC SECTOR WORKERS UNIONIZE (RICHARD FREEMAN & CASEY ICHNIOWSKI, EDS., 1988).

4. Impasse Procedures without Mandatory, Binding Arbitration

Interest arbitration is generally considered the *quid pro quo* for being denied the right to strike, so it is usually both mandatory and binding. *See, e.g., Snyder County Prison Board and County of Snyder v. Pennsylvania Labor Relations Board and Teamsters Local 764*, 912 A.3d 356, 357 (Pa. 2006). Still, in a few jurisdictions, interest arbitrators issue opinions that are merely advisory rather than binding. Also, a few states (e.g., Florida) which authorize collective bargaining but prohibit strikes have no step after mediation or fact-finding.

In a small number of jurisdictions, notably California, courts have relied on the older theory that mandatory, binding interest arbitration violates constitutional "non-delegation" principles (improperly shifting inherent government power to private parties). *See County of Riverside v. Superior Court*, 66 P.3d 718 (Cal. 2003). This case relied on specific language in the California state constitution, and it did not signal a change in the modern approach of rejecting non-delegation challenges. For an example of the clear majority approach (interest arbitration does not violate non-delegation principles), see *Office of Administration v. Penn. Lab. Rel. Bd.*, 528 Pa. 472 (1991).

Some states have binding, mandatory arbitration for some public employees, but not others. For example, Michigan uses binding arbitration for certain public safety workers, MICH. COMP. LAWS §§ 423.231–33 and §§ 423.271–87, but not for other public employees, MICH. COMP. LAWS § 423.207-207(a) (mediation is the final step for all other public employee).

5. Judicial Review of Interest Arbitration Decisions

The decisions of interest arbitrators may be appealed to court. Courts are usually fairly deferential to arbitrators, especially regarding factual findings. *See Hillsdale PBA Local 207 v. Borough of Hillsdale*, 137 N.J. 71 (NJ 1994) (the general standard of review for interest arbitrations is whether the award is supported by substantial credible evidence in the record as a whole). On the other hand, this standard is more stringent than for private-sector labor grievance arbitrations, or even commercial arbitrations, because interest arbitration is statutorily-mandated, public funds are at stake, and the decisions can affect the public. 137 N.J. 71, 82. In determining the level of deference, courts balance two sets of concerns. On one hand, arbitration decisions should at least normally be final to avoid delays, courts should defer to arbitrators who make very fact-specific determinations and are experts in the area, and discussing issues not significant in a particular dispute may seem unnecessary. On the other hand, legislatures have determined that, in public-sector interest arbitration cases, arbitrators should consider certain factors, and interest arbitration decisions implicate distribution of public goods as well as the relations of the employer and employees.

The most common reason for overturning an interest arbitration award is finding that the arbitrator did not properly consider the criteria the public-sector labor statute requires arbitrators to consider. Interesting issues arise when arbitrators felt that certain statutory criteria were not relevant or applicable in a given case or simply did not discuss them in the written decision. The majority and dissent in the case *In re Buffalo Professional Firefighters Association, Inc., Local 282, IAFF*, 850 N.Y.S.2d 744 (N.Y. App. Div., 2008), *vacated on other grounds, Arbitration Between Buffalo Professional Firefighters Association, Inc., Local 282, IAFF and Masiello*, 918 N.E.2d 887, 888 (N.Y. 2009), give both sides of this debate. In this case, a lower court had vacated an arbitration award on the grounds that the arbitrator did not sufficiently consider all the statutory criteria. On appeal, the court majority reversed. It explained that the statutory language did not specifically require arbitrators to make "express findings" on each of the statutory factors.

> Thus, the Legislature has not required arbitration panels to engage in unnecessary discussion in their awards of factors not raised by the parties or thought to be relevant by either the parties or the panel. Judicial review of public arbitration awards otherwise would devolve into mere

mechanical checklists, despite the fact that an award may appear on its face to be reasonable and to have a rational basis. 850 N.Y.S.2d 744, 749.

The dissent disagreed, relying in part on language in the statute preceding the specific criteria, which stated that in making determinations, arbitrators "shall specify the basis for its findings, taking into consideration, in addition to any other relevant factors, the following: ..." 850 N.Y.S.2d at 750.

Courts sometimes vacate interest arbitration awards if they violate other statutory requirements. Most importantly, arbitrators cannot issue awards on an issue that is not properly before them. Note here that permissive, as well as illegal, topics of bargaining may not be brought to interest arbitration. Also, arbitrators must use the type of interest arbitration the statute requires. *See, e.g., McFaul v. UAW Region* 2, 719 N.E.2d 632 (Oh. App. 1998) (vacating arbitration decision where the arbitrator did not choose the final offer of one side as required but instead awarded a compromise between the positions of the parties).

C. Legal Strikes

Although it remains the minority approach, many public employees have the right to strike in some states, including some large ones (e.g., California, Illinois, and Ohio). This right, however, is almost always more limited than the right of private-sector employees to strike.

1. Policy Arguments in Favor of Permitting Some Public Employees to Strike

Statutes authorizing a limited right to strike for some public employees were passed in the following states in the following years: Vermont (1967, municipal employees only); Montana (1969, nurses only); Pennsylvania (1970); Hawaii (1970); Oregon (1973); Alaska (1974); Minnesota (1975); Wisconsin (1977, municipal employees and teachers only); Illinois (1983); and Ohio (1983). In 2011, Act 10 in Wisconsin eliminated all public-sector strike rights in that state. Even in states with a broad right to strike, police and fire employees may not legally strike anywhere.

Some arguments in favor of a right to strike were made fairly early on in the history of public-sector labor statutes. In Pennsylvania, a 1968 report from the Governor's Commission to Revise the Public Employee Law of Pennsylvania concluded that a policy of simply banning all public-sector strikes was "unreasonable and unenforceable." It was based on an outmoded concept that all strikes against a sovereign were improper. The "consequences of a strike by a policeman are very different from those of a gardener in a public park." Further, the right to strike would strengthen the collective bargaining process. "It will be some curb on the possible intransigence of an employer; and the limitations on the right to strike will serve notice on the employee that there are limits to the hardships that he can impose." Indeed, a "carefully defined right to strike" would be a "safety valve that will in fact prevent strikes."

Others also argued that a strike threat can be a helpful tool in labor management relations, and, *contra* Wellington and Winter, public employers will not generally give in to public employee strikes. Some also stressed the blurring of lines between at least some private and public enterprises. *See, e.g.*, Kurt Hanslowe and John Acierno, *The Law and Theory of Strikes by Government Employees*, 67 CORNELL L. REV. 1055 (1982).

Interestingly, there is some evidence that legalizing public-sector strikes reduces their frequency. Professor Martin Malin found that in Ohio, and to a somewhat lesser extent in Illinois, the number of public-sector strikes significantly *decreased* after state laws made such strikes legal. The decline in Ohio was significant: an average of more than fifty-five strikes per year before the statute made strikes legal, but then an average of fewer than six strikes a year after strikes were legalized. Martin Malin, *Public Employees' Right to Strike: Law and Experience*, 26 MICH. J. OF LAW REF. 313 (1993). The effect Professor Malin described continued after his article was published. From 1993–1999, there were only a total of fifty public-sector strikes in Ohio, and from 2000–2010, only a total of forty-three. *See* Joseph Slater, *The Rise and Fall of SB-5 in Political and Historical Context*, 43 U. TOLEDO L. REV. 473, 481 (2012). Another study found that in general, "[s]trike costs, as measured by the incidence and length of strikes, are greatest in the absence of legislation requiring employees to bargain." Janet Currie and Sheena McConnell, *The Impact of Collective Bargaining Legislation on Disputes in the U.S. Public Sector: No Legislation May be the Worst Legislation*, 37 J. OF LAW AND ECONOMICS 519, 520–21 (1994).

2. Statutes Granting the Right to Strike

Statutes that grant public employees the right to strike often contain important similarities. Usually, unions must go through some alternative impasse procedures (mediation and/or fact-finding) before they are permitted to strike. Typically, even legal strikes will become illegal if they begin to threaten public health, safety, or welfare. Also, as noted, even states that permit most public employees to strike do not allow public safety employees (police, firefighters, and prison guards, most commonly) to strike.

However, there are often some important differences. For example, compare Ohio and Alaska, two states which permit most public employees to strike, but under somewhat different rules. In Ohio, employees who may strike (almost all except public safety employees and, as of 2025, faculty at state universities) must first go through mediation and fact-finding. Ohio Rev. Code §4117.14(C)(2), (3). In order to reject a fact-finder's recommendation, a union or employer must vote by a super-majority of three-fifths to do so, and if neither side rejects these recommendations, they form the basis of the contract. If one or both parties reject the recommendations, then the fact-finder's report will be made public. Ohio Rev. Code § 14(C)(6)(a). If the parties cannot come to an agreement within seven days after the publication of fact-finder's report, then public employees who are allowed to strike may legally strike, but even then, only after giving ten days' notice. Ohio Rev. Code § 14(D). Also, courts retain the power to enjoin otherwise legal strikes if and when it "creates clear and present danger to the health or safety of the public." Ohio Rev. Code §4117.16.

Alaska uses a different model, dividing public employees into three groups. The first group (mostly police, fire, and correctional workers) cannot legally strike. Alaska Stat. §23.40.200(b). The second group includes utility, snow removal, and sanitation employees, and employees in higher education. *Id.* §23.40.200(c). These employees may legally strike following an impasse, a secret ballot vote authorizing a strike, and exhausting mediation. But the strike is only permitted «for a limited time. The limit is determined by the interests of the health, safety, or welfare of the public.» If the strike threatens the health, safety, or welfare of the public, courts should enjoin it. *Id.* §23.400.200(c). The third group consists of all other public employees the statute covers. Employees in this third group generally may strike after a secret ballot vote. *Id.* §23.40.200(d). Employees of municipal school districts and state boarding schools, however, must go to advisory arbitration before voting to strike, may not strike until they have given seventy-two hours' notice, and cannot begin a strike until after a day of school with students in attendance has passed. *Id.* § 23.40.200(g).

3. Limits on Legal Strikes

Public-sector jurisdictions that allow strikes still follow private-sector rules on "unprotected" strikes. For example, "partial" strikes are illegal. *See, e.g.*, *East Cleveland Education Association v. SERB*, 12 Ohio Pub. Emp. Rep. ¶ 1219 (Oh.Ct. Common Pleas 1995).

In addition, as noted above, laws permitting strikes in the public sector usually have provisions allowing even strikes that were legal at their inception to be enjoined if the strike at some point threatens public health, safety, or welfare. This creates some tension: *all* strikes, by their nature, cause some inconvenience. At what point does an otherwise legal strike that causes some inconvenience become illegal because it threatens the health, safety, or welfare of the public?

Masloff v. Port Authority of Allegheny County, 613 A.2d 1186 (Pa. 1992), is a good example of a case wrestling with the application of the "health, safety, and welfare" exception. *Masloff* upheld an injunction against a strike by mass transit workers that was legal when it began. The lower court judge in *Masloff* enjoined this strike because of its "far-reaching effect" on "commercial, academic, medical, and social institutions." The Supreme Court of Pennsylvania noted that the relevant statute stated that strikes "shall not be prohibited unless or until such a strike creates a clear and present danger or threat to the health, safety, or welfare of the public." The statute also provided that if a court enjoined a strike that had started legally, the injunction order would have to require the parties to submit to binding interest arbitration. This type of statutory caveat is common.

The majority in *Masloff* let the injunction stand. It explained that "ordinary inconveniences resulting from a strike will not suffice to establish a clear and present danger," 613 A.2d 1186, 1191. But the majority distinguished situations "when such matters accumulate to such an extent, have continued for so long, or are aggravated by unexpected developments." *Id.* It noted that in the lower court, the city had introduced thirty witnesses, including blind, epileptic, professional, student, and blue-collar citizens, who testified as to the negative impact of the strike. The majority stated that medical services were delayed, citizens were endangered because they had to walk along public roads, and some had to find alternative living arrangements because of the inaccessibility of work, school, or day care. The majority rejected the union's argument that this is what one would normally expect in a transit workers strike. It stressed that ambulances, fire, and police services were "severely hampered" by the increased traffic congestion. *Id.*

Justice Larsen dissented. He first argued that all these effects were the normal, foreseeable consequences of a transit workers strike, and the legislature must have anticipated these effects when permitting these workers to strike. The "clear and present danger" language, the dissent continued, must refer to effects that are *not* the normal result of the covered employees striking. The dissent also disagreed with the majority as to whether the evidence actually showed any significant disruption of fire or police protection, or emergency medical services. If the normal inconveniences of a transit workers strike were sufficient to allow an injunction, the dissent concluded, how could these employees ever have an effective strike?

Other cases have created similar disagreements on this issue. If an otherwise legal teachers' strike threatens a loss of state subsidies to schools because the strike may cause a failure to comply with a statutory requirement of providing 180 days of instruction, does that threaten the public health, safety, or welfare? The New Jersey Supreme Court, in *Jersey Shore Educ. Association v Jersey Shore Area School District*, 548 A.2d 1202 (N.J. 1988), ruled that it did and upheld an injunction over two dissents.

D. Permanent Replacement of Strikers

While permanent replacement of strikers is an extremely important issue in the private sector, it has little to no importance in the public sector. While public employers may simply fire illegal strikers, in cases of legal strikes, only a very few decisions have even hinted that public employers could potentially use permanent replacements, and there is no reported case involving a public employer actually using permanent replacements. *See* Joseph Slater, *The "American Rule" that Swallows the Exceptions*, 11 EMP. RTS. & EMP. POL'Y J. 53, 86 (2007).

CHECKPOINTS

- Most public-sector laws bar strikes by public employees.
- Laws barring strikes typically include other forms of coordinated job actions such as the "blue flu."
- If a union engages in an illegal strike, individual strikers may be fined, disciplined (including discharge), and barred from future public employment, at least for a period of time.
- If a union engages in an illegal strike, courts may enjoin the strike, and enforce the injunction with both civil and, in some cases, criminal contempt sanctions. Other possible penalties against unions include forfeiture of the right to dues check-off and decertification.
- Jurisdictions are split as to whether private parties may sue unions who strike illegally for damages incurred because of the strike; the majority approach is not to allow such claims.
- Most public-sector labor laws bar strikes and provide alternative procedures to resolve bargaining impasses, specifically mediation, fact-finding, and interest arbitration.
- Mediation and fact-finding are usually mandatory but are not binding.
- Interest arbitration is usually mandatory and binding. In this process, the arbitrator sets the substantive terms of the labor contract, issuing decisions on the issues at impasse. In some jurisdictions, interest arbitration decisions are not binding.
- There are three basic models of interest arbitration: conventional (the arbitrator is allowed to "split the baby"); final offer, issue-by-issue (for each issue at impasse, the arbitrator may choose only the final proposal of one side); and final offer, total package (the arbitrator must choose all the proposals of either one side or the other).
- Public-sector labor statutes generally list criteria that interest arbitrators (and fact-finders) must consider in issuing their awards or recommendation. Usually, the most important of these factors are "comparable employees" and the employer's ability to pay.

- The decisions of interest arbitrators may be appealed to court. While courts are generally deferential, they will sometimes overturn awards, most commonly if the arbitrator did not use the criteria specified by the statute.
- Around a dozen states permit some public employees to strike. Often, although not always, statutes that permit strikes require unions and employers to engage in some impasse resolution procedures (mediation and/or fact-finding) before striking.
- Generally, even a legal strike may be enjoined if it begins to threaten the public health, safety, or welfare.
- Employers in the public-sector do not use permanent striker replacements as private-sector employers do.

CHAPTER 16

Secondary Activity and Recognitional Picketing

ROADMAP

- The distinction between primary and secondary activity
- The constitutional framework—secondary boycotts, picketing, and handbilling
- Overview of Section 8(b)(4)'s prohibition on secondary activity
- The meaning of unlawful means under Section 8(b)(4)
- The meaning of unlawful objectives under Section 8(b)(4)
- Consumer boycotts and consumer appeals
- The three provisos to Section 8(b)(4)
- Lesser-known unlawful objects
- The meaning of recognitional picketing under Section 8(b)(7)
- Section 10(l) injunctive relief and compensatory damages

When workers began to organize themselves in the nineteenth century, they quickly learned that leafleting (handbilling) and organizing boycotts and pickets were effective ways of communicating their message to the public and exerting economic pressure on employers to obtain their goals—better working conditions, shorter hours, job security, higher pay, and recognition. When direct pressure on their own employers (primary employers) proved inadequate to meet their goals, they began to exert pressure on customers of, and those doing business with, their employers. As discussed in Chapter 2, during the nineteenth and early twentieth centuries, businesses used criminal and civil conspiracy laws as well as judicial injunctions to repress such labor activity. This chapter discusses the modern legal relevance of these latter types of pressures, known as secondary activity, and the extent to which labor laws regulate picketing for recognition.

A. Basic Principles

1. What Constitutes Picketing

Labor picketing includes, but is not limited to, people patrolling a business entrance while carrying signs affixed to picket sticks. Handbilling or leafleting, without more, does not constitute picketing.

2. The Distinction between Primary and Secondary

Labor law often distinguishes between primary and secondary activity in determining whether union conduct is protected, permitted, or unlawful. Primary activity denotes concerted activity directed at an employer with whom the union has a labor dispute. Secondary activity denotes concerted activity directed at a third party who is not a party to the primary labor dispute. In the words of Judge Learned Hand:

> The gravamen of a secondary boycott is that its sanctions bear, not upon the employer who alone is a party to the dispute, but upon some third party who has no concern in it. Its aim is to compel him to stop business with the employer in the hope that this will induce the employer to give in to his employees' demands.

IBEW v. NLRB, 181 F.2d 34, 37 (2d Cir. 1950). For example, a union that represents employees of a newspaper publisher engages in primary activity when it strikes the publisher and secondary activity when it puts pressure on the firm that supplies the paper used in printing the publisher's newspapers. Whereas primary activity is generally considered protected activity under Section 7, secondary activity is not. The characterization also helps inform what types of concerted activities may be undertaken—including strikes, picketing, and boycotts.

B. The Constitutional Framework

The extent to which labor picketing has received constitutional protection under the First Amendment has varied. The height of constitutional protection came during the New Deal Era, when the Supreme Court drew a line between constitutionally protected picketing and unconstitutional picketing based on whether the picketing was accompanied by violence or property damage. In *Thornhill v. Alabama*, 310 U.S. 88 (1940), the Court declared unconstitutional a state statute criminalizing picketing. In that case, Union President Byron Thornhill was convicted under a state criminal statute for loitering and picketing a business to inform the public that the business was violating his members' federal statutory rights. Thornhill defaulted on the $100 fine and was sentenced to fifty-nine days in jail. The Alabama Court of Appeals upheld his conviction and lengthened his sentence to seventy-three days. *See Thornhill v. State*, 28 Ala. App. 527, 189 So. 913 (Ct. App. 1939) (affirming conviction), *rev'd sub nom. Thornhill v. Alabama*, 310 U.S. 88, 91 n.1 (1940). The U.S. Supreme Court reversed the conviction, holding that the statute unjustifiably abridged liberty of discussion. Although the state defended the statute on grounds of protecting the community from violence and breaches of the peace, it could show no actual "clear and present danger" to life, property, privacy, or peace thought to be "inherent in" labor picketing. *Id.* at 745–46.

The following year, in *AFL v. Swing*, 312 U.S. 321 (1941), the Court declared unconstitutional a state injunction against peaceful secondary picketing by unions. In that case, a beauty parlor asked a state court to enjoin the union's peaceful picketing of its establishment, alleging in part that the picketing was secondary because there was no labor dispute between the beauty parlor and the union. The case presented the question of whether a state could permanently enjoin peaceful persuasion merely because the enjoined picketers were not employees of the businesses they picketed. The Court held that a ban on "'peaceful persuasion' disentangled from violence and free from 'picketing en masse or otherwise conducted' so as to occasion 'imminent and aggravated danger,' ... is inconsistent with the guarantee of freedom of speech." *Id.* at 325–26.

Over the following fifteen years, the Court made a series of decisions that cut back on its constitutional protection of labor picketing. Those decisions culminated in *Teamsters Local 695 v. Vogt, Inc.*, 354 U.S. 284 (1957). In *Vogt*, the employer sought to enjoin the union's picketing, which was intended to persuade the employer's workers to join the picket line. *Vogt* started with the premise that all picketing done by a group is "speech plus." This premise is based on two beliefs. First, picketing involves patrol and inducement to action: "'Picketing by an organized group is more than free speech, since it involves patrol of a particular locality and since the very presence of a picket line may induce action of one kind or another, quite irrespective of the nature of the ideas which are being disseminated.'" *Id.* at 289. Second, picketing involves workers' exercise of economic power: When employees picket, they are exercising more than free speech rights. "They [are] exercising their economic power together with that of their allies to compel [an employer] to abide by union rather than by state regulation of trade." *Id.* at 292. According to the *Vogt* Court, a state may prohibit picketing that has an improper purpose. The Court found that the Wisconsin Supreme Court was justified in enjoining the peaceful picketing because the union's purpose in picketing—to coerce the employer to coerce its workers—was improper.

In contrast to labor picketing, the law more broadly protects leafleting or handbilling—a type of concerted activity in which workers distribute union literature. In *Edward J. DeBartolo Corp. v. Florida Gulf Coast Building & Construction Trades Council*, 485 U.S. 568 (1988) (*DeBartolo II*), the Court examined the question of whether the union peacefully handbilled businesses in a shopping mall in Tampa, Florida. Its primary dispute was with the construction company retained by the mall's owner to build a department store at the mall. The union's purpose was indisputably secondary: The union distributed handbills asking mall customers not to shop at any of the mall's tenants until the mall's owner publicly promised to use contractors who paid their employees fair wages and benefits. These circumstances resulted in the shopping mall owner filing charges with the NLRB alleging that the union violated Section 8(b)(4), discussed below, which makes most forms of secondary activity a union unfair labor practice (ULP). The main question was whether applying Section 8(b)(4)'s prohibition on secondary boycotts was unconstitutional where handbills (as opposed to pickets) constituted the means used to persuade people to boycott the mall tenants. Exploring the differences between handbilling and picketing, the Court answered that question in the affirmative. In the Court's view, unlike picketing, which is "a mixture of conduct and communication" that is coercive because it calls for an "automatic response to a signal," handbilling constitutes pure speech that calls for "a reasoned response to an idea." *Id.* at 580. Thus, whereas picketing may not receive constitutional protection based on the conduct associated with the speech, handbilling almost always receives constitutional protection as pure speech under the First Amendment.

Unions have become creative in staying on the permissible side of this free-speech line. For example, in *Tucker v. City of Fairfield*, 398 F.3d 457 (6th Cir. 2005), the court found that a union engaged in constitutionally protected conduct when it used an inflatable rat balloon measuring twelve feet high by eight feet in diameter as part of a labor protest. *Cf. Laborers' E. Region Org. Fund*, 346 N.L.R.B. 1251, 1265 (2006) (not passing on the administrative judge's finding that the union violated Section 8(b)(4)(i) when it used a rat display because, as the "functional equivalent of picketing," the rat "sent a signal to those who approached the entrance that a labor dispute was occurring and that action on their part was desired"). Courts are split on whether a labor-dispute-oriented mock funeral procession constitutes protected speech or picketing that can be more closely regulated and even prohibited. *Compare Sheet Metal Workers v. NLRB*, 491 F.3d 429, 437–38 (D.C. Cir. 2007) (holding mock funeral protected), *with Kentov v. Sheet Metal Workers*, 418 F.3d 1259, 1265 (11th Cir. 2005) (holding mock funeral unprotected). In *Sheet Metals Workers v. NLRB*, the court held that, although the union's purpose in conducting the mock funeral was to dissuade people from patronizing the hospital—the secondary employer in the union's dispute with nonunion contractors used by the hospital—the means used were uncoercive and therefore the conduct was protected. *Cf. Overstreet v. United Brotherhood of Carpenters*, 409 F.3d 1199 (9th Cir. 2005) (holding that the First Amendment protects a union that used a fifteen-foot stationary banner to shame the employer for not paying area standard wages). By contrast, in *Kentov*, the court found that when union representatives—one dressed as the Grim Reaper—patrolled near the hospital entrance carrying a coffin, their conduct was not protected because it was a mixture of conduct and communication intended to deter people from entering the hospital.

The final category of free speech cases involves union picketing or handbilling in areas open to the public, such as shopping malls. In *Hudgens v. NLRB*, 424 U.S. 507 (1976), the Court held that a shopping mall owner did not violate the First Amendment when he called the police to remove peaceful strikers from the mall under threat of arrest for criminal trespass. Although the union representatives were peacefully distributing handbills to discourage customers from shopping at a particular store in the mall because that store would not hire union contractors, the mall owner had a right, under state property law, to exclude people from its private property. Put simply, there was no state action. So why then, in *Fashion Valley Mall, LLC v. NLRB*, 42 Cal. 4th 850 (2007), did the California Supreme Court hold that the similar activity at a California mall was protected free speech under the California constitution? In contrast to the law of most states, California has a more lenient state action requirement for shopping malls, which are considered public forums. Therefore, the mall's prohibition against union handbilling in *Fashion Valley* was unconstitutional under the state constitution.

C. Section 8(b)(4) Prohibition against Secondary Labor Activity

1. Statutory Language

The statutory language of Section 8(b)(4) is unwieldy. Rather than taking a formalistic approach to Section 8(b)(4), the Board and the Court have been more concerned with interpreting Section 8(b)(4) considering its purpose—to ban some forms of secondary activity within constitutional limits while still protecting primary activity. *See* Section A, above. Accordingly, while it is important to match the statutory language with its interpretative meaning, students of secondary activity should not fret too much if they come away feeling as if the language and its meaning don't seem to match.

2. Deconstructing the Statutory Language

Deconstructing the statutory language in Section 8(b)(4) reveals that the law is divided into three parts: (I) unlawful means; (II) unlawful objects; and (III) provisos. To simplify, Section 8(b)(4) makes it unlawful for a union to use unlawful means (i, ii) to engage in one of four unlawful objects (A–D), subject to three provisos. This outline of the law looks something like this:

Section 8(b)(4) makes it a ULP for a union to—

I. Use *unlawful means* against (i) or (ii)

   (i) employees of a neutral employer; or

(ii) neutral employers

II. To obtain unlawful object (A), (B), (C), or (D)

(A) Forcing an employer to enter into a hot cargo agreement under Section 8(e);

(B) *Hallmark violations*: Forcing or requiring any person to cease dealing in the products of another employer or to cease doing business with another employer, or forcing any other employer to recognize or bargain with an uncertified union;

(C) Forcing any employer to recognize or bargain with a particular union if another union has been certified as the representative of its employees;

(D) *Jurisdictional disputes*: Forcing an employer to assign work to employees in Union A rather than to employees in Union B.

III. Subject to the following provisos

(1) Primary picketing or other primary activity proviso

(2) Sympathy strike proviso

(3) Publicity proviso

The following chart matches the statutory language with the simplified outline:

Deconstruction of NLRA Section 8(b)(4)

Statutory Language	Simplified Language
It shall be an unfair labor practice for a labor organization or its agents	It is unlawful for a union
	to use unlawful means (secondary strikes, boycotts, picketing) against
(i) to engage in, or to induce or encourage any individual employed by any person engaged in commerce or in an industry affecting commerce to engage in, a strike or a refusal in the course of his employment to use, manufacture, process, transport, or otherwise handle or work on any goods, articles, materials, or commodities or to perform any services; or	(i) employees of a neutral employer, or
(ii) to threaten, coerce, or restrain any person engaged in commerce or in an industry affecting commerce, where in either case an object thereof is—	(ii) a neutral party

	to obtain unlawful objects, including
(A) forcing or requiring any employer or self-employed person to join any labor or employer organization or to enter into any agreement which is prohibited by section 8(e) [subsection (e) of this section];	(A) forcing an employer to enter into a hot cargo agreement,
(B) forcing or requiring any person to cease using, selling, handling, transporting, or otherwise dealing in the products of any other producer, processor, or manufacturer, or to cease doing business with any other person, or forcing or requiring any other employer to recognize or bargain with a labor organization as the representative of his employees unless such labor organization has been certified as the representative of such employees under the provisions of section 9 [section 159 of this title]: **Provided, That nothing contained in this clause (B) shall be construed to make unlawful, where not otherwise unlawful, any primary strike or primary picketing;**	(B) causing a hallmark violation where the **primary activity proviso does not otherwise apply**
(C) forcing or requiring any employer to recognize or bargain with a particular labor organization as the representative of his employees if another labor organization has been certified as the representative of such employees under the provisions of section 9 [section 159 of this title];	(C) forcing any employer to recognize or bargain with a particular union if another union has been Board-certified, or
(D) forcing or requiring any employer to assign particular work to employees in a particular labor organization or in a particular trade, craft, or class rather than to employees in another labor organization or in another trade, craft, or class, unless such employer is failing to conform to an order or certification of the Board determining the bargaining representative for employees performing such work:	(D) interfering with a jurisdictional dispute;
	subject to the following provisos:
See Section 8(b)(4)(B) above	(1) Primary activity proviso,

Provided, That nothing contained in this subsection (b) [this subsection] shall be construed to make unlawful a refusal by any person to enter upon the premises of any employer (other than his own employer), if the employees of such employer are engaged in a strike ratified or approved by a representative of such employees whom such employer is required to recognize under this Act [subchapter]:	(2) Sympathy strike proviso, or
Provided further, That for the purposes of this paragraph (4) only, nothing contained in such paragraph shall be construed to prohibit publicity, other than picketing, for the purpose of truthfully advising the public, including consumers and members of a labor organization, that a product or products are produced by an employer with whom the labor organization has a primary dispute and are distributed by another employer, as long as such publicity does not have an effect of inducing any individual employed by any person other than the primary employer in the course of his employment to refuse to pick up, deliver, or transport any goods, or not to perform any services, at the establishment of the employer engaged in such distribution.	(3) Publicity proviso

3. Unlawful Means under Section 8(b)(4)

Section 8(b)(4) prohibits secondary activity—secondary strikes, secondary boycotts, and secondary picketing. This means generally that a union cannot strike, boycott, or picket an employer with whom it does not have a labor dispute. This section further fleshes out the unlawful means element of Section 8(b)(4).

a. The General Rule

Section 8(b)(4) makes it unlawful for a union to picket a secondary employer. For example, imagine the Widget-makers Union has a dispute with Johnson Widget Company, but rather than picketing Johnson, the Union decides to picket Gomez Metal Co., a supplier company, and Wang's Widgets & Gadgets, Inc., a company that sells the widgets that Johnson makes. The Union violates Section 8(b)(4) when it pickets Gomez Metal or Wang's Widgets & Gadgets unless some exception applies. The sections below explain those exceptions.

Section 8(b)(4) does not prohibit primary picketing at the primary employer even if it has effects on secondary employers. For example, Section 8(b)(4) does not prohibit primary picketing even though that picketing may have the effect of turning away delivery trucks at the gate of a construction site. *See* Section D.1 (discussing *NLRB v. International Rice Milling*) and Section C.3.c (discussing common site/reserve gate cases).

b. Ally Doctrine: Defining the Neutral Employer

The Board's court-approved ally doctrine provides guidance for determining whether the union is acting against the primary employer or an unconcerned neutral employer (the secondary employer). This characterization is important because union activity directed at a neutral is typically unlawful. If, however, the neutral itself behaves in a certain way, it could be stripped of its neutral status, thereby losing the protection of Section 8(b)(4). The court, in *Boich Mining Co. v. NLRB*, 955 F.2d 431 (6th Cir. 1992), explained the ally doctrine:

> A neutral employer may be stripped of its neutral status (1) if it performs "struck work" for the employer, i.e. work that it otherwise would not perform absent a strike, or (2) if the two employers become so closely entwined as to function essentially as a single entity.... In both instances, the union bears the burden of establishing that the two employers are allies under the Act.

Accordingly, a neutral employer becomes an ally—and therefore a lawful target for concerted activity—where it performs struck work or its actions entangle it sufficiently into the primary's business that the Board may consider them as acting in concert.

Douds v. Metropolitan Federation of Architects, 75 F. Supp. 672 (S.D.N.Y. 1948) provides an early example of prong (1) of the Board's ally doctrine. There, the primary firm (Company P) contracted out substantial amounts of work to a so-called neutral/secondary firm (Company S). As part of a proceeding to enjoin labor picketing, the court reviewed the following questions: (1) whether Company P's contract with Company S constituted "doing business together"; (2) whether the union had the unlawful objective of preventing Company P and Company S from doing business with one another; and (3) whether Company P and Company S were allies because Company S was performing struck work that it would not have performed absent the strike. The court held that because Company S was doing struck work that it normally would not do, it had become Company P's ally and, therefore, that the union could engage in lawful primary picketing of the ally.

AFTRA v. NLRB, 462 F.2d 887 (D.C. Cir. 1992), provides a counterexample of what it means for the primary and the secondary to be "so closely entwined as to function essentially as a single entity." There, the union, which was in a labor dispute with a TV station, picketed a third-party news company that happened to be owned by the same company that owned the TV station. The court held that the picketed third party was a neutral employer because the TV station and the news company operated as "separate autonomous entities," and the union did not have a labor dispute with the news company. Therefore, the union's conduct violated Section 8(b)(4). The union might not have violated the Act had it picketed just the owner, with whom it had the actual labor dispute.

c. Ambulatory Situs Picketing, Common Situs Picketing, and Reserve Gates

Sometimes it is difficult, if not impossible, for the union to picket only the primary employer because the primary employer's work site is mobile, and/or two employers, a primary and a secondary, occupy essentially the same location. This matters because union pickets of primary employers can have certain legal effects (e.g., turning away secondary employees) that would be illegal if the union were picketing a secondary employee. In such cases, the question becomes, essentially, who is the union *really* picketing?

In these cases, the Board has determined that,

> picketing ... the premises of a secondary employer is primary [and therefore permissible] if it meets the following conditions: (a) the picketing is strictly limited to times when the *situs* of dispute is located on the secondary employer's premises; (b) at the time of the picketing the primary employer is engaged in its normal business at the *situs;* (c) the picketing is limited to places reasonably close to the location of the *situs;* and (d) the picketing discloses clearly that the dispute is with the primary employer.

Sailors' Union of the Pacific (*Moore Dry Dock*), 92 N.L.R.B. 547, 549 (1950).

Moore Dry Dock illustrates the principles behind the ambulatory situs doctrine. In that case, the union, which represented ship crew members, had a primary labor dispute with Samsoc, the owner of the ship, the *S.S. Phopho.*

By way of background, when Samsoc entered into a six-year contract with the Kaiser Gypsum Co. to ship gypsum from Mexico to California, Samsoc entered into another contract with Moore Dry Dock to convert the *Phopho* into a vessel that could carry gypsum. To complete the conversion work, the *Phopho* was docked at the Moore shipyard. Samsoc hired foreign crew members at below-union wages to work on the *Phopho* while the ship was docked at the Moore shipyard. The union began to organize the *Phopho* crew and to seek recognition, thereby engaging in lawful recognitional picketing under Section 8(b)(7), discussed in Section G below. During the organizing campaign, the union picketed the *Phopho* at the Moore shipyard. Finding that the *Phopho* was an ambulatory work site of Samsoc, which was temporarily stationed at the Moore shipyard, a secondary worksite, the Board applied a four-factor test still used today. Applying that test, the Board held that the union's picketing was permissible (did not violate Section 8(b)(4)) because

(a) the picketing occurred at the secondary employer's workplace while the *Phopho*—the actual situs of the dispute—was docked there;
(b) the picketing occurred while the primary employer—Samsoc—was conducting its normal business on the *Phopho*;
(c) the union picketed at the yard entrance closest to where the *Phopho* was docked (the union selected that location after it was denied permission to picket at the dock where the *Phopho* was tied up); and
(d) the picket signs indicated that the union's dispute was with Samsoc—not with Moore and the union made no attempt to interfere with work in progress at Moore's shipyard.

Moore Dry Dock illustrates the significant thought that the Board and courts have put into the primary-secondary distinction to ensure that the government interferes as little as possible into a primary labor dispute while ensuring that unsuspecting neutrals remain unharmed.

The *Moore Dry Dock* factors became widely applied in the trucking industry in cases where unions would picket at pickup and delivery sites. Consequently, application of the *Moore Dry Dock* factors became prevalent in "reserve gate" cases, where union demonstrations would take place at the common entrance/exit to the primary situs used by secondary employees. Recall the rule from *International Rice Milling*—that a primary picket at a primary employer doesn't violate Section 8(b)(4) even if it has effects on secondary employees, such as turning them away at a firm's entrance. In response, employers created so-called reserve gates—entrances reserved only for secondary employees.

Local 761, IBEW v. NLRB (General Electric), 366 U.S. 667 (1961), exemplifies this type of case. In that case, General Electric operated a plant, known as the Appliance Park, where it manufactured electrical appliances. Appliance Park had several gates, which served as its only entrances/exits. To insulate G.E. employees from frequent labor disputes in which its contractors were involved, GE designated Gate 3-A as a reserve gate for use by independent contractors only. That gate was 550 feet away from the nearest gate available for G.E. employees, suppliers, and delivery workers. That gate was posted as follows: "Gate 3-A For Employees Of Contractors Only—G.E. Employees Use Other Gates." G.E. used independent contractors to perform work that its employees lacked the necessary skills to perform, and it was more economically efficient for the contractors to perform. The union was the bargaining representative of a unit of 7,600 G.E. production and maintenance workers. The union called a strike over twenty-four unsettled grievances with G.E. The union picketed all gates, including Gate 3-A, holding signs stating, "Local 761 On Strike G.E. Unfair."

General Electric presents the question of whether the union violated Section 8(b)(4) because, by picketing Gate 3-A, the union was enmeshing the independent contractors (neutral employees) in its labor dispute with G.E. The Board answered this question in the affirmative. The Court, however, remanded the case to determine whether Gate 3-A was indeed a "mixed gate," as the contractors themselves performed work integral to the functioning of Appliance Park. In remanding the case, the Court asked the Board to consider the following: where there is "a separate gate marked and set apart from other gates ... [1] the work done by the men who use the gate must be unrelated to the normal operations of the employer and [2] the work must be of a kind that would not, if done when the plant were engaged in its regular operations, necessitate curtailing those operations." *Id.* at 681. On remand, the Board concluded that the picketing at the reserve gate was primary, and therefore lawful, because the work of the independent contractors—installing shower rooms, repairing roads, enlarging the ventilation system, etc.—was "necessarily related to GE's normal operations." *Local 761, I.U.E.*, 138 N.L.R.B. 342, 346 (1962).

The common situs issue also arises in the context of contractors and subcontractors at construction sites. The seminal case is *NLRB v. Denver Building & Construction Trades Council*, 341 U.S. 675 (1951), discussed in the next section.

4. Unlawful Objectives under Section 8(b)(4)

Section 8(b)(4)(B) (formerly Section 8(b)(4)(A)) enumerates that section's so-called "hallmark" unlawful objectives. A union violates that section when it forces (i) the employees of a neutral employer or (ii) a neutral party to stop doing business with an employer with whom the union has a labor dispute. In other words, it makes it unlawful for "a union to induce employees to strike against or to refuse to handle goods for their employer when an object is to force him or another person to cease doing business with some third party." *Local 1976, United Bhd. of Carpenters v. NLRB*, 357 U.S. 93, 98 (1958). This section further fleshes out the unlawful object element of Section 8(b)(4).

a. Forcing a General Contractor to Fire a Nonunion Subcontractor

In *NLRB v. Denver Building & Construction Trades Council*, 341 U.S. 675 (1951), the Supreme Court defined the contours of Section 8(b)(4)(B). In that case, Doose & Litner, a union general contractor on a commercial building, awarded a subcontract for electrical work to Gould & Preisner, a nonunion firm, whose employees were the only nonunion employees on the project. Friction developed between union and nonunion workers, eventually resulting in union pickets at the construction site. Those pickets signaled to all union employees on the job to strike until otherwise ordered to return to work. For two weeks, the only workers to report for work were G&P's nonunion employees. General contractor D&L finally capitulated and terminated its contract with G&P, which had not yet finished the electrical work. The following day, the union removed the pickets, and the union employees returned to work. G&P filed charges against the union, alleging that the union struck the general contractor D&L to force it to cease doing business with nonunion subcontractor, D&L.

Denver Building & Construction Trades Council presented the question: who is the primary employer? Again, the answer to that question is significant because the union's conduct—strike activity—is lawful if it is directed against a primary employer and unlawful if it is directed at a secondary employer. If the general contractor D&L is the primary employer with whom the union has a dispute, then placing economic pressure on D&L to cease doing business with G&P is lawful. If, however, D&L is a neutral employer and G&P is the primary employer, then placing economic pressure on D&L to cease doing business with G&P is unlawful. The Court concluded that the union violated Section 8(b)(4) based on its finding that the union's primary dispute was with G&P for remaining nonunion. Given that D&L hired G&P to perform electrical work, the ally doctrine could have been applied here to make the picketing against D&L primary.

b. Forcing Employers to Boycott Another Employer's Products

In addition to prohibiting unions from using secondary pressure to force neutral firms to cease doing business with other firms, Section 8(b)(4)(B) prohibits unions from placing pressure on neutral employers to boycott another firm's products. Cases examining these issues often present the question of whether the union's conduct is an unlawful secondary boycott or whether it merely constitutes a request of managers to make lawful managerial decisions.

The main case on point is *NLRB v. Servette, Inc.*, 377 U.S. 46 (1964). There, the union was engaged in a primary labor dispute with Servette, a wholesale distributor of specialty items stocked by retail food stores. The union asked supermarket managers not to stock Servette goods during the strike. The union warned the managers that, if they did stock these items, the union representatives would handbill in front of their establishment and ask customers not to purchase items distributed by Servette. The court of appeals set aside the Board's order dismissing the complaint, alleging that the union violated Section 8(b)(4)(i) & (ii)—coercing neutral employers and their employees through the union's conduct. In the Board's view, the union's efforts to gain the support of supermarket managers did not constitute "induce[ment]" of an "individual" within the meaning of Section 8(b)(4). The court of appeals disagreed and explained that supermarket managers are statutory individuals and that the union's effort to enlist the aid of those managers constituted unlawful inducement. The Supreme Court agreed with the court of appeals that supermarket managers are statutory individuals but disagreed with the appeals court's conclusion that the union's efforts constituted unlawful inducement. Instead, the Court concluded that the Board reasonably found that the union merely asked "the managers ... to make a managerial decision which ... was within their authority to make." *Id.* at 51.

c. Consumer Boycotts and Consumer Appeals

Imagine picketers in front of a retail store asking customers not to buy a particular brand of clothing because that brand is made from child labor. That picketing constitutes a request for a consumer boycott. Most non-labor boycotts are lawful. Consumer boycotts organized by unions may be deemed unlawful, however, especially where the union engages in picketing. But not all labor-organized consumer boycotts are unlawful. For purposes of labor law only, secondary consumer boycotts that constitute "threaten, coerce, or restrain" within the meaning of Section 8(b)(4)(ii)(B) may be prohibited. The Board and reviewing courts have struggled with whether Congress intended to prohibit all consumer picketing at neutral employers—certainly problematic from a constitutional standpoint—or whether (and to what extent) the "threaten, coerce, or restrain" language should be more narrowly construed. The Supreme Court reviewed this question in two cases—*NLRB v. Fruit & Vegetable Packers, Local 760* (*Tree Fruits*), 377 U.S. 58 (1964), and *NLRB v. Retail Store Employees, Local 1001* (*Safeco Title Insurance Co.*), 447 U.S. 607 (1980).

In *Tree Fruits*, the union called a strike against fruit packers and warehouse workers who were selling Washington state apples to Safeway grocery stores. In furtherance of that strike, the union instituted a consumer boycott of Washington apples. Strikers and other union supporters placed two pickets in front of forty-five Safeway stores (and three picketers in front of another store). Placards and handbills clearly stated the union's request that consumers refuse to buy (boycott) Washington State apples because nonunion workers were packing those apples. Prior to the picketing, the union delivered a letter to each store manager explaining the nature of the picketing. The letter included a copy of the written instructions to the picketers, ordering them to remain peaceful and forbidding them from telling customers not to patronize the stores. The Board held that Section 8(b)(4) prohibits picketing in front of a neutral carrier of nonunion goods. The reviewing court rejected the Board's construction of Section 8(b)(4), holding that such picketing is prohibited only if the General Counsel could show that the picketing "threaten[ed], coerce[d], or restrain[ed]" in terms of economic loss. The court remanded to the Board to reopen the record to receive additional evidence.

The Supreme Court vacated the court's decision. As a threshold matter, the Supreme Court agreed with the lower court that Congress did not mean to prohibit all peaceful consumer picketing at secondary sites, particularly when that picketing "is limited, as here, to persuading Safeway customers not to buy Washington State apples when they traded in the Safeway stores." *Id.* at 63.

The Court disagreed with the lower court that the test for "to threaten, coerce, or restrain" is whether the neutral suffered or was likely to suffer economic loss. Instead, the Court concluded, "[a] violation of § 8(b)(4)(ii)(B) would not be established, merely because [the union's] picketing was effective to reduce Safeway's sales of Washington State apples, even if this led or might lead Safeway to drop the item as a poor seller." *Id.* at 72–73. Another way to look at *Tree Fruits* is that the union was merely picketing one of literally thousands of products that the supermarket carried. The chances that such actions could cause economic harm to the neutral supermarket were small.

By contrast, a larger number of an employer's products were involved in the consumer appeal in *NLRB v. Retail Store Employees, Local 1001 (Safeco Title Insurance Co.)*, 447 U.S. 607 (1980). In *Safeco*, the Court modified its holding in *Tree Fruits* when it held that picketing, which advocates for a boycott of a truly substantial portion of the neutral firm's business, is unlawful under Section 8(b)(4)(ii)(B). Here, Safeco Title Insurance Company was in the business of underwriting real estate insurance in the State of Washington. Safeco maintained close business relationships with only five local title companies. Over 90% of the title companies' business derived from the sale of Safeco insurance. When a labor dispute between Safeco and a union over contract negotiations arose, the union struck Safeco and picketed the company as well as the five title companies. The picketers distributed handbills asking customers to support the strike by canceling their Safeco insurance policies. Based on charges filed by Safeco and one of the title companies, the Board concluded that the union violated Section 8(b)(4)(ii)(B), rejecting the union's reliance on *Tree Fruits*. The D.C. Circuit, sitting *en banc*, refused to enforce the Board's order. The court agreed that the insurance companies were neutral parties but concluded that *Tree Fruits* left neutrals, who carry struck products, vulnerable to this type of boycott.

The Supreme Court reversed the lower court's decision on the grounds that it misapplied the statute. The Court distinguished *Tree Fruits* as a case involving a secondary boycott of struck products at a neutral business that carried many different products. In *Safeco*, the neutral insurance companies carried the boycotted product almost exclusively. Accordingly, requesting the neutral firms' customers to drop Safeco insurance (the struck product) was tantamount to putting the neutral firm out of business. In other words, the union's "secondary appeal against the central product sold by the title companies in this case is 'reasonably calculated to induce customers not to patronize the neutral parties at all.'" The Court expressed further concern about the "distinctly different" injury to Safeco compared to the injury at the grocery store in *Tree Fruits*.

> Product picketing that reasonably can be expected to threaten neutral parties with ruin or substantial loss simply does not square with the language or the purpose of § 8(b)(4)(ii)(B). Since successful secondary picketing would put the title companies to a choice between their survival and the severance of their ties with Safeco, the picketing plainly violates the statutory ban on the coercion of neutrals with the object of "forcing or requiring [them] to cease ... dealing in the [primary] produc[t] ... or to cease doing business with" the primary employer.

Id. at 614–15.

Students frequently ask why Safeco and the title insurance companies were not considered allies under the ally doctrine. The dissent says as much: "the single product secondary firm is likely to be the primary employer's strongest ally because of the alignment of their respective economic interests." *Safeco*, 447 U.S. at 623 (Brennan, J., dissenting). As this case illustrates, the line between product boycott and allyship is not easy to draw. Generally speaking, a neutral becomes an ally of a primary employer—and therefore loses its protected status as a neutral—when it takes on struck work that it ordinarily would not do but for the strike. Here, the neutral insurance companies did not take on any additional struck work and therefore did not ally themselves with the primary. The more difficult question then is where to draw the line between too few struck products to make an economic impact and just enough struck products to make an unlawful impact. Apples alone were not enough in *Tree Fruits*, but a company selling 90% of one type of title insurance was enough in *Safeco*. Predicting where the line exists between those two extremes is not a simple task.

D. The Three Provisos to Section 8(b)(4)

So far, we have been examining when secondary conduct is unlawful. Congress included three provisos to Section 8(b)(4) to clarify when such conduct is lawful.

1. Primary Activity Proviso

Congress added the primary activity proviso to the language of Section 8(b)(4)(B) to clarify that this section prohibits secondary—not primary—boycotts. The proviso states, "nothing contained in this clause (B) shall be construed to make unlawful, where not otherwise unlawful, any primary strike or primary picketing." The problem with Section 8(b)(4)'s original language was highlighted in *NLRB v. International Rice Milling*, 341 U.S. 665 (1951), where union picketers who were lawfully picketing their own employer were charged with a Section 8(b)(4)(ii)(B) violation because the strikers encouraged truckers employed by secondary employers from crossing the picket line to make a delivery to the primary employer. The Court held that such conduct does not constitute unlawful secondary inducement. *See* Section C.3.a., above. The congressional addition of the primary activity proviso incorporates the holding of *International Rice Milling* into the statutory language.

2. Sympathy Strike Proviso

Labor history is closely tied to the development of the sympathy strike—a strike in support of a primary strike. The sympathy strike constitutes a powerful means by which working-class members can support one another. The sympathy strike proviso protects the fundamental right of working-class members to support one another during labor disputes. Many of the most famous strikes in U.S. history were sympathy strikes. For example, during the Pullman Strike of 1894, railroad workers went on strike to support wildcat strikers who were protesting wage cuts at the Pullman Palace Car Company.

Although the jurisprudential history of this statutory language is confusing, the Board's most recent construction of this language can be distilled as follows: The sympathy strike proviso protects an employee's right "to honor another union's picket line." *See Torrington Construction Co.*, 235 N.L.R.B. 1540, 1541 (1978). This right is protected concerted activity under Section 7. *See, e.g., Children's Hospital Medical Center v. California Nurses Association*, 283 F.3d 1188, 1191–92 (9th Cir. 2002) (noting same and explaining that "[s]ympathy strikes are a means by which workers can demonstrate their solidarity with their 'brothers and sisters' who are engaged in a primary strike. '[R]espect for another union's picket line leads to a stronger labor movement.'") (citation omitted). This language would therefore cover the narrow form of a sympathy strike, such as the truck driver's refusal to cross a picket line to deliver goods to a retail store.

3. Publicity Proviso

The publicity proviso exempts otherwise prohibited secondary nonpicketing conduct (e.g., leafleting) where the communication is used for purposes of "truthfully advising the public ... that a product or products are produced by an employer with whom the labor organization has a primary dispute and are distributed by another employer." *Compare* Section 8(b)(7)(C) (proviso permitting picketing, which has the immediate purpose of truthfully informing the public that the employer does not hire union labor, even though its ultimate purpose may be to coerce the employer into recognizing it), discussed in Section G, below. As with much of Section 8(b)(4), the publicity proviso has been the subject of Supreme Court review. In *Edward J. DeBartolo Corp. v. NLRB*, 463 U.S. 147 (1983) (*DeBartolo I*), the union had a dispute with the shopping mall owner and its general contractor. The union peacefully distributed union literature (handbilled) to shopping mall tenants, asking their customers not to shop there until the mall's owner promised to use contractors who paid fair wages. The Board never reached the question of whether Section 8(b)(4)'s secondary boycott provisions prohibited the handbilling because it found that the handbilling was exempted by the publicity proviso. The Court reversed, holding that the publicity proviso did not protect the handbilling at issue because the purpose of the handbilling was to publicize a dispute between a union and a construction company, where the requested boycott included businesses with no relationship to the construction company. In other words, the union's request was not limited to publicizing the primary labor dispute with the construction company or the fact that the mall tenants were distributing the primary employer's goods because the mall tenants were not, in fact, "distributors" of the construction company's "products." The Court remanded the case to determine whether the handbilling violated Section 8(b)(4) and, if so, whether such application would be unconstitutional. The Court in *DeBartolo II*, discussed in Section B, above, held that such an application would be unconstitutional.

E. Other Unlawful Objects under Section 8(b)(4)

1. Hot Cargo Agreements and Work Preservation Clauses

Imagine the following scenario: A union proposes to an employer that bargaining-unit members will not have to handle struck work—products from other companies that are currently involved in a labor dispute and whose employees are on strike. The union's proposal did not violate Section 8(b)(4) as originally drafted because, although the clear intent of the clause was to affect secondary employers, the union could accomplish this goal through a contract with its primary employer.

Congress closed this loophole in 1959 when it added Section 8(e). Section 8(e) makes it a ULP for a union and an employer to enter into a hot cargo agreement—an agreement whereby the employer promises to refrain from handling, selling, or otherwise dealing with nonunion or struck products. Section 8(b)(4)(ii)(A) makes it a ULP for a union to threaten, coerce, or restrain an employer into executing a Section 8(e) agreement.

Neither Section 8(e) nor Section 8(b)(4)(ii)(A), however, reach work-preservation agreements: clauses in collective bargaining agreements (CBAs) that are intended to protect work historically performed by the bargaining unit. These clauses are standard in the construction industry. The case law in this area distinguishes between unlawful hot cargo agreements and lawful work-preservation clauses, and therefore typically calls for an interpretation of a CBA.

The seminal case is *National Woodwork Manufacturers Assoc. v. NLRB*, 386 U.S. 612 (1967). The clause at issue in that case, known as Rule 17, contained the following two sentences:

> No employee shall work on any job on which cabinet work, fixtures, millwork, sash, doors, trim or other detailed millwork is used unless the same is Union made and bears the Union Label of the United Brotherhood of Carpenters and Joiners of America. No member of this District Council will handle material coming from a mill where cutting out and fitting has been done for butts, locks, letter plates, or hardware of any

> description, nor any doors or transoms which have been fitted prior to being furnished on job, including base, chair, rail, picture moulding, which has been previously fitted....

Id. at 615 n.2. The first sentence, known as a union-label clause, is unlawful. The second sentence, known as a work-preservation clause, is lawful.

A union-label clause prohibits the employer's employees from using materials unless they are union-made. Union-label clauses generally constitute unlawful hot cargo agreements because they constitute an agreement between the employer and the union in which the employer promises not to have its workers handle nonunion materials. *See Carpenters District Council of Philadelphia (National Woodwork Manufacturers Assoc.)*, 149 N.L.R.B. 646, 655–56 (1964). The Board made that finding; the Union conceded as much and did not seek judicial review of that issue.

The second sentence, which prohibits the employer's employees from handling prefabricated doors, illustrates a lawful work-preservation clause intended to ensure that the employer's carpenters retain their job of door making. Throughout the twentieth century, the use of prefabricated doors replaced the skilled labor of carpenters. Unions relied on such work-preservation clauses to enhance carpenters' job security.

The Board has also found lawful work-preservation clauses where the union's intention was not to preserve work traditionally done by its members, but to acquire work for members that the members performed in the past. In the Board's view, obtaining this work has a primary purpose because it is "fairly claimable" by the union employees. In *Newspaper & Mail Deliverers' Union*, 298 N.L.R.B. 564, 566 (1990), the Board explained that "fairly claimable work is work that is identical to or very similar to that already performed by the bargaining unit and that bargaining unit members have the necessary skill and are otherwise able to perform." The conceptual distinction in these cases is that clauses aimed at preserving work a bargaining unit is doing and/or has traditionally done are mainly aimed at conditions at the primary employer. In contrast, clauses aimed at acquiring entirely new work are likely mainly aimed at secondary employers.

2. Jurisdictional Disputes

Imagine an employer assigns to Union A the work of unloading cargo from a certain ship. Union B claims that the employer's assignment of the work to Union A violates Union B's collective bargaining agreement with that employer. Union B pickets the employer in protest. This scenario is referred to as a jurisdictional or work-assignment dispute.

Section 8(b)(4)(D) makes it a ULP for a union to use economic pressure to force employers into assigning work to those they represent rather than to members of other bargaining units. Section 10(k) empowers the Board to hear such complaints in a special hearing, known as a 10(k) proceeding:

> Whenever it is charged that any person has engaged in [a ULP] within the meaning of [Section 8(b)(4)(D)], the Board is empowered and directed to hear and determine the dispute out of which such [ULP] shall have arisen, unless, within ten days after notice that such charge has been filed, the parties to such dispute submit to the Board satisfactory evidence that they have adjusted, or agreed upon methods for the voluntary adjustment of, the dispute....

29 U.S.C. § 160(k).

Together, Sections 8(b)(4)(D) and 10(k) establish procedures for protecting employers from becoming caught between the proverbial rock and a hard place—competing claims of rival unions demanding the right to perform the same work. *See NLRB v. Radio & Television Broadcast Engineers Union, Local 1212, IBEW* (*CBS*), 364 U.S. 573, 581 (1961). The Board holds the Section 10(k) hearing to identify "the real nature and origin of the dispute." *Teamsters Local 578* (*USCP-Wesco, Inc.*), 280 N.L.R.B. 818, 820 (1986), *aff'd* 827 F.2d 581 (9th Cir. 1987). If the Board determines that Section 8(b)(4)(d) has not been violated, then it will dismiss the charge without having issued a complaint. If, however, the Board determines that there are competing claims to the work, Section 10(k) "requires the Board to decide [such] jurisdictional disputes on their merits," meaning the Board must decide which union is "entitled to the disputed work." *CBS*, 364 U.S. at 579. Once the Board makes that determination, if the Board is satisfied that the parties are complying with its decision, it will dismiss the charge. Otherwise, it will issue a complaint, alleging a violation of Section 8(b)(4)(D).

F. Featherbedding

Section 8(b)(6) makes it an ULP for a union "to cause or attempt to cause an employer to pay or deliver or agree to pay or deliver any money or other thing of value, in the nature of an exaction, for services which are not performed or not to be performed." This section prohibits the practice of featherbedding—the practice of adopting make-work rules.

The history of featherbedding is inextricably linked to the history of work preservation. As technology has increasingly made more jobs redundant, workers through their unions have fought to retain those jobs. For years, unions were able to do that by persuading employers to agree to continue to pay the union workers for work that some might characterize as unnecessary. *American Newspaper Publishers Association v. NLRB*, 345 U.S. 100 (1953) illustrates this point. There, the Court recited the history of typesetters, a skilled profession in newspaper production during the nineteenth century. Typesetters used movable-type technology first developed in the mid-fifteenth century by Johannes Gutenberg. With the introduction of the linotype machine in the late nineteenth century, the job of composing the type gave way to those who could operate the linotype machine. The sole job remaining was for those composers who made the original form. Faced with this loss of work, the union in *American Newspaper Publishers Association* secured an agreement with the newspaper publishers to allow composers to set up duplicate originals. Performing "this 'made work' came to be known in the trade as 'setting bogus.' It was a wasteful procedure. Nevertheless, it has become a recognized idiosyncrasy of the trade and a customary feature of the wage structure and work schedule of newspaper printers." *Id.* at 103.

Section 8(b)(6) does not outright prohibit all featherbedding. "However desirable the elimination of all industrial featherbedding practices may have appeared to Congress, the legislative history of the Taft-Hartley Act ... demonstrates that when the legislation was put in final form Congress decided to limit the practice but little by law." *Id.* at 104. After reviewing the statutory language and legislative history of Section 8(b)(6), the Court, in agreement with the lower court, concluded that the practice of setting bogus did not constitute a ULP because, in these circumstances, the union was securing payment for union workers for work in fact performed. In a sense, the Court was restating an old contract adage that courts should not review the adequacy of consideration.

The Board, with court approval, has continued to narrowly construe Section 8(b)(6). For example, in *NLRB v. Gamble Enterprises, Inc.*, 345 U.S. 117,

123 (1953), the Court upheld the Board's finding that a union did not violate Section 8(b)(6) when it insisted that a theater hire local musicians in exchange for the union's consent that the theater could also hire traveling bands for other purposes. The Court upheld the Board's finding that the union's conduct did not violate the Act because "the union was seeking actual employment for its members."

G. Recognitional Picketing

1. Overview

Section 8(b)(7) regulates recognitional or organizational picketing ("recognitional picketing")—picketing to force an employer to recognize, or to force employees to select, a union. In particular, Section 8(b)(7) prohibits picketing, and even threatening to participate in picketing, which has a recognitional or organizational purpose, in the circumstances stated in subsections (A), (B), or (C), and subject to the two provisos to subsection (C). Picketing is recognitional for purposes of Section 8(b)(7) so long as one of its purposes is recognitional, even if the picketing has other objectives. In determining whether the picketing is recognitional, the Board reviews all the circumstances surrounding the union's overall conduct, not only the message on the pickets.

It is important to emphasize that Section 8(b)(7)'s ban is on recognitional picketing. Accordingly, Section 8(b)(7) does not proscribe other types of picketing, such as economic or area-standards picketing—activity to protest wages below the level set by union contracts in the locale—unless it also has a recognitional objective. *See, e.g., Retail Clerks Local 899* (*State-Mart, Inc.*), 166 N.L.R.B. 818 (1967) (holding that Section 8(b)(7)'s prohibitions on recognitional picketing did not apply where labor organizers picketed employer using signs informing the public that the employer did not pay area-standard wages, where there was no evidence that the union was in fact seeking recognition). Area-standards picketing is lawful under Section 8(b)(7) even if it has an effect of "induc[ing] any individual employed by any other person in the course of his employment, not to pick up, deliver or transport any goods or not to perform any services." 29 U.S.C. § 158(b)(7).

2. Unlawful Objectives

Section 8(b)(7) prohibits recognitional or organizational picketing under the following three circumstances. Subsection (A) bans recognitional or organizational picketing when the employer has lawfully recognized another union, and therefore, questions concerning representation (QCR) cannot be appropriately raised. Subsection (B) bars such picketing when a valid Board election has been held within the preceding twelve months. Subsection (C) provides that recognitional picketing that is not barred under (A) or (B) may not exceed thirty days unless a representation petition is filed within that period. Filing an election petition stays this limitation and the picketing may continue pending the outcome of the election. Congress enacted Subsection (C) to prevent blackmail picketing by a non-majority union—picketing for recognition that disrupts the employer's business for an extended period until the employer gives in to the union's demands. An employer who surrenders to a minority union under such a scenario violates Section 8(a)(2). *See* Chapter 8. Section 8(b)(7)(C) contains two provisos. The first proviso provides for expedited elections under certain circumstances described in Section G.3.a, above. The second proviso, described in Section G.3.b, immunizes informational picketing from the bans in subsections (A) and (B) unless the object of the informational picketing is to interfere with deliveries to the targeted employer.

a. Section 8(b)(7)(A)

Subsection (A) prohibits recognitional or organizational picketing when the employer has lawfully recognized another union, and therefore, a QCR cannot be appropriately raised. A union can defend a Section 8(b)(7)(A) allegation on two grounds, both of which show that a QCR can be appropriately raised. First, the picketing union can show that the incumbent union was not lawfully recognized. In this case, the picketing union must also timely file a Section 8(a)(2) charge. *See* Chapter 8, discussing the NLRA's prohibition on company unions. Second, the picketing union may show that the contract between the employer and the incumbent union does not bar a rival petition. *See* Chapter 10, discussing the Board's contract-bar rules.

b. Section 8(b)(7)(B)

Subsection (B) bars recognitional picketing when the Board has held a valid election within the preceding twelve months. The question of whether post-election picketing has an unlawful object turns on whether a valid election was held and whether that election occurred within the past 12 months.

The twelve-month period begins to run from the date that the Board certifies the results of the election. To defend against a Section 8(b)(7)(B) charge, the union must show that the election was invalid. *See* Chapter 10. A union that continues to picket after it loses a Board-conducted election violates Section 8(b)(7)(B).

c. Unreasonable Duration under Section 8(b)(7)(C)

Subsection (C) limits recognitional picketing to a reasonable period not to exceed thirty days, unless an election petition is filed before that period expires. The purpose of limiting peaceful, recognitional picketing to thirty days is to balance the employer's interest in ensuring that its business is not interrupted with the union's interest in using the picketing as an effective organizational tool—a primary purpose. In some cases, the Board limits the picketing to less than thirty days, such as when there is picket-line violence.

Insofar as thirty days is an outside limit, fewer than thirty days may, in some circumstances, be deemed unreasonable. For example, the Board has found that a union violates Section 8(b)(7)(C) when it engages in intermittent picketing over a twelve-month period. *See Local 3, Int'l Bhd. of Elec. Workers*, 325 N.L.R.B. 527, 529 (1998). A union also violates Section 8(b)(7)(C) when it engages in picket-line violence. *Retail, Wholesale & Dep't Store Union Dist. 65*, 141 N.L.R.B. 991, 999 (1963) (holding that the union, which engaged in twenty-six days of recognitional and organizational picketing without filing a petition, violated Section 8(b)(7)(C) by engaging in "picket-line acts, consisting ... of threats of physical violence, use of coercive and abusive language, blocking ingress and egress to and from struck premises"). Indeed, a union violates Section 8(b)(7)(C) when it engages in recognitional picketing of any duration where the unit it seeks is unlawful. *See Teamsters, Local 282*, 262 N.L.R.B. 528, 530 (1982) (holding that union violates Subsection (C) when it engages in recognitional picketing to admit both guards and non-guards to membership—a unit that is not appropriate under Section 9).

3. Section 8(b)(7)(C) Provisos

a. The First Proviso's Expedited Election Requirement

The first proviso to subsection (C) provides for an expedited election where the targeted employer files a Section 8(b)(7)(C) charge and the picketing union has filed a representation petition within a reasonable time after the picketing starts. This election requires no hearing and no showing of interest among the employees. Accordingly, the Region can hold a Section 8(b)(7)(C) election faster than a regular election. Without the charge, the Board will process an election petition filed during recognitional picketing along with routine representation procedures. This means that a union engaged in recognitional picketing can neither obtain an expedited election nor be rushed into one against its will.

In *International Hod Carriers, Local 840 (Blinne Construction Co.)*, 135 N.L.R.B. 1153 (1962), the Board analyzed the effect of employer ULPs on a union's Section 8(b)(7)(C) obligation to file an election petition to trigger an expedited election. The Board held that employer ULPs do not relieve the union from the filing requirement, explaining that, if the ULP charges were meritorious, the employer ULPs would serve as blocking charges, thereby delaying the expedited election until such time that an uncoerced election could be held. By contrast, if the ULPs were baseless, then the election would be held expeditiously. *Blinne Construction* also held that a majority union picketing for recognition cannot avoid a ULP under Section 8(b)(7) even though the purpose of Subsection (C) was to eliminate blackmail picketing by minority unions.

b. Informational Picketing Exception under the Second Proviso

The second or informational picketing proviso carves out a significant exception to Section 8(b)(7)'s ban on recognitional or organizational picketing, by permitting such picketing where two conditions hold. First, the picketing must be for the purpose of truthfully advising the public that the picketed "employer does not employ members of, or have a contract with a labor organization." Second, the picketing cannot interfere with deliveries to, or the performance of other services at, the picketed premises by employees of other employers. *See, e.g., NLRB v. Local 3, International Brotherhood of Electrical Workers*, 317 F.2d 193, 197 (2d Cir. 1963) (explaining that, in enacting the second proviso, Congress intended to protect "a comparatively innocuous species of picketing having the immediate purpose of informing or advising the public, even though its ultimate object was success in recognition and organization"). The *Local 3 IBEW* Court explained that lawful publicity picketing covers the dissemination of messages designed to influence individual members of the unorganized public. Informational or publicity picketing is permitted because its impact on the employer through individuals is weak, indirect, and non-coercive. By contrast, signal picketing—union picketing that signals to other labor groups and other workers not to work for the company—is not permitted under the second proviso of Section 8(b)(7)(C) because of its much greater impact on that employer's business. In short, informational picketing to members of the public is permissible unless it causes significant disruptions to the employer's business. At that point, the picketing becomes signal picketing, which the NLRA does not permit. Picketing that is exempt from Section 8(b)(7) under the informational picketing proviso is exempt even if such picketing also has a recognitional object.

H. Remedies: Mandatory Injunctive Relief under Section 10(l) and Compensatory Damages under Section 303

Section 10(l) authorizes injunctive relief for union violations of the secondary boycott and recognitional picketing sections of the NLRA. Section 303 permits an employer to sue in federal court for damages to its business or property caused by a union's violation of Section 8(b)(4). 29 U.S.C. § 187(b). This section focuses primarily on Section 10(l) injunctive relief.

Section 10(l) of the NLRA *requires* the Board to seek an injunction in a federal district court whenever there is reasonable cause to believe a violation of Section 8(b)(4)(A), (B), (C), or (D); Section 8(b)(7); or Section 8(e) has occurred. However, the Board may not seek an injunction under Section 8(b)(7) where a meritorious charge has been filed under Section 8(a)(2) alleging that the employer is dominating, interfering with, or supporting a union. Nor may a district court issue a temporary restraining order unless the petition for injunctive relief alleges "substantial and irreparable injury to the charging party will be unavoidable." 29 U.S.C. § 160. In any event, the temporary restraining order "shall be effective for no longer than five days."

Section 10(l) also instructs the district court to grant the Board's petition for an injunction if the Board had reasonable cause to believe that a violation of Section 8(b)(4), Section 8(b)(7), or Section 8(e) has occurred, and the court decides that injunctive relief is "just and proper." *See, e.g., National Mar. Union of Am., AFL-CIO v. Commerce Tankers Corp.*, 457 F.2d 1127, 1138 (2d Cir. 1972). For many years, various federal courts have had slightly different tests for determining whether injunctive relief is "just and proper," although most, if not all, seem to have interpreted the "just and proper" language as triggering a traditional equitable inquiry. *See, e.g., Overstreet v. United Bhd. of Carpenters & Joiners of Am., Local Union No. 1506*, 409 F.3d 1199, 1206 (9th Cir. 2005). For instance, the Seventh Circuit in *Kinney v. International Union of Operating Engineers, Local 150, AFL-CIO*, 994 F.2d 1271, 1275 (7th Cir. 1993) upheld the district court's application of the following four factors:

> (1) whether the petitioner had a reasonable likelihood of success on the merits; (2) whether the petitioner had an adequate remedy at law and/or would be irreparably harmed if the injunction did not issue; (3) whether the threatened injury to petitioner outweighed the threatened harm an injunction would have inflicted on defendant; and (4) whether the granting of a preliminary injunction served the public interest.

Courts are likely to review all Section 10(l) cases under this traditional four-part test for injunctive relief, in light of *Starbucks Corp. v. McKinney*, 602 U.S. 339, 345 (2024). There, the Court held that "district courts must use the traditional four-part test [likelihood of success on merits, irreparable harm, balance of equities, and public interest] when evaluating the Board's request for a preliminary injunction under § 10(j)." *See* Chapter 9, Section G.2.

Along these lines, Section 10(l) is often compared with Section 10(j) in other contexts. While the sections are similar in that they both provide procedures for seeking injunctive relief and both grant the district courts power to issue injunctive relief that they deem "just and proper," there are four main differences. First, Section 10(l) applies to union secondary conduct (boycotts, strikes, etc.); recognitional picketing; and jurisdictional disputes, whereas Section 10(j) applies to ULPs more generally. Second, Section 10(l) is mandatory: it compels the Board, upon reasonable cause, to seek injunctive relief. In contrast, Section 10(j) is discretionary, and permission must be received from the Board before a Section 10(j) injunction can be sought. Third and relatedly, the Board must seek injunctive relief when it has "reasonable cause to believe" that Section 8(b)(4), 8(b)(7), or 8(e) has been violated. In contrast, Section 10(j) contains no standard to trigger the injunctive relief request. Fourth, Section 10(l) relief must be sought before a complaint is even issued. Section 10(j) relief may not be sought until after the General Counsel has issued a complaint.

These differences are telling. "Section 10(l) reflects a Congressional determination that [these ULPs] ... are so disruptive of labor-management relations and threaten such danger of harm to the public that they should be enjoined whenever a district court has been shown reasonable cause to believe in their existence and finds that the threatened harm or disruption can best be avoided through an injunction." *Wilson v. Milk Drivers & Dairy Emp. Union, Local 471*, 491 F.2d 200, 203 (8th Cir. 1974).

CHECKPOINTS

- Labor law distinguishes between primary and secondary activity in determining whether union conduct is protected, permitted, or unlawful. Primary activity connotes concerted activity directed at an employer with whom the union has a labor dispute. Secondary activity connotes concerted activity directed at a third party who is not a party to the primary labor dispute—the unconcerned neutral.
- Labor picketing receives some constitutional protection under the First Amendment. The seminal labor picketing case is *Teamsters Local 695 v. Vogt, Inc.*, 354 U.S. 284 (1957), where the Court explained that picketing is not pure speech because it involves patrolling, inducement to action, and labor's exercise of economic power. As a mixed form of communication and conduct, it is entitled to some First Amendment protection but may be regulated.
- Section 8(b)(4) prohibits secondary activity—secondary strikes, secondary boycotts, and secondary picketing—activity directed against third-party, unconcerned neutrals who have no tie to the primary labor dispute.
- The Board's court-approved ally doctrine provides that a neutral employer may be stripped of its neutral status (1) if it performs "struck work" for the employer; or (2) if the two employers become so closely entwined as to essentially function as a single entity.
- The Board's court-approved ambulatory situs doctrine, as explained in *Moore Dry Dock*, holds that picketing the premises of a secondary employer is primary if (a) the picketing is strictly limited to times when the *situs* of dispute is located on the secondary employer's premises; (b) at the time of the picketing the primary employer is engaged in its normal business at the *situs*; (c) the picketing is limited to places reasonably close to the location of the *situs*; and (d) the picketing discloses clearly that the dispute is with the primary employer.

- Section 8(b)(4) prohibits unions from compelling (i) the employees of a neutral employer; or (ii) an unconcerned neutral party to stop doing business with the primary.
- Section 8(b)(4) prohibits unions from forcing a general contractor to fire a nonunion subcontractor.
- In cases where Firm A distributes Firm B's goods X, Section 8(b)(4) does not prohibit unions from asking Firm A's managers to boycott X even where the request is accompanied by the threat of handbilling Firm A's customers asking them not to purchase X.
- Section 8(b)(4) does not prohibit all peaceful consumer activity at secondary or neutral employers.
- Under *DeBartolo II*, asking the public not to patronize a secondary employer may not be done via picketing, but it may be done via handbilling. The Court thereby distinguishes between picketing, which is mixed form of communication and conduct that may not always receive constitutional protection, and handbilling, which almost always receives constitutional protection as pure speech under the First Amendment.
- Under *Tree Fruits*, Section 8(b)(4) generally permits unions to ask customers of a neutral or secondary firm to boycott a specific product made by the primary employer that is sold at the secondary's store. Section 8(b)(4) does not prohibit such picketing merely because the union's picketing reduces the secondary firm's sales.
- Under the *Safeco* exception to the *Tree Fruits* rule, however, Section 8(b)(4) prohibits picketing at the secondary store that sells the primary employer's product where the union's request to the secondary firm's customers to boycott the primary's product is tantamount to putting the secondary firm out of business.
- The primary activity proviso expressly exempts primary activity from Section 8(b)(4)(B)'s prohibitions.
- The sympathy strike proviso under Section 8(b)(4) protects an employee's right to honor another union's picket line.
- The Section 8(b)(4) publicity proviso exempts otherwise prohibited secondary conduct where the communication is used for purposes of publicity so long as the means is not picketing.

- Section 8(e) makes it a ULP for a union and an employer to enter into a hot cargo agreement—an agreement whereby the employer promises to refrain from handling nonunion products.
- Section 8(b)(4)(ii)(A) makes it a ULP for a union to threaten, coerce, or restrain an employer into executing a Section 8(e) agreement.
- Neither Section 8(e) nor Section 8(b)(4)(ii)(A) reaches work-preservation clauses.
- Sections 8(b)(4)(D) and 10(k) establish procedures for protecting employers from competing claims of rival unions demanding the right to perform the same work.
- Section 8(b)(6) purports to prohibit the practice of featherbedding—the practice of adopting make-work rules. However, the Supreme Court has so narrowly interpreted this section that many instances of featherbedding remain permissible.
- Section 8(b)(7) limits a union's right to engage in recognitional or organizational picketing—picketing an employer for the purpose of gaining recognition or organizing.
- Section 8(b)(7) bans recognitional picketing where there is no question concerning representation or a valid election took place in the past twelve months.
- Section 8(b)(7)(C) limits recognitional picketing to thirty days unless the union files an election petition. It permits informational picketing that truthfully advises the public that the picketed employer does not employ union workers, so long as the picketing does not interfere with third-party deliveries to that employer.
- An employer can request an expedited election under a proviso to Section 8(b)(7) that shortens the period of recognitional picketing but also requires the employer to forgo standard pre-election procedures.
- Remedies for violating these sections of the Act include injunctive relief under Section 10(1) and compensatory damages under Section 303 for Section 8(b)(4) violations.

CHAPTER 17

Grievance Arbitration

ROADMAP

- The grievance-arbitration process
- Typical issues that arise in grievances: just-cause dismissals, seniority, and past practices
- Judicial intervention in private-sector grievance arbitration
- Judicial injunctions to compel grievance arbitration
- Concurrent jurisdiction between arbitrators and the labor board
- Arbitration of federal statutory claims
- Public-sector grievance arbitration

This chapter addresses grievance arbitration, the process by which parties to a collective bargaining agreement (CBA) resolve disputes arising from a breach of that CBA. Interest arbitration—a process by which labor and management may resolve issues resulting from a bargaining impasse by presenting those issues to a neutral arbitrator—is not discussed here but rather in Chapter 13 on public-sector bargaining.

A. Overview of the Grievance-Arbitration Process

One of the main duties of unions is to bargain collectively with management with a view toward reaching an agreement and to execute any resultant agreement into a written CBA. Almost all CBAs have a grievance-arbitration clause. Administering that contract and adjusting grievances under the grievance-arbitration clause is another key duty of a union.

Grievance procedures are contractual. Accordingly, the precise structure of any shop's grievance-arbitration mechanism will vary from contract to contract. The typical grievance-arbitration clause establishes a multi-step procedure that culminates in arbitration. In step one, the grievant or union presents the grievance to their immediate supervisor or the lowest-level supervisor who has the authority to settle the dispute. Absent a resolution at step one, the grievance proceeds to step two, where it is typically presented to the step one supervisor's supervisor or the shop manager. The grievance typically moves up the chain through three or more steps, until it is presented to a high-level manager such as the Vice President or Director of Human Resources. In the absence of a resolution at the final grievance step, the union may choose to take the grievance to arbitration.

Most grievance-arbitration clauses are likely to share several common features. These clauses will typically create several layers of review but be designed to encourage communication and settlement at the lowest level of review. They will often contain strict time limits for filing grievances and answers at each step. A union's failure to timely file a grievance will serve as an employer's complete defense to the grievance at arbitration. Management's failure to respond to or answer a grievance will often be construed as a denial of the grievance.

B. Arbitration Selection Process

The two most prominent organizations to provide arbitrators are the American Arbitration Association (AAA) and the Federal Mediation and Conciliation Service (FMCS). Both organizations maintain a list of experienced arbitrators who are qualified to resolve disputes over the interpretation and application of CBAs. Both organizations can provide a list of appropriate names to the parties. Both organizations will appoint an arbitrator if the parties so request. To qualify as an arbitrator of workplace disputes, the arbitrator must have labor and employment subject-matter expertise and formal arbitration training. For example, AAA arbitrators are qualified, using the following four criteria: (1) area of expertise—labor, employment, and elections; (2) language capacity, including English, several romance languages, Arabic, and Chinese; (3) industry expertise; and (4) type of services, including fact-finding, mediation, and arbitration. According to the FMCS website, FMCS arbitrators must have "extensive and recent experience" with collective bargaining and be "capable of conducting an orderly hearing, … analyze testimony and exhibits and … prepare clear and concise findings and awards within reasonable time limits." Given these required qualifications, many arbitrators are lawyers.

C. Arbitration Issues

1. Contract Interpretation

Many grievances involve issues of contract interpretation. One way of thinking of arbitration is in terms of the parties purchasing an expert in contract interpretation.

2. Just Cause in Discipline and Discharge Cases

Most CBAs have a progressive disciplinary system, which culminates in an employee's right not to be discharged except for just cause (or some equivalent terms such as cause, good cause, reasonable cause, or proper cause). Sometimes the CBA defines just cause. Other times, the CBA gives either an exhaustive list (an employee may be fired for these reasons and only these reasons) or an incomplete list of offenses that constitute proper cause for discharge (an employee may be fired for just cause, which includes, but is not limited to, the following offenses …). And sometimes, the CBA merely states that an employee can be fired for just cause, without defining that term.

Deciding what constitutes cause in any of these circumstances is a matter of contract interpretation. Where the term just cause is left undefined in the CBA or is vaguely defined, the arbitrator must construe the contours of the contractual term, "just cause." Drafting the CBA in these ways presents the following legal question: What standard does the arbitrator use to determine what constitutes just cause?

The modern just-cause standard originated in *Enterprise Wire Co. and Enterprise Independent Union*, 46 Lab. Arb. 359 (1966) (Daugherty). There, in the context of determining whether an employer justly discharged an employee for excessive absenteeism and for noncompliance with job requirements, the arbitrator articulated what has come to be known as the Seven Tests of Just Cause:

a. Are company rules reasonably related to business efficiency, orderliness, safety, or the performance expectations of an employee in that position?
b. Did the employer warn the employee of the consequences of breaching company rules?
c. Before taking action to discharge the employee, did the employer investigate the matter to determine the employee's guilt?
d. Did the employer conduct that investigation fairly and objectively?
e. Did the investigation turn up substantial evidence of the employee's guilt?
f. Did company officials fairly and without discrimination apply the rules?
g. Did the company issue a degree of discipline reasonably related to the seriousness of the employee's offense and her past record?

a. Reasonable Rules

A firm is generally entitled to promulgate and enforce work rules to ensure that its business is run efficiently, orderly, and safely. The firm is also entitled to promulgate and enforce performance standards. (The extent to which the union has a say in work rules and performance standards is discussed in Chapters 11, 12, and 13.) Along these lines, an employee protected by a just-cause CBA provision can be fired for one of two reasons—misconduct or poor performance. The question of whether an employee has engaged in misconduct or has performed poorly often involves whether that employee has violated a work rule.

Before deciding whether an employee has violated a work rule (and thus might have engaged in misconduct) or whether an employee has performed poorly, an arbitrator may be called upon to determine whether those rules or standards are reasonable. In making their determination, an arbitrator may ask the following questions: (1) Is the rule or standard written in a manner that is easy to understand? (2) Has the firm consistently applied the rule or standard? (3) Has the firm ever disciplined an employee for violating this rule? (4) If so, under what circumstances? Some of these questions are relevant in determining not only whether the work rule itself is reasonable but also whether the employer has been applying that rule fairly. *See* Section C.1.f.

b. Notice

Just cause typically requires an employer to warn the employees that their conduct might result in discharge. There are two common ways in which the failure to warn arises. First, an employer might simply promulgate a rule at the time of its violation. In such cases, the employee would not understand that their conduct might result in disciplinary action. Second, an employer might have a work rule that has not been applied in a long time, if ever. In those cases, employees could also claim that they were not on notice that their conduct would result in discipline.

Another type of notice is embedded in the concept of progressive discipline. In such cases, an employer may not discharge an employee who has a clean record, absent egregious circumstances. Instead, the employer is obligated to give employees opportunities to correct their behavior before the employer can lawfully fire them. One variation of such discipline would look like this: the first offense results in an oral warning, the second offense in a written warning, the third offense in a suspension, and the fourth offense in discharge. There may be instances where notice is not required. For example, an arbitrator would likely rule in the employer's favor where the employer summarily fired employees for credibly threatening to blow up the workplace if management did not acquiesce to those employees' demands.

c. The Employer Investigated the Matter Before It Made the Decision to Discipline

Absent extraordinary circumstances, just cause requires the employer to investigate the matter thoroughly before imposing discipline. For example, an arbitrator might find that an employer unjustly discharged a grievant where it simply believes another employee's report about the grievant's misconduct, without conducting an independent investigation.

d. The Employer's Investigation Was Fair and Objective

Relatedly, the employer's investigation must be conducted fairly and objectively. For example, an arbitrator might find that the employer's investigation is unjust where the employer requests only one side of the story and ignores employee-witness reports.

e. Substantial Proof of Misconduct or Poor Performance

Before discharging an employee, an employer should have substantial evidence of misconduct or a record of poor performance. Such evidence often consists of documentation of previous misconduct or prior performance evaluations.

f. Equal Treatment

The concept of equal treatment plays a significant role in determining whether the employer had just cause to discipline or discharge the employee. In determining whether an employee has been treated without discrimination, the arbitrator will review the following:

(1) Has the employer applied its work rules consistently?

(2) Has the employer treated like situations alike? In other words, has the employer meted out the same or comparable discipline to similarly situated employees—those with similar conduct or performance records?

(3) Has the employer held all employees accountable to reasonable performance standards?

g. Proportionate Punishment

The arbitrator will also determine whether the punishment fits the crime. The arbitrator will determine whether there is a reasonable connection between the degree of discipline and the seriousness of the employee's offense, as well as their past record. This is a nuanced variation on the idea that employees should generally not be summarily dismissed for first-time offenses, but they can be summarily dismissed for egregious offenses such as endangering the lives of their co-workers.

h. Summary

The seven tests of just cause demonstrate that there is both a procedural and a substantive dimension to just-cause dismissal. As to process, an employer has a duty to provide whatever notice and opportunity to be heard that the parties have agreed upon and to engage in a fair and objective pre-decisional investigation. The employer should have substantial evidence to support its disciplinary decision. Such evidence goes to the merits of the decision and whether the employer's ultimate punishment was nondiscriminatory and proportionate to the offense. For these reasons, most CBAs provide for various steps in the grievance-arbitration process. There is also a substantive dimension to just-cause dismissal. The employer's duty to discharge an employee only for just cause typically encompasses a right to be fired only for two reasons—misconduct or poor performance—per reasonable work rules and reasonable performance standards.

Significantly, if the CBA "does not define 'just cause' and does not include a list of offenses that would lead to termination, then any reviewing court must defer to an arbitrator's interpretation of the scope and meaning of the just-cause provisions of the agreement." *IMC-Agrico Co. v. Int'l Chem. Workers Council of United Food & Commercial Workers Union, AFL-CIO*, 171 F.3d 1322, 1328 (11th Cir. 1999) (citing cases).

3. Seniority Rights

Seniority and reverse seniority have become important concepts in grievance arbitration. Unions typically try to negotiate seniority as a criterion for management actions. For example, unions might use seniority to choose annual leave, work assignments, or recall, and reverse seniority in cases of layoff. In contrast, management tries to negotiate as much discretion as possible in assigning work and making recall and layoff choices.

There are several types of seniority that a union can bargain for and, therefore, that can be used in distributing contractual benefits. For example, the CBA may require facility-wide seniority in determining annual work schedules, but unit-wide seniority for deciding who can take leave. This would allow all union workers to choose their work schedules based on seniority, while also allowing management to maintain holiday coverage in each job category.

4. Past Practice

Arbitrators also use past practice—"the understood and accepted way of doing things over an extended period of time"—to interpret contractual language in CBAs and to gain insight "into the nature of [the parties'] contractual rights and obligations." Richard Mittenthal, *Past Practice and the Administra-*

tion of Collective Bargaining Agreements, 59 MICH. L. REV. 1017, 1019, 1042 (1961). To qualify as legitimate, these unwritten, sometimes unspoken, practices must have clarity, consistency, longevity, repetition, acceptability, and mutuality. *Id.* at 1019. The longer standing, the clearer, and the more accepted the practice, the more likely the arbitrator is to find that the practice is binding. Union professionals use the term "common law of the shop" to refer to a set of practices that have these characteristics.

A past practice has the legal effect of incorporating that practice into the CBA. For all intents and purposes, the past practice becomes a term or condition of employment and, therefore, the employer cannot unilaterally change that term without bargaining with the union. For example, in *Phillips Petroleum Co.*, 24 Lab. Arb. 191, 194–95 (1955) (Merrill), the arbitrator found that providing electric service to employees for $1.00 per month was an established practice and therefore incorporated into the CBA as a continuing contractual obligation. Based on this finding, the arbitrator ordered the company to pay the grievants the difference between $1.00 per month and the amount the utility charged them.

Most arbitrators use past practice to help interpret a CBA or to fill in the gaps where a CBA is silent, but they will not use past practice to change the meaning of clear and unambiguous contractual language. *See Phelps Dodge Copper Products Corp.*, 16 Lab. Arb. 229, 223 (1951) (Justein) ("[p]lain and unambiguous words are undisputed facts. The conduct of the parties may be used to fix a meaning to words or phrases of uncertain meaning. Prior acts cannot be used to change the explicit terms of a contract"). Nor may the parties interpret the CBA in a manner that is contrary to the clear and unambiguous language of state law. For example, in *City of Palo Alto*, 107 Lab. Arb. 494, 499 (1996) (Riker), a city employee challenged their employer's refusal to grant them paid military service leave based on a twenty-five-year practice of granting paid leave notwithstanding contractual language that military leave is governed by state law, which in this case did not require paid leave. The arbitrator held that a past practice—to pay employees on military leave—cannot overcome the clear and unambiguous language of state law.

Past practices need not relate to a contractual subject. For example, an employer may give each employee a turkey every year as a Thanksgiving bonus. It is unlikely that the employer agreed in a CBA to give its employees turkeys for Thanksgiving. Yet such a clear, consistent, long-standing, repetitive, and acceptable act indubitably qualifies as a practice.

5. Obey Now and Grieve Later

Arbitrators have developed an obey-and-grieve principle according to which an employee must obey their superior's orders even if that order is in breach of the CBA. The purpose of this rule is famously expressed in *Ford Motor Co.*, 3 Lab. Arb. 779, 780–81 (1944) (Shulman), a case where the employer discharged the committee member for instructing production employees to refuse work assignments during a strike on the grounds that the work assignments themselves violated the CBA:

> The remedy under the contract for violation of right lies in the grievance procedure and only in the grievance procedure. To refuse obedience because of a claimed contract violation would be to substitute individual action for collective bargaining and to replace the grievance procedure with extra-contractual methods. And such must be the advice of the committeeman if he gives advice to employees. His advice must be that the safe and proper method is to obey supervision's instructions and to seek correction and redress through the grievance procedure....
>
> .... [T]he grievance procedure is prescribed in the contract precisely because the parties anticipated that there would be claims of violations which would require adjustment. That procedure is prescribed for all grievances, not merely for doubtful ones. Nothing in the contract even suggests the idea that only doubtful violations need be processed through the grievance procedure and that clear violations can be resisted through individual self-help. The only difference between a "clear" violation and a "doubtful" one is that the former makes a clear grievance and the latter a doubtful one. But both must be handled in the regular prescribed manner.

In furtherance of his view that management, not labor, has the authority to direct employees and, therefore, that the committee member's usurpation of that authority constituted misconduct, the arbitrator added that "production cannot wait for exhaustion of the grievance procedure" whenever a dispute arises. He based that declaration on his observation that the purpose of an industrial plant is "production," that someone in authority must "direct the manner in which [production] is to go on until the controversy is settled," and that authority is vested in [the supervisor]. This policy allows production to proceed while the grievance procedure is pursued. *Id.* at 781. Because committee members have no such vested authority, it was improper for him to direct the employees to stop production.

Interestingly, the arbitrator modified the committee member's discipline from a discharge to a layoff, not to exceed four days. The arbitrator did this in light of the evidence—the committee member's conduct was not different from that of other committee members—and, therefore, the employer's real reason for discharging the committee member was because it viewed him as a troublemaker. *See* Section C.2.f.

Several circumstances might justify disobeying a work rule or direct order. For example, an employee need not obey an unlawful rule, or one that creates a safety hazard for the grievant or another employee. *Id.* Nor must the grievant obey a rule in cases where obeying the rule would cause irreparable harm or where it is simply impossible to obey the rule, such as where the employer asks a disabled person to complete a task that cannot be completed because of the employee's disability.

D. Judicial Intervention in Private-Sector Grievance Arbitration

1. General Principles

Section 301 of the Labor Management Relations Act, 29 U.S.C. § 185, gives federal courts jurisdiction over CBA disputes between employers and unions. Section 301(c) provides:

> For the purposes of actions and proceedings by or against labor organizations in the district courts of the United States, district courts shall be deemed to have jurisdiction of a labor organization
>
> (1) in the district in which such organization maintains its principal office, or
>
> (2) in any district in which its duly authorized officers or agents are engaged in representing or acting for employee members.

Prior to the enactment of Section 301, unions lacked legal status to sue or be sued in federal court. Section 301(b) changes this, first by clarifying that unions and employers are "bound by the acts of their agents." The following sentence then confers the right to "sue or be sued." The final sentence in Section 301(b) provides:

> Any money judgment against a labor organization in a district court ... shall be enforceable only against the organization as an entity and against its assets, and shall not be enforceable against any individual member or his assets.

This final sentence makes impermissible certain remedies found permissible in the *Danbury Hatters' Case*, a.k.a. *Loewe v. Lawlor*, 208 U.S. 274 (1908) (*Loewe I*), and *Lawlor v. Loewe*, 235 U.S. 522 (1915) (*Loewe II*). (For a more in-depth discussion of these cases, *see* Chapter 2.) There, a union pursued a secondary-boycott strategy (*see* Chapter 16 for a discussion of secondary boycotts), a nationwide boycott, to put economic pressure on D.E. Loewe & Co., a fur hat manufacturer that operated as an open shop (union membership was not a condition of employment). The company sued the union under the Sherman Antitrust Act of 1890. The case was twice brought before the United States Supreme Court. In *Loewe I*, the Supreme Court held the Sherman Antitrust Act applied to union activities such as national boycotts. The remanded case also made its way to the United States Supreme Court, primarily on the question of damages. In *Loewe II*, the Court upheld the finding below that the union had violated the Sherman Act and that union members were jointly liable for treble damages. While Congress enacted legislation to immunize unions from antitrust violations, as later interpreted by the Supreme Court to implicitly exempt unions from antitrust laws, *see* Chapter 2, the rule that union members could be held liable for damages for the actions of union officials continued until the enactment of Section 301(b).

Judicial interpretations of Section 301(a) were originally more controversial because they raised the question of whether Section 301 is merely jurisdictional or also a source of substantive law. The express language of Section 301(a) converts these breach-of-contract cases into federal-question cases:

> Suits for violation of contracts between an employer and a labor organization representing employees in an industry affecting commerce as defined in this chapter, or between any such labor organizations, may be brought in any district court of the United States having jurisdiction of the parties, without respect to the amount in controversy or without regard to the citizenship of the parties.

By enacting Section 301, Congress conferred subject-matter jurisdiction on federal courts to hear disputes arising under CBAs.

In *Textile Workers Union v. Lincoln Mills*, 353 U.S. 448 (1957), the Supreme Court affirmed this interpretation of Section 301(a). There, the union addressed work-assignment disputes through the appropriate grievance steps provided for in the CBA. The employer denied those grievances at each step. Upon completion of the grievance steps, the employer refused to arbitrate the dispute, as provided for in the CBA. The Supreme Court held that a union could sue an employer for specific enforcement of an agreement to arbitrate and that a court could compel arbitration as a remedy for breach of the CBA's grievance-arbitration provisions. The Court added: "the substantive law to apply in suits under § 301(a) is federal law, which the courts must fashion from the policy of our national labor laws." *Id.* at 456. Thus, *Lincoln Mills* allows for the development of a federal common law under Section 301.

The Court has since further refined its interpretation of Section 301 jurisdiction. First, in *Dowd Box Co. v. Courtney*, 368 U.S. 502 (1962), the Court held that federal court jurisdiction over Section 301 lawsuits is concurrent with state court jurisdiction. Plaintiffs may, therefore, bring these suits in either federal or state court. Second, in *Smith v. Evening News Association*, 371 U.S. 195, 197 (1962), the Court explained that Section 301 removed the Board's exclusive authority to handle breach of collective-bargaining cases: "The authority of the Board to deal with an unfair labor practice which also violates a collective bargaining contract is not displaced by § 301, but it is not exclusive and does not destroy the jurisdiction of the courts in suits under § 301." Finally, in *Local 174, Teamsters v. Lucas Flour Co.*, 369 U.S. 95 (1962), the Court held that state courts exercising concurrent jurisdiction under Section 301 must apply federal law.

2. The Steelworkers Trilogy: Judicial Review of Arbitration Decisions

In a series of cases decided in 1960, the Court cemented the principle that arbitration is the cornerstone of this newly minted federal common law of CBAs. These cases—*American Manufacturing*, *Warrior & Gulf*, and *Enterprise Wheel*—have come to be known as the *Steelworkers Trilogy*, named for the United Steelworkers Union, a party common to all three cases.

American Manufacturing and *Warrior & Gulf* both concern the considerable deference judges give arbitrators in interpreting CBAs. In *Steelworkers v.*

American Manufacturing Co., 363 U.S. 564 (1960), an employee grieved an employer's decision to refuse to reinstate him based on a doctor's statement in a workers' compensation hearing that the employee's work-related injury rendered him partially disabled. At the grievance's final step, the employer refused to arbitrate the case because the parties had settled the case through the workers' compensation action. The lower courts sided with the employer on the grounds that either the workers' compensation settlement estopped the arbitration proceedings (district court) or the grievance was frivolous (Sixth Circuit). The Supreme Court reversed, explaining that it is the arbitrator's—not the court's—function to determine whether a contract dispute is subject to arbitration (arbitrability). The Court added: "Whether the moving party is right or wrong is a question of contract interpretation." *Id.* at 568. Interpreting the contract is the arbitrator's, not the court's, job. Thus, a grievance is arbitrable if it alleges a violation of the relevant CBA, even if on the merits the case is very weak, even "frivolous."

A similar issue arose in *Steelworkers v. Warrior & Gulf Manufacturing Co.*, 363 U.S. 574, 582–83 (1960). There, the employer refused to arbitrate a dispute over its decision to contract out maintenance work, allegedly in violation of the CBA. The legal issue for arbitration concerned the scope of the arbitration clause. The employer contended that its decision to contract out work was a strictly managerial function and that such decisions were expressly excluded from arbitration. The union disputed that narrow interpretation of the arbitration clause's scope. The Court ordered arbitration, holding that:

> An order to arbitrate the particular grievance should not be denied unless it may be said with positive assurance that the arbitration clause is not susceptible of an interpretation that covers the asserted dispute. Doubts should be resolved in favor of coverage.

Notably, by holding this dispute arbitrable, the Court was not interpreting the arbitration clause or siding with one party or the other. It was merely holding that the arbitrator, not the court, should determine the scope of the arbitration clause. The arbitrator decides the dispute's arbitrability. And even if the arbitrator decides that the dispute is arbitrable, it may still find in favor of the employer on the merits. Moreover, this case stands for the principle that grievable disputes are presumptively arbitrable, meaning that grievable disputes are arbitrable absent a CBA clause stating that a topic could be grieved but not arbitrated.

In *Steelworkers v. Enterprise Wheel & Car Corp.*, 363 U.S. 593 (1960), the Court examined the scope of judicial review of arbitration awards. In that case, the employer discharged several employees for engaging in a work stoppage to protest the discharge of a fellow worker. The arbitrator found that, although the work stoppage was improper under the CBA, the remedial discharges were not justified. The arbitrator modified the discharges to ten-day suspensions. The employer refused to comply with the arbitrator's decision, citing that the CBA expired before the award was finalized. The Fourth Circuit denied enforcement of the arbitrator's remedy on the grounds that arbitration awards beyond CBA expiration are unenforceable. The Supreme Court reversed, holding that courts did not have discretion to reject arbitration awards merely because they disagreed with the arbitrator's interpretation of the CBA. In so holding, the Court famously demarcated the roles of arbitrators and courts in deciding arbitration cases:

> [A]n arbitrator is confined to interpretation and application of the [CBA]; he does not sit to dispense his own brand of industrial justice. He may of course look for guidance from many sources, yet *his award is legitimate only so long as it draws its essence from the collective bargaining agreement.* When the arbitrator's words manifest an infidelity to this obligation, courts have no choice but to refuse enforcement of the award.

Simply put, the court must defer to the arbitrator's interpretation of the CBA and subsequent award "so long as it draws its essence from the collective bargaining agreement." *Id.* at 597. This makes it exceedingly difficult in practice to appeal an adverse arbitration judgment successfully.

3. Judicial Intervention to Protect Public Policy

As discussed above, arbitrators, not courts, determine the scope of arbitration clauses and whether a grievance is arbitrable. Moreover, judicial review of an arbitrator's interpretation of the CBA is narrow and must be upheld "so long as it draws its essence from the [CBA]." But what if the arbitration award draws its essence from the CBA but is repugnant to another important policy?

The Supreme Court has thrice visited the question of what standard it should use in reversing an arbitral decision. One key point to keep in mind in these cases is that the question is not whether the employee violated the law or public policy. The question is whether complying with the arbitrator's award would cause the employer to, e.g., violate the law. In *W.R. Grace & Co. v. Rubber Workers*, 461 U.S. 757, 764, 766 (1983), the Court refused to vacate an arbitration award "[u]nless the arbitral decision [fails to] 'draw its essence from the [CBA],'" or unless the contract, as interpreted by the arbitrator, "violate[d] some explicit public policy" that is "well defined and dominant" and is "ascertained 'by reference to … laws and legal precedents and not from general considerations of supposed public interests.'" Applying that standard, the Court refused to overturn an arbitral decision in favor of male employees, even though the arbitral decision conflicted with a settlement agreement between the employer and the Equal Employment Opportunity Commission (EEOC) regarding sex and race discrimination claims.

Applying the principle articulated in *W.R. Grace & Co.*—that the court's role is limited to determining whether the arbitral "award created any explicit conflict with other 'laws and legal precedents' rather than an assessment of 'general considerations of supposed public interests"—the Court, in *United Paperworkers International Union v. Misco, Inc.*, 484 U.S. 29, 43 (1987), also refused to vacate an arbitral award. In that case, the employer discharged an employee when it found marijuana in the employee's car, citing that the employee, whose job included operating dangerous machinery, violated the company's rule prohibiting drug possession. The arbitrator upheld the employee's grievance and ordered the company to reinstate the employee with backpay and full seniority. The lower court refused to enforce the arbitrator's award. In reversing the lower court, the Supreme Court explained:

> To conclude from the fact that marijuana had been found in [the employee's] car that [the employee] had ever been or would be under the influence of marijuana while he was on the job and operating dangerous machinery is an exercise in factfinding about [the employee's] use of drugs and his amenability to discipline, a task that exceeds the authority of a court asked to overturn an arbitration award.

Id. at 44–45. An arbitrator's "improvident, even silly, factfinding" is not "a sufficient basis" for a reviewing court to refuse to enforce an arbitration award. *Id.* at 39.

In *Eastern Associated Coal Corp. v. United Mine Workers, District 17*, 531 U.S. 57 (2000), the most recent Supreme Court case to examine the court's role in enforcing arbitral awards, the Court once again applied the *W.R. Grace & Co.* standard and refused to vacate an arbitral award. There, the employer sought to reverse the arbitrator's decision (1) finding that the employer had wrongfully discharged a truck driver who tested positive for marijuana twice in a sixteen-month period and (2) ordering backpay provided that the employee meet several conditions, including participating in a drug rehabilitation program. The Court rejected the company's argument that the arbitral award violated public policy found in Department of Transportation regulations, requiring random drug testing for truck drivers. In so holding, the Court explained that "the question to be answered is not whether [the employee's] drug use itself violates public policy, but whether the agreement to reinstate him does so." *Id.* at 63.

In summary, judicial review of arbitration decisions is exceedingly narrow, and for good reason. Federal labor policy favors channeling these breach-of-contract suits to arbitration to promote industrial peace and collective bargaining. Given the long history of judicial restraint of concerted activity (*see* Chapter 1), the congressional finding that repression of union activity results in industrial strife (*see* 29 U.S.C. § 151), and the fact that the parties have bargained for an arbitrator—not the courts—to decide their contractual disputes, limiting judicial review of arbitration decisions appears to be the wise choice. Indeed, it remains unclear under what circumstances courts would apply the public policy exception in cases where complying with the arbitrator's decision would not cause the employer to violate a law.

E. Judicial Injunctions to Support Grievance Arbitration

In *Sinclair Refining Co. v. Atkinson*, 370 U.S. 195 (1962), the Supreme Court held that Norris-LaGuardia's anti-injunction provisions generally prohibit federal courts from enjoining strikes in breach of a CBA's no-strike clause. The Court further refined its holding in *Boys Market, Inc. v. Retail Clerk's Union, Local 770*, 398 U.S. 235 (1970). There, the union and the employer were parties to a CBA containing a broad grievance-arbitration clause. A dispute arose when the employer allowed nonunion workers to perform bargaining-unit work. In protest, the union picketed the employer's premises. The employer filed suit in state court, requesting a temporary restraining order (TRO), a permanent injunction, and specific performance of the contract's arbitration provision. After the state court issued the TRO, the union removed the case to federal court and moved to quash the state court injunction. In response, the employer moved for an order compelling arbitration. The Court carved out an exception to Norris-LaGuardia's anti-injunction provision, by permitting federal courts to enjoin work stoppages in the following circumstances: (1) the work stoppage is subject to mandatory arbitration; (2) the court compels arbitration as a condition of issuing the injunction; (3) the work stoppage violates the CBA's no-strike promise; and (4) principals of equity favor the injunction. As the Court had previously held, the no-strike promise need not be explicit because the Court has read a no-strike promise into a contractual promise to arbitrate a dispute. *See Teamsters v. Lucas Flour Co.*, 369 U.S. 95 (1962). Applying these conditions, sympathy strikes—strikes in support of another union's dispute with an employer—are generally not enjoinable because the underlying dispute is between another union and an employer and therefore not arbitrable. *See Buffalo Forge Co. v. Steelworkers*, 428 U.S. 397 (1976).

Unions can also seek so-called "reverse *Boys Market* injunctions"—cases where the union asks the court to enjoin an employer from taking action that it believes violates the CBA. In general, the court will not issue such injunctions unless (1) the dispute is subject to mandatory arbitration; (2) the union can show actual or threatened irreparable harm; and (3) equities favor issuing the injunction. *See, e.g., Gen. Drivers & Dairy Employees, Local No. 563 v. Bake Rite Baking Co.*, 580 F. Supp. 426, 431 (E.D. Wis. 1984) (applying traditional equities analysis for issuing injunctive relief). The union need not show likelihood of success on the merits of the arbitration. It only needs to show that there is a genuine and sufficiently sound dispute to be arbitrated. *Id.* For example, a court is likely to issue a reverse *Boys Market* injunction where the employer is about to close a plant in violation of the CBA. In such a case, it would be hard, if not impossible, for the court to undo the sale, which would cause irreparable harm to all the workers who lost their jobs. For example, in *International Union, United Automobile, Aerospace & Agricultural Implement Workers of America-UAW v. Goodyear Aerospace Corp.*, 656 F. Supp. 1283, 1285 (N.D. Ohio 1986), the court issued a reverse Boys Market injunction to prevent the employer from entering into an asset purchase agreement with another firm unless the sales agreement included a successorship clause under which the purchasing entity agrees to subsume the seller's CBA. In enjoining such sales, the court found that the union's dispute with the company—namely, the company would breach the CBA if it sold its assets without including a successorship clause—was arbitrable and that the union was entitled to an injunction on ordinary equity principles. The union showed irreparable harm because under labor successor law, a purchaser or successor is free to reject a CBA and set initial terms and conditions of employment. The court also found that, on balance, the union would suffer more harm than the employer, based primarily on its finding that the employer had presented no evidence of harm related to the injunction.

F. Concurrent Jurisdiction between Arbitrators and the Labor Board

1. General Principles

As a general matter, arbitrators lack the authority to enforce the NLRA, and the Board lacks the authority to adjudicate disputes arising under a CBA. The Supreme Court ultimately decided a series of jurisdictional questions that this division of authority raises. First, under what circumstances can an arbitrator resolve an unfair labor practice (ULP)? This question arose in the context of whether an arbitrator has the authority to decide a work-assignment dispute between two unions. Under Section 8(b)(4)(D), it is a ULP for Union A to strike to force an employer to assign work to those employees that Union A represents rather than to employees represented by Union B. Normally, the Board is empowered through Section 10(k) to hear and resolve such disputes. In *Carey v. Westinghouse Electric Corp.*, 375 U.S. 261 (1964), the Court decided that the arbitrator had authority to resolve such a dispute, even though the arbitrator was essentially deciding the Section 8(b)(4)(D) issue. For a more thorough discussion of Section 10(k), see Chapter 16.

Second, does the Board have jurisdiction to construe a CBA to determine whether an employer violated Section 8(a)(5) when it unilaterally changes the terms of the CBA? In *NLRB v. C & C Plywood Corp.*, 385 U.S. 421 (1967), the Court held that the Board may construe the contract to determine whether the employer's conduct violated the statute. Later cases have held that the Board does not receive any deference from the courts of appeals on its construction of the contract, although it has the authority to construe the contract. This is because, unlike arbitrators, Board members do not have any more expertise in contract interpretation than do judges. *See, e.g., Retail Clerks International Association Local No. 455 v. NLRB*, 510 F.2d 802, 805 (D.C. Cir. 1975) ("[t]he

Board's argument to the extent it relies on contract interpretation alone, and not enunciation of policy, is entitled to no particular deference").

Third, does an employer violate Section 8(a)(5) when it refuses to furnish information relevant to resolving a grievance? In *NLRB v. Acme Industrial Co.*, 385 U.S. 432 (1967), the Court found a statutory violation here. For a more thorough discussion, see Chapter 11.

2. The Arbitral Deferral Doctrine

In *Acme Industrial Co.*, the Court examined the following question: Under what circumstances should the Board defer to an arbitration decision before deciding a question requiring contract interpretation? Suppose this question arises before arbitration has concluded. In that case, the Board must consider whether to hold the complaint in abeyance to allow the arbitrator to decide the question (pre-arbitral or *Collyer* deferral). If, however, the question arises after arbitration has concluded, the Board must decide whether to examine the issue *de novo* or to defer to the arbitrator's decision (post-arbitral or *Spielberg/Olin* deferral). This area is tricky because it presents a potential conflict between two significant federal policies—the federal labor policy granting exclusive, or at least primary, jurisdiction to the NLRB to decide the question of what constitutes a ULP and the federal labor policy favoring the arbitration of labor disputes.

Under the Board's *Collyer* deferral policy—as set forth in *Collyer Insulated Wire*, 192 N.L.R.B. 837 (1971), and *United Technologies Corp.*, 268 N.L.R.B. 557 (1984)—"certain charges must be deferred to the contractual grievance procedure if the conduct is cognizable under the grievance procedure, the grievance procedure culminates in final and binding arbitration and the charged party waives all timeliness defenses to the grievance." NLRB CASEHANDLING MANUAL (PART ONE): UNFAIR LABOR PRACTICE PROCEEDINGS § 10118.1(b) (updated Jun. 2025). Notwithstanding these guidelines, the Board has determined that deferral is inappropriate in the following circumstances:

- The charge alleges a violation of Section 8(a)(4) [for retaliation. *UFCW Local 1776*, 325 N.L.R.B. 908 (1998)];
- [T]he charge alleges [that] a party has failed to supply information in violation of [the duty to bargain in good faith under either] Section 8(a)(5) or 8(b)(3). *Clarkson Industries*, 312 [N.L.R.B.] 349, 353 (1993);

- The charged party's defense is not reasonably based on an interpretation of the [CBA]. *Oak Cliff-Golman Baking Co.*, 202 [N.L.R.B.] 614, 616–17 (1973) (*but see* GC Memo 02-05 regarding [pension] collection cases);
- The case involves the resolution of unit determination or other representation type issues. *St. Mary's Medical Center*, 322 [N.L.R.B.] 954 (1997).

NLRB Casehandling Manual (Part One): ULP Proceedings § 10118.1(a).

Under the Board's post-arbitral or *Spielberg/Olin* deferral policy, as set forth in *Spielberg Mfg. Co.*, 112 N.L.R.B. 1080 (1955), and *Olin Corp.*, 268 N.L.R.B. 573 (1984), the Board asks the Regional Office to determine whether the arbitration award meets the following standards:

- The arbitration proceedings were fair and regular;
- The parties agreed to be bound by arbitration;
- The arbitrator was presented with the facts relevant to resolving the ULP issue and considered that issue to the extent that the ULP and grievance issues were "factually parallel"; and
- The arbitrator's decision was not "clearly repugnant" to the purposes and policies of the NLRA.

The burden of proof rests with the party opposing deferral. If the award meets these standards, the charge should be dismissed. If the award does not meet such standards, the Region should complete the investigation and allow the case to proceed as normal. If the case reaches the Board, the Board will review the case under these standards. NLRB Casehandling Manual (Part One): ULP Proceedings § 10118.4.

G. Arbitration of Federal Statutory Claims

An employee might also raise claims that constitute a violation of both the CBA and another federal statute, such as Title VII of the Civil Rights Act of 1964 (Title VII) or the Fair Labor Standards Act of 1938 (FLSA). The Supreme Court has addressed this issue several times. Initially, in *Alexander v. Gardner-Denver Co.*, 415 U.S. 36 (1974), the Supreme Court was asked to decide whether an employee may litigate a race discrimination claim after the union arbitrated the claim and lost. There, the Court held that the two claims were independent of one another and therefore that the Title VII claim could proceed even though the employee lost at arbitration. The *Alexander* Court stressed that arbitration is not an appropriate means for vindicating statutory rights. *See also Barrentine v. Arkansas-Best Freight System*, 450 U.S. 728 (1981) (permitting the FLSA suit to go forward where no grievance had been filed under the CBA).

In the ensuing years, nonunion employers began requiring employees, as a condition of employment, to sign agreements requiring the arbitration of statutory employment claims. These agreements waived the employees' right to litigate statutory employment claims in state or federal court. This issue first reached the Court in *Gilmer v. Interstate/Johnson Lane Corp.*, 500 U.S. 20 (1991). There, the employer compelled its employee, Gilmer, to register as a securities representative with the New York Stock Exchange, whose NYSE registration application contained an agreement to arbitrate any dispute arising out of Gilmer's employment or termination of employment with Interstate. Seven years later, Interstate fired Gilmer, who was 62 years old. Gilmer pursued a discrimination claim in federal court under the Age Discrimination in Employment Act, 29 U.S.C. § 621 *et seq.* (ADEA). Relying on both the Federal Arbitration Act (FAA), which makes arbitration agreements "valid, irrevocable, and enforceable," 9 U.S.C. § 2, and the arbitration agreement incorporated into the NYSE registration, Interstate moved to compel arbitration. The district court denied that motion, based on two grounds: the Supreme Court's decision in *Alexander v. Gardner-Denver*, where the Court had previously concluded that arbitration is not the most appropriate means of vindicating statutory rights, and Congress's intention to protect victims of age discrimination from waiving the judicial forum. The Fourth Circuit reversed, resulting in a conflict among the circuits regarding the arbitrability of age-discrimination claims. The Supreme Court affirmed. Noting that the FAA embodies a strong federal policy favoring arbitration and acknowledging that arbitration is not the most appropriate means of vindicating statutory rights, the Court held the following: Where parties agree to arbitrate disputes arising under a statute, those disputes are arbitrable unless the party seeking judicial resolution of the dispute can show that Congress intended to preclude waiver of the judicial forum. Because Gilmer agreed to arbitrate all employment disputes, his ADEA claim was arbitrable unless he could show that Congress intended to preclude waiver of the judicial forum for ADEA claims. Finding nothing in the text of the ADEA, its legislative history, the statutory framework, or the statutory purpose to preclude arbitration of ADEA claims, the Court affirmed the Fourth Circuit's decision to compel arbitration.

Gilmer did not resolve all questions regarding the arbitrability of statutory employment law claims. *Gilmer*'s implicit conclusion—that employers can compel nonunion employees to arbitrate a claim under the ADEA—was later confirmed explicitly in *Circuit City Stores, Inc. v. Adams*, 532 U.S. 102 (2001). In that case, the Court held that Adams' state law employment discrimination claim was subject to compulsory arbitration because he signed an employment application that contained an agreement to arbitrate such disputes. Cases such as these do not resolve the question whether language in a CBA could ever bind union employees to arbitrate their federal statutory claims. The Court left open that question in *Wright v. Universal Maritime Service Corp.*, 525 U.S. 70 (1998), instead holding that union members' statutory employment claims could be forced into arbitration only if the waiver of judicial forum was clear and unmistakable. The Court found that the CBA provision in *Wright* did not meet this standard.

The Court squarely decided the question whether a union and an employer could waive employees' statutory rights in *14 Penn Plaza LLC v. Pyett*, 556 U.S. 247 (2009). There, the Court again reviewed whether relevant language in a CBA clearly and unmistakably waived the right of union employees to litigate a federal statutory claim. The CBA contained the following clause:

> § 30 NO DISCRIMINATION. There shall be no discrimination against any present or future employee by reason of race, creed, color, age, disability, national origin, sex, union membership, or any other characteristic protected by law, including, but not limited to, claims made pursuant to Title VII of the Civil Rights Act, the Americans with Disabilities Act, the Age Discrimination in Employment Act, the New York State Human Rights Law, the New York City Human Rights Code, ... or any other

> similar laws, rules, or regulations. *All such claims shall be subject to the grievance and arbitration procedures (Articles V and VI) as the sole and exclusive remedy for violations. Arbitrators shall apply appropriate law in rendering decisions based upon claims of discrimination.*

Id. at 252 (emphasis added). Here, the union arbitrated, and lost, the employees' grievance over a work assignment based in part on a disability discrimination claim under the Americans with Disabilities Act (ADA). The Court reversed the Second Circuit's decision to allow the case to proceed. Relying on *Gilmer*, the Court explained that "an agreement to arbitrate statutory antidiscrimination claims" waives the right to go to court so long as the waiver is "explicitly stated," i.e., clear and unmistakable. In relying on *Gilmer*, the Court clarified that whether the waiver is contained in a contract signed by an individual employee or a CBA is irrelevant. The Court, however, left open the question whether a CBA—which permits the union to block individuals from pursuing arbitration in cases where the union has voted not to arbitrate the case—can waive the individual's right to seek judicial remedies. The answer to this question is important because it is standard industry practice for CBAs to allow unions to block individuals from pursuing arbitration unless the union participates.

The courts have continued to erode an employee's rights to vindicate rights in a judicial forum. In *D.R. Horton, Inc.*, 357 N.L.R.B. 2277 (2012), *enf. den. in pertinent part*, 737 F.3d 344 (5th Cir. 2013). In that case, the employer made all existing and new employees sign the Mutual Arbitration Agreement (MAA), which made the following conditions of employment: (1) employees voluntarily waive all rights to a jury or bench trial regarding all claims between the employee and the employer; (2) all claims would be determined by final and binding arbitration; (3) the arbitrator would not have authority to fashion a class or collective action. *D.R. Horton, Inc. v. NLRB*, 737 F.3d 344, 348 (5th Cir. 2013). The third condition—the class-action/collective-action waiver—meant that employees could not pursue a class or collective action through either an arbitral or a judicial forum. One employee, Michael Cuda, who attempted to participate in a collective-action claim under the FLSA, filed charges with the NLRB, alleging that the collective-action waiver violated his Section 7 right to join with other employees to improve his working conditions through judicial and administrative proceedings. The Board ultimately held that the MAA violated the NLRA because employees would "reasonably interpret its language as precluding or restricting their right to file charges with the Board" and because it required employees "to waive their right to maintain joint, class, or collective employment-related actions in any forum." *Id.* at 349. The court denied enforcement of the Board's order, which it characterized as unique in prohibiting class-action waivers in arbitration agreements. While the court agreed that Section 7 protects an employee's right to join with other employees in this way and therefore that the company violated Section 8(a)(1) to the extent that the MAA discourages employees from filing charges with the NLRA, it enforced the MAA to the extent that it waives employees' right to class or collective action under other statutes. Nevertheless, other courts of appeals upheld the principle articulated in *D.R. Horton* that an employer-imposed arbitration agreement waiving an employee's right to join a collective action violates Section 8(a)(1).

The Supreme Court ultimately rang *D.R. Horton*'s death knell in *Epic Systems Corp. v. Lewis*, a consolidation of several cases, including *Murphy Oil USA, Inc.*, 361 N.L.R.B. 774 (2014), *petition granted in pertinent part sub nom. Murphy Oil USA, Inc. v. NLRB*, 808 F.3d 1013 (5th Cir. 2015), *aff'd sub nom. Epic Sys. Corp. v. Lewis*, 584 U.S. 497 (2018). In this case, the Court addressed, among other issues, the question whether employer-imposed arbitration agreements that bar individual employees from pursuing work-related claims on a collective basis in a judicial or any other forum violate Section 8(a)(1). The Board argued that these bans violate Section 8(a)(1) because they limit the employees' right to engage in concerted activities for mutual aid or protection under Section 7. They are, therefore, unenforceable under the Federal Arbitration Act's saving clause, under which agreements to arbitrate are enforced "save upon such grounds as exist at law or in equity." 9 U.S.C. § 2. The Court disagreed with the Board and concluded that Section 7 does not express "a clear and manifest congressional command to displace the Arbitration Act and outlaw agreements like" the one at issue. *Epic Systems Corp.*, 584 U.S. at 511.

H. Public-Sector Grievance-Arbitration Issues

Public-sector labor rules governing the relationship between arbitrators and courts are very similar, although three points should be made. First, although most state jurisdictions have adopted the Court's approach in the *Steelworkers' Trilogy* for deferring to the arbiter's decision as to whether a dispute is arbitrable, a few jurisdictions have remained skeptical of courts being quite as deferential to arbitrators in decisions that can affect the public. Second, although most public-sector jurisdictions have adopted the Court's approach of limiting judicial review of arbitral awards to the question of whether the award draws its essence from the contract, some public-sector jurisdictions have adopted a broader "public policy" exception to this approach than the Supreme Court has in private-sector cases. Third, public-sector CBAs often provide substantive rights and procedures that overlap with those granted under existing state laws, such as civil service and tenure laws. These laws are more likely to limit arbitrators in the public sector than in the private sector. For example, where a civil service law provides for an exclusive remedy, arbitration under the CBA is barred.

CHECKPOINTS

- One of a union's primary duties is to administer collective bargaining agreements (CBAs) and to resolve grievances.
- The grievance-arbitration process is a contractually agreed-upon procedure for resolving workplace disputes that encourages dispute settlement at the lowest level of authority but allows for escalation and resolution by a third-party neutral in case of dispute irreconciliation or bargaining impasse.
- There is both a procedural and a substantive dimension to just-cause dismissal. As a matter of process, the arbitrator inquires whether the employer followed the procedures outlined in the CBA. As a matter of substance, the arbitrator asks whether the employer proved that it discharged an employee for just cause, as that phrase is defined in the CBA. If the phrase is undefined, the arbitrator must construe the phrase.

- Unions and management often agree to use seniority in determining how to distribute scarce resources.
- Arbitrators use past practice to interpret CBAs. Past practice has been defined as "the understood and accepted way of doing things over an extended period of time." The concept of past practice is often used by arbitrators to determine the law of the shop and whether a change in terms and conditions of employment has occurred.
- Section 301(c) of the Labor Management Relations Act gives federal courts jurisdiction over CBA disputes between employers and unions.
- Section 301(b) confers on unions the right to sue and be sued.
- Section 301(a) confers subject-matter jurisdiction on federal courts to hear disputes arising under CBAs.
- Federal court jurisdiction over Section 301 lawsuits is concurrent with state court jurisdiction, but state courts exercising concurrent Section 301 jurisdiction must apply federal law.
- The *Steelworkers Trilogy* explains that national labor policy favors arbitration.
- The arbitrator, not the court, determines whether a contract dispute is arbitrable.
- Grievances are arbitrable if they allege a violation of the CBA, even if they are very weak or even "frivolous" on the merits.
- An issue is arbitrable if the contract can plausibly be read to make that issue arbitrable.
- A reviewing court must defer to the arbitrator's interpretation of a CBA and subsequent award "so long as it draws its essence from the [CBA]."
- Courts must also defer to the arbitrator's decision even if the employee violated the law or was contrary to public policy, so long as complying with the arbitrator's award does not cause the employer to violate the law or an "explicit public policy" that is "well defined and dominant" and is "ascertained 'by reference to ... laws and legal precedents and not from general considerations of supposed public interests.'"
- Courts may permissibly read a no-strike promise into a CBA that has a grievance-arbitration clause.

- The Court has carved out an exception to Norris-LaGuardia's anti-injunction provision, by permitting federal courts to enjoin work stoppages (*Boys Market* injunctions) in the following circumstances: (1) the work stoppage is subject to mandatory arbitration; (2) the court compels arbitration as a condition of issuing the injunction; (3) the work stoppage violates the CBA's no-strike promise; and (4) principals of equity favor the injunction.
- A court will issue a reverse *Boys Market* injunction—where the union asks the court to enjoin an employer from taking action that violates the CBA—where (1) the dispute is subject to mandatory arbitration; (2) it would be hard to undo the employer action; and (3) equities favor issuing the injunction.
- Arbitrators have the authority to resolve ULP questions that are entangled in contractual disputes that are the subject of the grievance.
- The Board has the authority to construe contractual language to resolve ULPs.
- Under the Board's *Collyer* pre-arbitral deferral policy, the Board will normally defer to the contractual grievance procedure if the conduct is grievable, the grievance procedure culminates in final and binding arbitration, and the charged party waives all timeliness defenses to the grievance.
- Under the Board's post-arbitral *Spielberg/Olin* deferral policy, the Board will defer to an arbitration decision if it meets the following criteria: (1) the arbitration proceedings were fair and regular; (2) the parties agree to be bound by arbitration; (3) the arbitrator was presented with the facts relevant to resolving the ULP issue and considered that issue to the extent that the ULP and grievance issues were "factually parallel"; and (4) the arbitrator's decision is not "clearly repugnant" to the NLRA.
- Both union and nonunion employees can waive their right to litigate federal statutory claims either by signing an express waiver or simply by being covered by a CBA that clearly and unmistakably waives that right.
- Most public-sector jurisdictions have adopted the *Steelworkers Trilogy*'s approach to deferring to arbitrators' decisions as to whether a

dispute is arbitrable and to deferring to arbitration awards unless the award does not draw its essence from the contract. A few state jurisdictions remain skeptical about granting so much deference to arbitrators in decisions that can impact the public.

CHAPTER 18

Labor Law Preemption

ROADMAP

- The constitutional origins of preemption doctrine
- Distinction between express and implied forms of preemption
- Guiding principles behind labor law preemption analysis
- Mandatory labor law preemption under *Garmon*
- Permissive labor law preemption under *Machinists*
- Section 301 preemption based on the existence of a CBA

A. Constitutional Origins of Preemption Doctrine

The preemption doctrine originates from the Supremacy Clause of the United States Constitution. That clause, found in Article VI of the Constitution, states: "This Constitution, and the Laws of the United States which shall made in Pursuance thereof... shall be the supreme law of the Land; and the Judges in every State shall be bound thereby, any Thing in the Constitution or Laws of any State to the contrary." The general idea here is that when federal and state law conflict, federal law trumps state law. Where federal labor law preempts state law, the state law and the court that seeks to enforce that law must give way to the federal scheme. Preemption doctrine, not only in labor law but also in many other areas of law, is a complex doctrine concerning the relative powers of the federal and state sovereigns in the United States. The idea of federalism—how power should be divided between the federal and state governments—is a closely related concept.

Over many decades, the United States Supreme Court has developed a taxonomy for the different types of preemption. First, preemption can either be express or implied. Express preemption exists when the federal law itself explicitly specifies the state law that it supplants. Many federal statutory schemes lack express preemption provisions. The National Labor Relations Act (NLRA) falls into this category. In such cases, preemption must be implied, and there are various subcategories of this type of preemption.

Implied preemption is typically divided into two broad categories: "field preemption" and "conflict preemption." Field preemption is the more expansive form, arising when courts conclude that Congress intended to occupy an entire regulatory area over which it has power. This intent is inferred from a federal scheme so comprehensive that it leaves no room for supplementary state regulation. When field preemption applies, all state laws within that domain are displaced, regardless of whether they directly conflict with federal law.

Conflict preemption represents a narrower form of implied preemption. It arises in two distinct scenarios: first, when an individual or entity cannot possibly comply with both federal and state law simultaneously—typically because the laws are in direct contradiction; and second, when the state law, even if not directly inconsistent, would frustrate Congress's purposes and objectives in enacting the federal statute. In either situation, the state law is preempted and cannot be enforced.

B. Preemption Doctrine and Labor Law Generally

1. Overview

The question of where labor law preemption fits within this larger preemption framework is not straightforward because it encompasses elements of both field preemption and conflict preemption within the broader preemption doctrine. The only apparent certainty is that the NLRA contains no express preemption provisions, nor does its legislative history offer any indication of the extent to which it was intended to displace state labor laws. Nevertheless, NLRA preemption has developed in a manner that is relatively aggressive compared to preemption under employment laws that establish a floor but not a ceiling for employee protections (e.g., the Fair Labor Standards Act (FLSA) minimum wage provisions permit states to set higher minimum wage rates). Furthermore, the NLRA differs from these other employment laws in that it preempts state laws that are more employee-friendly in the area of union-management relations.

The labor preemption doctrine governs the inherent tensions between federal labor statutes—most notably the NLRA—and state-level regulatory efforts that seek to influence employer-employee relations in contexts such as union organization, collective bargaining, and other forms of protected concerted activity, including strikes, picketing, and boycotts. In addition to the Supremacy Clause, discussed above, another federal constitutional provision comes into play with preemption doctrine. The Commerce Clause under Article I, Section 8 states that, "Congress shall have Power ... To regulate Commerce with foreign nations, and among the several States, and with the Indian Tribes." This clause has been interpreted since the 1930s and the New Deal Era to give Congress an almost limitless power to legislate in the labor relations area. And Congress has largely occupied the field of labor law (as discussed in more detail below). It could have also chosen to occupy the field of employment law entirely, but it has never chosen to do so. We know this not only because many state and local laws explicitly apply to the workplace that would have no force if Congress chose to occupy the labor relations field exclusively, but also because the NLRA itself contains one explicit exception to its typically robust preemptive effect by allowing state right-to-work laws concerning union security agreements (see Chapter 19 for a discussion of these laws). The problematic issue that remains, then, is discerning Congressional preemptive intent when considering the interaction between the NLRA and potentially inconsistent state labor laws or state court decisions.

2. Guiding Principles Behind Labor Law Preemption Analysis

Because it is not possible to understand the scope of labor law doctrine from the text of the NLRA itself, the Supreme Court has set forth two guiding principles or themes in its labor preemption decisions: (1) avoid conflicts in substantive rights and (2) protect the primary jurisdiction of the National Labor Relations Board (NLRB or Board). With respect to the first guiding principle, guarding against substantive conflicts between state and federal labor law, the Court has recognized four basic scenarios where such conflicts might exist: (1) state laws that restrict or potentially restrict the exercise of employee rights under Section 7 of the NLRA; (2) state laws that permit or even potentially permit conduct that is restricted by the unfair labor practice (ULP) provisions of Section 8; (3) state laws that provide a different or additional remedial scheme than federal labor law does; and (4) state laws that seek to regulate activity that Congress purposefully chose to leave unregulated and subject to the free play of economic forces.

The second guiding principle, the doctrine of primary jurisdiction, seeks to incorporate administrative law concepts into this area of labor law. The fundamental insight here is that Congress created the NLRB to administer and enforce the NLRA and has given the Board primary authority and responsibility (i.e., primary jurisdiction) to adjudicate disputes that arise under the statute. In practical terms, this dynamic requires parties to a labor dispute first to utilize the NLRB's processes to resolve their labor relations disputes, not courts or other agencies. This primary reliance on the NLRB is, in turn, premised on the NLRB's expertise and experience in resolving labor relations matters and on the importance of fashioning a coherent and uniform body of national labor law by which parties can predicate their future labor relations conduct.

Based on these two guiding principles, the Supreme Court has developed three preemption doctrines: (1) *Garmon* preemption; (2) *Machinists* preemption; and (3) Section 301 preemption. Each of these preemption doctrines is considered in turn.

3. Preemption Principles Apply Only to State Regulation, Not to Government Market Participation

Before delving into the preemption doctrines, it is crucial to recognize a key distinction drawn by the Supreme Court in labor law: while preemption principles may limit state regulatory actions, they do not apply when the government operates as a market participant. In *Building and Construction Trades Council of Metropolitan District v. Associated Builders and Contractors of Massachusetts/Rhode Island, Inc.* (*Boston Harbor*), 507 U.S. 218, 226–27 (1993), the Supreme Court held that the NLRA does not bar a state agency overseeing a construction project from requiring contractors to comply with specific terms of a labor agreement. The Court reasoned that "[w]hen a State owns and manages property, for example, it must interact with private participants in the marketplace. In so doing, the State is not subject to pre-emption by the NLRA, because pre-emption doctrines apply only to state *regulation*." *Id.* at 227 (emphasis in original). This decision underscores the principle that when the government acts as a market participant—rather than as a regulator—it is afforded greater flexibility to shape labor relations in pursuit of efficient project management and cost-effective outcomes.

In *Chamber of Commerce v. Brown*, 554 U.S. 60, 70 (2008), the Supreme Court reaffirmed and clarified its reasoning in *Boston Harbor*, stating: "[W]hen a State acts as a market participant with no interest in setting policy, as opposed to a regulator, it does not offend the pre-emption principles of the NLRA." To determine whether a state agency is acting in its capacity as a market participant, courts and the Board must evaluate whether the challenged conduct "was specifically tailored to one particular job, and aimed to ensure an efficient project that would be completed as quickly and effectively as possible at the lowest cost." *Id.* When this standard is met, NLRA preemption—under any of its doctrinal forms—does not constrain the state's action. This framework is particularly relevant when evaluating state-imposed labor requirements on publicly funded construction projects, where the line between regulation and participation can be nuanced.

C. *Garmon* or Mandatory Preemption Analysis

1. Introduction to *Garmon* Preemption

Consistent with the first three types of substantive rights conflicts discussed above, the Supreme Court held in *San Diego Trades Council v. Garmon*, 359 U.S. 236 (1959), that the NLRA preempts state laws that regulate conduct that Section 7 protects or *arguably* protects or that Section 8 prohibits or *arguably* prohibits. In other words, *Garmon* preemption arises when there is an actual or potential conflict between state workplace regulation and federal labor law. It does not matter whether one is considering a specific law that deals with labor relations or simply a rule of general application that only incidentally touches on labor relations. This is very much a conflict preemption doctrine based on the idea that it is impossible for parties to abide by both federal and state law in a given area. At the same time, the Court was clear that the primary jurisdiction of the NLRB in matters involving conduct subject to Sections 7 and 8 of the NLRA was of utmost importance.

In this vein, consider the use of the word "arguably" by the Court. Its use underscores the breadth of *Garmon* preemption. Indeed, *Garmon*'s "arguably" language indicates that as long as the assertion of NLRA protection or prohibition is not unreasonable in a given scenario, a state court is without authority to adjudicate the case under state law principles, even if the NLRB ends up deciding that the challenged conduct is not federally protected or prohibited. Moreover, even if the NLRB decides not to take jurisdiction over the case for a legitimate reason (e.g., for jurisdictional reasons), the state courts remain without power to adjudicate the dispute. Indeed, this is exactly what happened in *Garmon* itself when the Court concluded that California state courts lacked jurisdiction to intervene in a picketing dispute between the parties.

Keep in mind, however, that while both employers and unions can commit unfair labor practices under Section 8, only employees have protected rights under Section 7. To say that an activity is not punishable by the NLRA under Section 8 is not the same thing as saying that the activity is protected under Section 7. Although some employer advocates have made the argument that employers have free speech "rights" under Section 8(c) (discussed in Chapter 7), the better argument is that Section 8(c) does not provide rights but only precludes the use of employers' noncoercive speech as evidence of an unfair labor practice. Noncoercive employer speech is thus one of those activities in labor relations that is neither protected nor prohibited, even arguably so, by the NLRA and therefore not preempted under *Garmon*.

The Court has shown an unwillingness to resolve *Garmon* preemption disputes on an *ad hoc* basis. The preference is for a broad, prospective, categorical treatment of these preemption issues. Thus, preemption can apply where there exists conflict in substantive law, conflict in remedial schemes, or where primary jurisdiction issues are involved (e.g., where the primary power to interpret labor issues has been delegated to the Board).

Although *Garmon* preemption is supposed to provide a bright-line, categorical rule for what state laws and regulations are preempted by the NLRA, the Supreme Court has recognized at least one significant exception for mass picketing (i.e., where employees cannot freely come and go from an employer location) and threats of violence. In such situations, state regulation is permitted although the conduct at issue is also likely prohibited by Section 8 as an unfair labor practice. This is because such state laws against violence and mass pickets involve "interests so deeply rooted in local feeling and responsibility" that the Court has not found such state regulation preempted in the absence of express preemption provisions. *See UAW v. Russell*, 356 U.S. 634 (1958); *United Construction Workers v. Laburnum*, 347 U.S. 656 (1954). These cases typically involve conduct that amounts to a crime, an intentional tort, or both, and where the state interest in regulation is strong and obvious.

2. Specific U.S. Supreme Court Applications of *Garmon* Preemption

Two Supreme Court cases illustrate the broad categorical approach taken by the Court in *Garmon* preemption cases. In *Amalgamated Association of Street, Electric Railway & Motor Coach Employees of America v. Lockridge*, 403 U.S. 274 (1971), the Court, applying *Garmon*, held that the NLRA preempted a state court order reinstating a worker to union membership after he had been terminated for failing to pay union dues. The Court concluded that *Garmon* preemption applied because Section 8(b)(2) arguably prohibited the union's conduct. In another case concerning collective bargaining rights, *Local 24, International Teamsters v. Oliver*, 358 U.S. 283 (1959), an owner-operator of a truck sought to have a certain provision in the Teamsters CBA voided under state antitrust law, because it limited his ability to lease his truck to other interstate trucking companies. The state court entered a permanent injunction against the minimum rental provision, and the union responded by arguing that the NLRA preempted the state court injunction. The Court agreed with the Teamsters and found the state antitrust action preempted, because the contract provision was a mandatory subject of bargaining under Section 8(d), and employees' right to bargain over this subject was protected by Section 7.

Conversely, several cases before the Supreme Court have survived *Garmon* preemption. For instance, in *Farmer v. United Brotherhood of Carpenters and Joiners, Local 25*, 430 U.S. 290 (1977), the Court concluded that the NLRA did not preempt a tort action brought in state court by a union member against the union to recover damages for intentional infliction of emotional distress. Because the state had a substantial interest in regulation of that conduct, the Court concluded that the state's interest did not threaten the federal regulatory scheme for labor law. In a similar case, *Linn v. Plant Guard Workers*, 383 U.S. 53 (1966), the Court held that a Pinkerton manager's defamation claim against the union was not preempted because it did not involve protected activity under Section 7 and there was an overriding state interest in protecting residents from defamation. Most recently, in *Glacier Northwest, Inc. v.*

International Brotherhood of Teamsters, 598 U.S. 771 (2023), the Court held that the NLRA does not preempt the employer's state tort claims alleging that employee-concrete-truck drivers intentionally destroyed the employer's concrete during a strike when they abandoned their trucks, leaving the concrete to harden. *See id.* at 785. The Court explained that Section 7 does not arguably protect strike activity where the employees "fail to take 'reasonable precautions' to protect their employer's property from foreseeable, aggravated, and imminent danger due to the sudden cessation of work." *Id.* at 780.

In *Sears, Roebuck & Co. v. San Diego District Council of Carpenters*, 436 U.S. 180 (1978), the union had picketed Sears' use of a nonunion subcontractor to perform carpentry work in the store. A state court enjoined the picketing under state trespass law. Although the conduct could be seen as arguably prohibited recognitional picketing under Section 8(b)(7)(C), a prohibited jurisdictional dispute strike under Section 8(b)(4)(D), or arguably protected area standards picketing under Section 7 (all discussed in Chapter 16), the Court held that the state court action was not preempted under *Garmon*. Preemption did not exist, according to the Court, because: (1) the issues before the state court would not be the same issues before the NLRB, and thus, the Board's primary jurisdiction was not implicated; and (2) the union could have filed an unfair labor practice charge when Sears demanded the removal of the picket, but the union never filed a charge. Because the union had a fair opportunity to present the picketing issue to the Board, it had sufficient protection against the risk of error by the state court in coming to its trespass decision.

The Supreme Court has found *Garmon* conflict preemption principles to apply in cases concerning the selection of bargaining representatives. In *Brown v. Hotel & Restaurant Employees, International Union Local 54*, 468 U.S. 491 (1984), the New Jersey Casino Control Commission ordered the president and other officers of a union be removed from their offices because of their criminal convictions and association with members of organized crime. If the union refused, the Commission would bar the union from collecting dues from any of its members. On the issue of whether the NLRA preempted the state Casino Control Act provisions because they conflicted with Section 7 rights, the *Brown* Court found the law was not preempted because Congress had indicated that employees do not have an unqualified right to choose their union officials and that certain state disqualification requirements are compatible with Section 7.

D. *Machinists* or Permissive Preemption Analysis

1. Preemption of State Laws Where Congress Meant to Leave the Field Unregulated

When state laws seek to regulate activities that Congress has purposefully chosen to leave unregulated, the laws implicate another preemption doctrine. In *Machinists v. Wisconsin Employment Relations Commission*, 427 U.S. 132 (1976), the union was engaging in partial strike activity by working but putting economic pressure on the employer by refusing to work overtime. The state labor board enjoined this activity. The Court explained that the policy of federal labor law is to leave self-help activities available to the parties, subject only to the free play of economic forces. State interference with this scheme impermissibly altered the balance of power that occurs under a free play of economic forces. The Court therefore held that the NLRA federal statutory scheme, which implicitly left open to either party the use of lawful economic pressure to force the resolution of labor stalemates, preempted the contrary Wisconsin approach to this type of labor activity. *Machinists* establishes a separate strain of preemption doctrine known as "permissive preemption." This refers to the fact that permissible conduct that is neither prohibited nor protected by the NLRA may also be protected from state regulation.

Although not exactly field preemption, this doctrine encompasses a broad range of potential state labor law regulations because it applies wherever Congress intended to leave unregulated economic weapons neither expressly protected by Section 7 nor prohibited by Section 8. State law is therefore preempted under *Machinists* when it interferes with lawful economic pressure applied by either party. Where state laws have attempted to give additional economic power to one side or the other during the collective bargaining process, as some states have sought to do in the past, courts have found such laws preempted under *Machinists*.

For instance, in *Golden State Transit Corp. v. City of Los Angeles*, 475 U.S. 608 (1986), the union argued that the city should not grant a franchise to a cab company until a labor dispute between the union and the cab company had been settled. The city subsequently conditioned the franchise renewal on the cab company's settlement of the labor dispute by a specific date. The Court held that the NLRA preempted under *Machinists* the city's action in conditioning the cab company's franchise renewal on settlement of the labor dispute. More specifically, *Machinists* preemption precluded the city regulation because Congress intended the labor dispute between the parties to be unregulated. Consequently, the city was prohibited from imposing restrictions on either party's use of economic weapons.

In contrast with *Golden State Transit Corp.*, *Machinists* preemption was found inapplicable to the state misrepresentation and breach-of-contract claims of permanent replacement workers who lost their jobs after a strike settlement agreement returned all striking employees to their previous jobs. In *Belknap, Inc. v. Hale*, 463 U.S. 491 (1983), the Supreme Court concluded that allowing the contract claims would not impermissibly burden the employer's economic weapon of hiring permanent replacement workers during an economic strike.

Similarly, in *New York Telephone Co. v. New York State Department of Labor*, 440 U.S. 519 (1979), when an employer challenged a state unemployment system that provided benefits to employees absent from work during lengthy strikes, the Court disagreed with the employer that the unemployment compensation system conflicted with the federal labor policy of allowing the free play of economic forces to operate during the bargaining process. Instead, the Court upheld the law based on the legislative histories of the NLRA and the Social Security Act, which were enacted within six weeks of each other. In this vein, the Court concluded that Congress intended states to be free to decide whether to authorize such unemployment compensation payments as the tension between the Social Security Act and the NLRA suggested only a conflict between two federal statutes, as opposed to the normal preemption issue of a conflict between federal and state laws.

In all, *Machinists* preemption has proven to be just as broad as *Garmon* preemption, and it is also seen as vindicating the primary jurisdiction of the NLRB. Critics have maintained that *Machinists* preemption is based on rights that the Court discerns out of thin air and that are nowhere found in the NLRA. As such, these opponents maintain that *Machinists* preemption transforms employer economic power into federal statutory rights by giving such employer power the ability to preempt contrary state labor law protections.

2. Possible Limits on the Scope of *Machinists* Preemption

There have been several arguments made over the years for limiting the breadth of *Machinists* preemption doctrine. Courts have accepted some, but not all, of these arguments for limitations.

For instance, the *Machinists* preemption doctrine has not been restricted to the collective bargaining context. Courts have also applied it to the organizing context. The argument against preemption here is that the free play of economic forces is unsuited to the organizing environment where there is not a fair contest between unorganized employees and their much more economically powerful employers. The Supreme Court in *Chamber of Commerce v. Brown*, 554 U.S. 60 (2008), rejected this argument. There, the Court held that the NLRA preempted the California statute that prohibited grant recipients receiving more than $10,000 in state program funds from using such funds "to assist, promote, or deter union organizing." The Court's conclusion in *Brown* that *Machinists* applied in the organizing context is further bolstered by the language in *Metropolitan Life Insurance Co. v. Massachusetts*, 471 U.S. 724, 751 (1985), that "[*Machinists* cases] rely on the understanding that in providing in the NLRA a framework for self-organization and collective bargaining, Congress determined both how much the conduct of unions and employers should be regulated, and how much it should be left unregulated."

The *Brown* Court also struck down the argument that *Machinists* only applies to zones of activity left free from *all* regulation. According to this argument, the Board has regulated employer speech during organizing campaigns by forbidding speech on the eve of the election (discussed in detail in Chapter 7), Therefore, the field is not open to the free play of economic forces under *Machinists* preemption. The Court in *Brown* rejected this argument, finding that, although the NLRB has policed a narrow zone of speech to ensure free and fair elections under Section 9 of the Act, the general policy of Congress has been to prohibit regulation of noncoercive speech and to allow the free play of economic forces during the organizing process.

That leaves two additional restrictions to *Machinists* preemption that have found some traction. First, the Supreme Court has recognized an exception to *Machinists* preemption where the states traditionally have had great latitude under their police powers to legislate for the protection and health of all their citizens (similar to the exception that exists for areas of traditional state concern under *Garmon* preemption). Courts have interpreted this police power to encompass the broad authority for regulating the employment relationship to protect workers within the state. Accordingly, state laws that set minimum employment standards are not in conflict with the Act and should survive preemption.

For instance, in *Lockridge*, discussed above Section C.2, the Court held that lower courts "cannot declare pre-empted all local regulation that touches or concerns in any way the complex interrelationship between employees, employers, and unions; obviously, much of this is left to the States." More specifically, in *Metropolitan Life Insurance Co. v. Massachusetts*, the Court unanimously concluded that the NLRA did not preempt a Massachusetts-mandated health insurance benefit law. The Court reasoned that although state law required employee benefit plans to purchase benefits that the parties to a collective bargaining agreement did not wish to purchase, *Machinists* preemption was inapplicable. This was because the Massachusetts mandated benefit law did not alter the balance of power between the parties to the labor contract, and Congress's concern when enacting the NLRA was unrelated to local or federal regulation establishing minimum terms of employment. Since *Metropolitan Life*, state child labor laws, occupational safety and health laws, and minimum wage laws have all also survived NLRA preemption.

Second, some state laws arguably survive *Machinists* preemption based on the power of the state to regulate property interests that the NLRB does not displace. This potential exception to *Machinists* preemption law derives directly from the Court's holding in *Lechmere Inc. v. NLRB*, 502 U.S. 527 (1992) (discussed in more detail in Chapter 7), explaining the relationship between federal labor law and state property regulation: "[T]he right of employers to exclude union organizers from their private property emanates from state common law, and while this right is not superseded by the NLRA, nothing in the NLRA expressly protects it." *See Thunder Basin Coal Co. v. Reich*, 510 U.S. 200, 217 n.21 (1994).

Two important points can be derived from *Lechmere* and *Thunder Basin Coal*. First, the NLRA left most state property rights intact, even if such rights influence the balance of power in a labor dispute. Second, these same private property rights are not protected by the NLRA. This second point makes clear that *Garmon* preemption is not implicated where employers seek to use their property as they wish. The first point, in turn, clarifies that no form of labor preemption, *Garmon* or *Machinists*, comes into play when states decide to modify state property law rights that the NLRA never displaced. For instance, the ability to exclude nonunion representatives from employer property is not the kind of economic weapon that Congress intended to be available to employers. It is, therefore, subject to regulation by the states.

The Supreme Court applied this very same principle to the advantage of employers in *Lechmere* where it found that non-employee union organizers generally had no right to access employer property to solicit for union membership. The right to exclude these organizers did not derive from federal labor law, but rather from the state property rights of the employers. Thus, an employer can, consistent with federal labor law, use its state law property rights to its advantage in an organizing campaign, but a state is not barred from altering such rights. *See, e.g., Pruneyard Shopping Center v. Robins*, 447 U.S. 74, 84–88 (1980) (holding California State Constitution's grant of freedom to individuals to enter privately owned shopping mall and gather petitions did not violate property owner's First and Fifth Amendment rights under United States Constitution). It is simply a matter of states, by statutes, modifying the bundle of property rights that employers enjoy under state law. This is consistent with the understanding of the NLRB and federal courts that federal labor law operates against the background of state regulation of property rights and contract relations.

In short, both the minimum conditions and property rights exceptions to *Machinists* preemption may permit some state labor laws to survive preemption under *Machinists*. Even so, the scope of *Machinists* preemption is still quite expansive and more akin to field preemption than to conflict preemption.

E. Section 301 or CBA Preemption Analysis

Section 301 preemption is the third and final preemption doctrine. Section 301 preemption concerns disputes arising under existing CBAs. More precisely, Section 301 of the Labor Management Relations Act (or Taft-Hartley Amendments of 1947) permits parties to a labor dispute to enforce the terms of a CBA in federal or state court.

Although Section 301 on its face refers only to jurisdiction, it has been interpreted as authorizing federal courts to fashion a body of common law for the enforcement of CBAs to promote uniformity in this area of labor law. *See Textile Workers Union v. Lincoln Mills of Alabama*, 353 U.S. 448 (1957). Under *Lincoln Mills*, Section 301 not only confers subject matter jurisdiction on the federal courts, but it also directs the district courts to develop a federal common law of labor agreements. *See also* Chapter 17. Any state law that is inconsistent with federal common law under Section 301 is deemed preempted.

Section 301 preemption is a type of "complete preemption" and operates even if there is not a federal question under Section 301 on the face of the complaint. *See Avco Corp. v. Machinists*, 390 U.S. 557 (1968). This is a form of field preemption where Congress has chosen to completely occupy the field of federal labor law concerning the interpretation of CBAs. So even if a plaintiff does not bring a complaint directly under Section 301, and yet the cause of action concerns the interpretation of a CBA, the court will treat whatever state law claim has been brought as if it had been pled initially under Section 301. Complete preemption can be particularly important if the plaintiff files her state law claim in state court and the defendant wishes to remove the case to federal court based on complete preemption under Section 301. *See Metropolitan Life Ins. Co. v. Taylor*, 481 U.S. 58, 63–64 (1987) ("One corollary of the well-pleaded complaint rule developed in the case law ... is that Congress may so completely pre-empt a particular area that any civil complaint raising this select group of claims is necessarily federal in character. For 20 years, this Court has singled out claims pre-empted by § 301 of the LMRA for such special treatment.").

For instance, in *Allis-Chalmers Corp. v. Lueck*, 471 U.S. 202 (1985), the Supreme Court held that Section 301 preempts a state law tort action for bad-faith delay in making disability-benefit payments due under a CBA. The Court so concluded because the state law claim was inextricably intertwined with consideration of the labor contract's terms. By contrast, Section 301 preemption was found not to apply in the Supreme Court case of *Lingle v. Norge Division of Magic Chef, Inc.*, 486 U.S. 399 (1988). There, the Court considered whether an employee covered by a CBA that provided her with a contractual remedy for discharge could instead enforce her state law remedy for retaliatory discharge under Illinois Worker's Compensation law. The Court concluded that such a state remedy was not preempted by Section 301. It was true that the state law analysis of the employee's retaliatory discharge claim could lead to examination of some of the same issues that arise when interpreting the CBA itself. Nevertheless, the Court pointed out that Section 301 preemption only provides that federal law will be the basis for interpreting CBAs. The doctrine says nothing about the substantive rights a state may provide to workers when adjudication of those rights does not depend upon the interpretation of such agreements. Because the state law claim in *Lingle* could be resolved without interpreting the agreement itself, and particularly without interpreting the just cause provision of the CBA, the state law claim was considered independent of the CBA, and Section 301 preemption did not apply.

CHECKPOINTS

- Preemption analysis derives from the Supremacy Clause of the U.S. Constitution.
- Where federal labor law preempts state law, the state law in question and the state court that seeks to enforce it must give way in favor of the federal law.
- Ordinarily, general preemption can be either express or implied; but labor preemption is implied under the NLRA because of the lack of any express provisions or any inkling of legislative intent.
- Implied preemption can be either field preemption (occupying the whole field of law for the federal scheme) or conflict preemption (ousting state law where it is impossible to follow both federal and state law or where state law frustrates the purposes and objectives of federal law).
- Congress has almost completely occupied the field of labor relations (except for permitting state right-to-work laws) but has chosen not to preempt all laws governing employment under its Commerce Clause powers.
- The guiding principles behind labor law preemption analysis include the need to avoid conflicts in substantive rights and the need to preserve the primary jurisdiction of the NLRB (based on its expertise and the need for uniformity).
- Preemption principles apply only to government regulation, not to government conduct when acting as a market participant.
- Under *Garmon* preemption, the NLRA preempts state laws that regulate conduct that Section 7 protects or *arguably* protects or that Section 8 prohibits or *arguably* prohibits.
- An exception to *Garmon* preemption exists for state laws against mass picketing and violence where the state interest is strong and obvious.

- Under *Machinists* preemption, state laws that impermissibly interfere with the free play of economic forces and alter the balance of power between the parties to a labor dispute are preempted, even though there is no direct conflict with specific provisions of the NLRA.
- Courts have recognized limitations to *Machinists* preemption where state minimum employment standards or state property rights are implicated.
- Under Section 301 preemption, any state law or cause of action that is inconsistent with the federal common law involving the interpretation of CBAs is preempted.
- Congress has so completely preempted the interpretation of CBAs under Section 301 that any case raising state law claims involving these issues is necessarily federal in character and can be removed from state court to federal court.

CHAPTER 19

The Duty of Fair Representation and Union Security Clauses

ROADMAP

- The origins of the union's duty of fair representation (DFR)
- The substantive standards for determining whether a union has violated its DFR
- Procedures for DFR suits, and "hybrid DFR / § 301" suits
- Remedies in DFR suits, including in "hybrid" suits
- Variations on DFR rules in the public sector
- Evolution of rules regulating union security clauses, including both modern "right to work" rules and "agency fee" rules
- *Beck* and the right to object to dues money being spent on activities not related to collective bargaining
- *Janus:* all union security clauses in the public sector violate the First Amendment
- What courts have held is and is not related to collective bargaining
- Procedures unions and objectors must follow to provide and enforce rights under *Beck* and related precedent

---

A. Introduction

This chapter focuses on the relationship between unions and employees in the bargaining units that unions represent. It describes two distinct sets of rules: the union's duty of fair representation (DFR); and regulation of union security clauses (contract provisions obligating members of union bargaining units to pay some portion of dues to the union). Note, though, that while these cases feature union-employee relations, employers are also often involved. In DFR cases, they are often brought in as co-defendants in what are called "hybrid DFR/§ 301" claims. Also, since union security cases involve clauses in collective bargaining agreements, employers and their advocates should understand the restrictions on such clauses.

For DFR rules, almost all public-sector jurisdictions use rules essentially identical to those that have evolved under the NLRA. There are a few variations worth noting. As to union security clauses, prior to 2019, the rules in the public and private sector were also essentially the same, at least in effect. But in one of the most significant developments in all labor law since the first edition, in 2018, in *Janus v. AFSCME*, 575 U.S. 878 (2018), the U.S. Supreme Court reversed precedent that was more than forty years old and held that all public sector union security clauses violate the First Amendment. Law under the Railway Labor Act (RLA) and NLRA continues to be quite similar; indeed, many of the current rules were first developed in RLA cases.

B. The Duty of Fair Representation

1. The Creation of the Duty of Fair Representation

The rule that unions have a duty to represent bargaining unit members fairly originated in the private sector in the 1940s. This rule is not in the text of the NLRA or RLA. Rather, courts and the NLRB created DFR rules in the private sector. In the public sector, DFR rules are often, but not always, written into the relevant statute. Whatever the source of the rule, the justification for DFR rules is that they are a necessary corollary to the principle of exclusive representation. Because unions, not individual employees, deal with the employer on matters of wages, hours, and working conditions, unions should have a duty to handle those representation duties fairly and competently.

The first court rulings that the exclusive representative principle required unions to act fairly came in 1944. For example, *Steele v. Louisville & Nashville R. Co.*, 323 U.S. 192, 203 (1944), held that exclusive representation imposes on unions "the duty to exercise fairly the power conferred upon it on behalf of all those for whom it acts, without hostile discrimination against them." Using this logic, *Tunstall v. Locomotive Firemen*, 323 U.S. 210 (1944), concluded that union members had a right to be represented without racial discrimination. *Wallace Corp. v. NLRB*, 323 U.S. 248, 255 (1944), explained that unions under the NLRA have a duty to represent employees "fairly and impartially." *Ford Motor Co. v. Huffman*, 345 U.S. 330, 337 (1953), under the NLRA, stated that unions must make an "honest effort to serve the interests of all of those members without hostility to any." *Humphrey v. Moore*, 375 U.S. 335, 342 (1964), reaffirmed that a union's "broad authority" as an exclusive representative is accompanied by a "duty of fair representation."

Importantly, because the DFR is based on exclusive representation, unions have a duty to fairly represent employees who are members of the union bargaining unit, even if they are not actually union members (how this can be, and the consequences of this, are discussed further below). *See, e.g.*, *Smith v. Sheet Metal Workers Local 25*, 500 F.2d 741 (5th Cir. 1974).

2. Jurisdiction, Parties, Standards, and Damages

Because DFR rules were not set out in the statutory language of the NLRA, it was not initially clear how these cases should be handled. Were they ULPs, and if so, did the NLRB have jurisdiction in the first instance? What did plaintiffs need to prove? In cases where the union's alleged bad act involved failing to protect the employee from an employer's adverse action, how could employers be joined in the suits? For successful plaintiffs in such suits, how should courts divide plaintiff's damages between the union and the employer?

The NLRB took the position that DFR violations were ULP violations. *See, e.g.*, *NLRB v. Miranda Fuel Co.*, 140 N.L.R.B. 181 (1962), *enf. den. on other grounds*, 326 F.2d 172 (2d Cir. 1963); *Independent Metal Workers Local 1 (Hughes Tool Co.)*, 147 N.L.R.B. 1573 (1964). Courts have seemingly accepted this position. In *DelCostello v. International Brotherhood of Teamsters*, 462 U.S. 151, 170 (1983), while the Supreme Court declined to decide the issue squarely, it indicated support for this view: "even if not all breaches of the duty are unfair labor practices ... the family resemblance is undeniable, and indeed there is substantial overlap."

As the law developed though, it became clear that DFR cases would be handled differently than other types of ULP actions. The Supreme Court addressed this and other important questions listed above in *Vaca v. Sipes*, 386 U.S. 171 (1967). *Vaca* contains almost all the basic principles of modern DFR law, including the rule that permits plaintiffs to sue unions directly in court for DFR violations.

The facts in *Vaca* involved one of the most common types of DFR claims: a union refused to arbitrate an employee's grievance, which precluded the employee from pursuing the grievance further. *Vaca* first set out the substantive threshold for a DFR violation. The union's duty is to serve the interests of employees it represents "without hostility or discrimination toward any, to exercise its discretion with complete faith and honesty, and to avoid arbitrary conduct." *Id.* at 177. The Court majority then explained that even assuming a DFR is a ULP, plaintiffs making a DFR claim may go directly to court (unlike all other ULP claims, where the NLRB has initial jurisdiction). *Vaca* reasoned that courts had created the DFR doctrine, and so there was no fear of courts and the NLRB issuing conflicting rules on the issue. Also, *Vaca* noted that DFR cases typically involve reviewing the union's positions in negotiations and grievances, something the NLRB does not normally do. Further, the Court explained, as this case exemplified, plaintiffs in DFR suits often join employers as defendants pursuant to § 301 of the Taft-Hartley Act (Section 301 is discussed in Chapter 17 in more detail). Section 301 suits go directly to court, and, the court reasoned, it would be inefficient to have one part of essentially the same case before the NLRB and another part before a court.

As to this last justification, it is important to understand how and why DFR suits against unions are often joined with § 301 suits against employers. Many DFR cases are indeed similar to *Vaca* in that the employee's complaint is that the union did not handle the employee's grievance in a fair manner (e.g., deciding not to take it to arbitration for impermissible reasons). But of course what the employee is really concerned about is the employer's action (or inaction) that led to the grievance: the employee also believes the employer has violated the labor contract. A typical example involves an employer firing an employee, the employee believing that discharge was not for just cause under the labor contract, and the employee later being dissatisfied with the union's representation regarding the discharge. Thus, the employee believes the union has violated its DFR, but the employee also believes that the employer's discharge decision violated the labor contract under Section 301.

The general rule (*see* Chapter 17) is that employees and unions cannot bring claims that the employer violated the labor contract to court; the labor contract itself sets out a grievance and arbitration procedure which is generally the exclusive mechanism to challenge alleged violations of the contract. Further, labor contracts routinely provide that only the union, not the individual employee, can choose to take a grievance to arbitration. *Vaca* reasoned that while an employee is normally bound to this contractual process, the employee's duty in this regard should be waived if the union's DFR violation has made going through the contractual process futile or impossible. This would be true, for example, if the union violated its DFR by refusing to take a grievance to arbitration for an impermissible reason: the employee would therefore be unable to go to arbitration.

In short, in these cases, a suit by an employee against an employer for allegedly violating the terms of a labor contract can go directly to court, and the employee's suit against the union can be taken directly to court as well. Note that courts can hear the contract claim against the employer *only* if plaintiff shows that the union has violated its DFR. Thus, in these "hybrid DFR / § 301" cases, employers join with the union in arguing that the union did not violate its DFR. Because if the court holds that the union did not violate its DFR, then the employee cannot maintain the § 301 suit against the employer, because the case is no longer properly before the court.

Vaca also set out the substantive standard for determining when a union violates its DFR. The duty is violated only when the union's conduct is "arbitrary, discriminatory, or in bad faith." 386 U.S. at 190. The majority in *Vaca* rejected the idea that an employee has an absolute right to have a union take a grievance to arbitration. Unions should be able to weed out weak claims, and courts should not second-guess the union's discretion in this regard. In *Vaca*, the Court held that the union had satisfied its duty, as it had represented the employee through the fourth step of the grievance procedure, paid for his medical tests, and, when the tests were unfavorable to the union side, asked the employer to find light work for him.

The *Vaca* majority then turned to the remedies available in hybrid suits. It held that courts should divide damages between the employer and union, depending on the extent to which the acts of each caused the employee's harm and divide damages accordingly. This is discussed further below.

Justice Black, dissenting, noted that, under the rules set out by the majority, the finding that the union did not violate its DFR meant that the employee (in this and similar cases) could not sue the employer in court. Further, since the union had decided not to arbitrate the grievance, the employee had no forum to challenge the employer's decision. Justice Black suggested two alternatives to this approach. "Either the employee should be able to sue his employer for breach of contract after having attempted to exhaust his contractual remedies, or the union should have an absolute duty to exhaust contractual remedies on his behalf." *Id.* at 208. It is important to understand that these alternatives, outside of a partial exception in one public-sector jurisdiction (discussed below), are not the law.

Additional issues *Vaca* raised are discussed in the subsections below.

a. Going Directly to Court in DFR Cases without § 301 Claims

One reason *Vaca* gave for allowing DFR plaintiffs to go directly to court was that many DFR claims against unions were coupled with a § 301 claim against the employer, and it would be inefficient if the DFR claim had to go first to the NLRB while the § 301 claim went directly to court. But not all DFR suits also involve § 301 claims. In a DFR suit that did not involve a § 301 claim, should plaintiffs still be allowed to go directly to court? The Supreme Court answered that question in the affirmative in *Breininger v. Sheet Metal Workers International Association Local Union No. 6*, 493 U.S. 67 (1989).

In *Breininger*, plaintiff claimed that the union violated its DFR by discriminating against him in the way it ran a union hiring hall. Because no employer actions were involved, the NLRB and the court of appeals held that plaintiff's DFR action had to be brought before the NLRB initially. The Supreme Court reversed: "[W]e have never suggested that the *Vaca* rule contains exceptions based on the subject matter of the fair-representation claim presented, the relative expertise of the NLRB in the particular area of labor law involved, or any other factor." *Id.* at 76. Among other things, the Court reasoned, it would be impractical to distinguish among different types of DFR cases for this purpose. Thus, *all* DFR claims may be brought directly to court.

Note here that in DFR actions in which plaintiffs seek backpay for lost income due to the breach of the duty (true in almost all DFR cases), plaintiffs are entitled to a jury trial. *Teamsters Local 391 v. Terry*, 494 U.S. 558 (1990) (a splintered decision finding that DFR claims are "suits at common law" under the Seventh Amendment's historical analysis and thus, plaintiffs are entitled to jury trials).

b. Hybrid Claims and Exhaustion: Practical Impact

As discussed above, hybrid claims may start in court but are valid if and only if the union has violated its DFR. As Judge Easterbrook memorably put it, "a hybrid contract/DFR suit does not get to first base unless the worker shows that the union has abandoned him to the wolves." *Pease v. Production Workers of Chicago & Vicinity Local 707*, 386 F.3d 819, 823 (7th Cir. 2004). This rule has very important practical consequences.

Again, this generally means that if a union has *not* violated its DFR in a hybrid case, the employee has no further options. This is because first, in at least the vast majority of labor contracts, the union, not individual employees, decides whether to take a grievance to arbitration. Second, if the union has not violated its DFR, the employee cannot sue the employer in court for violating a provision in a labor contract enforceable by the grievance-arbitration procedure. So, if a union decides not to arbitrate a grievance, and in making that decision does not violate its DFR, the individual employee almost certainly will not be able to arbitrate the alleged contract violation or take the claimed violation to court.

Similarly, in hybrid claims, even if a plaintiff can show a DFR violation, the plaintiff will not be able to recover unless plaintiff also shows that the employer violated the contract. *See Vencl v. International Union of Operating Engineers, Local 18*, 137 F.3d 420, 424 (6th Cir. 1998).

As to the "exhaustion" theory, *Clayton v. International Union, United Automobile Workers*, 451 U.S. 679 (1981), allowed an additional possible hurdle for plaintiffs in hybrid cases. *Clayton* held that a union may require that an employee exhaust an internal appeals process before going to court if the employee wants to challenge the union's decision, e.g., on whether to take a grievance to arbitration. The internal appeals process must meet certain criteria: the employee must be able to receive a fair hearing, the procedure must allow the employee to receive full relief, and the process must not create unreasonable delays. The UAW has created a process that meets these criteria. *See Bell v. DaimlerChrysler Corp.*, 547 F.3d (7th Cir. 2008) (describing this process).

c. Substantive DFR Standards

In deciding what sort of bad, unfair, or incompetent union conduct violates the DFR, courts attempt to balance two sets of concerns. First, the system of exclusive representation gives the union the power to negotiate and enforce contract terms. While unions are generally democratic institutions, individuals who are in the minority may be consistently outvoted or ignored, sometimes for improper reasons. Also, because union officers are human beings, even when they have no bad intent, they sometimes make serious mistakes. At the same time, the NLRB and courts are not in the position to routinely second-guess the tactical decisions unions make. This is especially true since bargaining units contain a variety of employees with a variety of interests. Absent significantly unfair conduct, unions and their members should be able to make their own strategic choices.

Indeed, in its 1953 *Huffman* decision, the Supreme Court observed:

> Inevitably differences arise in the manner and degree to which the terms of any negotiated agreement affect individual employees and classes of employees. The mere existence of such differences does not make them invalid.... A wide range of reasonableness must be allowed a statutory bargaining representative in serving the unit it represents, subject always to complete good faith and honesty of purpose in the exercise of its discretion.

345 U.S. at 338.

Vaca stated that a union violated its DFR if its conduct was "arbitrary, discriminatory, or in bad faith." 386 U.S. at 190. After *Vaca*, some courts treated contract *administration* (grievance and arbitration handling) differently than contract *negotiation*. Also, some courts required intentional bad behavior to prove a DFR violation, *see, e.g., Olsen v. United Parcel Service*, 892 F.2d 1290 (7th Cir. 1990), while others allowed DFR claims based on ordinary negligence, *see, e.g., Dutrisac v. Caterpillar Tractor Co.*, 749 F.2d 1270 (9th Cir. 1983). Most cases fell somewhere in between. In *United Steelworkers of America. v. Rawson*, 495 U.S. 362, 372–73 (1990), the Supreme Court rejected the "ordinary negligence" standard for DFR cases.

The Supreme Court further standardized the rules in *Air Line Pilots Association, International v. O'Neil*, 499 U.S. 65 (1991). The facts in *ALPA* are fairly dense, but in short, plaintiffs claimed that the union entered into a settlement ending a strike that was so bad—arguably worse than no settlement at all—that it violated the union's DFR. The District Court ruled for the union on summary judgment, stating that "the agreement that was achieved looks atrocious in retrospect, but it is not a breach of fiduciary duty to badly settle the strike." *Id.* at 71. The Court of Appeals reversed, rejecting the union's argument that a DFR violation required intentional bad acts, and holding that there was at least a question of fact as to whether the union had acted in a way that was arbitrary or discriminatory.

The Supreme Court first agreed that DFR plaintiffs were not required to show intentionally bad behavior. Second, the Court rejected the union's argument—which was based on some appellate court precedent—that courts should be more deferential to union decisions in contract negotiations than in grievance and arbitration handling. The Court explained that it was hard to draw a bright line between those two categories in some cases, and some DFR cases were in neither category, *see, e.g., Breininger.* So, the standard for all DFR cases was whether the union's acts were arbitrary, discriminatory, or in bad faith.

The Court found that the union's acts in this case were neither discriminatory nor in bad faith. It then explained that the Court of Appeals had used too broad a definition of "arbitrary." To be "arbitrary," the Supreme Court held, the union's act must be outside "a wide range of reasonableness." 499 U.S. at 66, 67. The appellate court's approach was "flawed because it fails to take into account either the strong policy favoring the peaceful settlement of labor disputes ... or the importance of evaluating the rationality of a union's decision in light of both the facts and the legal climate that confronted the negotiators at the time the decision was made." *Id.* at 79.

This is a very deferential standard. Indeed, the Court noted that under this standard, even if it were true (as the Court of Appeals had found), that the settlement was worse than a unilateral surrender of the strike, this alone would not necessarily show that the settlement violated the union's DFR. The Supreme Court explained that enforcing the union's legal rights after a unilateral surrender would have required considerable litigation, while the settlement achieved some benefits for some employees immediately. In short, "even a bad settlement may be more advantageous in the long run than a good lawsuit." *Id.* at 81.

Thus, after *O'Neil,* the same standard is used for cases involving contract negotiation and contract administration. That standard is that a union violates its DFR if it acts in a manner that is "arbitrary, discriminatory, or in bad faith," with "arbitrary" defined as "outside a wide range of reasonableness."

Mere negligence is not enough to prove a DFR, but showing intentionally bad conduct is not required.

d. Most Common DFR Violations

The most common DFR violations involve the following types of behavior. First, intentional misconduct, such as dishonesty that prejudices the plaintiff, violates the DFR. *See, e.g., Beck v. Food & Commercial Workers Local 99*, 506 F.3d 874 (9th Cir. 2007) (union's unexplained failure to file a grievance after it promised plaintiff it would); *Lewis v. Tuscan Dairy Farms*, 25 F.3d 1138 (2d Cir. 1994) (union official intentionally misrepresenting to a plant's employees how seniority would be credited if plant were purchased).

Second, discrimination for personal or other invidious reasons violates the DFR. Of course, labor contracts routinely "discriminate" among employees on the basis of, e.g., skill, seniority, training, or education in terms of salary, potential for advancement, priority in layoffs, and other rights and benefits. This by itself does not violate the DFR. But invidious discrimination because of categories not relevant to the workplace is a violation. This includes discrimination on the basis of, e.g., race, sex, and religion (although in modern times most such cases would more typically be litigated under Title VII or other employment discrimination laws). Discriminating against an employee for personal reasons—union politics or just old-fashioned personal animosity—also may lead to a DFR violation. *See, e.g., Ramey v. District 141, IAM*, 378 F.3d 269 (2d Cir. 2004) (DFR violation where union discriminated against employees because they previously had supported another union).

Third, courts have held that missing a deadline for filing a grievance or requesting arbitration such that the claim may no longer be pursued is sufficiently "arbitrary" to support a DFR claim. This is true even if the union official in charge simply made a mistake. *Vencl v. Int'l Union of Operating Engineers Local 18*, 137 F. 3d 420, 426 (6th Cir. 1998).

On the other hand, the law remains clear that unions need not take every grievance to arbitration, even if the affected employee wants to arbitrate. Unions do not violate their DFR if they have investigated a case and determined in good faith that it is weak, *see, e.g., Williams v. Sea-Land Corp.*, 844 F.2d 17 (1st Cir. 1988), or if the costs of the arbitration would greatly outweigh the benefits of even a successful result, *see, e.g., Hamilton v. Consolidated Freightways*, 612 F.2d 343 (8th Cir. 1979).

What if a grievance involves a conflict between members of the bargaining unit? Suppose two employees are being considered for the same promotion and the contract lists criteria for the promotion, or the employer is trying to determine which employee was more at fault in an incident that could lead to different levels of discipline. In short, the union has a duty to fairly represent both bargaining unit members. Although it is not required to, the union may legally take the side of one employee over another, if it does so after doing a competent investigation and making a decision in good faith. *See Smith v. Hussmann Refrigerator Co.*, 619 F.2d 1229 (8th Cir. 1980).

As noted above, unions generally have a duty to fairly represent members of the bargaining unit who are not union members. Perhaps most importantly, unions cannot only arbitrate the grievances of actual union members or, under the NLRA, charge non-members for arbitration costs. Unions have an equal duty to arbitrate on behalf of bargaining unit members who are not union members. This is true even if a nonmember is paying a lesser amount of dues than are members, or in a right to work jurisdiction, no dues at all (limits on union security clauses and right to work rules are discussed in detail below). *See Abilene Sheet Metal v. NLRB*, 619 F.2d 332 (5th Cir. 1980) (refusing to represent grievant because of his nonmember status violated the union's DFR). In response to *Janus*, a few jurisdictions in the public sector have adopted some exceptions to these doctrines, which will be discussed below. Nor can unions intentionally discriminate against nonunion members in contract negotiations. Unions may, however, exclude nonmembers from contract ratification votes without violating their DFR. *Branch 6000, National Association of Letter Carriers*, 232 N.L.R.B. 263 (1977), *enf'd*, 595 F.2d 808 (D.C. Cir. 1979). Generally, though, the DFR extends equally to members and nonmembers. Recall this rule when reading the section below on union security clauses.

In some DFR cases, the union has taken the case to arbitration, and plaintiff alleges that the union did such a poor job at the arbitration, it violated its DFR. Unions need not provide lawyers or "lawyer-quality" representation at arbitrations, and negligent failure to make certain arguments does not itself violate the DFR. *See, e.g.*, *Cannon v. Consolidated Freightways Corp.*, 524 F.2d 290 (7th Cir. 1975).

Suppose, however, that a union has handled an arbitration so badly that it does violate its DFR, and also, not surprisingly, the employer won the arbitration. Should the DFR violation permit a court to vacate the arbitration award? In *Hines v. Anchor Motor Freight, Inc.*, 424 U.S. 554 (1976), the Supreme Court answered that question in the affirmative.

In *Hines*, the employer fired some employees because they allegedly had sought reimbursements for hotel expenses beyond what their receipts indicated. The arbitrator upheld the dismissal. It later came out that a clerk at the hotel had committed the fraud, not the employees, and also that this fact could have been discovered "with a minimum of investigation," which the union did not do. 424 U.S. 554, 559. The Court of Appeals found that the union had violated its DFR, but that the arbitration award upholding the discharge should not be disturbed both because of the finality provision in the contract's arbitration clause and because there was no evidence of employer misconduct at the arbitration. The Supreme Court, however, held that if the union had violated its DFR, the employee should not be bound by the finality provision (the Court did not decide whether the union actually had violated its DFR in this case). The Court noted that the employer was not blameless, because the employer could and should have made an adequate investigation into the facts before firing the employees. The Court did stress that arbitration decisions cannot be vacated or re-opened merely because new evidence was discovered later; the *Hines* rule only applies if the union violated its DFR.

e. Remedies for DFR and § 301 Violations

As noted above, *Vaca* held that in a hybrid DFR/§ 301 claim, damages should be apportioned between the employer and the union. The Supreme Court examined this issue in more detail in *Bowen v. U.S. Postal Service*, 459 U.S. 212 (1983).

In *Bowen*, the employer fired the plaintiff, but it was undisputed that had the union not violated its DFR and refused to take the case to arbitration, the employer would have later reinstated him. The District Court held that the employer was responsible for all the backpay up to the date when an arbitrator, but for the DFR, would have reinstated the employee, and that the union was responsible for backpay after that date. The Court of Appeals held that only the employer should be liable for backpay, not the union. The Supreme Court reversed the Court of Appeals and held that both parties responsible for plaintiff's harm should be responsible to make plaintiff whole. Thus, the union was liable for harms that occurred after the employee would have been reinstated but for the DFR. The Court remanded to the District Court for an allocation of damages. A four-justice dissent authored by Justice White would have made the employer responsible for all the damages, as the employer's wrongful act was the real cause of plaintiff's unemployment. *Hines* also reaffirmed that punitive damages are not available against unions in DFR cases.

3. Public-Sector DFR Rules

Rules concerning the DFR are almost always the same in the public sector as in the private sector. Again, public-sector statutes often contain these rules explicitly, unlike the NLRA, but they are substantively the same as the court-developed rules in the private sector. *See, e.g.*, OH. REV. CODE 4117.11(b)(6) (union ULP to "[f]ail to fairly represent all public employees in a bargaining unit"). In other public-sector jurisdictions without such statutory language, courts have followed the private-sector approach of creating DFR rules as a necessary corollary to exclusive representation. *See, e.g.*, *Belanger v. Matteson*, 346 A.2d 124 (R.I. 1975). The substantive standards are nearly always identical to private-sector rules. *See, e.g.*, *State ex rel. Hall v. State Employment Relations Board*, 912 N.E.2d 1120 (Oh. 2009); *Belanger, supra*. In a rare exception, Illinois requires intentional bad behavior by the union. *See* 115 ILCS 5/14(b)(1) (Educational Labor Relations Act); 5 ILCS 315/10(b) (Public Labor Relations Act).

As to procedures, many states follow the private-sector rule and allow plaintiffs to bring DFR claims either to the labor board or directly to court. *See, e.g.*, *Farber v. City of Paterson*, 440 F.3d 131 (3d Cir. 2006); *Demings v. Ecorse*, 377 N.W.2d 275 (Mich. 1985). In some jurisdictions, however, plaintiffs must bring DFR claims to the state agency initially. Note that in such jurisdictions, the labor board is generally empowered to grant relief against the employer as well. *See, e.g.*, *Piteau v. Board of Education of Hartford*, 15 A.3d 1067 (Conn. 2010); *Karahalios v. Nat'l Fed. of Federal Employees*, 489 U.S. 527 (1989) (federal sector). Finally, in some states, plaintiffs must bring DFR claims to court and cannot bring them to the labor board. *See, e.g.*, *Ziccardi v. Commonwealth of Pennsylvania*, 456 A.2d 979 (Pa. 1982).

As to substantive differences, unlike the private-sector rule, New Mexico allows punitive damages in certain DFR claims. *See Atkins v. United Steel Workers of America, Local 187*, 148 N.M. 442 (2010). Also, picking up on one of Justice Black's suggestions in *Vaca*, Alaska permits an employee to sue the employer for breach of a labor contract if the union refuses to arbitrate the employee's case, even if the union did not violate its DFR. *Casey v. Fairbanks*, 670 P.2d 1133 (Alaska 1983).

C. Union Security Clauses

1. Introduction

A "union security clause" is a provision in a labor contract that requires members of a union bargaining unit to pay at least some dues to the union representing them as a condition of employment. The text of the NLRA contains some rules regarding union security clauses, but in some important ways, the rules courts have developed in this area diverge from what might seem to be the most obvious reading of the statute. Thus, understanding the rules requires tracing their historical development and evolution. As with DFR rules, this involves reviewing some older cases interpreting the Railway Labor Act. Before 2018, union security rules under the RLA, NLRA, and in the public sector usually followed the same principles. In 2018, however, the *Janus* decision held that all union security clauses in the public sector violated the First Amendment.

Even before the NLRA was passed, unions attempted to negotiate union security clauses in contracts with employers. Many employers and some employees (disenchanted with the union that represented them or with unions in general) have opposed such clauses for an equally long period. Prior to the NLRA, unions often sought either the "closed shop"—an agreement that the employer would only hire people who were already members of the union—or the "union shop"—an agreement that an employee would have to join the union after being hired as a condition of employment. Employers often insisted on the "open shop"—refusing to agree to any sort of union security clause.

Today, neither the closed shop nor the union shop is legal anywhere in the private or public sectors. Under the NLRA, about half the states are "right to work" states in which no union security clause is legal. In jurisdictions that are not "right to work" in the private sector, the most that a union security clause can require is what is called an "agency shop" or "fair share" agreement. Such agreements cannot require objecting non-members—members of a union bargaining unit who both are not union members and who make proper objections—to pay that percentage of their dues that go to activities not related to collective bargaining. In states that have not adopted the right to work option, however, union security clauses may require all members of a union bargaining unit to pay the percentage of their dues that goes to activities related to collective bargaining.

These rules were not always this way. There have been various changes to legal rules along the way, often in the absence of any change in statutory or constitutional language.

2. Union Security from the NLRA to the Early 1960s

The original Wagner Act in 1935 did not contain any restrictions on union security arrangements. In 1947, however, the Taft-Hartley Act changed the law in this area in two important ways. First, it added Section 14(b) to the NLRA. Section 14(b) allows individual states to adopt "right to work" rules under which any form of union security clause in a labor contract is illegal. This is, interestingly, the only part of the NLRA that permits a state to vary a rule. As of this writing, twenty-six states have chosen the "right to work" option under Section 14(b): Alabama, Arizona, Arkansas, Florida, Georgia, Idaho, Indiana, Iowa, Kansas, Louisiana, Mississippi, Nebraska, Nevada, North Carolina, North Dakota, Oklahoma, South Carolina, South Dakota, Tennessee, Texas, Utah, Virginia, and Wyoming. Almost all these states became right to work states no later than the 1950s. The exceptions are Oklahoma (2001) and Indiana (2012).

The main argument against right to work rules is that it creates a free-rider problem because, as noted above, unions have a duty to fairly represent all members of the bargaining unit, regardless of whether the employee pays dues or not. Thus, in right to work jurisdictions, an employee may refuse to pay any dues, but a union cannot consider that fact when, e.g., deciding whether to handle that employee's grievance or arbitration or when negotiating protections, rights, and raises in a labor contract. The employee thus may receive valuable services (and services that are not free for the union to provide) without paying for them, including the benefits of a collective bargaining agreement. The main argument in favor of right to work rules is that the employee may not have wanted these services in the first place and should not be forced to pay for them as a condition of employment.

Second, Taft-Hartley amended Section 8(a)(3) to make the closed shop illegal everywhere. On the other hand, the language as amended appeared to explicitly allow the union shop. Section 8(a)(3) makes it an employer ULP to engage in:

> discrimination in regard to hire or tenure of employment or any term or condition of employment to encourage or discourage membership in any labor organization: *Provided*, That nothing in this subchapter, or in any other statute of the United States, shall preclude an employer from making an agreement with a labor organization ... to require as a condition of employment membership therein on or after the thirtieth day following the beginning of such employment or the effective date of such agreement, whichever is the later.... *Provided further*, That no employer shall justify any discrimination against an employee for non-membership in a labor organization (A) if he has reasonable grounds for believing that such membership was not available to the employee on the same terms and conditions generally applicable to other members, or (B) if he has reasonable grounds for believing that membership was denied or terminated for reasons other than the failure of the employee to tender the periodic dues and the initiation fees uniformly required as a condition of acquiring or retaining membership.

Also, the parallel language of Section 8(b)(2) appears to make the union shop legal. Section 8(b)(2) makes it a union ULP:

> to cause or attempt to cause an employer to discriminate against an employee in violation of subsection (a)(3) of this section or to discriminate against an employee with respect to whom membership in such organization has been denied or terminated on some ground other than his failure to tender the periodic dues and the initiation fees uniformly required as a condition of acquiring or retaining membership.

Thus, after Taft-Hartley, unions and employers under the NLRA operated under the assumption that while the closed shop was illegal, in jurisdictions that were not "right to work," a union security clause could legally require that, as a condition of employment, after an employee had been employed for thirty days, the employee was obligated to become a union member.

As indicated above, that is not the law today. Further changes came through court decisions.

3. *General Motors* and Membership "Whittled Down to Its Financial Core"

The first change in NLRA law came with *NLRB v. General Motors Corp.*, 373 U.S. 734 (1963). *General Motors* held that the union shop was legal. Significantly, though, it explained that "membership" for the purpose of a union shop did not mean literal membership, but rather only initiation fees and monthly dues. Specifically, "the burdens of membership upon which employment may be conditioned are expressly limited to the payment of initiation fees and monthly dues.... 'Membership' as a condition of employment is whittled down to its financial core." *Id.* at 742–43.

Essentially, this meant that in jurisdictions that were not right to work, a union security clause could require payment of full dues as a condition of employment but could not require an employee literally to join the union. In NLRA cases, this rule would last until the *Beck* case in the late 1980s (discussed below). Meanwhile, cases decided in other areas of labor law were setting the stage for changes in NLRA law.

4. Limitations on Union Security Clauses under the RLA

Before *General Motors*, the Supreme Court had created somewhat different rules for union security clauses under the Railway Labor Act, first in *Railway Employees Department v. Hanson*, 351 U.S. 225 (1956), and then in *International Association of Machinists v. Street*, 367 U.S. 740 (1961). *General Motors*, decided two years after *Street*, did not mention either case, so it appeared that RLA and NLRA rules were separate. Later cases, however, would bring RLA rules to the NLRA, so understanding modern NLRA rules requires understanding *Street*.

In *Street*, a union-security clause required employees to pay full dues to the union. The union, in turn, spent some of its dues income on political causes plaintiff employees opposed. The lower courts held that this violated the First Amendment's free speech provisions. The Supreme Court explained that it would avoid the constitutional question, given that it could interpret the statute in a way that avoided constitutional infirmity. The Court emphasized that the railway industry had a strong tradition of "voluntary unionism." 367 U.S. 740, 750. It noted that the statutory language (in relevant part quite similar to that in the NLRA quoted above), barred security clauses that required termination when lack of union membership was caused by anything other than failure to pay dues. The Court explained, however, that this showed a "congressional concern over possible impingements on the interests of individual dissenters." *Id.* at 766. The Court then noted that the main reason to permit union security clauses was to avoid the free rider problem discussed above. Given this justification, the Court reasoned, the RLA did not give unions "unlimited power to spend exacted money." *Id.* at 768. Specifically, "use to support candidates for public office, and advance political programs, is not a use which helps defray the expenses of the negotiation or administration of collective agreements...." *Id.*

Justice Frankfurter, writing for himself and Justice Harlan, dissented. This dissent argued that the statutory language authorized the full union shop and that this did not violate the First Amendment. It also stressed the "political activity of American trade unions in general and railroad unions in particular—activity indissolubly relating to the immediate economic and social concerns that are the raison d'etre of unions." *Id.* at 800. Further, the dissent found no constitutional issue, apparently because of a lack of sufficient state action:

> Congress has not commanded that the railroads shall employ only those workers who are members of authorized unions. Congress has only given leave to a bargaining representative, democratically elected by a majority of workers, to enter into a particular contractual provision arrived at under the give-and-take of duly safeguarded bargaining procedures.... When we speak of the Government 'acting' in permitting the union shop, the scope and force of what Congress has done must be heeded. There is not a trace of compulsion involved....

Id. at 807.

After *Street*, the rule under the RLA was that a union security clause could not require an employee to pay for political activities if the employee objected. So, if a union spent ten percent of its dues income on politics and ninety percent on "expenses of the negotiation or administration of collective agreements," a union security clause could only require an objecting employee to pay ninety percent of union dues.

5. Pre-*Janus* Rules on Union Security Agreements in the Public Sector

Fourteen years after *Street*, the Supreme Court set out rules for union security clauses in the public sector. While the rules in public employment derive from the First Amendment (because public employment does involve state action), the rules were, for forty years, essentially the same as in the private sector (where the Court derived the rules from statutory language).

Abood v. Detroit Board of Education, 431 U.S. 209 (1977), was the first major case in the public sector. It involved a challenge to Michigan's public-sector statute, which at the time permitted union-security clauses that required payment of full dues. The Court noted that the concerns on both sides of the union security issue were essentially the same in the public sector as in the private. Rejecting an argument by the plaintiffs, the Court found that public employees did not have a "weightier First Amendment interest than a private employee in not being compelled to contribute to the costs of exclusive representation." *Id.* at 210. Still, the plaintiffs had a First Amendment right not to be compelled (as a condition of employment) to fund political speech with which they disagreed. Thus, union security clauses could require dues payments for "collective-bargaining activities" but not for "ideological activities unrelated to collective bargaining." *Id.* at 236. The Court did not further elaborate as to which activities fell into which category. This would remain the rule in the public sector until *Janus* in 2018. In the period before 2018, as in the private sector, some public-sector jurisdictions chose to bar union security clauses, and other public sector jurisdictions did not.

6. Agency Fee Rules Finally Applied to the NLRA

Just over a decade after *Abood*, the Supreme Court applied the "agency fee payer" rules that had been used under the RLA in the public sector unions under the NLRA in *Communications Workers v. Beck*, 487 U.S. 735 (1988).

In *Beck*, the Court majority held that the rule in *Street* applied to the NLRA because the relevant statutory language in the NLRA is the same as in the RLA. The majority did not rely on the Constitution. It even cited *Steelworkers v. Weber*, 443 U.S. 193, 200 (1979), noting that *Weber* had found that an affirmative action clause in a private-sector CBA did not implicate state action. Still, constitutional concerns may be lurking in the background in *Beck* through its reliance on *Street*, which explained that it was interpreting the RLA to avoid constitutional issues.

As to the NLRA's statutory language, the *Beck* majority admitted that "§ 8(a)(3) permits an employer and a union to enter into an agreement requiring all employees to become union members as a condition of employment." 487 U.S. 735, 738. But, it continued, the "statutory question presented in this case" was whether the "financial core membership" as defined in *General Motors* "includes the obligation to support union activities beyond those germane to collective bargaining." *Id.* at 745. It did not, the majority explained, because the relevant language in the RLA was "nearly identical," *id.* at 746, as were the policy concerns. Thus, *Street* controlled. Also, the majority found no meaningful distinctions in the legislative histories of the relevant RLA and NLRA provisions, or in the histories of the railroad industries and the industries the NLRA covers.

The dissent by Justice Blackmun, joined by Justices O'Connor and Scalia, stressed that the statutory language in the NLRA seems explicitly to permit requiring full dues. Further, even if the language was ambiguous, the Court should defer to the NLRB's interpretation that would have allowed full dues. As to the legislative history, the dissent noted that the RLA did not allow union-security clauses until 1951; thus, the language in the RLA that is identical to that in the NLRA was added to the RLA four years after it was added to the NLRA. "It would surely come as a surprise to the legislators who enacted § 8(a)(3) to learn that, in discerning their intent, the Court listens not to their voices, but to those of a later Congress." *Id.* at 780.

Beck thus brought rules that already existed under the RLA and, at the time, the public sector, to the NLRA. Under these rules, a member of a union bargaining unit can avoid paying that portion of dues that go to activities which are not related to collective bargaining. This right can only be invoked by employees who are not actually members of the union. Also, the employee must make an affirmative objection to paying for such activities. Thus, such employees are sometimes referred to as "objecting nonmembers" or "nonmember objectors."

As noted above, while a union's DFR generally extends to members of the bargaining unit who are not members of the union, nonmembers may be excluded from contract ratification votes (although their interests must be considered in negotiations). Also, nonmembers may legally be excluded from votes on union officers. Thus, employees who wish to exercise rights under

Beck may not be able to take part in either type of vote. *See Kidwell v. Transportation Communications International Union*, 946 F.2d 283 (4th Cir. 1991).

The Supreme Court took on another issue involving the intersection of DFR and union security clause rules in *Marquez v. Screen Actors Guild, Inc.*, 525 U.S. 33 (1998). In *Marquez*, the plaintiff argued that a union violated its DFR by having a provision in a collective bargaining agreement that directly quoted the relevant statutory language from the NLRA on union security clauses. Arguably supporting the dissent in *Beck*, the plaintiff argued that this language completely misled her as to what her rights actually were under *Beck*. The Court rejected the DFR claim. "When we interpreted § 8(a)(3) in *General Motors* and *Beck*, we held that the section, fairly read, included the rights that we found. To the extent these interpretations are not obvious, the relevant provisions of § 8(a)(3) have become terms of art...." *Id.* at 46. Importantly, though, the Court added that unions must inform employees of their *Beck* rights in more easily understood language. The required notification is discussed in more detail below.

7. What Activities Are "Related to Collective Bargaining" and What Procedures Must Unions and Objectors Follow?

The cases above did not delve deeply into the issues of what activities by unions are related to collective bargaining, and what procedures should be followed in ensuring and enforcing rights under *Beck*, but other cases have.

The consequence of an activity not being related to collective bargaining is, pursuant to the rules above, that an objecting nonmember may not be "charged" that portion of their dues that go to that activity. Thus, activities that are related to collective bargaining are often called "chargeable" activities, while activities not related to collective bargaining are often called "non-chargeable" activities. *Beck*, quoting an RLA case, explained that chargeable activities were those "necessary to 'performing the duties of an exclusive representative of the employees in dealing with the employer on labor-management issues.'" *Beck*, *supra*, at 762–63, *quoting Ellis v. Brotherhood of Railway, Airline & Steamship Clerks*, 466 U.S. 435, 448 (1984).

Ellis also touched on the procedures unions must follow in these cases. *Ellis* held that a rebate method (charging full dues and then later giving refunds proportionate to non-chargeable expenses) was constitutionally improper, as "the union obtains an involuntary loan for purposes to which the employee objects." 466 U.S. 435, 444. The Court suggested that instead the union should use a method involving "advance reduction of dues and/or interest-bearing escrow accounts." *Id.* The Court gave some more details on how this could work in *Chicago Teachers Union Local No. 1 v. Hudson*, 495 U.S. 292 (1986) (discussed further below).

Ellis then addressed whether a variety of activities the union had engaged in were chargeable. Note that in this context, "related to collective bargaining" means the collective bargaining process broadly understood: actual negotiations, grievance and arbitration handling, and also activities that keep the union going as an institution are "related to collective bargaining." Thus, *Ellis* held that expenses for union conventions were chargeable, as conventions help the union set strategies and goals. Similarly, it held that union-sponsored social activities that were open to nonmembers were chargeable activities, as they help the union function (and here, the expenses were minimal). Litigation expenses were chargeable to the extent they had an impact on the objector's local. Union publications, on the other hand, were chargeable only to the extent that the publication reported on chargeable activities; the portion of a publication that reported on non-chargeable activities (e.g., politics) was not chargeable. Note here a practical point for unions: the cost of administering *Beck* rights (keeping track of what is and is not chargeable, doing audits and making reports regarding these issues, and litigating challenges while bearing the burden of proof to show that expenses are chargeable) may well exceed the cost of lost dues.

Perhaps the most interesting issue in *Ellis* involved whether expenses relating to organizing (or attempting to organize) other local unions were chargeable. The Court of Appeals had held that they were, because organizing efforts helped create a stronger union organization overall. *Ellis*, however, held that they were not, as the effect on the local with the objectors was too attenuated. The "free-rider rationale does not extend this far." As the next subsection shows, however, the NLRB has held that some organizing expenses are, in fact, chargeable.

a. More Recent Cases on What Activities Are Chargeable

Ellis remains almost entirely good law, but there are some recent developments involving organizing and other issues.

First, the NLRB has found that some organizing expenses are chargeable. In *Meijer, Inc.*, 329 N.L.R.B. 730 (1999), the NLRB found that expenses for organizing employees in the same competitive market were chargeable (the

Ninth Circuit ultimately upheld this ruling). In *Meijer*, the union with the objectors represented employees in a grocery store in Colorado, and the challenged expenses went to organizing campaigns in similar stores in the same geographical region. The NLRB distinguished *Ellis* on two grounds. First, the NLRB explained that *Ellis* was an RLA case, and *Meijer* involved the NLRA, and thus *Ellis* was not binding on this point. Distinguishing RLA and NLRA precedents is very unusual in this area. Second, the NLRB distinguished *Ellis* on the facts, noting that in *Meijer*, there was expert testimony that increasing unionization in this industry had raised wages in the industry. There was no such evidence in *Ellis*.

Meijer was a decision of the NLRB under President Clinton. Under President George W. Bush, the NLRB narrowed this rule in *Teamsters Local 75 (Schreiber Foods)*, 349 N.L.R.B. 77 (2007), *enf'd in rel. part, Pirlott v. NLRB*, 522 F.3d 423 (D.C. Cir. 2008). *Schreiber Foods* held that for organizing expenses to be chargeable, the union must provide evidence specifically showing "a direct, positive relationship between the levels of union-represented employees and the level of organization of employees of employers in the same competitive market." 349 N.L.R.B. at 77. In *Schreiber Foods*, the NLRB found that this standard had not been met. The testimony the NLRB found insufficient was to the effect that organizing other production and maintenance employees in Green Bay, Wisconsin would help a local union of production and maintenance employees in Green Bay, in part because the local labor market was relatively small. The NLRB found this insufficiently specific, as it was based only on general principles of labor economics.

The Supreme Court's next foray into what activities were chargeable came in *Lehnert v. Ferris Faculty Association*, 500 U.S. 507 (1991) (a public-sector case that remains valid precedent for the private sector). *Lehnert* held that a local teachers' union could charge objectors their proportion of the costs of chargeable activities of the union's state and national affiliates. Even if the activities of those parent bodies were not done *directly* for the benefit of the local, their expenses would be chargeable if there was some evidence that the activities might benefit the local. So, for example, the local could charge for a publication which the local's state body published (to the extent that publication reported on chargeable activities). However, the union still had the burden to show that expenses of parent bodies could benefit the local. Intriguingly, the Court held that the costs of preparing for a strike were chargeable, even though the strike would have been illegal under Michigan's public-sector labor law. On the other hand, the Court reaffirmed that electoral and other political activities (beyond lobbying a public body to ratify a contract) were not chargeable. Nor were public relations efforts designed to enhance the reputation of the teaching profession.

In *Locke v. Karass*, 555 U.S. 207 (2009), another public-sector case, the Court reaffirmed the *Lehnert* test for determining whether expenses by a national union are chargeable to local members. This case involved a national litigation fund, and the Court found the expenses were chargeable, as there was a reciprocal benefit to the local, since fees paid by all locals could be used in litigation for all locals.

b. Procedures in Union Security Clause Cases: Providing Information and Enforcing Rights

In *California Saw & Knife Works*, 320 N.L.R.B. 224 (1995), *enf'd sub. nom. International Association of Machinists v. NLRB*, 133 F.3d 1012 (7th Cir. 1998), the NLRB addressed several important issues regarding what sort of information the union must provide and how nonmember objectors may seek to enforce their rights.

First, unions must give notices of *Beck* rights to new employees, and either to any current employees who resign union membership or generally once yearly. Unions may require objections to be made in a 30-day window period once a year, but they may not require objections to be sent by certified mail, with each objection in an individual envelope. Unions must provide documentation listing all major categories of chargeable, non-chargeable, and if applicable, mixed expenses. The union must give objectors sufficient information to determine whether to challenge the dues deduction calculation. It is the union's burden to show that expenses it has charged are related to collective bargaining. The D.C. Circuit has required that an independent auditor perform the audits by which the union makes these calculations. *See Ferriso v. NLRB*, 125 F.3d 865, 870–71 (D.C. Cir. 1997).

The NLRB upheld the following process for handling objections. After receiving an objection, the union sends the objector information detailing and explaining the reduction in dues based on the previous year's expenses. After receiving this response, the nonmember objector has 30 days to file a challenge to these calculations.

While this case also upheld the union's requirement that challenges to the union's calculations must be arbitrated, the Supreme Court rejected such a requirement in *Air Line Pilots Association v. Miller*, 523 U.S. 866 (1998). The Court held that objectors had a right to go directly to court with these claims.

"[A]rbitration is a matter of contract and a party cannot be required to submit to arbitration any dispute which he has not agreed so to submit." *Id.* at 877.

The Supreme Court also set out important, if general, guidelines for procedures in *Chicago Teachers Union, Local No. 1 v. Hudson*, 475 U.S. 292 (1986). *Hudson* held that a "rebate" procedure was unconstitutional, as it did not ensure that the union would not use the nonmember objector's money for objectionable purposes. This case also held that the burden of proof to explain why all expenses were chargeable or non-chargeable was on the union.

If not a rebate, then what? *Hudson* indicated that placing the money in an escrow account would be constitutionally sound, and it even indicated that the union need not put all 100 percent of an objector's dues into the account, as that would deprive the union of access to some escrowed funds that it is unquestionably entitled to retain. The Court concluded that "an escrow for the amounts reasonably in dispute while such challenges are pending" would be sufficient. *Id.* at 310.

Beck rights continue to be controversial and politically charged. For example, consider two contrasting Executive Orders. Soon after he was inaugurated for his first term, on February 17, 2001, President George W. Bush signed Executive Order 13201. This Order required government contractors to post notices informing employees of their rights under *Beck*. Then, soon after he was inaugurated for his first term, President Barack Obama, on January 30, 2009, rescinded that order and substituted Executive Order 13496. This Order required government contractors to post notices informing employees of their rights to join (or refrain from joining) a union.

8. The Public Sector, *Janus*, and Statutory Changes

As noted above, in 2018, the Supreme Court reversed *Abood* and held that all union security clauses in the public sector violated the First Amendment. In the years before *Janus*, there were indications that some Justices were skeptical of *Abood*. *See Knox v. Service Employees Int'l Union, Local 1000*, 567 U.S. 298, 311 (2012) (Justice Alito opining that *Abood* was "something of an anomaly"); *Harris v. Quinn*, 573 U.S. 616 (2014) (*Abood* did not apply to home health care aides who were "not full-fledged public employees"). But these cases left *Abood* intact.

Finally, however, in 2018, the Supreme Court completely reversed *Abood* in *Janus*. The *Janus* majority stated that *Abood* (i) undervalued plaintiffs' First

Amendment interests by using insufficiently strict scrutiny; and (ii) overvalued the state's interest in union security clauses. As to the former, the majority rejected a comparison to the line of cases in which the Court allowed the government significant discretion in limiting the free speech rights of individual public employees because of the government's broad rights in its role as an employer. These cases include the rule that normal workplace grievances are not a matter of "public concern" and therefore cannot implicate the First Amendment. The *Janus* majority reasoned that the collective power of unions transformed speech about workplace matters normally outside the protection of the First Amendment into matters of public concern. The majority essentially held that *everything* a public-sector union bargains about is inherently a matter of public concern.

The majority also argued that *Abood* exaggerated the government's interest in "labor peace" and collective bargaining. The majority stated that in "right to work" jurisdictions, including but not limited to the federal sector, unions effectively represent their members through bargaining. The majority rejected the "free rider" argument, noting that unions in "right to work" jurisdictions still seek to become exclusive representatives, and thus they must see a benefit for themselves in that status. Intriguingly, the majority at least implied that states could alter DFR rules to allow unions to charge employees they represent who do not pay dues for the costs of arbitrations.

Justice Kagan's dissent, joined by Justices Breyer, Ginsburg, and Sotomayor, would have applied *stare decisis* because *Abood* had worked well in practice, had matched the Court's approach to the First Amendment rights of public employees generally, and was deeply entrenched in law and reality. Per *Abood*, employers receive significant benefits from bargaining with an exclusive representative (e.g., not having to deal with multiple unions). This system, in turn, requires unions to have adequate funding to avoid being decimated by free riders. The issue, the dissent argued, is whether unions will be *able* to be effective negotiating partners, not whether they want to be.

The dissent also stressed the Court's line of decisions on the free speech rights of individual public employees. It noted that government employers have substantial latitude to regulate employee speech, including the rule that the First Amendment does not protect speech relating to conditions of employment. It rejected the majority's "special rule" for union speech, noting there had been no exception giving special protection to speech involving policies that apply to groups of employees. Further, the dissent argued that the inquiry should not be whether the public is interested in public employee speech, but rather whether the speech was about and directed to the workplace. The dissent also raised challenging hypos involving groups of nonunion employees agitating for better benefits. Finally, the dissent maintained that even if union speech is a matter of public concern, under the First Amendment balancing test, the employer's interests should prevail.

Janus means, in short, that all of the public sector is "right to work" as a matter of constitutional law. It also held that unions must obtain affirmative consent, shown by "clear and convincing evidence," before they can deduct union dues from non-members' paychecks.

In the years preceding *Janus* to the present, there have been a variety of statutory changes regarding related rules, some disadvantaging unions but some favoring them.

First, a number of states have passed legislation limiting or eliminating the use of dues check-off for public-sector unions. Some of these laws bar dues check-off only for political expenses. Some apply to all unions, some only to certain unions. For example, in 2023, Florida SB 256 barred dues check-off for most public sector unions, but not public safety unions. *See generally* Ann Hodges, *Maintaining Union Resources in an Era of Public Sector Bargaining Retrenchment*, 16 Emp. Rts. & Emp. Pol'y J. 599, 603–04 (2012).

Second, on the other hand, in reaction to *Janus*, several states have amended their DFR rules or otherwise tried to ameliorate the effects on unions. Prior to *Janus*, Nebraska was a "right to work" state, but it stood alone in adding the following statutory language:

> If an employee who is not a member of the labor organization chooses to have legal representation from the labor organization in any grievance or legal action, such employee shall reimburse the labor organization for his or her pro rata share of the actual legal fees and court costs incurred by the labor organization in representing the employee in such grievance or legal action.

Neb. Rev. Stat. § 48-838(4).

Around the time of the *Janus* decision, some states adopted similar rules. New York amended its law to grant unions statutory rights to meet with new employees. Also, it amended its DFR rules to provide that unions did not have a duty of fair representation to provide nonunion members representation (i) during questioning by an employer, (ii) in statutory or administrative proceedings or to enforce statutory regulatory rights, or (iii) in any stage of a grievance, arbitration or other contractual process concerning the evaluation or discipline of a public employee where the non-member is permitted to proceed without the employee organization and be represented by his or her own advocate." N.Y. CIV. SERV. LAW § 209-a(2). In 2023, California enacted Assembly Bill 2556 which, among other things, authorizes firefighter unions to charge non-dues-paying bargaining unit members for the reasonable costs related to providing individual representation. In a more modest measure, New Jersey passed a bill that facilitates union communication with bargaining unit members and also bars public employers from encouraging bargaining unit members from resigning from the union. 2018 N.J.A. 3686.

More generally, tensions between DFR principles and union security rules, and tensions between the institutional rights and concerns of unions and the rights and concerns of individual members of union bargaining units, will continue to exist. These tensions will likely lead to more litigation, political battles, and some new rules in the public sector.

CHECKPOINTS

- The duty of fair representation was created by courts in the private sector.
- Under the NLRA, plaintiffs may bring DFR claims directly to court; they may, but are not required to, bring the claim initially to the NLRB.
- When plaintiffs allege the employer has violated a labor contract and the union has violated its DFR regarding the alleged contract violation, plaintiffs may join the employer as a defendant in a "hybrid DFR/§ 301" claim. But the claim against the employer may only go forward if plaintiff shows that the union has violated its DFR.
- In such "hybrid" suits, if the plaintiff is successful, both the union and the employer must pay damages to the extent that the acts of each caused plaintiff's harm.
- A union violates its DFR if its actions are in bad faith, discriminatory, or arbitrary. Arbitrary means "outside a wide range or reasonableness." These cases typically involve intentional misrepresentation, discrimination because of personal animosity, or gross negligence such as missing a deadline for filing a grievance.

- The DFR does not require unions to arbitrate all grievances, or to treat all members of the bargaining unit equally in all ways. Unions have considerable discretion to choose strategies in bargaining and contract administration. Thus, they may refuse to arbitrate grievances because, e.g., a case is weak, and unions may negotiate contracts that, e.g., give greater compensation to employees with more skill, training, or seniority.
- Unions generally have the same DFR duties to members of their bargaining unit who are not union members as they do to those who are union members.
- Public-sector jurisdictions generally follow private-sector DFR rules, although a few variations exist.
- A "union security clause" is a clause in a labor contract that obligates employees to pay at least some portion of dues as a condition of employment.
- Under the NLRA, about half the states have chosen to be "right to work" jurisdictions. In such jurisdictions, union security clauses are illegal, and thus a member of a union bargaining unit who is not a member of the union does not have to pay any dues.
- Even in jurisdictions that are not "right to work," a union security clause may not require that a member of a union bargaining unit actually join the union.
- Per the *Beck* case, in jurisdictions that are not "right to work," a union security clause may not compel a member of the bargaining unit who is not a member of the union to pay that portion of dues that go to activities that are not related to collective bargaining, if the member objects
- "Related to collective bargaining" includes the bargaining process, grievance and arbitration handling, and activities that sustain unions. The biggest example of an activity that is not related to collective bargaining is politics.
- Unions are required to notify employees of their rights under *Beck* and give them enough information to determine whether to make an objection.

- Unions have the burden of proof to show which of their activities are and are not related to collective bargaining, and they also must calculate relevant totals and percentages of expenditures on each activity.
- Unions may not give "rebates" after the fact to objectors. Rather, they generally must use an advance rebate or escrow system.
- In the public sector, before *Janus* in 2018, the rules were essentially the same as under the NLRA. But *Janus* held that all union security clauses in the public sector violated the First Amendment.
- In recent years, some states have passed laws covering public sector unions on related topics: e.g., restricting the use of dues check-off for political purposes or in general; or limiting the DFR obligations of public-sector unions to nonunion-members.

CHAPTER 20

Successorship

ROADMAP

- Who is a successor under Board successorship law?
- Substantial business continuity
- Substantial and representative complement
- At what point is the bargaining obligation triggered?
- When a successor must subsume its predecessor's contractual obligations: the perfectly clear successor's limited duty
- Successor's liability for its predecessor's unfair labor practices
- The duty to bargain versus the duty to arbitrate in successorship cases

---

Business entities frequently change their business form. Sometimes, those changes are as simple as a change in corporate name, such as from James Smith Company to Smith Company. At other times, a merger between two business entities occurs, or one firm acquires another, or perhaps one firm purchases all the business assets of another. Labor issues can arise from these changes. For example, if A, which is nonunion, merges with B, which is union, under what conditions, if any, does the union still represent the employees of B? Under what circumstances is the employer legally obligated to recognize the union? Under what circumstances is the employer obligated to assume the collective bargaining agreement (CBA) that the union negotiated with B? To answer questions concerning the labor consequences of business transformations, it is necessary to review the labor law concept of successor.

A. What Is a Successor?

For purposes of federal labor law, a legal successor is an employer that is obligated to bargain with a union where the following two conditions have been met:

1. There is "substantial business continuity" between the two enterprises, the putative successor and its predecessor; and
2. The employer has hired a "substantial and representative complement" of employees, *Fall River Dyeing & Finishing Corp. v. NLRB*, 482 U.S. 27 (1987).

1. Substantial Business Continuity

In determining whether there is substantial business continuity between the putative successor and its predecessor, the Board examines the following three factors:

a. Is the business of both employers essentially the same?
b. Are the employees of the new company doing essentially the same jobs in the same working conditions under the same supervisors?
c. Does the new entity have the same production process, produce the same products, and basically have the same body of customers?

When examining these factors, the Board is mindful of the question whether "those employees who have been retained will understandably view their job situations as essentially unaltered." *Fall River Dyeing & Finishing Corp.*, 482 U.S. 27, 43 (1987) (quoting *Golden State Bottling Co. v. NLRB*, 414 U.S. 168, 184 (1973)).

NLRB v. Burns Int'l Security Servs., Inc., 406 U.S. 272 (1972), provides a straightforward example of substantial business continuity. In that case, Wackenhut Corp. provided security for Lockheed, an aerospace corporation specializing in aircraft design and manufacturing with substantial military contracts. The United Plant Guards (UPG), which represented Wackenhut's guards, had recently executed a three-year CBA with Wackenhut. That contract was due to expire in April 1970. In spring 1968, Burns won a bid for the next security services contract. Burns chose to retain 27 Wackenhut guards and to bring 15 of its guards from other Burns facilities for a total of 42 guards. Burns provided the Wackenhut guards with membership cards from the American Federation of Guards (AFG), with whom Burns had a collective-bargaining relationship. Burns announced that it "'could not live with' the existing contract between Wackenhut and the union." Burns refused to recognize UPG, but it did recognize AFG.

Burns presented two main questions: whether the employer had a duty to bargain with UPG rather than AFG, and whether the employer had a duty to subsume the contract that Wackenhut had with UPG. Those questions are discussed below. However, the facts of this case provide a nice example of substantial business continuity, which was not the focus of *Burns*. Applying the Board's substantial continuity test, the Court held that Burns was a successor because (1) the business of both employers—guard services—is essentially the same; (2) Burns' employees are doing essentially the same jobs—guard jobs—as Wackenhut employees; and (3) Burns provides the same service—security services—as did Wackenhut.

The Court focused on the substantial continuity test in *Fall River Dyeing & Finishing Corp. v. NLRB*, 482 U.S. 27 (1987). There, the predecessor (Sterlingwale) operated a textile dyeing and finishing plant for 30 years. The predecessor engaged in two production processes: the converting process, whereby the predecessor bought unfinished fabrics, dyed and finished them, and then sold the finished products to apparel manufacturers; and commission dyeing, whereby the predecessor dyed and finished customer-owned products according to their customers' specifications. For most of that time, the predecessor had a collective-bargaining relationship with the union. The most recent CBA was due to expire in 1981. In the late 1970s, the textile-dyeing business began to suffer from foreign competition and adverse economic conditions. As a result, in 1982, the predecessor laid off all its production employees, primarily because its converting process was no longer financially viable. It retained only a skeletal crew of workers and supervisors to ship goods on remaining orders and to maintain the company's building and machinery. During this production hiatus, the predecessor's president liquidated the company's inventory and sought a business partner to help revive the business. In late summer, the predecessor went out of business. A few months later, the predecessor's former vice president of sales and the president of a former customer formed Fall River Dyeing & Finishing Corporation, which acquired the predecessor's plant, real property, and equipment. By September 1982, Fall River began operating out of the predecessor's former plant and started hiring employees. Soon thereafter, Fall River hired 12 supervisors, 8 of whom had been the predecessor's supervisors and 3 of whom had been the predecessor's employees. By mid-January 1983, Fall River had also hired 55 workers for an initial production shift, 36 of whom were former employees of the predecessor. During this time, Fall River engaged exclusively in commission dyeing.

The Court upheld the Board's conclusion that there was substantial continuity between Fall River and its predecessor. Applying the Board's three-factor substantial continuity test, the Court upheld the Board's findings that (1) Fall River's business—commission dyeing—was essentially the same as its predecessor's; (2) Fall River's employees were doing the same jobs because they were operating the same machines under the direction of the same supervisors; and (3) Fall River's production process was the same as its predecessor's. The Board, with the Court's approval, examined these questions from the employees' viewpoint.

A seven-month hiatus between the predecessor's business demise and Fall River's takeover and restart of the new business complicated the substantial continuity question. The Court found, however, that from the employees' perspective, the hiatus was less than seven months because the predecessor maintained a skeletal crew for part of the time and because the other factors so strongly pointed in the direction of continuity. Although a long hiatus often accompanies business discontinuity, the hiatus's length is not so much a cause of business discontinuity as it is an effect. For example, a long hiatus may be caused by changes in production, which can disrupt business continuity.

Everfresh Beverages Inc., 323 NLRB 357 (1997), *enf'd mem.* 162 F.3d 1162 (6th Cir. 1998), provides another example of substantial business continuity. In that case, National Beverage purchased Everfresh Beverages, a company that bottled and sold (nonretail) beverages. At the time of the sale, Everfresh was a debtor in bankruptcy. On the day the sale was executed, National Beverage officials informed Everfresh employees that National Beverage had acquired their company, and they were all discharged from Everfresh; however, National Beverage would consider hiring each of them. The following morning, National Beverage interviewed employees for the very same jobs from which they had just been discharged. National Beverages rehired all the same supervisors and eventually added three more supervisors—all of whom had been bargaining-unit employees for Everfresh. National Beverage continued to operate using the same machinery, equipment, and production methods. The only difference in operations was that Everfresh Beverages discontinued one of its production lines. National Beverages also sold the same product to approximately two-thirds of the same customers. In this case, the Board easily found substantial business continuity, as the only difference between

Everfresh, the predecessor, and National Beverages, the successor, was in the decreased production volume, which had resulted in some lost customers.

2. Substantial and Representative Complement of Employees

The Supreme Court settled the substantial and representative complement question in *Fall River*, 482 U.S. 27. The doctrine grew up amidst several questions raised by *Burns*: (1) Whose majority—the successor's or the predecessor's—triggers the bargaining obligation? (2) At what time should the Board count this majority? and (3) When, if at all, did the union have to demand bargaining? In partial answer to questions one and two, the Board devised its substantial and representative complement test. The Board considers the following three factors in determining whether the successor has hired a substantial and representative complement:

- at the time that the employer has hired a substantial and representative complement, a majority of the successor's bargaining unit workers must be composed of employees who formerly had worked for the predecessor;
- "whether the job classifications designated for the operation were filled or substantially filled, and whether the operation was in normal or substantially normal production"; and
- "the size of the complement on that date and the time expected to elapse before a substantially larger complement would be at work, ... as well as the relative certainty of the employer's expected expansion."

Fall River Dyeing & Finishing Corp., 482 U.S. at 49 (quoting *Premium Foods, Inc. v. NLRB*, 709 F.2d 623, 628 (9th Cir. 1983)). The substantial and representative complement test does not answer the timeliness of a union's bargaining demand, which is a separate inquiry discussed below.

a. A Majority of the Successor's Employees Worked for the Predecessor

Concerning the question—whose majority?—the Court explained that "[a]fter *Burns*, there was some initial confusion ... [whether] work force continuity would turn on whether a majority of the successor's employees were those of the predecessor or on whether the successor had hired a majority of the predecessor's employees." *Fall River*, 482 U.S. at 47 n. 12. The Court concluded that workforce continuity would turn on whether a majority of the successor's employees were former employees of the predecessor. Simply put, the Board is balancing the Section 7 rights of employees who voted for and have been protected by union representation and those employees who did not vote for this union. Accordingly, the critical ratio here is the number of former union employees (predecessor's employees) to the total number of employees hired by the successor (total number of successor's employees).

The following two scenarios illustrate the first criterion regarding majority hire without the complicating factor of when to conduct the headcount.

- Scenario A: Company P has one production line with 100 employees. Company S hires a total of 300 employees, including all 100 of the predecessor's employees. Answer A: Company S is not a successor. Even though it hired all 100 of P's former employees, 100 employees is not a majority of the 300 employees hired in total.
- Scenario B: Company P has three production lines with 300 employees. Company S downsizes to one production line and hires a total of 100 employees, all of whom previously worked for Company P. Answer B: Company S is a successor because 100 percent of its employees formerly worked for P.

Notwithstanding these rules, under the Board's forfeiture doctrine, employers may not engage in discriminatory hiring practices to avoid their bargaining obligations under *Burns*. As the Board has explained:

> The fundamental premise for the forfeiture doctrine is that it would be contrary to statutory policy to confer *Burns* rights on an employer that has not conducted itself like a lawful *Burns* successor because it has unlawfully blocked the process by which the obligations and rights of such a successor are incurred.... [T]he *Burns* right to set initial terms and conditions of employment must be understood in the context of a successor employer that will recognize the affected unit employees' collective-bargaining representative and enter into good-faith negotiations with that union about those terms and conditions.

Advanced Stretchforming Int'l, Inc., 323 N.L.R.B. 529, 530 (1997) (quotation marks, citation omitted), *enf'd* 233 F.3d 1176 (9th Cir. 2000). To illustrate, assume the successor wishes to hire all 50 of its predecessor's employees. Also assume that it only wants to hire 90 employees in total but instead hires 100 employees to get around the substantial and representative majority requirement. In these circumstances, the Board will normally find that such an employer has violated the Act and will order the employer to bargain with the union over terms and conditions of employment.

The following two prongs—regarding (b) job classifications/production and (c) stability of the complement—help to answer the timing question—at what point should the Board count the complement?

b. Were the Job Classifications Designated for the Operation Filled or Substantially Filled, and Was the Operation in Normal or Substantially Normal Production?

In determining whether job classifications were substantially filled and whether operations were in substantially normal production, the Board must decide when to take the snapshot. This is important for establishing both numbers in the ratio—predecessor's employees to total number of successor employees—especially the denominator in that ratio.

This factor is often at issue in the successor context, where one business is purchasing another business in economic distress. This is precisely the situation in *Fall River*. There, the Board selected a time at which the successor "'had hired employees in virtually all job classifications, had hired at least fifty percent of those it would ultimately employ in the majority of those classifications, and … employed a majority of the employees it would eventually employ when it reached full complement.'" *Fall River*, 482 U.S. at 52 (quoting court of appeals decision). The Court further noted that, at this time, the successor had reached normal production.

Everfresh Beverages, discussed above, also provides some insight into this factor. There, the Board took the snapshot when the successor, which had purchased a business in bankruptcy, had restarted two of the three production lines. The Board reasonably found substantially normal production, considering that all job classifications had been filled and that production was up and running.

c. The Size of the Complement on That Date and the Time Expected to Elapse before a Substantially Larger Complement Would Be at Work, ... as Well as the Relative Certainty of the Employer's Expected Expansion

This factor—the complement's size on the date that a snapshot of the workforce is taken—is also a question of timing. The Board must decide on what date it will count the workers to determine whether a substantial and representative complement exists. *Everfresh Beverages, Inc.*, 323 N.L.R.B. 357 (1997), *enf'd mem.* 162 F.3d 1162 (1998), discussed above, illustrates this timing aspect of the substantial and representative complement doctrine. Recall in that case, the successor, which had purchased a business in bankruptcy, was able to operate two of the three production lines in less than one week. Moreover, essentially all the employees working for that successor were, in fact, former Everfresh employees. The Board reasonably found substantially normal production (factor two in the test described above), considering that all job classifications had been filled and that production was up and running. The disputed question then for the Board was solely one of timing—at what point in time should the Board count the number of employees? Should the Board wait for the successor to expand its business, as it claimed that it would, or should it take the snapshot now, when its production was at two-thirds capacity?

The successor made the claim that the lost production line was temporary and that it was going to rapidly expand business. In other words, the head count was premature. The Board, with court approval, found that the successor failed to meet its burden of substantiating that defense because the successor placed no evidence on the record to show that its stated plans to expand were anything more than "wishful thinking": "There is no documentation that sales were increasing or were expected to increase. Nothing to indicate a firm foundation on which to base a legitimate projection requiring increased production and the hiring of additional employees." *Id.* at 360.

d. The Union's Continuing Demand

Normally, the union demands bargaining to trigger the employer's duty to bargain. The successorship context complicates matters. Difficulty in fixing the time at which to take the snapshot raises the question of what happens if the union requests bargaining before the successor has hired a substantial and representative complement. The Board has held that a premature bargaining demand does not defeat the employer's bargaining duty.

The Court in *Fall River* upheld as reasonable the Board's continuing demand rule in the successorship context:

> The successor's duty to bargain at the substantial and representative complement date is triggered only when the union has made a bargaining demand. Under the continuing demand rule, when a union has made a premature demand that has been rejected by the employer, this demand remains in force until the moment when the employer attains the substantial and representative complement.

Fall River, 482 U.S. at 52 (internal quotation marks omitted).

B. The Bargaining Obligation

To sum up, a successor is obligated to bargain with the predecessor's union if the following three conditions are met:

1. There is substantial business continuity between the successor and the predecessor;
2. The employer has hired a substantial and representative complement; and
3. The union has requested bargaining.

A successor who meets these conditions but fails to recognize and bargain in good faith with the union violates § 8(a)(5) of the National Labor Relations Act. A premature bargaining demand does not disturb the parties' bargaining obligation.

C. Successor Bar Rule

The successor bar rule is a policy the Board has developed regarding a successor's bargaining obligation. Under this rule, "once a successor's obligation to recognize an incumbent union has attached (where the successor has not adopted the predecessor's contract), the union is entitled to a reasonable period of bargaining without challenge to its majority status through a decertification effort, an employer petition, or a rival petition." *St. Elizabeth Manor, Inc.*, 329 N.L.R.B. 341, 344 (1999). For decades, the Board has oscillated between having a successor bar rule and not having one. *Contrast Ugl-Unicco Serv. Co.*, 357 N.L.R.B. 801 (2011) (successor bar); *and St. Elizabeth Manor, Inc.*, 329 N.L.R.B. 341 (1999) (same), *with MV Transp.*, 337 N.L.R.B. 770 (2002). In *Hospital Menonita de Guayama, Inc. v. NLRB*, the D.C. Circuit thoroughly examined the Board's successor bar rule and affirmed it. 94 F.4th 1, 11 (D.C. Cir.), *cert. granted, judgment vacated and remanded*, 145 S. Ct. 982 (2024). However, after the Court decided *Loper Bright Enterprises v. Raimondo*, 603 U.S. 369 (2024) (overturning *Chevron* and holding that courts must use "independent judgment in deciding whether an agency has acted within its statutory authority"), the Court vacated the judgment of the D.C. Circuit and remanded the case for further consideration in light of *Loper Bright*.

D. The Perfectly Clear Successor's Limited Duty to Assume the Predecessor's Contract

Even if the legal successor meets those standards, it is generally not obligated to assume the CBA, unless certain circumstances apply. It is well settled that a successor is free to set initial terms and conditions of employment for the predecessor's employees without bargaining with the incumbent union. *Burns*, 406 U.S. at 298–99. The successor's privilege to set those initial terms and conditions of employment, however, is not absolute. Where it is "perfectly clear" that the successor employer intends to retain all or substantially all its predecessor's unionized employees as a majority of its workforce under the same terms as their previous employment, then the successor becomes a "perfectly clear successor" and is legally obligated to bargain with the union before altering any terms or conditions of employment. *Id.* at 294–95.

The Supreme Court explained the perfectly clear successor doctrine in *Burns*, 406 U.S. at 294–95 (emphasis added):

> Although a successor employer is ordinarily free to set initial terms on which it will hire the employees of a predecessor, there will be instances in which it is *perfectly clear* that the new employer plans to retain all of the employees in the unit and in which it will be appropriate to have him initially consult with the employees' bargaining representative before he fixes terms.

In *Spruce Up Corp.*, 209 N.L.R.B. 194, 195 (1974), *enf'd mem.* 529 F.2d 516 (4th Cir. 1975), the Board interpreted the *Burns* perfectly clear exception as applying in the following two circumstances: (1) where the new employer has "actively or, by tacit inference, misled employees into believing they would all be retained without change[s]," and (2) "where the new employer … has failed to clearly announce its intent to establish a new set of conditions prior to inviting former employees to accept employment." Thus, under *Spruce Up*, an employer that is "silent about its intent with regard to the existing terms and conditions of employment" is a "perfectly clear" successor if it "clearly indicated it would be hiring the predecessor's employees" before announcing changes. *Canteen Corp.*, 317 N.L.R.B. 1052, 1053 (1995), *enf'd* 103 F.3d 1355 (7th Cir. 1997).

Canteen Corp. illustrates the Board's perfectly clear exception. There, before assuming control of the predecessor's business, the successor engaged in several talks with the union and personally contacted every one of its predecessor's employees, asking each one to apply for employment. During those talks with the union, the successor and the union discussed which sample contract they would use in negotiating a new CBA. The parties agreed to a probationary period for all employees and a time for the initial bargaining session. In these circumstances, the court held that the successor violated Section 8(a)(5) & (1) when it offered employment to some of the predecessor's employees at a drastically reduced wage without first bargaining with the union. The court based its decision on *Burns* itself, finding that "[a] new employer must consult with the union when it is clear that the employer intends to hire the employees of its predecessor as the initial workforce." *Canteen Corp.*, 103 F.3d at 1362.

The *Everfresh Beverages* factual scenario, slightly altered, illustrates this concept. Say that, instead of interviewing the employees and setting initial terms, National Beverage officials called all the employees into a meeting on Friday afternoon and announced the following: "National Beverage just bought your company. You all are to report to work on Monday as scheduled. All of you will retain your jobs and all terms of employment will remain unaltered." In such a case, National Beverages would be the perfectly clear successor to Everfresh Beverages, and it could not change any terms or conditions of employment without first bargaining with the union.

E. The Successor's Duty to Assume the Predecessor's Liability

In 1973, the Court examined the obligations of a successor employer, this time in the context of liability for a predecessor's unfair labor practices (ULPs). In *Golden State Bottling Co. v. NLRB*, 414 U.S. 168 (1973), Golden State Bottling Company unlawfully discharged employee, Kenneth Baker, in violation of Section 8(a)(3). *See Golden State Bottling Co.*, 147 N.L.R.B. 410 (1964), *enf'd NLRB v. Golden State Bottling Co.*, 353 F.2d 667 (9th Cir. 1965). The Board's order ran against Golden State's "officers, agents, successors, and assigns." *See id.* at 411. In 1968, Golden State sold its soft-drink bottling business to All American Beverages, which was fully aware of the Board's order against Golden State. Thereafter, following a backpay specification proceeding, 29 C.F.R. §§ 102.52–102.59, the Board issued a supplemental order running against Golden State and its successor, All American Beverages. *Golden State Bottling Co.*, 187 N.L.R.B 1017, 1025–26 (1971) (supplemental decision and order directing All American Beverages to reinstate employee Baker and ordering both firms to jointly or severally pay backpay in the amount of $16,497 plus interest), *enf'd Golden State Bottling Co. v. NLRB*, 467 F.2d 164 (9th Cir. 1972) (per curiam).

Golden State squarely presents the question "whether the bona fide purchaser of a business, who acquires and continues the business with knowledge that [its] predecessor has committed an [ULP] in the discharge of an employee, may be ordered by the [NLRB] to reinstate the employee with backpay." *Golden State Bottling Co., Inc. v. N.L.R.B.*, 414 U.S. 168, 170 (1973). The Court held that the Board does not exceed its statutory power under Section 10(c) of the Act, 29 U.S.C. § 160(c), when it issues a reinstatement and backpay order against a bona fide successor. *Golden State Bottling Co.*, 414 U.S. at 176–77. The Court added that Rule 65(d) of the Federal Rules of Civil Procedure, regarding persons bound by injunctive orders, does not bar judicial enforcement of Board orders that run against successors who were not parties to the original proceedings. *Id. at* 177–80. The Court explained:

> Rule 65(d) "is derived from the common-law doctrine that a decree of injunction not only binds the parties defendant but also those identified with them in interest, in 'privity' with them, represented by them or subject to their control." ... Persons acquiring an interest in property that is a subject of litigation are bound by, or entitled to the benefit of,

> a subsequent judgment, despite a lack of knowledge. RESTATEMENT OF JUDGMENTS § 89, and comment c (1942); *see* 1 J. STORY, EQUITY JURISPRUDENCE § 536 (14th ed. 1918).

Golden State Bottling Co., 414 U.S. at 179 (internal citations omitted). Applying those common-law principles here, the Court held that "a bona fide purchaser, acquiring, with knowledge that the wrong remains unremedied, the employing enterprise which was the locus of the unfair labor practice, may be considered in privity with its predecessor for purposes of Rule 65(d)." *Id.* at 180.

F. The Duty to Arbitrate versus the Duty to Bargain in the Successorship Context

The first Supreme Court case to examine successorship principles is *J. Wiley & Sons, Inc. v. Livingston*, 376 U.S. 543, 546–51 (1964). This Section 301 action to compel arbitration, 29 U.S.C. § 185, presents the question whether a successor, which has merged with its predecessor, must arbitrate claims under a CBA between the union and the predecessor. Here, the CBA did not contain a successorship clause binding future owners to the CBA's terms. It did include a clause requiring the employer to make payments into the union's pension fund. One week before the expiration of the CBA, the union filed this motion to compel arbitration because the successor refused to recognize the union or make the payments under the CBA. The Court found that the duty to arbitrate survived here, even though there was no privity between the union and the successor, because (1) there was business continuity between the two firms and (2) the successor knew about the union's claims before it merged with the predecessor. The Court did not undertake a full-fledged successorship analysis, however, because this case predates *Burns*.

A few years after *Burns* was decided, the same issue was raised in *Howard Johnson Co. v. Detroit Local Joint Executive Board, Hotel & Restaurant Employees*, 417 U.S. 249 (1974), in which a union filed a Section 301 action to compel arbitration by the new owner. In this case, the Court held that the duty to arbitrate did not survive an asset-purchase agreement (whereby the purchaser bought its predecessor's business—a Howard Johnson's Hotel that the predecessor had been operating) because there was no business continuity between the new firm and its predecessor. Although the new firm continued to operate a Howard Johnson's restaurant and hotel, it did not hire any of its predecessor's supervisors and very few of its predecessor's employees. The union filed an action to compel arbitration on the question of whether the employer should have hired all its predecessor's employees.

The Court distinguished *J. Wiley* on two grounds. First, *J. Wiley* involved a merger of one firm into another against a state law backdrop, making the surviving corporation liable for the obligations of the disappearing corporation. No such state law protections or obligations were available in *Howard Johnson*. Second, the disappearance of the original entity in *J. Wiley* meant that the employees would have no means of enforcing vested benefits unless the arbitration could proceed against the surviving corporation. By contrast, in *Howard Johnson*, the union could enforce its claims against the predecessor, which continued as a viable entity with substantial assets. To the extent that the union was disputing the new firm's right to hire a new workforce, that dispute was at odds with the successorship doctrine established in *Burns*, which—absent anti-union motive—allows new firms to set initial terms and conditions of employment.

CHECKPOINTS

- Under *Fall River*, a legal successor is obliged to bargain with the union under the following conditions: (1) there is substantial continuity; (2) the employer has hired a substantial and representative complement; and (3) the union has requested bargaining.
- The Board examines the following three factors in determining whether there is substantial business continuity between the new firm (successor) and its predecessor: (1) Is the business of both employers essentially the same? (2) Are the employees of the new company doing essentially the same jobs in the same working conditions under the same supervisors? and (3) Does the new entity have the same production process, produce the same products, and basically have the same body of customers?
- When examining the three factors of substantial continuity, the Board is mindful of the question whether "those employees who have been

retained will understandably view their job situations as essentially unaltered."

- The Board considers the following factors in determining whether a substantive and representative complement exists: (1) "whether the job classifications designated for the operation were filled or substantially filled, and whether the operation was in normal or substantially normal production"; (2) "the size of the complement on that date and the time expected to elapse before a substantially larger complement would be at work, ... as well as the relative certainty of the employer's expected expansion"; and (3) whether, at the time that the employer has hired a substantial and representative complement, a majority of the successor's bargaining unit workers were composed of employees who formerly had worked for the predecessor.
- Under the Board's forfeiture doctrine, employers may not engage in discriminatory hiring practices to avoid their bargaining obligations under *Burns*.
- A premature bargaining demand does not defeat a union's claim that the employer is required to bargain with it.
- The Board oscillates between having a successor bar, which entitles a union to a reasonable period of bargaining with a successor without challenge to its majority status, and not having such a bar.
- Under *Burns*, even if the legal successor meets those tests, it is not obliged to assume its predecessor's CBA, absent certain circumstances.
- In *Burns*, the Court observed that "[a]lthough a successor employer is ordinarily free to set initial terms on which it will hire the employees of a predecessor, there will be instances in which it is *perfectly clear* that the new employer plans to retain all of the employees in the unit and in which it will be appropriate to have him initially consult with the employees' bargaining representative before he fixes terms."
- The Board interpreted the *Burns* perfectly clear exception as applying in the following two circumstances: (1) where the new employer has "actively or, by tacit inference, misled employees into believing they would all be retained without change[s]," and (2) "where the new employer ... has failed to clearly announce its intent to establish a new set of conditions prior to inviting former employees to accept employment."

- The bona-fide purchaser of a business, who acquires and continues the business with knowledge that its predecessor has committed a ULP, may be ordered by the NLRB to remedy that ULP.
- Under *J. Wiley*, the duty to arbitrate survives successorship to the extent that such claims are vested. Nevertheless, as the Court explained in *Howard Johnson*, the duty to arbitrate may not survive where there is no business continuity.

CHAPTER 21

The Intersection of Labor and Antitrust Law

ROADMAP

- The historical use of antitrust law by employers to thwart union activity
- The statutory exemption for certain anticompetitive union actions that do not involve non-labor groups
- The nonstatutory exemption for certain types of anticompetitive union bargaining
- The nonstatutory exemption for certain anticompetitive employer actions that occur as part of the collective-bargaining process

---

Labor law's protection of collective action stands in stark contrast to antitrust law and its prohibition against economic actors' joining together to gain an anticompetitive advantage. Indeed, the goal of unions is to obtain enough control over the supply of employees to extract gains for the employees. As a result of the conflict between union attempts to use economic power to restrict the supply of employees and the antitrust laws' prohibition against certain anticompetitive activity, Congress and the courts have carved out various labor exemptions to antitrust law. This chapter explores how these exemptions operate.

A. The Early History of Unions and Antitrust Law

For decades, the conflict between labor unions and antitrust law was severe. As discussed in Chapter 2, employers, with help from the courts, used antitrust law as a key means of attacking unionization in late 1800s and early 1900s. This problem became so acute that one of Congress's first labor statutes attempted to reduce the federal courts' ability to intervene in labor disputes.

In 1890, Congress enacted the Sherman Antitrust Act. Section 1 of the Sherman Act provides: "[e]very contract, combination in the form of trust or otherwise, or conspiracy, in restraint of trade or commerce among the several States ... is declared to be illegal." 15 U.S.C. § 1. A violation of this provision is classified as a felony and is subject to treble damages and jail time. Employers enjoyed remarkable success using this provision against labor unions, particularly when unions boycotted the employers in an attempt to induce them to use union workers. *See, e.g.*, *Loewe v. Lawlor*, 208 U.S. 274 (1908) (the Danbury Hatters case, described in Chapter 2).

The employers' success in Danbury Hatters and similar antitrust actions took a heavy toll on unions and their organizers. The specter of a conviction and personally crippling treble damage awards helped to stifle much labor organizing activity. The antitrust and conspiracy litigation, in addition to widespread violence connected to labor disputes (most resulting from employer repression of union activism), made any effort to unionize a workforce a risky proposition.

In 1914, however, Congress attempted to rein in what it viewed as a business-friendly judiciary by amending the Sherman Act. Among other reforms, Section 6 of the Clayton Antitrust Act declared that:

> the labor of a human being is not a commodity or article of commerce. Nothing contained in the antitrust laws shall be construed to forbid the existence and operation of labor ... organizations, instituted for the purposes of mutual help, ... or to forbid or restrain individual members of such organizations from lawfully carrying out the legitimate objects thereof; nor shall such organizations, or the members thereof, be held or construed to be illegal combinations or conspiracies in restraint of trade, under the antitrust laws.

15 U.S.C. § 17. Section 20 of the Clayton Act also imposed significant restrictions on the ability of courts to issue injunctions against labor organizing

activity, which had been another significant tool to fight unions. Although the Clayton Act appeared to provide a significant benefit to labor unions, in *Duplex Printing Press Co. v. Deering*, 254 U.S. 443 (1921), the Supreme Court narrowly interpreted the labor provisions by holding that Congress intended only to make clear that the antitrust laws do not make otherwise lawful union activity illegal. In other words, the Court in *Duplex Printing* held that the Clayton Act did not provide any exemptions for union activity that had previously been considered illegal under the Sherman Act.

The Court's narrowing of the Clayton Act led Congress to enact the Norris-LaGuardia Act of 1932 (discussed in Chapter 2), which prevented federal courts from enjoining, among other things, most nonviolent union activity. Many states enacted similar restrictions on state courts' ability to issue labor injunctions under what have been called "baby Norris-LaGuardia acts."

B. Antitrust Labor Exemption for Unions

Following the enactment of the Norris-LaGuardia Act, the Supreme Court softened its application of antitrust law to union activity. Most notably, in *United States v. Hutcheson*, 312 U.S. 219 (1941), the Court clarified that antitrust law has a much narrower application when unions are involved. In *Hutcheson*, the International Association of Machinists struck and boycotted Anheuser-Bush's products to protest the employer's hiring of members of a competing union. The employer sued the Machinists for violating the Sherman Act, but the Supreme Court rejected the suit. The Court emphasized the Norris-LaGuardia Act's prohibition against federal court injunctions that limit union activities related to a labor dispute. According to the Court, through the Norris-LaGuardia Act, Congress mandated a policy "that the allowable area of union activity was not to be restricted, as it had been in the *Duplex* case, to an immediate employer-employee relation." *Id.* at 231. Thus, the Norris-LaGuardia Act exempted the Machinists' boycott—which was peaceful conduct related to a labor dispute—from liability under the Sherman Act. However, the Court restricted this exception to cases in which "the union acts in self-interest and does not combine with non-labor groups." *Id.* at 232. This restriction and its exception came to be known as the "statutory labor exemption" to antitrust law.

Although the statutory exemption was a significant development, its limited value was due to the fact that it does not apply when unions and employers work together to resolve a labor dispute. *See Allen Bradley Co. v. Local Union No. 3, IBEW*, 325 U.S. 797, 808 (1945) (holding that Section 6 of the Clayton Act's reference to "mutual help" did not include unions' use of "employer-help"). The Court subsequently addressed this gap by developing what is called the "nonstatutory labor exemption." This exemption was rooted in two cases, *United Mine Workers of America v. Pennington*, 381 U.S. 657 (1965), and *Local Union No. 189, Amalgamated Meat Cutters v. Jewel Tea Co.*, 381 U.S. 676 (1965).

Pennington involved an agreement between the United Mine Workers and two large mining companies to raise the standard wage for miners under an industry-wide collective bargaining agreement. This activity occurred during a time when too much coal was being mined. As a result of this surplus, part of the agreement's goal was to close down smaller coal mining companies that were part of the multi-employer bargaining unit (see Chapter 10 for a discussion of multi-employer bargaining), but could not afford the wage increases as well as the larger companies. The statutory antitrust exemption did not apply because the union combined with the large mining companies, which were part of a "non-labor group" that could not take advantage of the exception under *Hutcheson*.

However, the Court held that there was a nonstatutory labor exemption to the antitrust laws that did apply. In particular, the Court held that the agreement's focus on wages went to the heart of the parties' duty to bargain under the NLRA. Therefore, although the agreement contemplated using the parties' market power, it did so through "elimination of competition based on wages among the employers in the bargaining unit, which is not the kind of restraint Congress intended the Sherman Act to proscribe." 381 U.S. at 664. The Court concluded that it was "beyond question" that a union can make a wage agreement with a multi-employer bargaining unit and, based on its own decision rather than an agreement with an employer, seek the same wages from other employers without violating antitrust law. *Id.* In contrast, a union cannot take advantage of the exemption if it enters into an agreement with a multi-employer bargaining group to pressure employers not in that bargaining group to accept a certain wage. In other words, an agreement limited to parties amid collective bargaining may enjoy an antitrust exemption, but if that agreement extends, or attempts to extend, an anticompetitive measure to groups that are not parties, the exemption does not apply.

On the same day as *Pennington*, the Court applied the nonstatutory exemption in *Jewel Tea*. In that case, a union and a multi-employer bargaining group reached an agreement setting the permissible number of hours for butchers. One of the employers objected to the restriction on hours, but a union strike threat pressured it to sign on. The Court applied the nonstatutory labor exemption and held that it applied to the union's actions. Key to this holding was the finding that the union pressured the employer on its own accord, rather than as part of an agreement with the other employers. Accordingly, the union did not run afoul of *Pennington's* warning that the nonstatutory exemption will not apply to unions that act with one set of employers to force other employers to agree to certain conditions of employment. As the Court held, the hours agreement at issue in *Jewel Tea* is a mandatory subject of bargaining and, therefore, "the unions' successful attempt to obtain that provision through bona fide, arm's-length bargaining in pursuit of their own labor union policies, and not at the behest of or in combination with non-labor groups, falls within the protection of the national labor policy and is therefore exempt from the Sherman Act." 381 U.S. at 689–690. In contrast, if the union's bargaining activity, which included a strike threat, had focused on a nonmandatory subject, then the nonstatutory exemption would not have applied.

Underlying both *Pennington* and *Jewel Tea* was the idea that the nonstatutory exemption was predicated on a need to harmonize the policies of both labor and antitrust law. In *Connell Construction Co. v. Plumbers and Steamfitters Local Union 100*, 421 U.S. 616 (1975), the balance between these two statutory schemes swung against a union. *Connell* involved a general contractor that subcontracted work both to employers that used union labor and those that did not. The union successfully picketed the general contractor to force it to subcontract only to employers that had signed a contract with the union. The agreement between the union and general contractor was a hot cargo clause that violated Section 8(e) of the NLRA (discussed in Chapter 16). The general contractor sued the union, arguing that its pressure violated the antitrust laws. The Court held that the nonstatutory exemption did not apply in *Connell*, primarily because of the Section 8(e) violation. When balancing the policies of labor and antitrust law, the Section 8(e) issue both undermined the labor law interests and enhanced the antitrust law interests. This was because the "substantial anticompetitive effects" of the agreement between the union and general contractor "would not follow naturally from the elimination of competition over wages and working conditions. It contravenes antitrust policies to a degree not justified by congressional labor policy, and therefore cannot claim a nonstatutory exemption from the antitrust laws." *Id.* at 625. In other words, because the anticompetitive agreement was unlawful under labor law, the nonstatutory exemption did not apply.

Underscoring these labor antitrust cases is the reality that the labor exemption is limited to formal unions (see Chapter 8 for a discussion of a "labor organization"). This can present risks for various types of workers or government attempts to protect them. For instance, organizations that represent gig workers who are not statutory employees, such as the Uber Guild, which represented drivers in New York, could face the risk of antitrust liability because it is not a formal union. Moreover, in 2015, Seattle enacted an ordinance that provided collective-bargaining rights to Uber and other on-demand drivers. The Chamber of Commerce challenged the ordinance on the ground, among others, that it permitted the independent-contractor drivers to price-fix in violation of antitrust laws. Although the district court rejected the challenge, holding that the ordinance was exempt from antitrust liability under the "state immunity" doctrine, the Ninth Circuit disagreed and held that the case could proceed. *See Chamber of Commerce v. City of Seattle*, 90 F.3d 769 (9th Cir. 2018). However, Seattle subsequently amended the ordinance, which mooted the case. But there was no question that the labor antitrust exemption did not apply because the ordinance covered independent contractors who were not statutory employees and could not form a formal union.

C. Antitrust Labor Exemption for Employers

The previous section discussed unions' ability to avoid antitrust violations via the statutory and nonstatutory exemptions. But unions are not alone, as employers also have uses for such an exemption. Take, for example, professional sports leagues. These leagues function as multi-employer bargaining units that, among other things, represent a group of employers (team owners) in their dealings with players' unions. Like unions, employers will often make agreements among themselves about work-related matters. However, agreements like these risk violating antitrust laws.

In *Brown v. Pro Football, Inc.*, 518 U.S. 231 (1996), the Supreme Court addressed whether employers also enjoy an antitrust exemption. *Brown* involved a dispute between the National Football League (NFL) and the NFL

Players Association. The parties' collective bargaining agreement expired and, during negotiations for a new agreement, the NFL offered a proposal that would allow teams to start "developmental squads" made up of new players who did not make the regular team but could occasionally play in games as substitutes for injured regular players. The NFL proposed a fixed weekly salary for developmental players; the union rejected that proposal and insisted that the developmental players be able to negotiate their salaries and receive similar benefits and protection as regular players. The parties' negotiations reached an impasse, after which the NFL unilaterally implemented the developmental squad program, with its proposed weekly salary. The NFL also informed the teams that they must pay the exact same weekly amount or face disciplinary action.

The developmental squad players sued the NFL and teams, alleging that the agreement to pay a fixed weekly salary violated Section 1 of the Sherman Act. The district court held that no antitrust exemption applied and sent the case to a jury, which awarded treble damages of over $30 million. The Supreme Court overturned the award, holding that the NFL and teams were exempt from liability under the Sherman Act.

The Court began by emphasizing that the policy reasons for providing unions with a nonstatutory antitrust exemption applied to employers as well. By enacting "the labor statutes, Congress ... hoped to prevent judicial use of antitrust law to resolve labor disputes.... The implicit ('nonstatutory') exemption interprets the labor statutes in accordance with this intent, namely, as limiting an antitrust court's authority to determine, in the area of industrial conflict, what is or is not a 'reasonable' practice." *Id.* at 236–37. This policy reflects the fact that collective bargaining often involves a group of employers, like a group of employees, that reach an agreement among themselves about work-related matters, and that agreement can restrict competition in some fashion.

Having recognized a nonstatutory antitrust exemption for employers, the Court then addressed the exemption's scope. The basic parameters of the exemption apply to conduct that is related to employers' lawful bargaining activity. The Court held that the NFL's agreement to implement and to enforce fixed developmental league wages fit under this definition because:

> That conduct took place during and immediately after a collective-bargaining negotiation. It grew out of, and was directly related to, the lawful operation of the bargaining process. It involved a matter that the

> parties were required to negotiate collectively. And it concerned only the parties to the collective-bargaining relationship.

Id. 250. In other words, because the NLRA considers employers' post-impasse implementation of terms to be lawful (see Chapter 12) and "an integral part of the bargaining process," an agreement among employers to engage in such conduct should be exempt from antitrust liability.

As the Court emphasized, however, the exemption has limits. One limitation might occur when the agreement in question is significantly distant in time or circumstances from the collective-bargaining process. For instance, as the Court noted, if there is an "extremely long" impasse followed by the multiemployer group becoming defunct, the exemption may not apply.

The Court cited another example of a situation that might remove employers' antitrust exemption, which will be familiar to sports fans: the union's decertification. As the Court in *Brown* stressed, if the collective-bargaining relationship collapses, then the labor law interests that would normally shield employers from antitrust liability also fall away. Professional athletes, among other employees, have used this theory to their advantage either by threatening to decertify their union or by actually doing so. When this happens, the teams are then faced with a risk of substantial antitrust liability if they agree among themselves to take any action that limits players' wages or other terms and conditions of employment. Recently, however, teams have been more forceful in challenging this practice, arguing that it is a sham because the union is decertifying in name only and is still acting as the employees' representative.

In a related development, the NCAA—facing antitrust liability on various fronts—has begun to allow collegiate players to earn more money. One proposal to allow the NCAA to regulate this new phase of collegiate sports without violating antitrust laws is to encourage unionization of athletes. There are hurdles to a collective-bargaining regime, such as collegiate athletes' status as employees, and the fact that many major college sports programs are public universities, and therefore generally covered by state public-sector labor statutes that vary widely in terms of what, if any, collective bargaining rights public employees have. But it is a development worth monitoring.

Sports collective bargaining has also raised another possible protection for employers against antitrust suits. In 2011, the NFL and the players' union were involved in contentious negotiations over a new collective bargaining agreement. Aware that the NFL planned to lock out the players as soon as the current agreement expired, the players voted to renounce the union as their representative (and the union "voluntarily decertified") before that happened. The next day, the NFL locked out the players, several of whom then sued for an injunction against the lockout, arguing that it violated antitrust law. The district court agreed with the players and issued a preliminary injunction against the lockout. However, the Eighth Circuit reversed the district court, holding that the Norris-LaGuardia Act prohibited courts from issuing injunctions against employer lockouts. *See Brady v. National Football League*, 644 F.3d 661 (8th Cir. 2011). This ruling was novel in that the Norris-LaGuardia Act was originally intended to prevent federal court interference with *union* action. This question still remains in some doubt, as the parties settled before the matter could be brought to the Supreme Court.

CHECKPOINTS

- Section 1 of the Sherman Act prohibits contracts and other agreements to restrain trade or commerce.
- The Supreme Court narrowly interpreted Congress' attempt in the Clayton Act of 1914 to permit unions and groups of employees to act in their mutual interest and to limit courts' ability to enjoin union activity.
- In 1932, Congress enacted the Norris-LaGuardia Act, which prohibited federal courts from enjoining most nonviolent union activity. Many states passed similar "baby Norris-LaGuardia" acts to similarly restrict state courts.
- In *United States v. Hutcheson*, the Supreme Court recognized a "statutory labor exemption" to antitrust law that applies when a union acts in its own interest and not in combination with non-labor groups, including employers.
- Later, the Court recognized the "nonstatutory labor exemption," which permits unions to act with employers to set wages and other noncompetitive conditions of employment.
- The nonstatutory exemption applies to a union's decision—made on its own accord—to pressure an employer to agree to certain conditions of employment that are mandatory subjects of bargaining.

- The nonstatutory exemption does not apply to an agreement between a union and a group of employers to pressure another group of employers to accept certain wages or other conditions of employment.
- The nonstatutory exemption does not apply to an anticompetitive agreement between a union and employer that violates the NLRA.
- Employers can also take advantage of the nonstatutory exemption if their anticompetitive conduct is related to, but not too distant from, lawful collective bargaining.
- Unions, with varying success, have voluntarily decertified during labor disputes to preclude employers from using the nonstatutory exemption.

Mastering Labor Law Master Checklist

Chapter 1 • Introduction to Private and Public Sector Labor Law

- ☐ Scope of labor law
- ☐ Differences between private and public-sector labor law
- ☐ Objectives of this book

Chapter 2 • History and Background of Labor Law in the Private and Public Sectors

- ☐ History of unions before development of modern labor law
- ☐ Issues addressed by National Labor Relations Act and public-sector labor laws
- ☐ Basic structure of private and public-sector labor laws

Chapter 3 • Overview of the National Labor Relations Board's Organization and Its Unfair Labor Practice and Election Procedures

- ☐ Description of National Labor Relations Board
- ☐ Discussion of the Board's unfair labor practice and election functions
- ☐ Process for bringing cases in front of Board

Chapter 4 • Jurisdiction of the NLRA

- ☐ Employers covered by, and excluded from, the NLRA

- ☐ Employees covered by, and excluded from, the NLRA and public sector laws (some of which do not exclude supervisors or have much narrower definition than the NLRA)
- ☐ Other employee exemptions under NLRA and issues of extraterritoriality

Chapter 5 • Section 7 Rights to Engage in Protected Conduct: Union Employees

- ☐ Distinction between protected and unprotected activities under Section 7
- ☐ The three elements that constitute protected activity: concertedness, ends, means
- ☐ *Weingarten* rights and the meaning of employee disloyalty

Chapter 6 • Section 7 Rights to Engage in Protected Conduct: Nonunion Employees

- ☐ Increasing importance of nonunion employees' Section 7 rights
- ☐ Individual and group concerted action
- ☐ Social media issues involving nonunion employees' concerted activities
- ☐ Employee pay-secrecy rules and the interaction of the NLRA with other laws

Chapter 7 • Organizing a Union: Section 8(a)(1) Unfair Labor Practices

- ☐ Facially neutral work rules that may conflict with employees' labor rights
- ☐ Employer property rights and employee communication rights under Section 8(a)(1)
- ☐ Employer speech and communication rights under Section 8(c)
- ☐ Employer interference with employee Section 7 rights under Section 8(a)(1)

Chapter 8 • Employer Domination or Interference of a Labor Organization: Section 8(a)(2) Unfair Labor Practices

- ☐ Section 8(a)(2)'s prohibition against employer domination and assistance

- ☐ Definition of labor organization under Section 2(5)
- ☐ Limitations on recognition of non-majority unions under Section 8(a)(2)

Chapter 9 • Employer Discrimination: Section 8(a)(3) Unfair Labor Practices

- ☐ Section 8(a)(3) prohibition against individual-based union discrimination
- ☐ Distinction between Section 8(a)(1) and 8(a)(3) discrimination cases
- ☐ Distinction between individual and group discrimination cases
- ☐ Distinction between pretext and dual-motive discrimination cases
- ☐ Special issues concerning salts, partial shutdowns, and runaway shops

Chapter 10 • The Representation Election

- ☐ Election procedures under the NLRA and public-sector election rules
- ☐ Bars to conducting NLRA elections
- ☐ Bargaining-unit determinations, election objections, and withdrawal of recognition
- ☐ Representation without an election
- ☐ Decertifying a union

Chapter 11 • The Duty to Bargain: Exclusivity and Good Faith Bargaining

- ☐ Exclusivity principle, majority rule, and the prohibition against direct dealing
- ☐ Distinctions between "good faith" and "bad faith" bargaining
- ☐ Duty to provide information, impasses, and public-sector bargaining rules

Chapter 12 • The Duty to Bargain in the Private Sector: Subjects of Bargaining

- ☐ Distinction between mandatory and permissive subjects of bargaining
- ☐ Special bargaining scope issues: subcontracting, shutdowns, runaway shops
- ☐ Bargaining procedures, retired workers, and bargaining remedies

Chapter 13 • Subjects of Bargaining in the Public Sector

- ☐ Distinction between scope of bargaining in public and private sectors
- ☐ Statutory balancing test vs. laundry list approach to public-sector bargaining
- ☐ Restrictions on bargaining, effects bargaining, and public-sector bargaining remedies

Chapter 14 • Employer Responses to Concerted Union Activity: Private Sector Strikes and Lockouts

- ☐ The right to strike and employer responses to employee concerted activities
- ☐ Permanent replacements and *Laidlaw* rights of permanently replaced employees
- ☐ *Great Dane* framework and group, inferential Section 8(a)(3) cases

Chapter 15 • Resolving Bargaining Impasses in the Public Sector

- ☐ Prohibition against strikes in the public sector and remedies for illegal strikes
- ☐ Alternative dispute procedures for resolving bargaining disputes
- ☐ Interest arbitration and standards of court review
- ☐ Legal public sector strikes in some states

Chapter 16 • Secondary Activity and Recognitional Picketing

- ☐ Distinction between primary and secondary activity
- ☐ Constitutional issues involving pickets, boycotts, and handbilling
- ☐ NLRA sections 8(b)(4) and 8(b)(7) on secondary boycotts and recognitional picketing

Chapter 17 • Grievance Arbitration

- ☐ Grievance arbitration process in the private and public sectors
- ☐ Typical issues that arise during grievance process
- ☐ Standards of judicial review and relationship between arbitrator and NLRB

Chapter 18 • Labor Law Preemption

- ☐ Discussion of origins of preemption doctrine and different forms of labor preemption
- ☐ Guiding principles behind labor law preemption doctrine
- ☐ *Garmon* preemption, *Machinists* preemption, and Section 301 preemption

Chapter 19 • The Duty of Fair Representation and Union Security Clauses

- ☐ The duty of fair representation
- ☐ Procedures, substantive standards, and remedies for DFR claims
- ☐ Union security clauses, *Beck* objection rules, and right-to-work laws
- ☐ Public sector union security clauses unconstitutional under *Janus*

Chapter 20 • Successorship

- ☐ The meaning of a successor under Board successorship doctrine
- ☐ Substantial business continuity and substantial and representative complement tests
- ☐ The duty to bargain vs. the duty to arbitrate in successorship cases

Chapter 21 • The Intersection of Labor and Antitrust Law

- ☐ The impact of antitrust law on labor law in historical perspective
- ☐ Statutory and nonstatutory labor exemptions to antitrust law
- ☐ Antitrust labor exemptions for employers in the sport industry

Index

U